Interdisciplinarity and archaeology

Interdisciplinarity and archaeology

Scientific interactions in nineteenth- and twentieth-century archaeology

edited by

Laura Coltofean-Arizancu and
Margarita Díaz-Andreu

Oxford & Philadelphia

Published in the United Kingdom in 2021 by
OXBOW BOOKS
The Old Music Hall, 106–108 Cowley Road, Oxford OX4 1JE

and in the United States by
OXBOW BOOKS
1950 Lawrence Road, Havertown, PA 19083

© Oxbow Books and the individual contributors 2021

Paperback Edition: ISBN 978-1-78925-466-2
Digital Edition: ISBN 978-1-78925-467-9 (ePub)

A CIP record for this book is available from the British Library

Library of Congress Control Number: 2020952177

All rights reserved. No part of this book may be reproduced or transmitted in any form or by any means, electronic or mechanical including photocopying, recording or by any information storage and retrieval system, without permission from the publisher in writing.

Printed in the United Kingdom by Short Run Press

Typeset by Versatile PreMedia Services (P) Ltd

For a complete list of Oxbow titles, please contact:

UNITED KINGDOM	UNITED STATES OF AMERICA
Oxbow Books	Oxbow Books
Telephone (01865) 241249	Telephone (610) 853-9131, Fax (610) 853-9146
Email: oxbow@oxbowbooks.com	Email: queries@casemateacademic.com
www.oxbowbooks.com	www.casemateacademic.com/oxbow

Oxbow Books is part of the Casemate Group

Front cover: © Wirestock | Dreamstime.com
Back cover: Classification of stone implements from the Drift. Plate IV in John Evans, 'Account of some further discoveries of flint implements in the Drift on the Continent and in England', *Archaeologia* 1862, xxxix; 57–84.

Contents

List of contributors vii

1. Interdisciplinarity in archaeology – a historical introduction 1
   Margarita Díaz-Andreu and Laura Coltofean-Arizancu

2. Two sides to the coin: erudition and natural history from
   antiquarianism to archaeology in the work of John Evans 23
   Nathan Schlanger

3. Non-spectacular exceptions: faunal remains and bone artefacts
   in nineteenth-century Hungarian archaeology 43
   Laura Coltofean-Arizancu

4. From plants to pollen, from Europe to Spain: looking at interdisciplinarity
   in archaeology 69
   Margarita Díaz-Andreu

5. Archaeology and interdisciplinarity in the Irish Free State in the 1930s:
   the role of the Committee for Quaternary Research 97
   Mairéad Carew

6. Interdisciplinarity? The word and the practice in the history of Swiss
   wetland archaeology 117
   Géraldine Delley

7. In search of interdisciplinarity in Portuguese archaeology:
   notes on the 1960s 133
   Ana Cristina Martins

8. Science and archaeology in Italy: a difficult marriage 157
   Alessandro Guidi

9. Archaeology and the Armed Forces in Spain from the nineteenth to the twenty-first century 181
   Francisco Gracia Alonso

10. The decline of epistemology in archaeology: comments on an ongoing discussion 203
    Oscar Moro Abadía and Emma Lewis-Sing

List of contributors

MAIRÉAD CAREW
University College Dublin, Ireland

LAURA COLTOFEAN-ARIZANCU
Universitat de Barcelona, Spain

GÉRALDINE DELLEY
Laténium and University of Neuchâtel, Switzerland

MARGARITA DÍAZ-ANDREU
ICREA and Universitat de Barcelona, Spain

FRANCISCO GRACIA ALONSO
Universitat de Barcelona, Spain

ALESSANDRO GUIDI
Roma Tre University, Italy

EMMA LEWIS-SING
Memorial University of Newfoundland, Canada

ANA CRISTINA MARTINS
IHC-FCSH NOVA – Pólo Universidade de Évora | Uniarq-UL

OSCAR MORO ABADÍA
Memorial University of Newfoundland, Canada

NATHAN SCHLANGER
École nationale des Chartes and UMR Trajectoires, France

Chapter 1

Interdisciplinarity in archaeology – a historical introduction

Margarita Díaz-Andreu and Laura Coltofean-Arizancu

Abstract

This chapter outlines the history of scientific interactions in archaeology since the early years of its professionalisation in the nineteenth century. It shows that multidisciplinary and interdisciplinary pursuits already existed in the practice of archaeology in the early years of the discipline. It is argued that nineteenth-century archaeology practitioners were already open to exchanges with other fields of knowledge. This was due firstly to their multilevel training and secondly to the less strictly delimited disciplinary boundaries. These interactions, however, often represented isolated cases that were not consolidated into research traditions or the establishment of sub-disciplines. That would mostly occur after the First World War, and particularly after the Second World War, when archaeology's approach to other disciplines was led by a strong belief in the hard sciences and resulted in an increasing development of interdisciplinarity. The last two decades have witnessed the success of interdisciplinary approaches in archaeology, an accomplishment that is changing the training within the discipline and archaeological practice. Rather than focusing its attention on a few countries, this chapter aims to contribute to a global history of interdisciplinarity in archaeology.

Keywords: history of archaeology; disciplinarity; interdisciplinarity; multidisciplinarity; archaeometry; archaeological sciences.

Introduction

In the last two decades, the term 'interdisciplinarity' has become increasingly important for funding bodies and institutions. This can be observed on an international, European, national and local level. Archaeology has not been an exception and, as a result – or probably in parallel with – we have witnessed the birth of new branches within the discipline. These include archaeozoology, archaeobotany, archaeoacoustics, geoarchaeology and archaeometallurgy, in addition to others that are not preceded by the 'archaeo-' prefix, such as palynology within archaeology. However, as will be seen in this volume, in archaeology – as in many other branches of knowledge – interdisciplinarity is far from being something novel, as it has been taking place since its very inception as a discipline. Despite this, most histories of archaeology treat the historical development of the discipline largely in isolation, separated from most of the other sciences. In contrast to the occasional links with anthropology and philology that are suggested by some authors, in this volume it will be argued that from the very first years of professionalisation in the nineteenth century, archaeology has shared much with a wide variety of disciplines, ranging from the hard, natural and social sciences to the humanities. Moreover, the role played by interdisciplinary – as well as multidisciplinary – cooperation has been essential to the development of archaeology as we know it today.

This introductory chapter will offer an explanation of the common but often ambiguous and misused concepts relating to interdisciplinarity. These include not only the term interdisciplinarity, but also discipline, multi- and pluridisciplinarity and transdisciplinarity. A historical outline of multidisciplinary and interdisciplinary practices in archaeology will consider four major periods: the nineteenth century; the first half of the twentieth century until the end of the Second World War; the post-war years until the 1980s; and the past forty years. This overview will include an examination of the earliest collaborations between archaeologists, collectors, antiquarians and colleagues from other fields, such as naturalists, geologists and palaeontologists, among others. The first steps towards interdisciplinarity in its current understanding will be then explored. Our historical outline will end with some comments on the explosion of specific, narrow specialisations within archaeology – those with the prefix 'archaeo-' and others – in the twenty-first century.

Defining concepts
Interdisciplinarity

Interdisciplinarity, multidisciplinarity, pluridisciplinarity and transdisciplinarity are all related concepts that derive from the same word: 'discipline', a 'body of knowledge or skills that can be taught and learned' (Alvargonzález 2011, 387) that has 'its own background of education, training, procedures, methods and content areas' (Berger 1972, 25). Discussions as to how all these terms should be understood have been present in the literature since September 1972, when a Seminar on Interdisciplinarity in Universities was organised at the University of Nice in France by the Centre for Educational Research and Innovation (CERI) of the Organisation for Economic Cooperation and Development (OECD), with the support of the French Ministry of Education. The seminar resulted in the report entitled *Interdisciplinarity: problems of teaching and research in universities* (Apostel *et al.* 1972) edited by a group of researchers led by Leo Apostel from the

University of Ghent. That report provided a complex analysis of the concept of interdisciplinarity, as well as its impact on teaching and research in relation to society. In this report, interdisciplinarity was considered to be

> an adjective describing the interaction among two or more different disciplines. This interaction may range from simple communication of ideas to the mutual integration of organising concepts, methodology, procedures, epistemology, terminology, data, and organisation of research and education in a fairly large field. An interdisciplinary group consists of persons trained in different fields of knowledge (disciplines) with different concepts, methods, and data and terms organised into a common effort on a common problem with continuous intercommunication among the participants from the different disciplines (Berger 1972, 25–26).

There are various typologies of interdisciplinarity (Klein 2017). In the so-called 'shared interdisciplinarity', 'groups tackle aspects of a complex problem' but this does not necessarily imply collaboration. In 'cooperative interdisciplinarity', however, collaboration is required (Klein 2017, 23–24). Apart from shared and cooperative interdisciplinarity, there are other types, such as methodological and theoretical interdisciplinarity. The first aims 'to improve the quality of results, typically by borrowing a method or concept from another discipline to test a hypothesis, to answer a research question, or to help develop a theory' (Bruun *et al.* 2005, 84 in Klein 2017, 24). However, if this does not lead to a major shift in the borrowing discipline's practice, the relationship between the two fields can be described as *auxiliary*. Conversely, the connection becomes *supplementary* when the methodological input of one of the disciplines turns out to be long-lasting and complex (Klein 2017, 24–25).

With regard to theoretical interdisciplinarity, which is considered to be more authentic than its methodological counterpart, Julie Thompson Klein explains that this 'connotes a more comprehensive general view and epistemological form embodied in creating conceptual frameworks for analysing particular problems, integrating propositions across disciplines, and synthesizing continuities between models and analogies' (2017, 25). There are several forms of theoretical interdisciplinarity depending on the degree of integration, such as generalising, integrated, conceptual, structural and unifying (Klein 2017, 22). Among these, some authors consider the integrated form as the purest and highest level of interdisciplinarity. In integrated interdisciplinarity, 'concepts and insights of one discipline contribute to problems and theories of another ... Individuals may also find their disciplinary methods and theoretical concepts modified as a result of cooperation, fostering new conceptual categories and methodological unification' (Klein 2017, 25–26). There is also a form of hybrid interdisciplinarity, in which interdisciplinary relationships merge and, through institutionalisation, transform into a subdiscipline (Klein 2017, 27).

Multidisciplinarity, pluridisciplinarity and transdisciplinarity

In contrast to interdisciplinarity, which entails the integration of knowledge from other different disciplines and, in addition, teamwork on various levels of collaboration, Julie Thompson Klein describes multidisciplinarity as a juxtaposition of various disciplines that, however, 'remain separate, retain their original identity, and are not questioned' (Klein 2017, 23). In a multidisciplinary approach, the knowledge from various disciplines is combined and consulted rather than integrated to resolve a matter. Therefore, multidisciplinarity widens knowledge, but does not necessarily modify the relations between disciplines; neither does it imply collaboration between specialists from different backgrounds.

Pluridisciplinarity is a very similar term to multidisciplinarity and the two are often confused. The main difference between them is that while the disciplines involved in a multidisciplinary relationship are not normally interconnected, in pluridisciplinarity they are 'assumed to be more or less related' (Berger 1972, 25). The closeness or distance between disciplines translates into 'epistemological proximity' or 'epistemological distance' (Choi and Pak 2008, E42). Epistemological proximity allows disciplines to form groups or 'knowledge subsystems', the best-known examples being those of the natural sciences, the social sciences and the humanities (Choi and Pak 2008, E42). Physics and chemistry, for example, are epistemologically closer and therefore belong to the same knowledge subsystem. However, they are epistemologically further from history and languages that, for their part, are also epistemologically close and belong to a distinct knowledge subsystem. Based on this explanation, the juxtaposition between physics, history and music would form a multidisciplinary relationship, while that between physics, chemistry and biology would be pluridisciplinary.

The last term to define in this section is transdisciplinarity, in whose meaning Julie Thompson Klein identifies four 'trend lines'. The first entails achieving a unity of different sciences that transcends disciplines, while the second sees transdisciplinarity in the form of various conceptual frameworks (*e.g.* Marxism, phenomenology, structuralism, feminist theory, etc.) that restructure knowledge 'by metaphorically encompassing parts of material fields that disciplines handle separately'. In its third sense, transdisciplinarity is seen as antidisciplinarity, as questioning traditional disciplinarity and being influenced by movements bringing social change. Finally, the fourth trendline focuses on the problem-solving potential of transdisciplinarity in lifeworld matters (Klein 2017, 29–30).

A sea of terms

Since the early discussions in 1972, the exact meaning of interdisciplinarity and all the other terms has been much debated. This has resulted not only in nuanced definitions and classifications but also unfortunately in much confusion (Frodeman 2017, 3; Klein 2017, 21). This confusion has led to the current situation in which these terms may be interchanged (Alvargonzález 2011, 387; Klein 2017, 21, see also comments by Pombo 2008 in Martins, this volume) and there is often no concordance between their use in theory and practice (Klein 2017, 21). Referring to the ambiguities entailed by the terms 'interdisciplinarity' and 'transdisciplinarity' – and we would add 'multidisciplinarity' and 'pluridisciplinarity' (at least in the case of archaeology) – Robert Frodeman considers that they 'have served a strategic function. In both cases they have allowed academics to gesture toward conducting research that's more relevant than "normal" disciplinary knowledge, while avoiding the painful task of actually working with people outside the academy' (Frodeman 2017, 4). As proposed at the start of the next section, when a historical overview is provided, the confusion increases, as these terms have been proposed for today's science and are not always easy to apply to a historical study.

Interdisciplinary collaborations in nineteenth-century archaeology

The concepts defined in the previous section – discipline, interdisciplinarity and multi-, pluri- and transdisciplinarity – imply the existence of a discipline. However, the question of when archaeology became established as a discipline is not easy to answer. The opening to the public of museums with antiquities dates back to the eighteenth century, beginning with the Museo Capitolino in 1733, although the boom in foundations of this type of institution only took place a century later (Díaz-Andreu 2020a, 35–39, 42–55). Moreover, the first chair of archaeology was founded in Leiden in 1818, but neither that nor the few others that were established in the following decades had continuity. Furthermore, although more university chairs were created in the second half of the nineteenth century (Díaz-Andreu 2007, passim), it was not until the following century that institutionalisation became firmer in this type of centre and even then mostly in Europe and North America. All these creations in the eighteenth century, and especially in the nineteenth century, indicate that everything related to archaeology was in flux: as a concept archaeology itself was in transformation and, at the same time, teaching about antiquities was being organised. It is only with this fluid understanding and an awareness that archaeology was a discipline in formation, that it is possible to confront the history of interdisciplinarity in archaeology during the nineteenth century.

Today we consider as an amateur or avocational archaeologist anyone who earns a living in another trade or profession while practising archaeology without an official archaeology degree (or a degree accepted for entry into the archaeology profession). In the nineteenth century, however, the situation was more complex, first of all because in most countries such a university degree did not yet exist. The vast majority of those who became involved in archaeology made their living in other professions, although today we include them in the histories of archaeology and call them archaeologists. In addition to them, there were also a few individuals who obtained positions that today we would consider more appropriate for the qualification of archaeology professionals. They were those working in institutions in which their labour was related to antiquities: museums, universities and the few nascent archaeological services such as monument commissions and the like. In most instances not even those professionals had been trained in degrees that would have been considered suitable today. In both cases, among professionals and avocational archaeologists, the great diversity of their training resulted in a transfer of knowledge from one emerging discipline to another.

The transfer of knowledge between these emergent disciplines, however, did not always entail the collaboration between different colleagues. Rather, it may have been personalised in one single individual; for example, the lawyer who applied what he had learned about legislation to the study of Roman law or the geologist who used his geological knowledge to understand archaeological stratigraphy. In the nineteenth century, professionals who placed their professional wisdom at the service of archaeology included members of disciplines with a large component of the hard, natural and medical sciences (architects, biologists, doctors, engineers, geologists, palaeontologists and zoologists); individuals working in the humanities (anthropologists, historians of art, geographers, lawyers and philologists); and public servants, priests, businessmen and members of the army. Alessandro Guidi and Laura Coltofean-Arizancu emphasise this variety of backgrounds in relation to the development of prehistoric archaeology in Italy and Hungary. The same situation can be seen elsewhere, for example, in Britain (Van Riper 1993; O'Connor 2007); in Canada (Killan 1998); in Denmark (Kristiansen 2011); in Germany (Sommer and Struwe 2006; Brather 2008); and in the United States (Gifford and Rapp Jr 1985; Kehoe 1998). A similar diversity is found in the colonial world (Malarkey 1984; Mitchell 1998).

Interestingly, the exchange of knowledge between disciplines also occurred among individuals interested in different archaeological periods, or even the same individual having developed an interest in different periods in archaeology. Nathan Schlanger illustrates this point in his chapter by analysing how John Evans (1823–1908), trained in numismatics by his father, applied the methodologies used to classify and describe coins to the study of lithics. Ultimately, his experience in numismatics was decisive in establishing that the flint tools discovered by the French antiquarian Jacques Boucher de Perthes (1788–1868) were authentic and human-made (Schlanger, this volume). The majority of those practising archaeology in the nineteenth century were avocational archaeologists, although their importance decreased proportionally throughout the nineteenth century in direct relation to the professionalisation of the discipline.

To our knowledge, the first example of what would today be considered an interdisciplinary project, with scholars from different disciplines joining efforts, took place in Denmark. We are referring to the first and later the second *køkkenmøddingkommission* (Kitchen Midden Commission) in a period that has been called the first scientific revolution in archaeology and was characterised as having 'parallel, and related, scientific breakthroughs of cultural, biological and geological evolution' (Kristiansen 2014, 14). Also known as the Lejre Commission, the first involved the collaboration between a naturalist, a geologist and an archaeologist between 1848 and 1869. Using the concept described in the previous section, we could consider the first Kitchen Midden Commission as 'cooperative interdisciplinarity', *i.e.* that in which collaboration is required. The Danish commission debated how to interpret correctly the stratigraphy found in one specific type of archaeological context, shell middens (Kristiansen 2002; Gron and Rowley-Conwy 2018; see also Díaz-Andreu this volume). This group effort was unique at the time, unique at least until the creation of the second Kitchen Midden Commission in 1893.

Beyond Scandinavia there were also some examples of interdisciplinary/multidisciplinary collaborations. In Hungary, for example, influenced by the first Kitchen Midden Commission, Flóris Rómer commissioned the archaeozoological analysis of faunal remains found in archaeological contexts at the zoology department of the University of Pest (Coltofean-Arizancu, this volume). In Switzerland there were also collaborations between archaeologists and members of other disciplines. Thus, the research undertaken on lake-dwellings led to cooperation between archaeologists, botanists and zoologists who examined the exceptionally well-preserved organic remains recovered from wetlands (Menotti 2004; Delley, this volume, and also Delley and Kaeser 2013).

In the nineteenth century, interdisciplinary collaborations also occurred in excavations. Multidisciplinary teams were formed for the excavations of both ancient Rome and Greece. In the former, Napoleon III, after buying the Villa Farnese, commissioned the Roman engineer and architect Pietro Rosa to uncover the old imperial palaces in 1861 (Cooley 2006). In Italy it is also worth mentioning the role of the architect Giacomo Boni in developing an understanding of how to interpret geological layers and buildings (De Santis and Fortini 2014). In the case of German archaeology it is possible to see interdisciplinary collaborations in excavations, as noted from 1877 at Olympia and from 1882 at Troy, where archaeologists hired architects and engineers, thus creating a precedent for later German-led digs (Marchand 1996; Ceserani 2008; Eberhardt 2008). The interdisciplinary approach of the German Archaeological Institute by not drawing a clear divide between classical archaeology and classical philology has also been highlighted by Christian Jansen (2008). In the case of Hungary, archaeologist Jenő Nyáry organised a multidisciplinary team for the analysis of the various archaeological finds from excavations carried out in 1876 at the Neolithic Aggtelek Cave, including expertise in botany, chemistry, geology, mineralogy, petrography, physical anthropology, dentistry and zoology (Coltofean-Arizancu, this volume).

In summary, in the nineteenth century the diversity of the training of the individuals engaged in archaeology, combined with unclear boundaries between disciplines, seems to have provided a fertile ground for multidisciplinary and interdisciplinary practices, and for the exchange and implementation of ideas, theories, concepts and methods. The nineteenth century was when the earliest cross-fertilisations between archaeology and other disciplines took place, sometimes personified by individuals who had two or more interests (disciplinary specialisations) and, with increasing impetus in the last decades of the century, as collaborations between archaeologists and members of other disciplines. At the time, however, those exchanges did not necessarily result in long-lasting interdisciplinary collaborations and traditions, nor in the birth of other disciplines, as would happen in the twentieth century, especially after the Second World War.

Twentieth-century interdisciplinarity up to the end of the Second World War (1900–1945)

In many respects, the social base of archaeology in the early decades of the twentieth century was similar to that of the previous period: the number of avocational archaeologists was proportionally larger than that of professionals. However, the foundations of archaeology as a solid discipline were set in this period. There was a clear move towards the institutionalisation of the discipline in prehistoric as well as classical archaeology (Callmer *et al.* 2006; Dyson 2006). It is also possible to see a preoccupation with establishing methodologies, as indicated by the publication of books such as Flinders Petrie's *Methods and Aims in Archaeology* (1904) and the creation of a chair of Methods and Practice in Archaeology at the University of Liverpool in 1906 (Díaz-Andreu 2020b, 43). This concern for methods would ultimately set the basis for a more official institutionalisation of interdisciplinary practice.

Continuing with the tradition established in the nineteenth century, Palaeolithic archaeology, perhaps more so than the archaeology of any other chronological period, showed a very high degree of interdisciplinarity. This is clearly exemplified by alluding to the Institute of Human Palaeontology (IPH) set up in Paris in 1910 and its mirror institutions in Spain and Italy opened in 1912 and 1913 respectively. All three institutions had an interdisciplinary nature from the start. Thus, the chairs created at the IPH were for Palaeontology, Prehistoric Ethnology and Geology. At the Italian Committee for Research in Human Palaeontology there were anthropologists, physicists and prehistorians. In this volume, however, Guidi explains that the journals he has analysed reveal a decrease in the degree of interdisciplinarity with the natural sciences in the interwar period that he links to the rise of the fascist regime. The other institution clearly influenced by the IPH was the Spanish Commission for Palaeontological and Prehistoric Research (CIPP) made up of scholars who worked in palaeontology and prehistoric archaeology. One of the main figures in the institution, Eduardo Hernández Pacheco, had a chair in natural sciences, whereas the other, Hugo Obermaier, became a professor in the Humanities faculty at the University of Madrid (Díaz-Andreu 2014).

At the other end of the chronological spectrum, in classical archaeology, scholars were also in contact with members of other disciplines. This can be seen in the foreign schools, where archaeologists worked together with historians of art, architects and philologists (Vian 1992). It is also worth mentioning the collaboration between archaeologists and geographers on projects such as the Map of Roman Britain (1924), the seed of a wider international project: the Tabula Imperii Romani (Map of the Roman Empire) beginning in 1934 (Plácido, Sánchez Palencia and Cepas 1993). Another collaboration in this first part of the century was that established between archaeologists and engineers or members of the armed forces in relation to aerial photography, initially for classical sites (Gerster and Trümpler 2007; Reubi 2011), a cooperation that would continue in the second half of the century (Brown 2004; Gracia, this volume).

As noted for the case of the nineteenth century, in the early decades of the twentieth century archaeological excavations constituted an ideal place for interdisciplinarity. In prehistoric archaeology, the excavation of the lake-dwellings continued to provide an excellent platform for the exchange of knowledge and collaboration between different disciplines. In Germany, archaeological sites in the Federsee basin benefited from the work of palynologists, dendrochronologists and zoologists (Keefer 1992; Delley 2015a). In Britain, the creation of the Fenland Committee in Cambridge was also an excellent example of an explicit desire for collaboration between members of different disciplines. As Pamela Jane Smith explains, the first meeting held in 1932 'brought together a dozen individuals with a shared interest in the English Fenland, the region of low-lying wetlands north of Cambridge which promised special opportunities for geological, botanical, and archaeological field research' (Smith 1997, 13). In memoirs written at the time, one of the committee members, Charles W. Phillips, argued that 'it was being increasingly realized that major archaeological problems could only be solved with speed and efficiency by co-operative effort' (in Smith 1997, 13).

After the First World War, a series of associations was created with the purpose of bringing together professionals from different disciplines, including archaeology. One of them was the Commission for Quaternary Research set up by the Moscow Academy of Sciences in 1927. This new association aimed to build bridges between geology, botany, zoology, geography and archaeology to study the Pleistocene and published a bulletin from 1929. A year after the foundation of the Soviet association a similar one was set up on a European level under the name of Association for the Study of Quaternary Europe, later known as INQUA (The International Union for Quaternary Research) (Alexandrowicz 2006; Smalley 2011).

At the very end of the period under consideration in this section the interest in interdisciplinarity led some institutions to hire individuals whose specialisation was considered important for archaeology, a movement that was especially marked in the 1930s. Examples of this in the Netherlands, Ireland and England illustrate this point. Firstly, we can mention the case of Albert Egges van Giffen, a zoologist and biologist who was granted a chair of prehistory at Groningen and Amsterdam between 1930 and 1954 (Waterbolk 1999). Another case is that of the Danish Professor Knud Jessen, an expert in palaeobotany, who was invited by the director of the National Museum of Ireland to lead the research of the Committee for Quaternary Research in the 1930s. This committee played a pivotal role in fostering interdisciplinary practices in the Irish Free State (Carew, this volume). The hiring during the Second World War of a German refugee in England, the geologist Frederick Zeuner (1905–1963), first as an honorary professor of geochronology and later as a salaried professor at the Institute of Archaeology of the University of London (Simpson 2000–01; Díaz-Andreu 2012, 148-152) is a further example. All three indicate a limited, but open attitude towards interdisciplinarity on an institutional level that had moved from archaeology related to the Palaeolithic in the 1910s to other periods in the 1930s.

The second scientific revolution in archaeology: interdisciplinarity after the Second World War (1945–2000)

The seeds of what happened after the Second World War had been planted in the preceding years and were ironically linked, at least in the United States, to the deep economic crisis that followed the Wall Street Stock Market Crash of 1929. Channelled through the New Deal programme of public works, relief funding led to many new jobs in archaeology and the entry of a younger generation into the profession. 'Much of the progress since 1935 stems from the vitality, ingenuity, and imagination of this dedicated generation of archaeologists' (Johnson 1961, 3), explained Frederik Johnson (1904–1994), one of the members of that generation born between 1900 and 1915. He was described as one of the pioneers

> in developing modern interdisciplinary studies when in 1939 he organized some 15 scientists in various fields into a cooperative group to study the archaeological remains recovered from the excavation of a 4,000-year-old fishweir under Boylston Street in downtown Boston (MacNeish 1996, 270).

During the Second World War this generation experienced first-hand the success of having placed science at the service of the war effort, an achievement that gave it a new image in the eyes not only of the public but, importantly, of the funding bodies.

The end of the Second World War would, therefore, be the context that marked the beginning of the second scientific revolution in archaeology (see Kristiansen 2014), a revolution particularly notable for the advent of radiocarbon dating in archaeology (Taylor 2000; Delley 2015b). In a speech given at the 100th anniversary meeting of the Archaeological Institute of America in 1979, the method's discoverer, Willard F. Libby, described those early years. He explained that 'after four years of intensive work on war-time problems, we had a tendency to lean towards problems of no particular application and to try to get away from the intensive concentration characteristic of military research' (Libby 1980, 1019). This was behind the idea of focusing his research on something that would have been defined during the war as 'fully useless', which was how 'to use the cosmic rays to measure human history and time for geological events' (Libby 1980, 1019). He thanked his many archaeological collaborators in the early days of radiocarbon dating and stated that the development of his method would not have been possible without them, and in particular without Egyptologists (Libby 1980; see also Marlowe 1980). The radiocarbon dating method achieved immediate success and a series of radiocarbon dating laboratories emerged throughout the Western world (Hawkes 1986; Delley 2015a, ch. 1; Djindjian 2016, 127).

The interdisciplinary relationship formed between archaeologists and physicists was not the only one in those years. Those from the previous period continued and expanded within the same favourable attitude towards science created during the war and maintained in the post-war years. In this auspicious atmosphere, *Archaeometry* (1958) became the first interdisciplinary journal in archaeology and

Science in Archaeology (Brothwell and Higgs 1963) one of the first textbooks inspired by interdisciplinarity. As these definitions appeared in the United Kingdom, in France we note the introduction of such terms as 'archéometrie' (Djindjian 2016; Bellot-Gurlet and Dillmann 2018). The new impetus in interdisciplinarity does not mean that specialists had it easy. This is illustrated by reading the foreword of the first issue of *Archaeometry*, a journal written on a typewriter that started life as a humble institutional bulletin. This first volume was 'not intended to by-pass the normal channels of publication', rather, its aim was to 'provide a rapid means of circulating the results of completed research, to record partially successful projects which are not worthy of normal publication', and 'to give interim reports on some of the work in progress in the laboratory' (Hall, Kraay and Emeleus 1958, 1). The contributions of this first issue included a series of interdisciplinary texts related to chemistry, magnetic field dating, magnetic prospection, geomagnetic survey and neutron activation analysis (see also Pollard 2008, 191). They would all have been in publication appendixes, or as parts of an article that went unsigned by the authors of the analyses. They were considered not as part of archaeology, but as an example of what at the time were called 'auxiliary sciences' could contribute to the knowledge about the past produced by archaeologists. As the editors of the *Journal of Archaeological Science* explained in their historical overview in 2015, during those early years

> scientific techniques were still often envisaged as something additional, practiced by specialists largely placed outside the field, and whose expertise was only called on when required – or as an entertainment for curious scientists towards the end of their career (Torrence, Martinón-Torres, and Rehren 2015, 1).

Thus, we can see how the interdisciplinary knowledge some scholars were producing was resisted by some of their colleagues who considered it to be multidisciplinary, leading to the study of the same past but not quite at the level of traditional archaeology and therefore demoted as 'auxiliary'. Despite encountering a degree of resistance, the exchange of interdisciplinary knowledge in archaeology continued unabated and took place not only in publications but also in conferences, such as the International Symposia on Archaeometry organised by Martin Aitken (Oxford) from 1962 (López Varela 2019, xlv) and, a few years later, a symposium on the Impact of the Natural Sciences on Archaeology held by the Royal Society and the British Academy in 1969. Presentations dealt with archaeological chronology, archaeological site detection and artifact chemistry (Allibone 1970).

In this context of a willingness to strengthen links between archaeology and other sciences, but at the same time never fully perceiving these collaborations as part of the discipline, archaeologists continued to reinforce their previously established collaborations with other scientists in the natural sciences. The Second World War did not only have an effect on a newly found faith in science as discussed above, but, at the same time and not necessarily in contradiction, the war also led to a rebuff of industrialism and the nineteenth-century belief in progress. This rejection became more profoundly felt with the

Cold War conflicts in Korea and Vietnam and the series of ecological disasters that occurred during those years (Carson 1962; Molina and Rowland 1974). This fostered the interest in the environment, further developing a trend that had emerged, as seen above, during the first scientific revolution in archaeology in the nineteenth century, and then had been continued in the early twentieth century collaborations between archaeologists, biologists and geologists (Pişkin and Bartkowiak 2018). This interest even reached countries outside the centres of power at the time, as seen by the opening of an Institute of Palaeobotany at Lucknow (Uttar Pradesh, India) in 1946, in which fossil plants and plant evolution also in archaeological periods were analysed (Jha 2005). In addition to many publications (but not journals), congresses were organised, including one on *The Domestication and Exploitation of Plants and Animals* in 1968 in London (Ucko and Dimbleby 1969).

In the early post-war years, the incorporation of women represented an important step in the social composition of the interdisciplinary community. Despite its relevance, however, women's integration was far from unproblematic and it is worth noting that it took place particularly in fields that were not very popular at the time. Palynology in southern Europe is a good example, with the biologist Madeleine van Campo (1920–?), the archaeologist Arlette Leroi-Gourhan (1913–2005) (who always worked on a voluntary basis at the Museum of Man), the geologist Josette Renault-Miskovsky (1938–2018) in France and Josefina Menéndez Amor (1916–1985) in Spain. The last of these always published on matters related to archaeology with her former supervisor in the Netherlands, Frans Florschütz (1888–1965) and was only appointed a professor a few months before her death. The example of palynology is not as random as it may seem at first; not only was it not as popular in southern Europe as it was in the north, but it was also in the south that women entered interdisciplinarity and not other fields that were definitively perceived as male domains, such as metallurgy, radiocarbon dating or chemistry.

The new concern for science, of turning archaeology into a science with a capital 'S' (Flannery 1973; Moro Abadía and Lewis-Sing, this volume), was of particular importance in the most developed countries. Following two research trips to the United States in the late 1950s, the Spanish archaeologist Luis Pericot (1899–1978) published on his experience. Interestingly, he commented that:

> To say that the methods used by American archaeologists are the most advanced, would not be saying anything new. The whole secret of this lies in the collaboration of the scientists, geologists, chemists, pedologists, geographers, that the institutions have, while in our old countries it is not always easy to count on their cooperation (Pericot 1959, 8).

This is an accurate reflection of the atmosphere in that country in the years immediately prior to the explosion of the New Archaeology.

With the birth of the New Archaeology, collaboration was not only explicitly embraced and fostered, but also a new type of partnership appeared: that of archaeology and philosophy of science. New archaeologists, led by Lewis Binford (Binford and Binford 1968), pleaded for greater emphasis to be placed on scientific methods in archaeological research aimed at transforming archaeology into science. They were very much influenced by the work of philosophers of science like Carl Gustav Hempel, Wesley Salmon and Richard Braithwaite, as well as Thomas Kuhn and David Bloor (Moro Abadia and Lewis-Sing, this volume). The connection made between archaeology and philosophy led to an interest in archaeological theory that clearly separates the development of interdisciplinarity in the archaeology of the English-speaking countries from all others. Even when their teams worked outside their own countries, their ideas did not become influential, partly, it should be said, because they did not collaborate much with local archaeologists. An example of this can be seen in the limited influence of the British and American teams working in Spain from the 1960s to the 1980s (see Díaz-Andreu, this volume). However, from the 1970s the rise of English as an international language assisted the export of the way of doing archaeology, created mainly in the United States and the United Kingdom, to the rest of the world, in a process that took place mainly from the 1980s. This export mainly referred to the theories and archaeological practice fostered by the New Archaeology (or, as it was known in the United Kingdom and later everywhere, processual archaeology). However, by the 1980s, the New Archaeology label was clearly in decline and the scientific status of archaeology was being contested by the self-denominated post-processual archaeologists (Hodder 1982; 1985).

Beyond the English-speaking world, the term 'New Archaeology' or processual archaeology was only used by the very few archaeologists who were somehow connected to the United States or the United Kingdom. This does not mean, however, that the interest in interdisciplinarity elsewhere was less important. In parallel to the flurry of new/processual archaeology projects, there were many other countries where interest in interdisciplinary relations between archaeology and the sciences was key during those years. In France (and Italy) Sébastien Plutniak has studied the cooperation between archaeologists, and engineers and mathematicians (Plutniak 2016; 2017), as well as with geologists and biologists in places like Paris with Leroi-Gourhan (Schlanger 2015), Bordeaux with François Bordes (Delpech and Jaubert 2011), Marseille with Henri de Lumley or Montpellier with Jean-Louis Vernet, among others. Importantly, not all of them were archaeologists who sought the help of specialists in other sciences. Some were members of the other sciences, such as Vernet, who trained young archaeologists to answer questions raised in his own science, botany. This also took place in Germany at institutions such as the Institut für Palaeonatomie, Domestikationsforschung und Geschichte der Tiermedezin (Institute for Palaeoanatomy, Domestication Research and History of Veterinary Medicine) at the University of Munich, which undertook much research into archaeological fauna found at sites on the Iberian Peninsula and elsewhere. The role of the German Archaeological Institute in bringing interdisciplinarity to other countries such as Portugal and Spain and, up to a point, influencing local archaeologists, is highlighted by Martins and Díaz-Andreu in their chapters. In Portugal, Martins also mentions the collaborations of local archaeologists with geologists, geographers, geomorphologists, physical anthropologists, zoologists, botanists, physicians and chemists, as well as the importance of societies, journals and congresses (Martins, this volume).

In the final years of the period under discussion in this section some changes would be crucial for the history of interdisciplinarity in archaeology. For the first time it began to be common for archaeology departments to train students in both archaeology and the many interdisciplinary branches already present in the discipline. Thus, there was an increase in the number of young professionals 'with enough archaeological training to spot meaningful research problems, and enough scientific training to pursue them' (Killick and Young 1997, 518). This did not occur only in the United Kingdom and the United States, but also in parts of Europe including Spain (Díaz-Andreu and Portillo 2021), Japan in Asia (Killick and Young 1997, 519), and Mexico in Latin America (Barba and Lazos 2004).

From archaeometry to archaeological science: the third scientific revolution in archaeology

In the 2000s, archaeologists began to talk about 'archaeological science', a term that increasingly came to replace that of archaeometry. The new concept was not that new, as Lewis Binford had used it in the early 1980s (Binford 1987), but by the 2000s it had been practically forgotten for two decades. The appearance of the 'new' term was not the only change: in 1999 the theoretical archaeologist Mathew Johnson had already commented that 'I shall put forward my personal view that the whole thrust of recent theory has made a division of archaeological activity into "science-based archaeology" and "everybody else" increasingly artificial' (Johnson 1999, xi–xii). At the time, this comment sounded odd, coming as it did from a member of the post-processual line. Nevertheless, Johnson has now been joined by many others with a solid theoretical background, including Kristian Kristiansen who, in 2014, suggested that archaeology was going through a Third Science Revolution (Kristiansen 2014). In his view, the process of fragmentation within post-processual archaeology has been paralleled by the return of many archaeologists to quantitative methods and science-based knowledge, in what he defines as a revised form of the processual approach. The application of novel quantitative and modelling methods by processing large databases in areas such as genomics and strontium isotope analyses is producing new possibilities for theory-led interpretations. Archaeology, he argues, has a need for 'theorizing that is more integrated in actual modelling' (Kristiansen 2014, 25). A shift in archaeology has also been acknowledged by archaeological scientists. In 2015 David Killick commented that

> The practice of archaeology has been utterly transformed over the last fifteen years by an infusion of new (or greatly improved) scientific methods. These have made it possible to ask many new questions, and have produced a marked revival of interest in archaeological questions that had previously lapsed for lack of firm evidence (Killick 2015, 242).

These new methods had come together with a wave of enthusiasm for archaeological science that has led publications such as the *Journal of Archaeological Science* to grow in size by up to seven-fold in the last three decades (Killick 2015, 243).

Today, the successful integration of interdisciplinary practices in archaeology is largely debated among archaeologists (*e.g.* Ion 2017; Sørensen 2017; Furholt 2018), as well as the future of interdisciplinarity itself (*e.g.* Frodeman *et al.* 2017). According to osteoarchaeologist and anthropologist Alexandra Ion, archaeology is still on its way towards interdisciplinarity (Ion 2017, 194) and considers that

> Instead of attempting to make archaeology more objective and science–like, taking it towards mathematical models, we should embrace exactly what made it strong and a source of inspiration for decades: its contextual, and genealogical reasoning approach. What others pick up about archaeology as its strength, from Foucault to psychoanalysis, from digital humanities terminology to the public's imagination, is its ability to construct a narrative by grounding material traces (Ion 2017, 193).

The fervour in archaeological science has led to hybrid interdisciplinarity through which interdisciplinary relationships have been institutionalised and transformed as subdisciplines, *i.e.* archaeozoology, archaeometallurgy, etc. However, the enthusiasm for archaeological science and its integration into departments of archaeology is not fully global, due in large part to economic factors. The cost of archaeological science has led to a concentration of those practising interdisciplinary approaches mainly in economically powerful countries. The cost of laboratories and the number of professionals needed, for example, has not allowed the institutionalisation of interdisciplinarity in many countries in Africa (Killick 2015, 246) (for other examples around the world see Paredes Umaña and Erquicia Cruz 2013, table 1).

This volume

This volume includes several studies of the relationship between interdisciplinarity and archaeology in Europe and elsewhere in the nineteenth and twentieth centuries. Despite the fact that interdisciplinary cooperation has been essential in the development of archaeology as we know it today, as can be seen in the account provided in the previous pages, its role and influence have been largely ignored in the histories of the discipline (some exceptions have been mentioned above and can be seen in this chapter's bibliography). Importantly, beyond a few historians of archaeology who have dealt with interdisciplinarity, there also are many authors who have shown an interest in reconstructing the past of their own interdisciplinary branch of archaeology (see, for example, Gifford-Gonzalez 2018; Pişkin and Bartkowiak 2018; Troels-Smith, Jessen, and Mortensen 2018; López Varela 2019).

The authors of this volume include acknowledged scholars in the history of archaeology. Together they reconstruct fragments from the history of scientific interactions in nineteenth- and twentieth-century archaeology on a European and global level. The following nine chapters cover a wide range of topics. Some of them deal with interdisciplinarity in archaeology on a more general level by analysing its relationship with a number of other sciences (*e.g.* zoology, botany, physical anthropology, geology, palynology) in countries including the Irish Free State (Chapter 5), Switzerland (Chapter 6), Portugal (Chapter 7) and Italy (Chapter 8). Other chapters discuss the incorporation of particular disciplines such as palynology (Chapter 4) and zoology (Chapter 3) into archaeology, using specific countries (*i.e.* Spain and Hungary) as case studies. Several others focus on the contribution of organisations (*e.g.* the Committee for Quaternary Research in the Irish Free State) and journals (*e.g. O Arqueólogo Português* in Portugal) to explore interdisciplinarity and multidisciplinarity in archaeological practice. Chapter 2 uses the work of a scholar, John Evans, as a starting point for examining the intersection between antiquarianism, archaeology, the natural sciences and numismatics. Other chapters theorise on the use of the term 'interdisciplinarity' in archaeology and its reflection in the disciplinary practice (Chapters 6 and 7), as well as on the role of epistemology and philosophy of science (Chapter 10) in archaeological theory and practice. And last but not least, the influence of the army is also discussed in the development of underwater and aerial archaeology in Spain (Chapter 9). Apart from their contribution to the history of archaeology, the chapters of this volume also outline new and fascinating topics for future research. They will bring about a better understanding of the development, evolution and future of multidisciplinarity and interdisciplinarity in archaeology.

Acknowledgements

Most of the chapters included in this book were first presented in the one-day conference 'Towards interdisciplinarity. A historical analysis of the transfer of knowledge and techniques between disciplines (19th and 20th centuries)', organised within the framework of the InterArq project in Barcelona in June 2019. Most of the papers presented on that day that related to Spain were subsequently published in a special issue of the *Veleia* journal (Díaz-Andreu and Coltofean 2020). That publication was complemented by a book that, for the first time in the history of interdisciplinarity in archaeology, compiled the life experiences of almost fifty scholars from different generations who are either Spanish or based in Spain. It provides a very rich panorama of the development of archaeological science in Spain since the 1970s (Díaz-Andreu and Portillo 2021). The InterArq research project (HAR2016-80271-P) (interarqweb.wordpress.com) is funded by the State Research Agency (AEI) and the European Regional Development Fund (ERDF, EU). We are grateful to Margarita Gómez Salas de Schetter for designing the book cover.

References

Alexandrowicz, S.W. (2006) The Polish initiative in the creation of the International Union for Quaternary Research (INQUA). In M. Kokowski (ed.) *The Global and the Local: The History of Science and the Cultural Integration of Europe. Proceedings of the 2nd ICESHS Conference, Cracow*

September 6-9 2006, 194–197. Cracow, The Press of the Polish Academy of Arts and Sciences. Online.

Allibone, T.E., ed. (1970) *The Impact of the Natural Sciences on Archaeology*. London, British Academy.

Alvargonzález, D. (2011) Multidisciplinarity, interdisciplinarity, transdisciplinarity, and the sciences. *International Studies in the Philosophy of Science* 24 (4), 387–403.

Apostel, L., Berger, G., Briggs, A. and Michaud, G., eds (1972) *Interdisciplinarity: Problems of Teaching and Research in Universities*. Paris, Centre for Educational Research and Innovation (ERIC_ED061895).

Barba, L. and Lazos, L. (2004) La formación de los laboratorios de arqueometría en el Instituto de Investigaciones Antropológicas. In A. Benavides, L. Manzanilla and L. Mirambell (eds) *Homenaje a Jaime Litvak*, 33–44. México DF, Instituto Nacional de Antropología e Historia; Instituto de Investigaciones Antropológicas–UNAM.

Bellot-Gurlet, L. and Dillmann, P. (2018) Archéométrie une discipline du passé ou un enjeu interdisciplinaire pour l'avenir? Réflexions issues du bilan de 40 ans de colloques du GMPCA. *ArcheoSciences* 42 (1), 77–83.

Berger, G. (1972) Opinions and facts. In L. Apostel, G. Berger, A. Briggs and G. Michaud (eds) *Interdisciplinarity: Problems of Teaching and Research in Universities*, 21–74. ERIC_ED061895. Paris, Centre for Educational Research and Innovation.

Binford, L.R. (1987) Data, relativism and archaeological science. *Man* 22, 391–404.

Binford, S.R. and Binford, L.R., eds (1968) *New Perspectives in Archaeology: An Overview of the New Scientific Techniques and the New Theoretical Points that are Changing the Course of Archaeological Inquiry*. Chicago, New York, Aldine, Atherton.

Brather, S. (2008) Virchow and Kossinna. From the science-based anthropology of humankind to the culture–historical archaeology of peoples. In N. Schlanger and J. Nordbladh (eds) *Histories of Archaeology: Archives, Ancestors, Practices*, 318–334. Oxford, Berghahn Books.

Brothwell, D. and Higgs, E. (1963) *Science in Archaeology: A Comprehensive Survey of Progress and Research*, 1st edition. London, Thames & Hudson.

Brown, K. (2004) Aerial archaeology of the Tavoliere. The Italian Air Photographic Record and the Riley Archive. *Accordia Research Papers* 9, 123–146.

Bruun, H., Hukkinen, J., Huutoniemi, K. and Klein, J.T. (2005) *Promoting Interdisciplinary Research: The Case of the Academy of Finland Publications of the Academy of Finland. Series #8/05*. Helsinki, Academy of Finland.

Callmer, J., Meyer, M., Struwe, R. and Theune-Vogt, C., eds (2006) *The Beginnings of Academic Pre- and Protohistoric Archaeology (1830-1930) in a European Perspective*. Berlin, Verlag Marie Leidorf (Berliner Archäologische Forschungen 2).

Carson, R. (1962) *Silent Spring*. Boston, Houghton Mifflin.

Ceserani, G. (2008) Wilamowitz and stratigraphy at Capua: telling the Story of an unlikely pair in the history of archaeology. In N. Schlanger and J. Nordbladh (eds) *Histories of Archaeology: Archives, Ancestors, Practices*, 75–87. Oxford, Berghahn Books.

Cooley, A.E. (2006) French excavations on the Palatine Hill. The investigations by Pietro Rosa for Napoleon III. *Classical Review* 56 (1), 207–208.

Choi, B.C.K. and Pak, A.W.-P. (2008) Multidisciplinarity, interdisciplinarity, and transdisciplinarity in health research, services, education and policy: 3. Discipline, inter-discipline distance, and selection of discipline. *Clinical and Investigative Medicine* 31 (1), E41–E48.

De Santis, A. and Fortini, P. (2014) Giacomo Boni un approccio multidisciplinare all'archeologia. In A. Guidi (ed.) *150 anni di preistoria e protostoria in Italia*, 301–308. Studi di Preistoria e Protostoria I. Firenze, Istituto Italiano di Preistoria e Protostoria.

Delley, G. (2015a) Au-delà des chronologies. Des origines du radiocarbone et de la dendrochronologie à leur intégration dans les recherches lacustres suisses. *Archéologie Neuchâteloise 53*. Neuchâtel, Office du patrimoine et de l'archéologie.

Delley, G. (2015b) The long revolution of radiocarbon as seen through the history of Swiss lake-dwelling research. In G. Eberhardt and F. Link (eds) *Historiographical Approaches to Past Archaeological Research*, 95–114. Berlin, Edition Topoi.

Delley, G. and Kaeser, M.-A. (2013) Archéologie et botanique: un aller-retour Suisse-Egypte en classe diachronique. In C. Jacquat and I. Rogger (eds) *Fleurs des pharaons*, 113–131. Hauterive, Laténium.

Delpech, F. and Jaubert, J., eds (2011) *François Bordes et la préhistoire. Colloque international François Bordes, Bordeaux, 22-24 avril 2009*. Paris, Editions du Comité des travaux historiques et scientifiques (Documents préhistoriques 29).

Díaz-Andreu, M. (2007) *A World History of Nineteenth-Century Archaeology. Nationalism, Colonialism and the Past. Oxford Studies in the History of Archaeology*. Oxford, Oxford University Press.

Díaz-Andreu, M. (2012) *Archaeological Encounters. Building Networks of Spanish and British Archaeologists in the 20th Century*. Newcastle, Cambridge Scholars.

Díaz-Andreu, M. (2014) Transnationalism and archaeology. The connecting origins of the main institutions dealing with prehistoric archaeology in Western Europe: the IPH, the CIPP and the CRPU (1910–1914). In A. Guidi (ed.) *150 anni di preistoria e protostoria in Italia*, 163–177. Studi di Preistoria e Protostoria I. Firenze, Istituto Italiano di Preistoria e Protostoria.

Díaz-Andreu, M. (2020a) *A History of Archaeological Tourism. Pursuing Leisure and Knowledge from the Eighteenth Century to World War II*. New York, Springer.

Díaz-Andreu, M. (2020b) Towards archaeological theory: a history. In P. Díaz-del-Río, K. Lillios and I. Sastre (eds) *The Power of Reason, the Matter of Prehistory. Papers in Honour of Antonio Gilman Guillén. Edited by Pedro Díaz-del-Río, Katina Lillios and Inés Sastre*, 41–53. Bibliotheca Praehistorica Hispana. Madrid, Consejo Superior de Investigaciones Científicas.

Díaz-Andreu, M. and Coltofean, L. (2020) Dossier: historia de la interdisciplinaridad en Arqueología. *Veleia* 37, 13–175.

Díaz-Andreu, M. and Portillo, M., eds (2021) *Arqueología e interdisciplinaridad: la microhistoria de una revolución en la arqueología española (1970-2020)*. Barcelona, Universitat de Barcelona.

Djindjian, F. (2016) The revolution of the sixties in prehistory and protohistory. In G. Delley, M. Díaz-Andreu, F. Djindjian, V. Fernández, A. Guidi and M.A. Kaeser (eds) *History of Archaeology - International Perspectives*, 125–144. British Archaeological Reports. Oxford, Archaeopress.

Dyson, S.L. (2006) *In Pursuit of Ancient Pasts: A History of Classical Archaeology in the Nineteenth and Twentieth Centuries*. New Haven, Yale University Press.

Eberhardt, G. (2008) Methodological Reflections on the History of Excavation Techniques. In N. Schlanger and J. Nordbladh (eds) *Histories of Archaeology: Archives, Ancestors, Practices*, 89–96. Oxford, Berghahn Books.

Flannery, K.V. (1973) Archaeology with a capital S. In C.L. Redman (ed.) *Research and Theory in Current Archaeology*, 47–58. New York, Wiley.

Frodeman, R., Klein, J.T. and Pacheco, R.C.S., eds (2017) *The Oxford Handbook of Interdisciplinarity*, 2nd edition. Oxford, Oxford University Press.

Furholt, M. (2018) Massive migrations? The impact of recent aDNA studies on our view of third millennium Europe. *European Journal of Archaeology* 21 (2), 159–191.

Gerster, G. and Trümpler, C. (2007) *The Past from Above: Aerial Photographs of Archaeological Sites*. Los Angeles, Getty Publications.

Gifford, J.A. and Rapp Jr, G. (1985) The early development of archaeological geology in North America. In E.T. Drake and W.M. Jordan (eds) *Geologists and Ideas: A History of North Amercian Geology*, 409–421. Boulder, Col, Geological Society of America.

Gifford-Gonzalez, D.P. (2018) The emergence of zooarchaeology. In D.P. Gifford-Gonzalez (ed.) *An Introduction to Zooarchaeology*, 19–50. New York, Springer.

Gron, K.J. and Rowley-Conwy, P. (2018) Environmental archaeology in Southern Scandinavia. In E. Pişkin, A. Marciniak and M. Bartkowiak (eds) *Environmental Archaeology. Current Theoretical and*

Methodological Approaches, 35–74. Interdisciplinary Contributions to Archaeology. New York, Springer.

Hall, E.T., Kraay, C.M. and Emeleus, V.M. (1958) Foreword. *Archaeometry* 1, 1–15.

Hawkes, C.F.C. (1986) The research laboratory: its beginning. *Archaeometry* 28, 131–132.

Hodder, I. (1982) Theoretical archaeology: a reactionary view. In I. Hodder (ed.) *Symbolic and Structural Archaeology*, 1–16. New Directions in Archaeology. Cambridge, Cambridge University Press.

Hodder, I. (1985) Postprocessual archaeology. In M.B. Schiffer (ed.) *Advances in Archaeological Method and Theory, vol. 8*, 1–23. New York, Academic Press.

Ion, A. (2017) How interdisciplinary is interdisciplinarity? Revisiting the impact of aDNA research for the archaeology of human remains. *Current Swedish Archaeology* 25, 177–198.

Jansen, C. (2008) The German Archaeological Institute between transnational scholarship and foreign cultural policy. In N.d. Haan, M. Eickhoff and M. Schwegman (eds) *Archaeology and National Identity in Italy and Europe 1800-1950*, 151–182. Fragmenta 2, Journal of the Royal Netherlands Institute in Rome. Turnhout, Brepols.

Jha, N. (2005) Permian palynology in India – past, present and future. In *Challenges in Indian Palaeobiology. Current Status, Recent Developments and Future Directions. Diamond Jubilee National Conference, 15-16 November 2005, BSIP, Lucknow. Abstract Book*, 48–49. Lucknow, Birbal Sahni Institute of Palaeobotany.

Johnson, F. (1961) A quarter century of growth in American Archaeology. *American Antiquity* 27 (1), 1–6.

Johnson, M.H. (1999) *Archaeological Theory: An Introduction*. Oxford, Blackwell.

Keefer, E., ed. (1992) *Die Suche nach der Vergangenheit. 120 Jahre Archäologie am Federsee*. Stuttgart, Württembergisches Landesmuseum.

Kehoe, A.B. (1998) *The Land of Prehistory: A Critical History of American Archaeology*. London, Routledge.

Killan, G. (1998) Toward a scientific archaeology: Daniel Wilson, David Boyle and the Canadian Institute 1852-96. In P.J. Smith and D. Mitchell (eds) *Bringing Back the Past: Historical Perspectives on Canadian Archaeology*, 15–24. Mercury Series Number 158. Quebec, Canadian Museum of Civilization.

Killick, D.J. (2015) The awkward adolescence of archaeological science. *Journal of Archaeological Science (Special Issue: Torrence, R., Martinón-Torres, M. & Rehren, T. (eds) Scoping the Future of Archaeological Science: Papers in Honour of Richard Klein)* 56, 242–247.

Killick, D.J. and Young, S.M.M. (1997) Archaeology and archaeometry: from casual dating to a meaningful relationship? *Antiquity* 71, 518–524.

Klein, J.T. (2017) Typologies of interdisciplinarity: the boundary work of definition. In R. Frodeman (ed.) *The Oxford Handbook of Interdisciplinarity*, 21–34. 2nd edition. Oxford, Oxford University Press.

Kristiansen, K. (2002) The birth of ecological archaeology in Denmark: history and research environments 1850–2002. In A. Fischer and K. Kristiansen (eds) *The Neolithisation of Denmark. 150 Years of Debate*, 11–31. Poole, Orca Book.

Kristiansen, K. (2011) A social history of Danish Archaeology (Reprint with New Epilogue). In L.R. Lozny (ed.) *Comparative Archaeologies. A Sociological View of the Science of the Past*, 79–108. New York, Springer.

Kristiansen, K. (2014) Towards a new paradigm? The Third Science Revolution and its possible consequences in archaeology. *Current Swedish Archaeology* 22, 11–71.

Libby, W.F. (1980) Archaeology and radiocarbon dating Paper delivered at the one hundredth anniversary meeting of the Archaeological Institute of America, December, 1979. Boston, Massachusetts. *Radiocarbon* 22 (4), 1017–1020.

López Varela, S.L. (2019) The encyclopedia of archaeological sciences: bridging archaeological scholarship and science. In S.L. López Varela (ed.) *The SAS Encyclopedia of Archaeological Sciences*, xliv–l. New York, Wiley-Liss.

MacNeish, R.S. (1996) Frederik Johnson (1904–1994). *American Antiquity* 61 (2), 269–273.

Malarkey, J. (1984) The dramatic structure of scientific discovery in colonial Algeria: a critique of the journal 'Société archéologique de Contantine (1853–1876). In J.-C. Vatin (ed.) *Connaissances du Maghreb: sciences sociales et colonisations*, 137–160. Recherches sur les sociétés méditerranées. Paris, Centre national de la Recherche Scientifique.

Marchand, S. (1996) *Down from Olympus. Archaeology and Philhellenism in Germany, 1750–1950*. Princeton, New Jersey, Princeton University Press.

Marlowe, G. (1980) W.F. Libby and the archaeologists, 1946–1948. *Radiocarbon* 22 (3), 1005–1014.

Menotti, F. (2004) *The Lake in Prehistoric Europe. 150 Years of Lake-Dwelling Research*. London, Routledge.

Mitchell, P.J. (1998) The South African stone age in the collections of the British Museum: content, history and significance. *South African Archaeological Bulletin* 53, 26–36.

Molina, M. and Rowland, F. (1974) Stratospheric sink for chlorofluoromethanes: chlorine atom-catalysed destruction of ozone. *Nature* 249, 810–812.

O'Connor, A. (2007) *Finding Time for the Old Stone Age: A History of Palaeolithic Archaeology and Quaternary Geology in Britain, 1860–1960*. Oxford, Oxford University Press.

Paredes Umaña, F. and Erquicia Cruz, J.H. (2013) Los conceptos de pasado histórico, Estado y patrimonio como elementos indispensables para la elaboración de una biografía crítica de la arqueología salvadoreña. *Identidades* 6, 9–31.

Pericot, L. (1959) Impresiones arqueológicas de mis últimos viajes a América. *Boletín Americanista (Barcelona)* 1, 7–21.

Petrie, W.F. (1904) *Methods and Aims in Archaeology*. London, Macmillan.

Pişkin, E. and Bartkowiak, M. (2018) Environmental archaeology: what is in a name? In E. Pişkin, A. Marciniak and M. Bartkowiak (eds) *Environmental Archaeology. Current Theoretical and Methodological Approaches*, 1–14. Interdisciplinary Contributions to Archaeology. New York, Springer.

Plácido, D., Sánchez Palencia, J. and Cepas, A. (1993) El mapa del mundo romano. In A. Jimeno, J.M.d. Val and J.J. Fernández (eds) *Inventarios y Cartas Arqueológicas. Homenaje a Blas Taracena, Soria, 1991*, 57–64. Valladolid, Junta de Castilla y León.

Plutniak, S. (2016) Interests on the margins of the disciplines: computing, engineers and archaeologists in France (1950–2000). In G. Delley, M. Díaz-Andreu, F. Djindjian, V. Fernández, A. Guidi and M.A. Kaeser (eds) *History of Archaeology - International Perspectives*, 220–232. British Archaeological Reports. Oxford, Archaeopress.

Plutniak, S. (2017) *The Archeological Operation. A Sociohistorical Perspective on a Discipline facing Automatics and Mathematics. France, Spain, Italy, Second Half of the 20th Century*. Paris, École des hautes études en sciences sociales.

Pollard, A.M. (2008) Archaeometry 50th anniversary issue editorial. *Archaeometry* 50 (2), 191–193.

Pombo, O. (2004) *Interdisciplinaridade: ambições e limites*. Lisboa, Relógio D'Água.

Reubi, S. (2011) Unveiling the truth? Aerial photographs and the social sciences in interwar France. In F. Link and U. Dörk (eds) *Geschichte der Sozialwissenschaften im 19e und 20. Jh*. Berlin, Duncker & Humbolt.

Schlanger, N. (2015) L'insaisissable technologie d'André Leroi-Gourhan. Des tendances et des faits des années 1930 à l'après-guerre. In P. Soulier (ed.) *André Leroi-Gourhan, l'homme, tout simplement*, 103–116. Travaux de la MAE. Paris, Boccard.

Simpson, G. (2000–01) Remembering Frederick Zeuner and others at the Institute of Archaeology. *Archaeology International* 2000–01, 9–10.

Smalley, I. (2011) Notes for a History of INQUA – the International Union for Quaternary Research (Association pour l'etude du Quaternaire, Internationale Quartarvereinigung, etc). *Loess Letter* 65, 1–23.

Smith, P.J. (1997) Grahame Clark's new archaeology: the Fenland Research Committee and Cambridge Prehistory in the 1930s. *Antiquity* 71, 11–30.

Sommer, U. and Struwe, R. (2006) Bermerkungen zur prehistorischen Archäologie an deutschen Universitäten im 19. Jahrhundert. In J. Callmer, M. Meyer, R. Struwe and C. Theune-Vogt (eds) *The Beginnings of Academic Pre- and Protohistoric Archaeology (1830-1930) in a European Perspective*, Berliner Archäologische Forschungen 2. Berlin, Verlag Marie Leidorf.

Sørensen, T.F. (2017) The two cultures and a world apart: archaeology and science at a new crossroads. *Norwegian Archaeological Review* 50 (2), 101–115.

Taylor, E.R. (2000) The introduction of radiocarbon dating. In S. Nash (ed.) *It's about Time. A History of Archaeological Dating in North America*, 84–104. Salt Lake City, University of Utah Press.

Torrence, R., Martinón-Torres, M. and Rehren, T. (2015) Forty years and still growing: *Journal of Archaeological Science* looks to the future. *Journal of Archaeological Science (Special Issue: Torrence, R., Martinón-Torres, M. & Rehren, T. (eds) Scoping the Future of Archaeological Science: Papers in Honour of Richard Klein)* 56, 1–8.

Troels-Smith, J., Jessen, C. and Mortensen, M.F. (2018) Modern pollen analysis and prehistoric beer – a lecture by Jørgen Troels-Smith, March 1977. *Review of Palaeobotany and Palynology* 259, 10–20.

Ucko, P.J. and Dimbleby, G.W., eds (1969) *The Domestication and Exploitation of Plants and Animals. Research Seminar in Archaeology and Related Subjects, London University, 1968*. London, Gerald Duckworth.

Van Riper, A.B. (1993) *Men among the Mammoths. Victorian Science and the Discovery of Human Prehistory. Science and its Conceptual Foundations*. Chicago, London, The University of Chicago Press.

Vian, P., ed. (1992) *Speculum Mundi*. Roma, Centro internazionale di ricerche umanistiche, Unione Internazionale degli Istituti di Archeologia, Storia e Storia dell'Arte in Roma, Presidenza del Consiglio di Ministri (Storia e cultura).

Waterbolk, H.T. (1999) Albert Egges van Giffen 1884–1973. In T. Murray (ed.) *Encyclopedia of Archaeology. The Great Archaeologists*. vol 1, 335–356. Santa Barbara, ABC-CLIO.

Chapter 2

Two sides to the coin: erudition and natural history from antiquarianism to archaeology in the work of John Evans

Nathan Schlanger

Abstract

An inexorable progression is often posited between antiquarianism, with literary or humanistic propensities, and archaeology, a triumphantly interdisciplinary and positive pursuit on par with the natural sciences. This historiographical commonplace rather overlooks the practical and theoretical sophistication inherent in antiquarian studies, and it also naturalises retrospectively the dominance of the natural sciences, notably palaeontology and geology, as the sole possible grounds for interdisciplinarity. The challenging transition from antiquarianism to archaeology is embodied by John Evans (1823-1908), polymath, businessman, geologist and numismatist. While debating Cesar's account of Roman Britain, Evans developed a highly original 'natural history of coins'. Ten years prior to Darwin's book, it confirms the early enlistment of organic and genealogical metaphors in the interpretation of human history. It also underlies Evans' decisive 1859 contribution to the establishment of high human antiquity, by recognising in Boucher de Perthes' flint finds in the Somme valley distinctive products of human industry, as if they were coins.

Keywords: history of archaeology; interdisciplinarity; antiquarianism; natural history; numismatics; stone tools; John Evans; Boucher de Perthes; Charles Darwin; Pitt Rivers.

Introduction

As the nineteenth century drew to a close, John Evans was invited to preside over the 67th annual meeting of the British Association for the Advancement of Science (BAAS), held in July 1897 in Toronto, in the Dominion of Canada. His presidential address at this pageant of imperial science, partly swansong and partly summary of his long and distinguished career, explored 'the links that connect the past with the present'. It also included, in its preliminaries, some incisive comments on the distinction between antiquarianism and what he termed 'Archæology proper':

> It is no doubt hard to define the exact limits which are to be assigned to Archæology (sic) as a science and Archæology as a branch of History and Belles-Lettres. A distinction is frequently drawn between science on the one hand, and knowledge or learning on the other [...].
>
> It must however be acknowledged that a distinction does exist between Archæology proper, and what, for want of a better word, may be termed Antiquarianism. It may be interesting to know the internal arrangements of a Dominican convent in the middle ages [...] or to decide whether some given edifice was erected in Roman, Saxon, or Norman times. But the power to do this, though invoking no small degree of detailed knowledge and some acquaintance with scientific methods, can hardly entitle its possessors to be enrolled among the votaries of science.
>
> A familiarity with all the details of Greek and Roman mythology and culture must be regarded as a literary rather than a scientific qualification; and yet when among the records of classical times we come upon traces of manners and customs which have survived for generations, and which seem to throw some rays of light upon the dim past, when history and writing were unknown, we are, I think, approaching the boundaries of scientific Archæology (Evans 1898, 3–4).

The author of these claims, we should acknowledge outright, was himself a leading explorer of such archaeological boundaries. By then rich in achievements and honours, Sir John Evans (1823–1908) had been assiduously pursuing throughout his adult life his activities as gentleman scientist and entrepreneur (see his daughter Joan Evans 1943 for main biographical details, as well as recent appraisals in Sherratt 2002; O'Connor 2007; MacGregor 2008a; 2008b; Schlanger 2010; 2011, on which later parts of this chapter are based). As this chapter will further attest, his contributions to the advancement of numismatics, prehistoric archaeology and quaternary geology were outstanding: they were also particularly well disseminated in Britain and worldwide, through numerous publications, public lectures and official engagements with leading learned societies, such as the Society of Antiquaries of London and the Royal Society (see Fyfe 2015). All the while, Evans also deployed his impressive work ethics, managerial skills and technical nous at his uncle's paper and envelope factory, joining the mill in his youth to become a partner and son-in-law to the owner. Without doubt, John Evans can rightly be considered a 'polymath' – especially if, going beyond casual usage, this qualifier is not reduced to a mere celebratory accolade (admittedly all the more merited in our own age of narrow specialisms). 'John Evans, polymath' should above all denote a potential accomplishment, an intellectual disposition, a deeper-level opportunity for cross-fertilising different and even remote domains and practices. This could occur by bringing insights from science and business under a common heading, or indeed by bringing together hitherto unconnected areas of scientific enquiry. This was the case with Evans' and Prestwich's 'auditing' and 'stocktaking' claims surrounding the acceptance of high human antiquity in 1859 (see Schlanger 2010), and also with Evans' 'Victorian industrial culture' and his concerns with invention, design, calibration and patents (as discussed by Bulstrode 2016, and see MacGregor 2008a). Moreover, so I claim, it was upon such polymathic connections (albeit in ways that were not necessarily fully conscious, thought out or followed through) that Evans contributed so decisively to the making of prehistoric archaeology.

If so, the above quoted statements require a second reading. Limited to their strategic aims, and recalling the feverish context of the BAAS meeting, these claims follow the well-worn disciplinary ploy of promoting one's own newly favoured position by, *inter alia*, distinguishing, demarcating and eventually denigrating other or 'previous' approaches. Such a denigrating practice is not without its long-lasting consequences, but at present a closer look at these claims and their author cannot fail to highlight a paradoxical irony – which might be conveyed, to anticipate a classic historical (or at least literary) reference below, as: '*Tu quoque Evans?*'. Our polymath protagonist was after all a key actor in the propagation of both 'literary' and 'scientific' perspectives. Moreover, the retrospective distinctions he posited in his 1897 speech actually seem to undermine the very foundations of his seminal archaeological accomplishment. A critical appraisal of Evans' works will rather show that his ground-breaking contribution to the study of 'History that is not written' (Evans 1882a; 1882b; Roberts and Barton 2008) (Fig. 2.1) was first and foremost secured as an antiquary, that is, as an expert on ancient coinage fully conversant with ancient historical sources, belles-lettres and suchlike old-fashioned branches of learning.

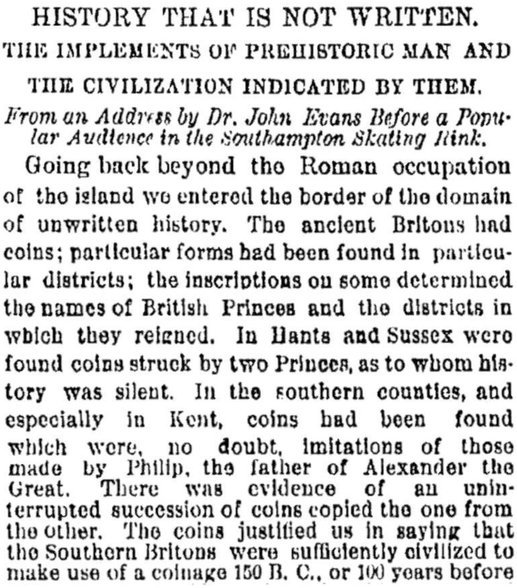

In fact, there are here two polymathic or interdisciplinary stories for us to unravel in the following pages, partly linked and yet also surprisingly disconnected. The first episode, starting in 1850, concerned Evans' remarkable contribution to the field of numismatics itself, where he was able to shed new light on a thoroughly familiar object – ancient coins – through an unprecedented recourse to natural history. The second episode, from 1860 onwards, related to Evans' successful transformation of a set of finds hitherto considered to be rather insignificant – ancient stone implements – into an essentially new object of scientific inquiry: a transformation that took place, I will argue, through the well-established lens of numismatics.

> HISTORY THAT IS NOT WRITTEN.
> THE IMPLEMENTS OF PREHISTORIC MAN AND THE CIVILIZATION INDICATED BY THEM.
> *From an Address by Dr. John Evans Before a Popular Audience in the Southampton Skating Rink.*
> Going back beyond the Roman occupation of the island we entered the border of the domain of unwritten history. The ancient Britons had coins; particular forms had been found in particular districts; the inscriptions on some determined the names of British Princes and the districts in which they reigned. In Hants and Sussex were found coins struck by two Princes, as to whom history was silent. In the southern counties, and especially in Kent, coins had been found which were, no doubt, imitations of those made by Philip, the father of Alexander the Great. There was evidence of an uninterrupted succession of coins copied the one from the other. The coins justified us in saying that the Southern Britons were sufficiently civilized to make use of a coinage 150 B. C., or 100 years before

Figure 2.1. 'History that is not written. The implements of prehistoric man and the civilization indicated by them'. From an address by Dr John Evans before a popular audience in the Southampton skating rink (The New York Times 1882, September 17) (Evans 1882a).

The first interdisciplinary turn – the natural history of coins

As if going against the (historical) order of things, coins had long preceded stone implements as objects of curiosity and of methodical inquiry in western scholarship. The same goes in the sequence of Evans' own research interests. Initiated early on to numismatics by his father, Evans had become by the 1840s a serious connoisseur and collector of British and Roman coins, and also an active, well-respected member of the numismatic community. The first of his many publications, in the 1850 issue of the *Numismatic Chronicle* (1850), was followed fifteen years later by a magisterial compendium on *The Coins of the Ancient Britons* (1864), itself updated two decades later with a substantial *Supplement* (1890) (see especially Jersey 2008). More details on Evans' numismatic practices will emerge throughout this paper, but it can be agreed at present that the bulk of his contribution was resolutely classificatory and descriptive. In his numerous publications, Evans used rather painstaking empirical Victorian prose to identify, compile, compare, systematise, localise and illustrate as accurately as possible many hundreds of individual coins from findspots and collections across the country.

In addition to this undeniably solid input, however, Evans also pursued throughout his life a far more radical and distinctive interpretative argument, concerning the existence, characteristics and date of coinage in pre-Roman Britain. As initially posed in numismatic circles, the problem could not have been of a more traditional 'literary' bend. It derived from Julius Caesar's remark in *De Bello Gallico* (V, 12), whereby 'Utuntur aut aere aut annulis ferreis ad certum pondus examinatis pro nummis' ('They use either brass, or rings of iron adjusted to a certain weight, instead of money', quoted and discussed in Evans (1875, 478, and see de Jersey 2008)). Should this 'pro nummis' be taken to imply that the pre-Roman native tribes did not master the practice of coinage? Evans' own position, forcefully set in his 1850 paper 'On the date of British coins', and unwaveringly reiterated throughout his life (see Fig. 2.1), was that such textual references in ancient sources (whatever their possible readings) should always be confronted with 'the testimony of the coins themselves' (Evans 1875, 478). Indeed, once he had organised and interpreted the numismatic evidence to his satisfaction, Evans was convinced that coinage in Britain long antedated the first Roman invasion of 55 BC. Furthermore, he argued it had as its prototype a circa 300 BC Macedonian stater of Philip II – or more probably some Gaulish (continental) imitation of this currency, reaching Britain through commercial exchanges or mercenaries' pay. By assessing the changing designs on the coins and their diminishing weight, he was able to place selected coins on a plate so as to 'show how, from this prototype, by means of successive imitations of imitations, a number of new and totally distinct types arose, until their original was quite lost sight of' (Evans 1850, 133). While an 'exact numismatic succession' was still lacking, the reader was invited to 'trace' well-oriented changes and admit that 'from No. 2 to No. 3 [top centre down to right, in Fig. 2.2] the transition is easy […] from this [No. 8] we arrive at No. 9, which is the perfect Verulam type' (Evans

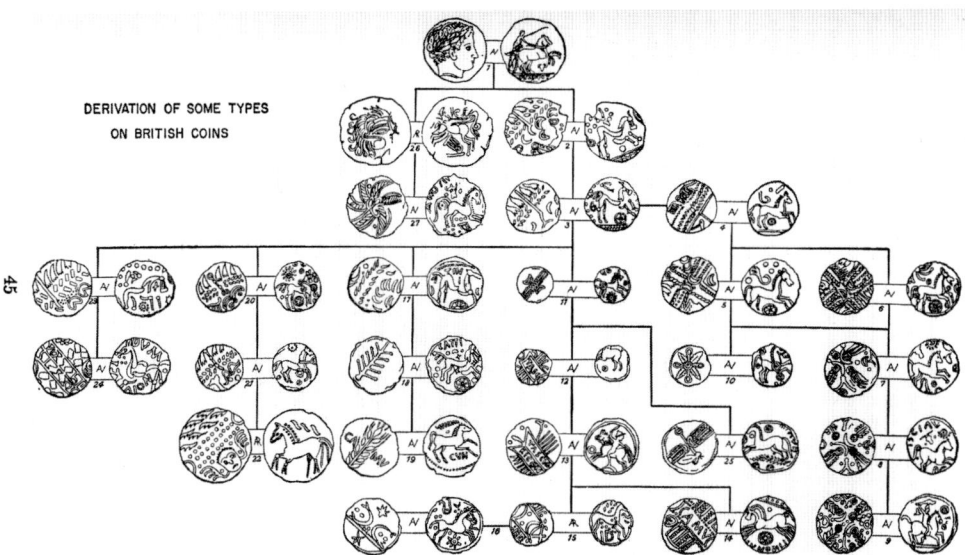

Figure 2.2. The derivation of some types of British coins by John Evans. Plate I in 'On the date of British coins' (Numismatic chronicle 1850, xii).

1850, 133). This whole process from the initial prototype to its latest imitation (at Roman contact) took time, and Evans could estimate, in response to the initial question, that British tribes have been producing coins already some 100 or 120 years prior to Cesar's landing.

This postulated process of transformation, linking incremental formal similarities and historical affinities, places Evans' interpretation along something of a watershed in western scholarship. On the one side, such expectations of 'gradual degeneration' dovetailed with the classical model promoted nearly a century earlier by Johann Joachim Winckelmann (1717–1768) in his *History of Ancient Art* (1764). The German historian of art and antiquarian had indeed argued that occidental civilisation, following its emergence in fifth-century BC Greece, had spread northwards through successive and more or less successful phases of creative imitation, until the aspired neo-classicism of his times. Moreover, the terminology Evans applied in this 1850 paper to coins and their transformations – including such notions as 'varieties', 'derivations', 'metamorphoses', 'succession', 'pedigrees' or 'descent' – proved highly compatible with organicist conceptions of selection, be they artificial (by breeders improving their stock, for example) or natural.

Intimations of Darwinism

Evans' own leanings in the 1850 publication seemed to be amply confirmed a decade later, upon the publication of Charles Darwin's *Origins of Species* (1859). Besides appearing to draw on the same 'language of nature' (see Beer 1983; Jordanova 1986), Evans also moved in Darwin's intellectual circles, notably via his friend the banker, politician and anthropologist John Lubbock (1834–1913). Be it as it may, Evans could readily cash in on these latest naturalist conceptions, and quite consciously recast what might have remained a historicist or morphological numismatic elaboration into a far bolder methodological and theoretical claim. Thus, in *The Coins of the Ancient Britons*, he stated that: 'Among barbarous nations the laws which regulate the types of coinage of this kind, consisting of successive copies of copies of a given original, are much the same as those which, according to our best naturalists [*i.e.*, Darwin], govern the succession of types in the organic kingdom' (Evans 1864, 27–28).

Further examples of such theoretical recasting can be found throughout Evans' publications. For example, in an 1875 paper eloquently titled 'The coinage of the ancient Britons and natural selection' he stated that 'the succession of the types of the [native British] coins followed certain laws, to a great extent analogous to those by which the evolution of successive forms of organic life appear to be governed' (Evans 1875, 476). Fifteen years later, in 1890, when he came to publish his *Supplement* (to *The Coins of the Ancient Britons*), Evans added a retrospective comment:

> In fact, I attempted [in 1850] to apply the principles of 'evolution' and 'natural selection' to numismatic inquires; and when, ten years afterwards, Darwin's great work on the origins of species was published, I found that I had been approaching the study of the barbaric art on much the same lines as those which he had conducted in his far more important inquiries into the hidden secrets of nature (Evans 1890, 421).

And again in 1897, in Evans' already quoted presidential address at the Toronto BAAS, he was keen to point out his prescience in enlisting evolution to numismatics:

> In arranging the chronological sequence of these coins, the evolution of their type – a process almost as remarkable, and certainly as well defined, as any to be found in nature – has served as an efficient guide. I may venture to add that the results obtained from the study of the morphology of these series of coins were published ten years before the appearance of Darwin's great work on the 'Origins of Species' (Evans 1898, 4–5).

Interdisciplinary references

Despite the slight ambiguity in Evans' position, clamouring to be a Darwinian *avant la lettre* while retrospectively claiming allegiance to its strength, the message broadcast throughout was consistent enough. And yet, this interdisciplinary convergence lends itself to several readings. Firstly, at one level, we have here some hitherto little considered elements relevant to the debated issue of Darwinism and archaeology, and more generally nineteenth-century recourse to the natural sciences. The overall historiographical impression (which is not contested here) is that Darwinism, with its entailed notions of 'selection', 'struggle' or 'decent with modification', had actually been slow to percolate into prehistoric archaeology, and had little discernible impact on the acceptance and subsequent study of high human antiquity in the 1860s. The introduction into archaeology of explicitly typological thinking (that is, of a classificatory system guided by serial, developmental or chronological expectations) is generally attributed to the Swedish scholars Hans Hildebrand and Oscar Montelius, who made occasional reference to Darwin's work in the 1870s (Gräslund 1987, 99 ff.; Riede 2006). Here Evans could – and actually did – claim some priority, as when he completed the sentence quoted above from the 1890 *Supplement* on 'Darwin's great work' with the following comment:

> Since the time this method of inquiry was adopted in the case of British coins [Evans is undoubtedly alluding here to his own 1850 publication] it has been found of service in connection with other series, and I may call attention to two interesting papers by Mr C.F. Keary[1] on 'The morphology of coins' which have been published in the Numismatic Chronicle [1885, 1886]. Dr. Hans Hildebrand has also followed the same method in investigating the history of some of the earliest Scandinavian coins. In his ethnological researches General Pitt Rivers has found, in the form and ornamentation of implements, an almost analogous development with that which has prevailed among coins (Evans 1890, 422).

A second comment takes us to an altogether different direction. As intriguing as were these transformative patterns, Evans' primary concern was really with the *historical* potential of these 'successive stages [...] for placing the various coins in even approximate chronological order', thereby providing time depth for British coinage. Thus, in his 1875 paper on natural selection, Evans took particular pride at having shed light 'on one of the obscurest portion of the history of this country', showing that Britain's native inhabitants were rather less barbarous and more civilised than previously portrayed. His concluding hope was that:

> a more favourable impression of our ancestors or predecessors in this country at the time of Caesar's invasion has been created than that which commonly prevailed. He [Evans] hoped that they would no longer be regarded as the merest savages 'who stained themselves blue, sat under the mistletoe, and indulged in obscene rites', and who burnt the living in wicker baskets, instead of, in accordance with the modern view, burying their dead in those useful articles [wicker baskets], for the manufacture of which Britain was famous even in Roman times (Evans 1875, 487).

This final comment was undoubtedly tongue-in-cheek. The cropping up of entrepreneurial and promotional instincts here is nevertheless quite revealing, as is Evans' much broader antiquarian agenda – post-druidic, William Stukeley-inspired – for the study of pre-Roman Britain. This brings us to the third and possibly most paradoxical consideration regarding Evans' transformational scheme: its generalisation and applicability *beyond* its numismatic hearth. We saw in the 1890 quote above how Evans applauded the input of his friend, the ethnographer and archaeological collector General Augustus Henry Lane Fox (1827–1900, known since 1880, and retrospectively, as Pitt Rivers). They repeatedly exchanged on these topics, and Pitt Rivers readily acknowledged the 'prototypical' inspiration provided by Evans' numismatic proposals for his own conception of ethnographic series (Schlanger 2010) (Fig. 2.3). This recognition, by the way, extended to the succeeding generation of British anthropologists and museum curators, such as Henry Balfour and Alfred Court Haddon, who both cited Evans' numismatic plate as a source (Balfour 1893, viii, 30 passim; Haddon 1895, 313).

Evans, for his part, appeared more nuanced. At some point, he did state that: 'no doubt this theory of descent with variations holds good with regards to most of the appliances of man' (1875, 482). Moreover, in the preface of his 1881 book on *Ancient Bronze Implements*, he went so far as to convey this expectation as a petition of principle:

> It may by some be thought that a vast amount of useless trouble has been bestowed in figuring and describing so many varieties of what were after all in most cases the ordinary tools of the artificer, or the common arms of the warrior or huntsman, which differed from each other only in apparently unimportant particulars. But as in biological studies minute anatomy often affords the most trustworthy evidence as to the descent of any given organism from some earlier form of life, so these minor details in the form and character of ordinary implements, which to the cursory observer appear devoid of meaning, may, to a skilful archaeologist, afford valuable clues by which the march of the bronze civilisation over Europe may be traced to its original starting-place (Evans 1881, v).

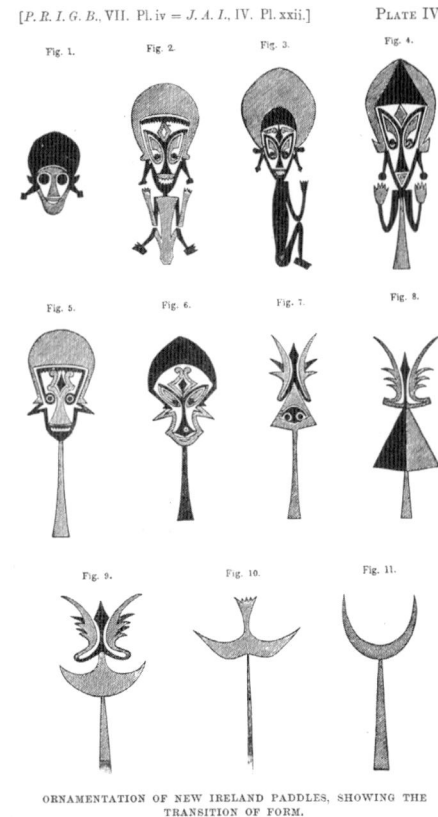

Figure 2.3. 'Ornamentation of New Ireland paddles, showing the transition of form', Plate IV (in Fox 1875, iv; reproduced from Pitt Rivers 1906).

And yet, whatever might have been Evans' success at examining bronze implements and ornaments in this light (see MacGregor 2008b), it is striking to note that he never really sought (and at times, as we shall see, actually resisted) to apply these interdisciplinary insights to the archaeological domain he had so skilfully made his own – the study of ancient stone implements.

The second interdisciplinary episode – the numismatics of flints

Indeed, intriguingly enough, Evans' decisive contribution to the study of worked flints, and to the emerging domain of prehistoric archaeology as a whole, was not actually grounded on the latest naturalist methods (he had brought to the fore). Rather, this contribution was built on the far more traditional and basic tool-kit of numismatics.

In other words, it was first and foremost *by considering flints as if they were coins* that Evans made of them new objects of scientific inquiry and vital sources of unwritten history. Let us then examine in some detail this archaeological contribution, before concluding with its interdisciplinary implications.

Evans' first encounter with stone implements took place in the spring of 1859 when, together with quaternary geologist and wine merchant Joseph Prestwich (1812–1896), he visited Northern France on behalf of the Geological Society. A local antiquarian at Abbeville, Jacques Boucher de Perthes (1788–1868), had for long been claiming to find evidence for the high, even 'antediluvian', antiquity of humankind. The visiting Englishmen examined the evidence at first-hand and gathered sufficient 'moral and collateral testimony' to be convinced of the coexistence of genuine human-made stone implements associated with fossil bones of extinct species in undisturbed 'drift' deposits. The relevant scientific authorities in France and in England (including the Society of Antiquaries and the Royal Society) soon followed suit, and prehistoric archaeology was launched on its course. The famous events surrounding the debates and acceptance of high human antiquity in the 1860s are detailed in, among others, Grayson (1983) and Hurel and Coye (2011). On the precursor figure of Boucher de Perthes, see mainly Aufrère (1940) and Cohen and Hublin (1989), and a new interpretation of his motivations and contributions in Schlanger (2015).

Evans, it must be emphasised, joined the trip as a recognised specialist. His brief – as he confirmed in his initial report to Prestwich on 25 May 1859 – was to study the flint implements contained in these quaternary deposits by 'regarding them from an antiquarian rather than a geological point of view'. More specifically, Evans was to seek between these newly-claimed Drift specimens and the better-known Celt implements some identifiable differences or resemblances 'which may consist in material, form or workmanship' (Evans 1859, 310, and see Evans 1860, 287) – these being, as it happens, precisely the criteria he had been applying for over a decade now to the study of coins (*e.g.* Evans 1850, 135). Through various physical and conceptual displacements, Evans proved able – often quite implicitly, and in ways that were not recognised as such by his contemporaries nor indeed by later commentators – to transfer some well-established methodological and interpretative stances from one domain of antiquarian expertise to another, new, nascent, still to be fully defined. These wide-ranging transfers touched notably on the *documentation* of ancient stone implements, their *authentication* and their *interpretation*.

Documenting authenticity

Together with the above criteria of material, form and workmanship, which served to structure scientific observations, Evans drew extensively on the documentary strategies of numismatics. For example, the notions of 'striking' and 'wrought', part of the technical vocabulary of numismatics, soon found themselves applied to stones, as in 'the best-wrought forms of flint implements', or 'flakes […] struck off, and wrought into shape' (see Evans 1860, 280, 289; 1872, 22, 292, 573 ff.). While Evans may not have been the first to use such terms, he was clearly drawing here on his specialised numismatic understanding – all the more so that he saw some telling affinities between the striking of coins and the striking of flints. More broadly, Evans emulated from numismatics the art of consistent, normalised, disciplined scrutiny. Appearing so small and so similar to one another, coins required rather more than sweeping impressions or overviews to become intelligible. From the Renaissance onwards, and upon the more systematic approach expounded by Joseph Hilarius Eckhel (1737–1798) in his *Doctrina numorum veterum*, numismatic practitioners were making sense of coins by methodically preparing and examining them, submitting each to the same descriptive gaze and set of criteria (*e.g.* metal, size, weight) in order to record their condition and dimensions, and to appraise their eventual specificities, markings or defects. Consistently applied and accompanied by particularly detailed illustrations, these preliminary procedures made it possible to refer the coins under study to their 'issues' and 'types' (as etched on the dies from which they had been struck) and then seek their historical or aesthetic affinities (for further discussion and references on numismatic practices see Schlanger 2010; 2011, as well as archaeological considerations in Kemmers and Myrberg 2011; Barrett 2012; Myrberg-Burström 2019).

This 'scrupulous accuracy' in documentation was also a reflection of deep-seated concerns regarding authenticity. Over the past two and a half millennia of their existence, coins have been repeatedly tampered with, clipped, imitated and faked – and this not simply as collectible items for duping unsuspecting amateurs (as might be false Greek marbles or Etruscan vases), but also, with infinitely more serious repercussions, as would-be items of valid currency insidiously introduced within the monetary economy. The discipline of numismatics was from the onset particularly attentive to this question, all the more so in the nineteenth century when its practitioners' base, traditionally composed of erudite collectors and art historians, broadened up to include also liberal professions and businessmen, keen on enhancing their own moral standing. Evans was one of those, and early in his career he experienced firsthand the need to fend off accusations regarding the dubious character of some coin he had acquired: 'I can only say that I never saw a coin with less cause for suspicion about it. Its patina, weight, workmanship, and the manner in which it came into my possession, all place its authenticity beyond any doubt' (Evans 1856, 164, and see Evans 1864; 1866).

Such a vigilant probity, involving shape, material, workmanship and provenience, was extended to the study of ancient stone implements. Here, the stakes were double. First and foremost was the question of the *artificial* status of candidate exemplars, as it was important to ascertain whether they were at all man-made objects, deliberately produced and shaped, or on the contrary misleading 'plays of nature' due to geological or mechanical factors, mere 'angular fragments broken by ice-action', as they were once dismissed by a famous commentator (see below). The second question surrounding stone implement concerned their *integrity* as genuinely ancient objects, rather than falsifications by modern forgers, sometimes deliberately 'planted' in quaternary layers by unscrupulous workmen. Evans was in fact uniquely placed, as a numismatist, to seek and assess the 'characteristics of authenticity' displayed by candidate exemplars (Evans 1859, 310). His attentiveness clearly transpires in his remark that 'many of the implements [of the Somme valley] have a coating of carbonate of lime forming an adherent incrustation upon them: this (…) is for those weapons what the patina is for bronze coins and statues, a proof of their antiquity' (Evans 1860, 297) – a revealing comment attesting to the transfer of a concept and its relevance from one antiquarian domain to another. The same applies to Evans' interest in the processes of flint implement manufacture, an interest that of course echoed his industrialist concerns. Their very forgery, so he argued, the very fact that they could be replicated, actually militated in favour of their artificial character, and against those who would ignore them as natural forms. Similarly, Evans' recourse to ethnographic occurrences of stone-working and use among the Aztecs, the Eskimo and the Australian Aborigines followed (albeit more thoroughly and with better defined objectives) the antiquarian interest in 'savage analogies' pursued by such scholars as Lafitau and Jussieu in the mid-eighteenth century – an antiquarian imagination which, as Evans himself intimated above, informed many reconstructions of pre-Roman, druidic Britain (Evans 1875, 487, quoted above, and see Piggott 1989; Schnapp 1996; 2002; as well as Manias 2015). Equally pertinent were Evans' visits, closer to home, to the Brandon gunflint-works, his employment of a Suffolk flintknapper, and again his own precocious recourse to experimental flintknapping, including live replications and demonstrations for his peers. All these were undertakings that secured Evans his lasting reputation as the incontrovertible authority on the reproduction and classification of ancient stone implements (Evans 1869; 1872, 13 ff., and see appreciations in White 2001; O'Connor 2007; Roberts and Barton 2008; Lamdin-Whymark 2009).

Interpretations

As it happens, also the classificatory and interpretative dimensions of Evans' stone implement studies proved to be thoroughly influenced by numismatic considerations. From his first visit to the Somme valley onwards, Evans' investigation of the 'character' of the flint finds was specifically oriented to their broader chronological implications. Besides providing some confirmation on the existence of the Stone Age (within the then still-controversial tripartite scheme of Stone, Bronze and Iron Ages) (see Gräslund 1987; Rowley-Conwy 2007; Blanckaert 2017), his classification also posited a structuring dichotomy, within this Stone Age, between the Celt and the Drift periods. From the onset, Evans saw it as his most important task:

> to point out wherein these implements from the drift resemble or differ from those in some degree analogous with them, which are so frequently found in this country and on the Continent, and are usually considered to be the work of the primitive, or as for convenience sake I will call them, the Celtic inhabitants of this part of Europe (Evans 1859, 130).

This Celt/Drift distinction, soon renamed by John Lubbock and known thereafter as the 'Neolithic' and 'Palaeolithic' periods (Lubbock 1865), embodied for Evans a simultaneously technological and tactile differentiation between 'polished' and 'unpolished' stone implements – clearly echoing the then prevailing numismatic distinction between coins 'inscribed' and 'uninscribed'. Focusing on the unpolished flints and their cutting edges, he distinguished between three main types: '1. Flint flakes, apparently intended for arrow-heads or knives. 2. Pointed weapons, analogous to lance or spear heads. 3. Oval or almond-shaped implements presenting a cutting edge all round' (Evans 1859, 1860; see Fig. 2.4). Leaving aside the flakes, considered to be chronologically non-diagnostic, Evans specified that both the 'pointed' and 'oval' implements belonged to the Drift period. However, surprisingly, no sooner had he identified these supposedly clear-cut and diagnostic types of implements than he set to tone down and belittle their distinctions. These implements may 'for convenience sake be classed under three heads, though there is so much variety among them that the classes, especially the second and the third, may be said to blend or run one into the other'. This made it difficult literally and figuratively to draw any 'decided line of demarcation' between the acute and the round-pointed forms, given that so many specimens 'occupied an intermediate position'. Moreover, 'what character of point an implement would have' was in fact 'to a considerable extent a matter of accident' related to difficulties posed by the nature and quality of the raw materials used (Evans 1862, 77; 1872, 561, 566–567).

The conception of variability invoked here actually bears the hallmark of numismatics: drawing on the systematic scrutiny of magnified micro-scale traits, it advanced some ready-made intelligibility in terms of *minting* considerations. As Evans had discussed at length in his numismatic writings (notably Evans 1864, 34, 43–45), the technical processes of coin manufacture in ancient times were such that no exemplars produced were ever exactly identical. Causes for variability included the specific properties of the raw materials (metals) refined and alloyed, the weight, shape and conditioning of the blanks (flans), their positioning and centring on the obverse (anvil) die, the placement and orientation of the reverse (punch) die above them, the force, angle and repetition of the striking blow, and so on. The whole sequence was repeated for each coin struck from each die used (as they wore down and cracked) and then again for each 'type' produced by the minting authorities. And as with coins, so with flints,

> it seems doubtful whether it is worthwhile to insist much on these subdivisions of form, many of which must, no doubt, have resulted from the manner in which the flint happened to break during the process of manufacture. Though, therefore, I have here attempted a somewhat detailed classification, I by no means wish it to be supposed that I consider each form of implement to have been specially made to serve some special requirement, as is the case with many of the tools and weapons of the present day. I am far more ready to think that only two main divisions can be established, though even these may be said to shade off into each other; I mean pointed implements for piercing, digging, or boring, and sharp-edged implements for cutting or scraping (Evans 1872, 567).

2. Two sides to the coin

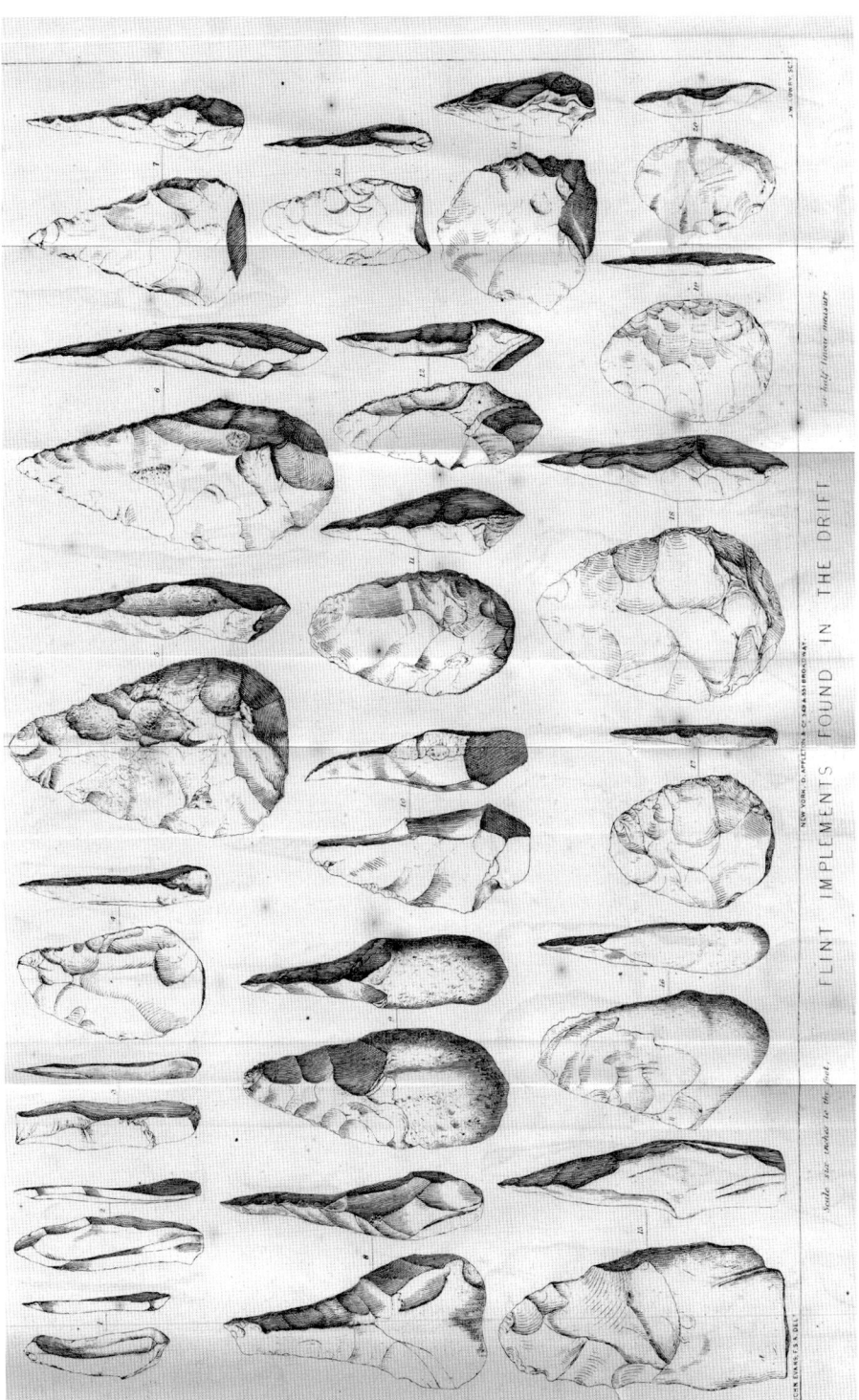

Figure 2.4. Classification of stone implements from the Drift. Plate IV in John Evans, 'Account of some further discoveries of flint implements in the Drift on the Continent and in England', Archaeologia 1862, xxxix; 57–84. Items 1 to 4 would be 'flakes', 5 to 10 'pointed', and 11 to 20 'oval'.

Conclusions

By considering flints as if they were coins, by documenting them, assessing their authenticity, and interpreting them in the lights of numismatics, Evans contributed more than any scholar, certainly throughout the nineteenth century, to advance the study of these flints – and could go no further. It is true that some of Evans' propositions, notably regarding the morphology of handaxes ('pointed' or 'oval'), have been the subject of some attention over the years (Roe 1968; Goren-Inbar and Gonen 2006). Likewise, there is no doubt that contemporary research has been moving beyond morphological and typological observations to pay increasing attention to technological considerations, including the knapping properties and uses of raw materials as well as the sequences and *chaînes opératoires* of their production. These were in fact questions of process and productivity to which Evans, with his (paper) manufacturer's acumen, had clearly been attentive to (see also Bulstrode 2016). Nevertheless, it seems that Evans did not really seek to 'complete the triangle': having looked at numismatics through the prism of natural history, and having then examined flints from the perspectives of coins, he did not take a synthetic step further to consider the option that subsequently became a leitmotif of prehistoric research – the natural history of stone implements.

Much as he was familiar with the terminology of selection, descent, transformation and progress – as we recall, a familiarity claimed in the study of coins ten years before the works of 'our best naturalists' – Evans hardly sought to apply this particular language to flints, and nor did he ever mention Darwin, 'evolution' or 'natural selection' in the context of prehistoric studies and stone artefacts. Moreover, while Evans may have approved Pitt Rivers' attempt, explicitly inspired from his own work, to put in series the ornaments of Melanesian paddles (Fig. 2.3, see above), he quite clearly disapproved the extension of this perspective to stone implements. Indeed, Pitt Rivers, as if enthralled by these laws of sequence and continuity he was fleshing out, had proposed to assemble also a series of stone implements, ranging from the oldest known (from St Acheul and the English river drifts, but also from Southern Africa and India) to recent ethnographic exemplars. 'By selecting specimens, and arranging them in order from left to right, I [Pitt Rivers] have endeavoured to trace the transition from the drift type to the almond-shaped celt type', showing how 'almost imperceptibly' they pass through 'numerous gradations of form', so that, 'in casting the eye from left to right along the upper row of diagram No. 1 (Plate XII), it will puzzle the acutest observer to determine where the Drift type ends, and that of the Celt begins' (Pitt Rivers 1868, as published in Pitt Rivers 1906, 103 ff.). For his part, however, Evans consistently rejected this particular vision, with its emphasis on continuity rather than classification, and likewise he remained sceptical of the claims advanced by Pitt Rivers upon his excavations at Cissbury. On the contrary, argued Evans, 'a glance at the figure will at once show how different in character they are', in shape and in mode of manufacture, exhibiting a 'complete gap between the River-drift and the Surface Stone Periods, so far as any intermediate forms of implements are concerned' (Evans 1872, 560). This complete gap, in turn, reinforced the hypothesis favoured by Evans (possibly of biblical or diluvial inspiration) whereby there has been a total population replacement between the Palaeolithic (drift) and Neolithic (celt) inhabitants of the country.

Back in 1860, Evans' initial ambition for the study of stone implements had been 'from the examination of ancient remains, to recall into an ideal existence days long since passed away, to trace the conditions of a previous state of things, and, as it were, to repeople the earth with its former inhabitants' (Evans 1860). We can now recognise that the frames of reference on which he more or less implicitly drew for 'repeopling the earth' were actually those of ancient history and classical studies, and not of the natural sciences. In fact, Evans rather seems to have proceeded as if his sources were of a historical, recorded nature. He thus projected a Julius Caesar-inspired quest for princely districts and ancient tribal boundaries deep back into the Stone Age. This is how we can understand his extension of a 'gazetteer' approach from numismatics to *Ancient Stone Implements* (1872). As he attempted to pin-point the provenance of flint tools within pseudo-political territorial entities, he left in the process little scope or need for such 'naturalist' considerations as raw material quality, availability or geomorphology. Similarly, with his manufacturer's technological and accident-based interpretation of situational variability (extended from coins to flints), Evans hardly saw throughout his career any need to identify or explore long-term broad-ranging developmental trends. This included, most obviously, the patterns championed at that time on the continent by Gabriel de Mortillet (1821–1898), the engineer-turned-museum curator whose periodisation of the Stone Age into Acheulean, Mousterian and Aurignacian industries not only confirmed that human-made objects were the best makers of civilisation, but also amply demonstrated the universal laws of human progress and development (Evans 1872, 430 ff.; Mortillet 1873; and see Richard 2008; Schlanger 2013; 2014).

Otherwise, but for a small terminological substitution, our protagonist remained true to himself. When he first set out to contribute to the establishment of high human antiquity, Evans had asserted the need to consider flints 'from an *antiquarian* point of view' – and we now know how important and indeed invaluable such an antiquarian, numismatic-based, accuracy-driven perspective has been for the development of prehistoric archaeology. If further confirmation is still needed, we need only to compare Evans' conclusions in 1859 with those reached, at the same time and regarding the same set of objects, by none other than Charles Darwin. Writing to his friend Joseph Hooker in June of that year, upon the confirmation of Boucher de Perthes' claims by the scientific establishment, Darwin could casually admit his previous scepticism (Charles Darwin to Joseph Dalton Hooker, 22 June 1859, Darwin Correspondence Project, 'Letter no. 2471', http://www.darwinproject.ac.uk/DCP-LETT-2471):

> I was glad to hear about Prestwich's paper [to the Royal Society]. My doubt has been (& I see Wright has inserted same in Athenæum) whether the pieces of flint are really tools: their numbers make me doubt; & when I formerly looked at Boucher de Perthes' drawings I came to the conclusion that they were angular fragments broken by ice-action.

With antiquarian eyes, Evans saw these flints for what they were, and drew on his numismatist-cum-businessman's authority to convince the scientific community thereafter. Some forty years later, in his valedictory presidential speech at the Toronto BAAS, he could advance with only a slight shift in vocabulary that 'it falls strictly within the province of the *archæologist* to judge whether given specimens were so wrought or not' (Evans 1898, emphasis added). For our part, in conclusion, we clearly need to recognise and take on board the fact that prehistoric archaeology has emerged and developed and grown *with* antiquarianism, and not *vis a vis* or *against* it. Like most scholars of his times, Evans was part 'professional' and part 'amateur', and the fact that his scientific reward was measured in official recognition rather than in contractual salary made it possible for him to move between and across disciplines, generating this polymathic interdisciplinarity that proved so fecund. In historiographic and disciplinary terms, it may have proved convenient for Evans, and for generations of prehistorians and archaeologists ever since, to emphasise their 'interdisciplinary' affinities with the 'natural' life- and earth-sciences. This has entailed a series of intellectual, methodological, academic, organisational and financial connections whose implications are still very much with us today, in the current topography of knowledge. Yet, as I have argued, Evans' own foundational case clearly helps us grasp that this master narrative of natural science dominance is neither innocuous nor devoid of biases and limitations. We have seen, on the contrary, that the study of human antiquity on the basis of objects, vestiges and material traces has always been, to greater or lesser degrees, significantly related to the achievements of historical and humanistic learning (see Schnapp 1993; 2002; Miller 2017). It is only by acknowledging these proximities and intersections that will we be able to truly expand the boundaries of interdisciplinarity, and reach out for a better understanding of humanity, past, present and future.

Acknowledgements

This chapter was written within the framework of the InterArq research project (HAR2016-80271-P) (interarqweb.wordpress.com) subsidised by the State Research Agency (AEI) and the European Regional Development Fund (ERDF, EU).

Note

1 In 'The morphology of coins', the numismatist, historian and later novelist Charles Francis Keary (1848-1917) advanced his own explanation as to why coins, specifically, could be understood as 'a chapter in natural evolution': this was because, unlike tools or implements 'coins have to perform no special function in relation to natural forces' – they are purely symbolic and arbitrary in character (Keary 1885).

References

Aufrère, L. (1940) Figures de préhistoriens, I. Boucher de Perthes. *Préhistoire* 7, 7–134.
Balfour, H. (1893) *The Evolution of Decorative Art. An Essay upon its Origin and Development as Illustrated by the Art of Modern Races of Mankind.* New York, Macmillan.

Barrett, K. (2012) Writing on, around, and about coins: from the eighteenth-century cabinet to the twenty-first-century database. *Journal of Museum Ethnography* 25, 64–80.

Beer, G. (1983) *Darwin's Plots: Evolutionary Narrative in Darwin, George Eliot and Nineteenth-Century Fiction*. Cambridge, Cambridge University Press.

Blanckaert, C. (2017) Nommer le préhistorique au XIXe siècle. Linguistique et transferts lexicaux. *Organon* 49, 57–103.

Bulstrode, J. (2016) The industrial archaeology of deep time. *The British Journal for the History of Science* 49, 1–25.

Cohen, C. and Hublin, J.-J. (1989) *Boucher de Perthes. Les origines romantiques de la préhistoire*. Paris, Belin.

Darwin, C. (1859) *On the Origin of Species*. London, John Murray.

Evans, J. (1850) On the date of British coins. *Numismatic Chronicle* 12, 127–137.

Evans, J. (1856) Errors respecting the coinage of ancient Celtic kings of Britain. *Numismatic Chronicle* 18, 161–165.

Evans, J. (1859) On the form and nature of the flint-implements (letter to J. Prestwich, 25 May 1859). In J. Prestwich, On the occurrence of flint-implements, associated with the remains of animals of extinct species in beds of a late geological period, in France at Amiens and Abbeville, and in England at Hoxne: appendix A. *Philosophical Transactions of the Royal Society* 150, 310–312.

Evans, J. (1860) On the occurrence of flint implements in undisturbed beds of gravel, sand and clay. *Archaeologia* 38, 280–307.

Evans, J. (1862) Account of some further discoveries of flint implements in the Drift on the Continent and in England. *Archaeologia* 38, 57–84.

Evans, J. (1864) *The Coins of the Ancient Britons, Arranged and Described by John Evans F.S.A., F.G.S. and Engraved by F.W. Fairholt, F.S.A*. London, Quaritch.

Evans, J. (1866) On the forgery of antiquities. *Notices of the Proceedings of the Royal Institution of Great Britain* 4, 356–365.

Evans, J. (1869) On the manufacture of stone implements in prehistoric times. In *Third International Congress of Prehistoric Anthropology and Archaeology, 1868, London and Norwich*, 191–193. London, Longmans.

Evans, J. (1872) *The Ancient Bronze Implements, Weapons and Ornaments of Great Britain*. London, Longmans, Green, Reader and Dyer.

Evans, J. (1875) The coinage of the ancient Britons and natural selection. *Notices of the Proceedings of the Royal Institution of Great Britain* 7, 476–487.

Evans, J. (1881) *The Ancient Bronze Implements, Weapons and Ornaments of Great Britain and Ireland*. London, Longmans, Green & Co.

Evans, J. (1882a) History that is not written. The implements of prehistoric man and the civilization indicated by them. (From an address by Dr. John Evans before a popular audience in the Southampton skating rink). *The New York Times* September 17.

Evans, J. (1882b) Unwritten history and how to read it. (A lecture to the working classes…). *Nature* 26, 513–516, 531–533.

Evans, J. (1890) *The Coins of the Ancient Britons: Supplement*. London, Quaritch.

Evans, J. (1898) Presidential address. In *Report of the 67th Meeting of the British Association for the Advancement of Science held at Toronto in August 1897*, 3–20. London, John Murray.

Evans, J. (1943) *Time and Chance: The Story of Sir Arthur Evans and his Forebears*. London, Longman.

Fox, A.H.L. (1875) On the Principles of Classification Adopted in the Arrangement of His Anthropological Collection, Now Exhibited in the Bethnal Green Museum. *The Journal of the Anthropological Institute of Great Britain and Ireland* 4, 293–308.

Fyfe, A. (2015) Journals, learned societies and money: philosophical transactions, ca. 1750–1900. *Notes & Records. Royal Society* 69, 277–299.

Goren-Inbar, N. and Gonen, S. (2006) *Axe Age. Acheulian Tool-making from Quarry to Discard*. London, Equinox.
Gräslund, B. (1987) *The Birth of Prehistoric Chronology*. Cambridge, Cambridge University Press.
Grayson, D.K. (1983) *The Establishment of Human Antiquity*. New York, Academic Press.
Haddon, A.C. (1895) *Evolution in Art as Illustrated by the Life-Histories of Designs*. London, Walter Scott Press.
Hurel, A. and Coye, N., eds (2011) *Dans l'épaisseur du temps. Archéologues et géologues inventent la préhistoire*. Paris, Muséum national d'Histoire naturelle (Publications scientifiques du muséum).
Jersey, P.d. (2008) Evans and ancient British coins. In A. MacGregor (ed.) *Sir John Evans (1823-1908). Antiquity, Commerce and Natural Science in the Age of Darwin*, 152–172. Oxford, Ashmolean Museum.
Jordanova, L. (1986) *Languages of Nature. Critical Essays on Science and Literature*. London, Free Association.
Keary, C.F. (1885) The morphology of coins. I. The Greek family. *Numismatic Chronicle* 5, 165–249.
Kemmers, F. and Myrberg, N. (2011) Rethinking numismatics: the archaeology of coins. *Archaeological Dialogues* 18, 87–108.
Lamdin-Whymark, H. (2009) Sir John Evans: experimental flint knapping and the origins of lithic research. *Lithics* 30, 45–52.
Lubbock, J. (1865) *Prehistoric Times: As Illustrated by Ancient Remains and the Manners and Customs of Modern Savages*. London, Williams & Norgate.
MacGregor, A., ed. (2008a) *Sir John Evans 1823-1908: Antiquity, Commerce and Natural Science in the Age of Darwin*. Oxford, Ashmolean Museum.
MacGregor, A. (2008b) Sir John Evans, model Victorian, polymath and collector. In A. MacGregor (ed.) *Sir John Evan 1823-1908. Antiquity, Commerce and Natural Science in the Age of Darwin*, 1–38. Oxford, Ashmolean Museum.
Manias, C. (2015) The problematic construction of 'Palaeolithic Man:' The Old Stone Age and the difficulties of the comparative method, 1859–1914. *Studies in History and Philosophy of Biological and Biomedical Sciences* 51, 32–43.
Miller, P.N. (2017) *History and its Objects: Antiquarianism and Material Culture Since 1500*. Ithaca, NY, Cornell University Press.
Mortillet, G.d. (1873) Classification des Ages de la Pierre. In *Congres International d'Anthropologie et d'Archeologie Prehistoriques, 6e Session, 1872*, 432–459. Bruxelles, Muquardt.
Myrberg-Burström, N. (2019) Money, coins and archaeology. In R. Naismith (ed.) *Money and Coinage in the Middle Age*, 231–263. Leiden, Brill.
O'Connor, A. (2007) *Finding Time for the Old Stone Age: A History of Palaeolithic Archaeology and Quaternary Geology in Britain, 1860-1960*. Oxford, Oxford University Press.
Piggott, S. (1989) *Ancient Britain and the Antiquarian Imagination*. London, Thames & Hudson.
Pitt Rivers, A.H.L.F. (1868) Primitive warfare, Part II: On the resemblance of the weapons of early man, their variation, continuity, and development of form. *Journal of the Royal United Services Institution* 12, 399–439.
Pitt Rivers, A.H.L.F., ed. (1906) *The Evolution of Culture and other Essays by the late Lt. Gen. A. Lane-Fox Pitt-Rivers [compiled and edited by John L. Myres]*. Oxford, Clarendon Press.
Richard, N. (2008) *Inventer la Préhistoire. Les débuts de l'archéologie préhistorique en France*. Paris, Vuibert Adapt-Snes.
Riede, F. (2006) The Scandinavian connection: the roots of Darwinian archaeology in 19th-century Scandinavian archaeology. *Bulletin of the History of Archaeology* 16 (1), 4–18.
Roberts, A. and Barton, N. (2008) Reading the unwritten history: Evans and ancient stone implements. In A. MacGregor (ed.) *Sir John Evans (1823-1908). Antiquity, Commerce and Natural Science in the Age of Darwin*, 95–115. Oxford, Ashmolean Museum.
Roe, D.A. (1968) British Lower and Middle Palaeolithic handaxe groups. *Proceedings of the Prehistoric Society* 34, 1–82.

Rowley-Conwy, P. (2007) *From Genesis to Prehistory. The Archaeological Three Age System and its Contested Reception in Denmark, Britain and Ireland*. Oxford, Oxford University Press.

Schlanger, N. (2010) Series in progress: antiquities of nature, numismatics and stone implements in the emergence of prehistoric archaeology. *History of Science* 48 (3/4 (161)), 343–369.

Schlanger, N. (2011) Coins to flint. John Evans and the numismatic moment in the history of archaeology. *European Journal of Archaeology* 14, 465–479.

Schlanger, N. (2013) One day hero. Jules Reboux at the crucible of prehistory in 1860s Paris. *Complutum [special issue: Moro Abadía, O. & C. Huth (eds) Speaking materials. Sources for the History of Archaeology]* 24 (2), 73–88.

Schlanger, N. (2014) Gabriel de Mortillet. 1821–1898. Classifying human cultural evolution. In B. Fagan (ed.) *The Great Archaeologists*, 28–30. London, Thames & Hudson.

Schlanger, N. (2015) Boucher de Perthes au travail. Industrie et préhistoire au XIXe siècle. In K. Raj and O. Sibum (eds) *Histoire des sciences et des savoirs, Tome 2 Modernité et globalisation*, 267–283. Paris, Le Seuil.

Schnapp, A. (1996) *The Discovery of the Past*. London, British Museum Press.

Schnapp, A. (2002) Between antiquarians and archaeologists – continuities and ruptures. *Antiquity (special section: 'Ancestral Archives. Explorations in the History of Archaeology')* 76, 134–140.

Sherratt, A. (2002) Darwin among the archaeologists: the John Evans nexus and the Borneo Caves. *Antiquity (special section: 'Ancestral Archives. Explorations in the History of Archaeology')* 76, 151–157.

White, M.J. (2001) Out of Abbeville: Sir John Evans, Palaeolithic patriarch and handaxe pioneer. In S. Milliken and J. Cook (eds) *A Very Remote Period Indeed: Papers on the Palaeolithic Presented to Derek Roe*, 242–248. Oxford, Oxbow Books.

Winckelmann, J.J. (1764) *Geschichte der Kunst des Alterthums*. Dresden, Walther.

Chapter 3

Non-spectacular exceptions: faunal remains and bone artefacts in nineteenth-century Hungarian archaeology

Laura Coltofean-Arizancu

Abstract

This chapter explores the scientific interest in the faunal remains and bone artefacts discovered in archaeological contexts in nineteenth-century Hungary. It does so by means of a content analysis of key publications and archival documents that offers an overview of the Hungarian archaeological scene at the time. The chapter demonstrates that animal remains and bone artefacts were common and widely circulating finds in nineteenth-century Hungary. However, they were regarded as less important than other finds, such as tools and weapons made of stone and especially metal. Faunal remains were frequently identified but unless they were found in exceptionally interesting and important contexts or were in private collections, their examination rarely went further. Their value was usually seen as utilitarian and their potential for reconstructing human-environment interactions was less understood. Although incipient archaeozoological investigations were already being carried out in nineteenth-century Hungarian archaeology, it would not be until the second half of the twentieth century that a consistent interest in archaeozoology became prevalent.

Keywords: history of archaeology; animal remains; bone artefact; archaeozoology; scientific collaboration; multidisciplinarity; interdisciplinarity; 1876 CIAAP Congress; Hungary.

Introduction

'Zooarchaeology' and 'archaeozoology' are terms that basically define the branch of archaeology that examines animal remains found at archaeological sites (Reitz and Wing 2008, 1–6; Gifford-Gonzalez 2018, 3, 9–11). Both terms were introduced after the Second World War and are used in a variety of ways across the globe. Thus, 'archaeozoology' is especially used in central and south-eastern Europe and Asia, while the term 'zooarchaeology' is preferred in western Europe, North America (Bartosiewicz 2001, 76; Reitz and Wing 2008, 4) and the English-speaking countries in general. Each term denotes distinct approaches to the interpretation of faunal remains found in archaeological contexts. Zooarchaeology is considered to approach the study of faunal remains from a cultural point of view, while archaeozoology does so from a more biological (Mengoni Goñalons 1988, 73; Bartosiewicz 2001, 77; Reitz and Wing 2008, 4), evolutionary and ecological perspective (Gifford-Gonzalez 2018, 10). These outlooks have also been influenced by the various political, economic, social and cultural contexts in which archaeology has developed as a discipline. The term 'archaeozoology' also indicates that 'this discipline has traditionally been developed and practised by natural scientists (palaeontologists, veterinarians etc.), who added the adjective "archaeo-" when defining the specific aspect of their zoological work' (Bartosiewicz 2001, 77; see also Bartosiewicz and Choyke 2002, 118). The term therefore implies a certain degree of collaboration between different disciplines, thus setting the ground for the multidisciplinary and interdisciplinary practices that will be explored throughout this chapter. Given that the geographical focus of this contribution is Hungary, a country located in central-eastern Europe, the term 'archaeozoology' will be used throughout the following pages.

Global histories of the development of zooarchaeology or archaeozoology as an archaeological branch have been outlined by the zooarchaeologists Simon J.M. Davis (1987/1995), Elizabeth Reitz and Elizabeth Wing (2008) and Diane Gifford-Gonzalez (2018), as well as by Ivana Živaljević (2013). Apart from these more general overviews, most of the histories of the subdiscipline focus on its evolution in specific countries or regions. These include Argentina (*e.g.* Mengoni Goñalons 1988, 72–76; 2007; 2010), Australia (*e.g.* Cosgrove 2002), Canada (*e.g.* Driver 1993; Stewart 1993; 2002), the Caribbean (*e.g.* Grouard 2010), China (*e.g.* Jing 2002), Hungary (*e.g.* Bartosiewicz 2001; 2017, 101–102; Bartosiewicz and Choyke 2002), Germany (*e.g.* Becker and Benecke 2001), Greece (*e.g.* Trantalidou 2001), Israel (*e.g.* Horwitz 2002), Latin America (Mengoni Goñalons *et al.* 2010), Mexico (*e.g.* Corona-M 2002a; 2002b; 2008), the Netherlands (*e.g.* Çakirlar *et al.* 2019), North America (*e.g.* Crader 2002; Lyman 2012; 2015; 2018) and Spain (*e.g.* Morales Muñiz 2002). The history of archaeozoology in Hungary and, to some extent, in the Carpathian Basin, has been traced by the archaeozoologist László Bartosiewicz (Bartosiewicz 2001; 2017, 101–102; Bartosiewicz and Choyke 2002). His publications mostly deal with the advancement of this subdiscipline in the twentieth century, with special attention paid to the period following the Second World War, although he has also offered brief accounts of the first archaeozoological studies in nineteenth-century Hungary (Bartosiewicz and Choyke 2002, 118–119; Bartosiewicz 2017, 101). Despite the fact that the existing literature points to the roots of the subdiscipline in this period, most of the above-mentioned contributions have in common their chronological focus on the twentieth century and the sparse information about early archaeozoological studies in the nineteenth century, although there are some exceptions (*e.g.* Davis 1987/1995, 19–21; Mengoni Goñalons 2007, 13–15; Corona-M 2008; Reitz and Wing 2008,

14–17; Bartosiewicz 2020, 1–2). This gap in research is understandable, as zooarchaeology/archaeozoology as we know it today developed especially in the second half of the twentieth century. Moreover, investigation of the nineteenth century would require thorough archival and library research, which is not high on archaeozoologists' and zooarchaeologists' list of priorities.

This chapter aims to explore the interest in analysing faunal remains and bone artefacts discovered in archaeological contexts in nineteenth-century Hungary. It will fill a gap in the research and literature on primeval archaeozoological/zooarchaeological studies in that century. The focus is on Hungary as one of the countries with the longest archaeozoological traditions in Europe (Bartosiewicz 2017, 101). By analysing the content of nineteenth-century scientific literature and archival documents (*i.e.* correspondence), the chapter will assess the ways in which Hungarian scholars of the time considered, studied and interpreted faunal remains and bone artefacts and how they published them in books and journals and displayed them at events. It will also examine the contexts in which the encounters between archaeologists and zoologists, palaeontologists and other natural scientists occurred in the nineteenth century and led to archaeozoological investigations and publications.

The chapter first provides general information about the state of archaeology in nineteenth-century Hungary and introduces the archaeozoological studies of the time known from the already existing literature. It then assesses how animal remains and bone artefacts were presented in the first Hungarian handbook of archaeology written by Flóris Rómer in 1866. The way in which faunal remains were integrated into the programme of a major archaeological event organised in Budapest in 1876 – the 8th International Congress of Prehistoric Anthropology and Archaeology – is evaluated by looking at the conference proceedings and the exhibition catalogue. The overview of Hungarian archaeology written in 1897 by the director of the Hungarian National Museum, Ferenc Pulszky, is also analysed. The chapter continues by evaluating the inclusion of faunal remains and bone artefacts in the articles of the two leading Hungarian archaeological journals of the time – *Archaeologiai Közlemények* and *Archaeologiai Értesítő* – until 1899[1]/1900. It also includes an examination of the contribution of two collectors and archaeologists, Jenő Nyáry and Zsófia Torma, in fostering the analysis of zoological and other archaeological finds. The chapter concludes with a discussion of the overall image of archaeozoological studies in nineteenth-century Hungary and the various directions from which multidisciplinary and interdisciplinary collaborations may have emerged in archaeology.

Archaeology and the study of faunal remains in nineteenth-century Hungary

Subsumed to a European-wide nationalist sentiment (Díaz-Andreu 2007), Hungarian archaeologists were not only concerned with recovering the remains of the past, but also with the ethnic roots and origins of the Hungarian nation (Bartosiewicz, Mérai and Csippán 2011, 280, 282–284). These were particularly important in forging a strong national identity that was necessary to gain independence from the Habsburg Empire. In 1867, the Austro-Hungarian Compromise resulted in the creation of the Dual Monarchy of Austria and Hungary, which led to the political consolidation and economic development of Hungary. As part of the latter, roadbuilding (see, for example, Dudás 1885, 394), railway development and river regulation were carried out all over the country, bringing to the surface numerous archaeological sites and finds that increased the interest in archaeology on an unprecedented scale (Bartosiewicz, Mérai and Csippán 2011, 280–281). This is also the period when the institutionalisation of archaeology began in Hungary. The establishment of the Hungarian National Museum (Magyar Nemzeti Múzeum) in 1802 by Count Ferenc Széchényi (1754–1820) and of several archaeological societies was part of this process. The museum also had a numismatic and antiquities collection from 1814. In 1846, János Luczenbacher (1796–1871), better known as János Érdy, was hired by the museum. His role in Hungarian archaeology was particularly important, as he was the first to undertake excavations at archaeological sites on a regular basis and to publish his results, for example in the *Akadémiai Értesítő* (Academic Reports) journal. Through his work, he 'laid the foundations of prehistoric archaeology in Hungary' (Vékony 2003, 17).

The two major Hungarian archaeological journals of the time, *Archaeologiai Közlemények* and *Archaeologiai Értesítő* – both of which will be analysed later in this chapter – were also founded in this period, the former in 1859 and the latter in 1868 by a scholar who will be discussed below, the clergyman Flóris Rómer (1815–1889). Both journals presented the most recent advances in the field of archaeology and were published in Pest (one of the two parts of the capital, Budapest, united in 1873) by the Archaeological Committee (Archaeologiai Bizottmány) of the Hungarian Academy of Sciences (Magyar Tudományos Akadémia) (Vékony 2003, 18). Whereas *Archaeologiai Közlemények* ceased to exist in 1899, *Archaeologiai Értesítő* did not (indeed, it is still the leading archaeology journal in Hungary today). Before the foundation of these two journals, articles related to archaeology were published, for example, in the *Tudományos Gyűjtemény* (Scientific Collection) journal (1817–1841) (Vékony 2003, 17), which gathered contributions from various scientific disciplines (Anonymous 1817, IV–XII).

Classical archaeology was at the centre of scholarly interest in nineteenth-century Hungary (Bartosiewicz, Mérai and Csippán 2011, 280), along with medieval antiquities and monuments (Rómer 1873, 55). However, prehistoric archaeology also began to receive attention before the middle of the century (see, for example, Rómer 1873) and especially after 1876, when the 8th International Congress of Prehistoric Anthropology and Archaeology (Congrès international d'anthropologie et d'archéologie préhistoriques; henceforth CIAAP) was held at the Hungarian National Museum in Budapest. Prehistoric archaeology appears to have been the driving force behind several multi- and interdisciplinary collaborations at the time, which also included the analysis of faunal remains. As Bartosiewicz (2017, 101) explains, 'the earlier the [chronology of the] site, the more archaeologists have enlisted the help of natural scientists trained in biological disciplines.' The first archaeozoological article, in the sense of an 'osteological study with historical connotations' (Bartosiewicz and Choyke 2002, 118), was published in Hungary during this time by the palaeontologist Ferenc Kubinyi (1796–1874) in the 1859 issue of the *Akadémiai Értesítő* journal under the title 'A teve és a ló, állat- és őslénytani s a Magyarok keletröl kijövetelére vonatkozólag történelmi tekintetben' ('The camel and the horse, a zoological, palaeontological and historical perspective on the arrival of Hungarians form the East'). This was followed by a second article written by the naturalist Nándor Báthory (1838–1905) and published in *Archaeologiai Közlemények* in 1868.

The driving force behind Hungarian archaeology at that time was a Benedictine monk, Flóris Rómer, who is regarded as its 'father' (Vékony 2003, 17; Bartosiewicz, Mérai and Csippán 2011, 280). Trained as a naturalist, he focused most of his attention on archaeology, although he continued to pursue his interest in the natural sciences. In 1863, he began to lecture on 'historical archaeology' at the University of Pest (Vékony 2003, 17–18) and in 1868 he was appointed a professor, imparting classes on multiple periods and disciplines (Vékony 2003, 18; Bartosiewicz, Mérai and Csippán 2011, 280). In 1869, he also became a keeper at the Hungarian National Museum (Vékony 2003, 18). Together with Ferenc Pulszky, the museum's director, he was the main force behind the organisation of the CIAAP Congress of 1876 in Budapest (Coltofean 2015, 1036–1044; 2016, 79–87; 2017, 331–333). He also actively contributed to the founding of many archaeological societies and museums in the country, as well as the *Archaeologiai Értesítő* journal (Vékony 2003, 18). His first major book, *A Bakony. Természetrajzi és régészeti vázlat* (*The Bakony. A natural history and archaeological sketch*), was published in 1860. It is interesting to note that he placed archaeology next to the natural sciences in the title of this volume. He did not integrate his natural history observations into those of archaeology and history, discussing each of them separately. However, he did not exclude the two in an effort to 'preserve the valuable relics' of the Bakony hilly area and to encourage their research (Rómer 1860, II). He also authored the first handbook of Hungarian archaeology (Rómer 1866), a volume to which we will return later in this chapter.

In the nineteenth century, archaeological activity in Hungary generally focused on cataloguing (Vékony 2003, 19) and describing finds from collections and excavations, and less on their interpretation. This practice was placed by Ferenc Pulszky in the context of a larger international movement (see Trigger 2006, 131–132) with the end aim of comparing the archaeological finds of different regions in Europe:

> The first task of prehistorians was to gather and publish the finds in each country, in order to establish through their comparison the similarities and differences of each territory and thus show how certain common or related aspects had spread from one territory to another and how they influenced each other. This work has not only begun everywhere, but it is largely finished, and the international congresses on prehistory especially served this purpose, where archaeologists of different countries participated and with the exhibitions organised on the occasion of the congresses they gained an overview of all the finds known so far. Among the

Scandinavian prehistoric archaeologists, Worsaae, Montelius, Sophus Müller, Hildebrand, Unsedt and most recently Söderberg travelled across Europe and scrutinised the prehistoric relics in different museums. In certain countries, prehistoric archaeology associations were formed and scientific journals were founded, in which the discovered objects were published. The relics of the Bronze Age were also published in larger works (Pulszky 1897, 133).

Following this line, compiling and presenting the representative artefacts for various periods in monographs was precisely the aim of the archaeologist József Hampel (1849–1913), Flóris Rómer's successor at the Hungarian National Museum and the University of Pest (*e.g.* Hampel 1876a; 1886–1896; 1895; 1896).

Despite the fact that the existing literature mainly highlights the activity of Flóris Rómer for nineteenth-century Hungarian archaeology (*e.g.* Vékony 2003; Bartosiewicz, Mérai and Csippán 2011), the picture was in fact much more varied. Although he was indeed the driving force behind archaeological research in Hungary, he directly or indirectly inspired and encouraged others to investigate the past and thus established a wide network of archaeological researchers across the country. Archival documents show that there was a dynamic network of enthusiastic scholars and collectors with multiple and diverse backgrounds who shared a common interest in the past and actively contributed to the development of archaeological research in Hungary. This network facilitated the discussion and exchange of ideas from various fields and the analysis of archaeological finds using methods from other disciplines (Coltofean 2016, 109–222; 2017, 334–341), which gradually led to multi- and interdisciplinary collaborations. These practices are best reflected in the correspondence of the actors involved, as well as in their publications in the main Hungarian archaeological journals.

Faunal remains and bone artefacts in the first Hungarian handbook of archaeology

In order to understand why and how analyses of faunal remains were undertaken in Hungarian archaeology in the nineteenth century, we must explore how animals and their bones were perceived in the scientific imagery related to prehistory and historical periods, and how this perception was then translated into the archaeological practice. In order to do so, in this section the ways in which faunal remains and bone artefacts were presented and illustrated in the first handbook of archaeology in Hungary, *Műrégészeti kalauz* (*Guide to Archaeological Objects*), will be examined. The guide was published in 1866 under the auspices of the Archaeological Committee of the Hungarian Academy of Sciences and consisted of two parts. The first, written by Flóris Rómer, was devoted to prehistoric archaeology ('Őskori műrégészet') and dealt with 'the antiquities before the Christian era' (Rómer 1866, IV). It discussed 'the most diverse barbarian and Roman relics' with a special focus on finds that were common both to Hungary and other regions (Rómer 1866, IV). The second part was written by the art historian, architect and doctor Imre Henszlmann (1813–1888) and discussed medieval architecture. A third section on medieval ecclesiastical sculpture and painting was also commissioned and assigned to the bishop and art historian Arnold Ipolyi (1823–1886) (Rómer 1866, IV), but it seems that it was never published. The Hungarian Academy of Sciences saw it necessary to publish and disseminate this volume in order to provide the public with the guidelines they needed to ensure the preservation and protection of the country's artistic and historical heritage (Rómer 1866, III). The book was a brief overview of the national and international archaeological knowledge of the time and included the latest recommendations for its practitioners. Thus, its content can be considered as representative of the archaeological theory and practice of mid-nineteenth-century Hungary.

In the handbook, Flóris Rómer mainly wrote about animals in the chapter on the Stone Age, which he described as 'a time whose children lived with ancient animals which are partly extinct today' (Rómer 1866, 6). Animals were seen as providers of the very basic necessities for life, from food to clothing. Their value was therefore utilitarian (Živaljević 2013, 1139). Given the scarcity of faunal analyses in Hungarian archaeology at the time the handbook was published, Flóris Rómer's description of the lives and diet of prehistoric peoples was probably based on his readings, ethnographic analogies with 'savage islemen' (Rómer 1866, 7) and his own observations in the field:

> I found many such turtle shells next to Garam-Kövesd, on one of the high banks of the Garam river, whose upper part [of the shells] bear the traces of breakage, so they were used while still being alive, and in large quantities in such a place, where the red clay and ash deposit under the mould, and the presence of red deer antler and sheep jaw show: that the owners of the many potsherds which can be found on today's plough land did not refrain from eating shells besides the meat of four-legged animals, when the area was still covered by a lake (Rómer 1866, 7, footnote).

Flóris Rómer had no formal training in zoology but his background as a naturalist, along with his vast knowledge, allowed him to make 'archaeozoological' observations in the field. Imagination probably also played an important role in depicting the picture of a period about which little was known and research into which was at its dawn in Hungary and elsewhere in Europe.

Flóris Rómer's handbook shows that, unless visually impressive or discovered in exceptional contexts, unworked animal bones received less attention than other finds at the beginning of the second half of the nineteenth century. Their potential for reconstructing human-environment interactions had not yet been realised. It is therefore not surprising that faunal remains were usually seen as just another raw material used for producing tools and weapons:

> The inhabitants of this time did not only work the stone, but also the pointed bones which were skilfully broken and edged with stones (Fig. 22); these could be used as spearheads, and [...] as harpoons; the fish bones as needles and perforators; the end of antlers as handles and, when pierced, as hammers; the horns of cattle as drinking vessels, etc. (Rómer 1866, 15).

There was a hierarchy of tools and weapons, in which those made of bone ranked lower than those of stone and metal. This is also illustrated by the fact that Flóris

Rómer devoted only one two-paragraph section to describing prehistoric bone tools. Of these paragraphs, only the first is really about bone tools (Rómer 1866, 15). In comparison, the section about stone tools, for example, is a little over seven pages long and consists of three subsections (Rómer 1866, 8–15). In a footnote belonging to the aforementioned paragraph, Flóris Rómer mentioned that he had participated in a session of doctors and naturalists in Bratislava (today the capital of Slovakia, but then in Austria-Hungary). This was, in fact, the annual meeting of the Hungarian Physicists and Nature Explorers that he regularly attended (Vékony 2003, 18). There he organised an archaeological exhibition of more than a thousand objects. In this exhibition, he explained that

> the antler tools from Magyarád (Hont County) were especially striking – similar ones are mentioned by Worsaae in Denmark – (Fig. 23. 24 and 25) and were displayed with the typical potsherds and the so-called kitchen middens, especially the remains of turtle shells – which were exhibited by the pharmacist Boleman from Levice on the last day of the exhibition, which is why it was too late to include them in the list of exhibits (Rómer 1866, 15, footnote).

Flóris Rómer was so impressed by these finds and their similarity to those from the Danish kitchen middens that he sent them for archaeozoological analysis to the zoology department of the University of Pest. He did not mention this in his handbook, but his name can be found in one of the first archaeozoological studies published in Hungary by the naturalist Nándor Báthory in the journal *Archaeologiai Közlemények* (Báthory 1868). That article is devoted entirely to the identification and description of the animal remains exhibited at the aforementioned meeting in Bratislava. They were examined by the article's author under the direction of the zoologist Tivadar Margó (1816–1896) who, as we will see later in this chapter, was also a member of the 1876 CIAAP Congress organising committee in Budapest. Báthory also explained that the examination of the finds had been requested by Flóris Rómer, as it was considered 'exceptionally important not only for our country, but for the whole of Europe' (Báthory 1868, 73). This example excellently illustrates the impact of the first Danish Kitchen Midden Commission (*køkkenmøddingkommission*; for more information, see Gräslund 1987, 34–38; Kristiansen 2002), organised between 1849 and 1869, on archaeological practice across Europe (see further details in Díaz-Andreu, this volume). It also shows how archaeological knowledge and innovations, including incipient interdisciplinary practices, circulated through reading scientific literature. In this particular case, it was through the work of the archaeologist Jens Jacob Asmussen Worsaae (1821–1885), who was one of the commission members and whose name was mentioned by Flóris Rómer in the quotation above.

The illustrations included in Flóris Rómer's part of the handbook are also worth analysing. Of the 156 illustrations he included, only five were related to bone tools: a hatchet in a red deer antler (Rómer 1866, 10, No. 9), a wooden awl in a bone handle (Rómer 1866, 15, No. 22), two bone tools (Rómer 1866, 15, No. 23–24) and a red deer antler hammer (Rómer 1866, 15, No. 25). It is interesting to note that all the bone objects selected for illustration were tools generally dated by the author to the Stone Age. There are no illustrations of animal bones in their purest form as biofacts, only of those that had been worked by humans and transformed into tools. The only other artefacts in the handbook that are somehow related to the animal world are some seashell beads dated by Flóris Rómer to the Bronze Age (Rómer 1866, 132, No. 88). There are also few illustrations of human bones. There are only four drawings of burials – two from the Stone Age (both of the same burial but with different details; Rómer 1866, 21, No. 32–33), one from the Iron Age (Rómer 1866, 76, No. 118) and one Roman (Rómer 1866, 93, No. 131). Looking at the handbook's list of illustrations, it is evident that preference was given to the depiction of artefacts such as tools made of stone and especially of bronze, followed by pottery. This tells which types of artefacts were considered important in Hungarian archaeology in the mid-nineteenth century. Those chosen for illustration had to be carefully selected and those appearing in publications were usually considered to be representative of a certain period, especially given the high cost of publishing a book and even more so with such a large number of illustrations (Rómer 1866, IV–V; see also Coltofean 2016, 101; 136; 183; 2017, 345).

Another part of the handbook that reveals information about the attitude to faunal remains and bone artefacts in the mid-nineteenth century is its first annex. In it, Flóris Rómer provided a set of brief instructions on how to excavate and preserve various archaeological finds, from potsherds to metal artefacts (Rómer 1866, 102–107). He emphasised that

> we must preserve even the smallest and least remarkable [artefact] piece, because even if it does not have an immediate value by itself, it will gain value when compared with other similar pieces; its value grows from a local and historical point of view, as this way collections become more complete, more interesting and, most importantly, more instructive! (Rómer 1866, 107).

Despite this careful attitude towards the recovery of artefacts, neither animal bones nor bone tools are mentioned in the annex and no guidelines are offered on how to handle and preserve them following their excavation. Human bones, however, did appear in the context of burials, which had to be carefully excavated. Moreover, Flóris Rómer advised on the meticulous recovery and recording of every element in the funerary inventory: 'we have to collect the jewellery, weapons and domestic tools lying under or next to the body, and scrupulously record the place each piece was found' (Rómer 1866, 105). In this quotation, the objects in the tomb were hierarchically listed according to the importance and value that was given to them at the time (*i.e.* jewellery – weapons – domestic tools). It is worth noting that, once again, faunal remains are not enumerated among the finds worthy of being recorded, although they are frequently present in burials and were considered among the most common finds for prehistoric times.

Regarding the bibliography included in the handbook, the list consisted of a selection of publications providing information about Hungary and its neighbouring countries that could be used as a starting point for those interested in acquainting themselves with prehistory. Two examples are the books authored by Jens Worsaae, *Dänemarks Vorzeit durch Alterthümer und Grabhügel beleuchtet* (Copenhagen, 1844) and *Zur Alterthumskunde des Nordens* (Leipzig, 1847). As previously shown, Jens Worsaae influenced Flóris Rómer's decision to commission the analysis of animal remains. Apart from those books, the publications of antiquarian and archaeological institutions and societies were also important in his work and he listed several of their 'Mittheilungen' and 'Memoirs' (*e.g.* Mémoires des antiquaries du Nord; Mittheilungen der kk. Central-Comm; Proceedings of the Society of Antiquaries) (Rómer 1866, 112, footnote). Most of the literature used by Flóris Rómer was published in Hungary, Germany, the Nordic countries (*e.g.* Denmark) and Belgium, as well as a few publications from Russia and England. As can be seen, his bibliography had an international flavour and was a good reflection of the archaeological knowledge of the time. This seems to indicate that his attitude to faunal remains and bone artefacts was not just personal or local but part of a wider standpoint.

Animal remains and bone artefacts at the 1876 CIAAP Congress

In 1876, the 8th International Congress of Prehistoric Anthropology and Archaeology (CIAAP) was held in Budapest at the Hungarian National Museum. This was an event of major importance for Hungarian archaeology as it meant its international recognition (Hampel 1902, 10; Bartosiewicz, Mérai and Csippán 2011, 282; Coltofean 2015, 1036; 2016, 78; 2017, 331). The congress led to the acknowledgement of prehistoric archaeology as a distinct discipline in Hungary and to its inclusion in the curricula of the universities in Budapest and Kolozsvár (Bartosiewicz, Mérai and Csippán 2011, 282; Coltofean 2015, 1036; 2016, 79; 2017, 331). The CIAAP Congress in 1876 was attended by numerous encyclopaedic scholars and was an excellent opportunity for discussions and establishing contacts. It also increased opportunities for building and strengthening national, international and interdisciplinary collaborations. This section examines the inclusion of faunal remains and bone artefacts in the papers delivered at the congress sessions, as well as in the archaeological exhibition that was organised on the occasion of this scientific event.

It is worth mentioning that the congress organising committee, with Ferenc Pulszky as its president and Flóris Rómer as secretary (Compte-rendu 1877, V–VI; Coltofean 2015, 1036; 2016, 79; 2017, 331), was highly multi- and pluridisciplinary. The only 'pure' archaeologist was József Hampel, who at the time represented a new and younger generation of archaeologists. Other members had various backgrounds and specialised in multiple fields simultaneously, including medicine (*e.g.* Lajos György Arányi, Imre Henszlmann, József Lenhossék), anatomy and physical anthropology (*e.g.* József Lenhossék), art history (*e.g.* Imre Henszlmann, Arnold Ipolyi), architecture and literary criticism (*e.g.* Imre Henszlmann), literature (*e.g.* Imre Henszlmann, Gyula Forster), philology (*e.g.* Finály Henrik), law (*e.g.* Pál

Hunfalvy, Lajos Candid Hegedüs), ethnology and linguistics (*e.g.* Pál Hunfalvy), theology (*e.g.* Arnold Ipolyi), mining engineering and geology (*e.g.* József Szabó), as well as chemistry (*e.g.* Vince Wartha)[2]. What is especially important for this chapter is that a zoologist, Margó Tivadar, was also a member of the organising committee. As seen in the previous section, it was under his supervision that Nándor Báthory carried out the archaeozoological analysis of the animal remains from Magyarád. Most of these scholars were also full or corresponding members of the Hungarian Academy of Sciences and some of them were also involved in politics. The organising committee also included authorities, such as the head of the National Post Office, the principal and deputy mayors of Budapest, and privy councillors. Some of these politicians were also interested in history and archaeology and had their own collections (*e.g.* Szalay Ágoston, a privy councillor). It is therefore possible to note a certain predisposition towards interdisciplinarity in assembling the event's organising committee. These diverse backgrounds allowed its members to approach archaeology from the perspective of different disciplines. This was also reflected in the congress programme, which had a varied subject matter and was also attended by scholars specialising in different fields.

The proceedings of the 1876 CIAAP Congress

The CIAAP Congress held in 1876 resulted in the publication of three volumes (Compte-rendu 1877; Rómer 1878; Hampel 1886) that allow us to see the papers that were delivered at the event, the debates that took place, and the latest ideas and theories that were circulating at the time. The congress had nine themes that reflect a prevalent interest in artefacts, such as stone and metal tools and weapons, as well as human remains. The latter were considered significant as they were able to provide information on the ethnicity of the peoples who inhabited the territory of Hungary in the past and therefore serve the country's national and political interests. Less attention was paid in the programme to pottery and animal bones. This does not mean, however, that animal remains were absent from the papers and debates. One of the papers by the Italian geologist and palaeontologist Giovanni Capellini, 'Les traces de l'homme pliocène en Toscane' ('The traces of the Pliocene man in Tuscany'), was particularly important (Capellini 1877). In it, he attempted to argue that humans had already existed in the Pliocene, using as evidence the bones of a cachalot (*Physeter macrocephalus*, the largest of the toothed whales) with cut marks discovered in Tuscany. In this example, we can see that animal bones, especially those of large animals, were used as dating elements. Capellini interpreted the marks as being man-made, as they could not be attributed to the teeth of any animal. The whale remains generated heated debates, with John Evans and Paul Broca arguing that the marks could still have been made by animals (Capellini 1877). Capellini's paper was significant as it could have brought much earlier evidence of human presence. This was an intensively debated topic at the time, in which the cut marks on animal bones played an important evidential role (see Trigger 2006, 142–143).

The archaeology exhibition organised at the 1876 CIAAP Congress

During the CIAAP Congress in 1876, an exhibition of archaeological finds from public and private collections in Hungary and beyond was organised at the Hungarian National Museum (Hampel 1876b, III; Coltofean 2015; 2016, 78–94; 2017, 333). The exhibition's catalogue (Hampel 1876b) illustrates, on the one hand, which archaeological finds the collectors considered to be important enough to be sent for exhibition and, on the other, the objects the event organisers selected to be displayed before the academic community and the general public. The exhibition catalogue included a detailed enumeration of the objects presented in the display cases. Looking at them, the attention given to tools and instruments compared to other types of artefacts, such as pottery, is striking. Bronze tools and weapons were considered especially interesting, followed by those of stone. Bones were rarely mentioned among the exhibited objects, although human bones, especially crania, were more frequent than those of animals. The latter rarely appeared in their pure state (*e.g.* mammoth teeth) in the exhibition. Nevertheless, they were included in the exhibition in a worked form, as bone tools. Among them, a particular preference was shown for antler tools. In fact, two antler hammers are the only bone artefacts illustrated in the catalogue (Hampel 1876b, 28, fig. 16; 130, fig. 129). This shows that more attention was paid to objects that were more spectacular in appearance or, in a way, more familiar in shape and material for the people of the time (*e.g.* a metal toolset).

The objects displayed in the exhibition illustrate the main themes of the congress. At the same time, they reflect the *status quo* of archaeological knowledge in that period. The congress, however, shook the state of the art in Hungary and the ideas discussed were later reflected on in publications, especially the *Archaeologiai Közlemények* and *Archaeologiai Értesítő* journals. The 1876 CIAAP Congress also generated greater interest in faunal remains in Hungary and this can be seen in the increasing number of articles mentioning them in journals, as discussed below.

Faunal remains and bone artefacts in an overview of archaeological knowledge in late nineteenth-century Hungary

In 1897, thirty years after the first Hungarian archaeology handbook, Ferenc Pulszky (1814–1897) published *Magyarország archaeologiája* (*The Archaeology of Hungary*). The book was the result of the 1889 call by the president of the Hungarian Academy of Sciences, Baron Eötvös Lóránd, to publish overviews that would comprise the existing knowledge in various fields (*e.g.* geography, history and grammar) considered to be essential for the country (Pulszky 1897, 1). Ferenc Pulszky accepted the mission to write such a book about archaeology. The two volumes of this major work aimed to reflect the archaeological knowledge that existed at that time in Hungary but discussed in the wider context of European archaeology. Therefore, this volume is essential for understanding archaeological practice, theory and discourses in late-nineteenth-century Hungary and, in our case study, whether the attitude to faunal remains and bone artefacts had changed in any way since 1866, the year in which Flóris Rómer's handbook had been published.

The first volume of Ferenc Pulszky's book, which this contribution focuses on, consisted of four chapters devoted to the Stone Age (especially the Neolithic), the Copper Age (a concept that he introduced in Hungary[3]), the Bronze Age and the Iron Age, the last of which ended with two sub-chapters devoted to Roman finds. The second volume was divided into two parts. The first dealt with the archaeological remains of the migration period, while the second included art history studies from the time of King Saint Stephen (1000/1001–1038) to that of the Holy Roman Emperor Joseph II (1765–1790). Looking at the table of contents from the first volume, it is evident that not much had changed in the attention given to faunal remains since the mid-nineteenth century. Apart from the chapter on the Iron Age, each chapter began with a characterisation of the period under discussion and was followed by various sub-chapters devoted to artefacts that were considered representative. What is striking in Ferenc Pulszky's book is that, compared to Flóris Rómer's handbook, he placed even more emphasis on metal artefacts (*i.e.* tools, weapons, jewellery and coins). His attention focused on tools and weapons made of stone and especially metal. Pottery only appeared in the title of one sub-chapter related to the Bronze Age, while bone artefacts, as well as animal and human bones, were not mentioned anywhere in the contents. However, they were present to a certain extent in the list of illustrations and plates. Of the 122 illustrations included in the first volume, ten depicted artefacts or features (*e.g.* kitchen middens) related to animal remains and bone artefacts, but only in connection with the Neolithic and the Copper Age. Unworked animal bones did not appear at all among the illustrated objects. In the case of the plates, out of 99 only one depicted a bone artefact (Pulszky 1897, 18, plate II) and another a feature ('shell mound with contracted skeletons' near Mugem in Portugal) with faunal remains (Pulszky 1897, 19, plate III). Even when writing about the Danish kitchen middens, Ferenc Pulszky was so focused on the tools and weapons found in them that, in contrast to Flóris Rómer, he paid less attention to the animal remains that had made them so famous:

> The kjökkenmöddings of the Danish are kitchen middens on the seaside, in which large numbers of nicely knapped and partly polished flint knives, scrapers, arrowheads and daggers were found together with seashells, fishbones, and the bones of animal and bird species that still live today (see No. 12 and Plate III). It is remarkable that these stone tools and weapons were all made from flint types, just like in the Palaeolithic; however, these are much more varied. Potsherds do not occur in these kitchen middens, but the dog, as the first domestic animal, already appears in the companionship of hunter and fisher peoples. Similar waste heaps were found in Portugal, also on the seaside (see Plate III) (Pulszky 1897, 19).

The attention given to faunal remains and bone artefacts changed in the actual content of Ferenc Pulszky's book, where they were more frequently mentioned than in Flóris Rómer's handbook. This might indicate that as finds they were taken more seriously than before. However, less importance was still given to animal remains than to any artefact. They were more significant as finds when they were worked in the form of tools and weapons, especially when made of antlers and long bones. Both animal remains and bone tools often appeared in enumerations of archaeological finds from different sites, as in the example below related to the Földvárhalom site:

> In the ash deposits there were also fragments of stone axes, deer antler hammers, bone knives, needles, awls and scrapers used for stripping off animal skins to make clothing; this is where the small clay animal figurines, spindle whorls and clay cones were also found. Apart from these objects, large numbers of various animal bones and skulls emerged from the mound, which can *certainly* be considered domestic waste (Pulszky 1897, 32; italics added).

As the quotation also shows, animal remains were easily interpreted as domestic waste without any further consideration. Their potential for understanding human-environment interactions had not yet been acknowledged. However, as we will see later in this chapter, some collectors were aware of this possibility and tried to explore it. Ferenc Pulszky continued to see animal remains only as finds that provided information about the type of food ancient peoples consumed and how their bones were used as a raw material for making tools, weapons and jewellery. This idea was well illustrated in the excerpt below, in which he describes life during the Neolithic:

> The Neolithic peoples already had permanent houses [...]. From the excavated remains of these settlements we can see that, apart from hunting and fishing, they also knew about agriculture; they also had domestic animals, which we see not only from animal bones found between ramparts and ditches, but they already made animal figures from clay and burnt them; we recognise among them the dog, the sheep, the pig, the bullock and, what is more, even the horse. Their tools and weapons were made of polished stone [...]. Mixed with these stone tools we also find bone tools, harpoons, hammers from red deer antlers, knives from the ribs of deer, needles, awls from other deer bones, skates and net weights from the leg bones of ox [...] and as jewellery they used the perforated teeth of wild boar and red deer, clay balls, punctured shells, as well as beads and bracelets from the thick shell of *dentalium* and *tridacna* (Pulszky 1897, 21; italics added).

In many of Ferenc Pulszky's enumerations of finds, the animal remains were attributed to species. This indicates that, up to a point, they were subjected to at least basic zoological and taxonomic identification. In fact, this was necessary, as the bones of certain animals were at some point used for dating and establishing periods in prehistory and Ferenc Pulszky was aware of this (cf. Worsaae's division of the Stone Age into an early and later period, the kitchen middens as well as deer antler and bone artefacts being typical of the first; Pulszky 1897, 17; Gräslund 1987, 35–38). However, no information was given about those responsible for the zoological identifications, the criteria they used or the context in which they were applied. This can be seen in the example given below:

> The bones which were found in this mound are especially of red deer; the awls, needles and hammers were made of these; then [bones] of pig, turf bullock (*Bos longifrons*); from the latter, which is now completely extinct, there is a skull with a perforated forehead, which allowed the removal of the brain; apart from these, horse teeth, bear teeth, roe deer bones and various genera of snails and shells (Pulszky 1897, 34; italics added).

Failing to include the names of those who had carried out the analysis was not an uncommon practice at the time and we also see it in publications related to other finds. Speaking about the site of Lengyel, Ferenc Pulszky regretted the absence of a Rütimeyer in Hungarian archaeology: 'They found thousands of animal bones here; it would be desirable if one of our naturalists paid such attention to their accurate identification, like the one that made Rütimeyer's name so famous in Switzerland' (Pulszky 1897, 36). This quote seems to indicate that he was waiting for the initiative of natural scientists to examine faunal remains found in archaeological contexts. It also gives the impression that archaeozoological analyses had never been carried out in Hungary. In addition, in his book he does not mention the archaeozoological studies that had been carried out by then in the country, for example by Nándor Báthory, László Örley or even by Ludwig Rütimeyer of the remains from the Aggtelek cave (detailed later in the chapter).

Faunal remains and bone artefacts reflected in Hungarian archaeology journals

As mentioned earlier in this chapter, the two leading archaeology journals in nineteenth-century Hungary were *Archaeologiai Közlemények* and *Archaeologiai Értesítő*. They both give an overview of the Hungarian archaeological scene of the time. They reveal, for example, that many excavations took place in nineteenth-century Hungary in which animal and human remains, as well as bone artefacts, were common finds. They also show that the practitioners of archaeology were very active and strived to keep up to date with the archaeological excavations, discoveries, theories and methods of the time, as well as with the latest literature in the field, both in Hungary and abroad. This is especially reflected in sections such as 'Archaeological Literature' (Régészeti irodalom), 'Archaeological Library' (Régészeti könyvtár), 'Overseas' (Külföld), and 'Inland scientific institutions and finds' (Hazai tudományos intézetek és leletek) in the journal *Archaeologiai Értesítő*.

The analysis of the contents of the two journals' issues revealed that none of the contribution titles included keywords such as 'zoology', 'palaeontology' and 'fauna'. *Archaeologiai Közlemények* does not include the word 'animal' either. The word 'bone', however, does appear in two of its titles: the archaeozoological study by Nándor Báthory (1868) and an article by Flóris Rómer (1873). Of these two, only Nándor Báthory's focused on animal remains, while the other dealt with human bones. Conversely, in *Archaeologiai Értesítő*, the word 'animal' recurs in three titles that are, in fact, three different parts of the same contribution on medieval sculpture fragments portraying humans and animals (Gerecze 1895a; 1895b; 1895c). In addition, the word 'bone' appears in six titles (Kršnjavi 1886; 1887; Strzygovszki 1891; Kárász 1894; Semper 1896; Endre 1899), although none of them in relation to zoological analyses. We can therefore conclude that in the nineteenth century only one article entirely devoted to archaeozoology was published in those journals (Báthory 1868). There were, however, other articles with sections that highlighted the importance of animal remains and their potential for reconstructing the fauna of the past and various aspects of human evolution (*e.g.* Majláth 1873).

The panorama changes when looking beyond the titles of the articles in the two journals. Their actual content shows that faunal remains and artefacts, especially bone tools, were frequently mentioned. They were common archaeological finds that, as in Ferenc Pulszky's book (1897), usually appeared in enumerations along with various types of artefacts. They were often also briefly described and identified, as in the example below:

> The following species were identified by the author [József Szombathy] among the bone materials: 1. *Equus caballus L.* apart from several jaw fragments [there were] more than 100 molars, which indicate a medium-sized specimen. 2. *Cervus tarandus L.* 3 molars several limb fragments. 3. *Cervus elaphus L.* teeth, leg fragments and antler parts; 4. *Cervus capreolus L.* 5. *Sus scrof. L.* it was probably a short specimen, its molars are represented by its jaws. 6. *Lepus variabilis Pall* (alpine hare) skull, jaw fragments and numerous leg parts. 7. *Cricetus frumentarius Pali* with a left maxilla. 8. *Vulpes vulgaris Briss.* broken limb bones. 9. *Lupus vulgaris Briss.* one metacarpus and the lower arm, the tibia of a dwarf owl species.
>
> Apart from these, in the cave's disturbed deposit there were many more recent bones from different body parts of goat, domestic pig, hare, goose and hen (Téglás 1881, 327).

In the quotation above archaeologist Gábor Téglás mentioned that the animal remains found in the Diravica cave were identified by the archaeologist conducting the excavations, József Szombathy (who also excavated the Palaeolithic site near Willendorf where the 'Venus of Willendorf' was discovered). The journals show that in the nineteenth century animal remains were not only identified by zoologists, but also by archaeologists and excavators in general, regardless of their background. This is another point that can also be seen in Ferenc Pulszky's book. The accuracy and complexity of the bone identification and analysis depended on the authors' knowledge of animal anatomy and taxonomy. Commonly mentioned bones were those of horse and dog (*e.g.* Varázséji 1880). Special attention was paid to horse remains in burials as they were often considered to indicate the presence of Magyars in Hungary and therefore served to explore ethnic roots:

> The Hungarian-ness of the finds is proven by the fact that horse skeletons were found everywhere, which especially points to horse people; based on the coins found in some of the burials, the finds can be dated to the 9th and 10th centuries, then the territory of our country was inhabited by Slavs and Magyars and their relatives, but we know that Slavs were not horse people, while the Magyars were world-famous for this; therefore we cannot consider them other than Magyar, which is also proven by the stirrup irons, which show that they could only be Avar or Magyar (Varázséji 1880, 334).

The journal editions also reveal that animal remains and bone artefacts were very present in society and circulated widely. This is especially illustrated by the issues of *Archaeologiai Értesítő*, which usually included reports on the latest donations received by the Hungarian National Museum's Department of Coins and Antiquities (Érem- és régiség osztály). The reports are impressive and show that many Hungarians, from both within and outside archaeology, donated various finds to the museum. Animal remains, bone artefacts (especially tools) and shells frequently appeared in these donations, which shows that they were considered significant, at least up to a certain point. Apart from being included in donations, faunal remains and bone artefacts were also sold. Reporting on his excavations at a prehistoric site in Szombathely in 1876, the teacher Vilmos Lipp mentioned that 'the [animal] bones, supposedly along with plenty of bone tools, were sold by the workers in our absence' (Lipp 1876, 95). This example highlights that these archaeological finds also had a certain financial value attached to them and that not only the practitioners of archaeology were aware of their importance, but also laypersons. They were probably selling them because they knew about the increasing interest in archaeology and the growing number of collectors and archaeological associations that were acquiring archaeological finds.

There were also occasions on which both human and animal remains were intentionally and unintentionally broken and/or scattered by workers or local peasants, either during excavations or agricultural work (*e.g.* Varázséji 1880, 336; Pintér 1886, 45; Melhárd 1886, 231; Szendrei 1889, 374; Sándorfi 1890, 71). This occurred because bones were considered unimportant or because workers did not want their tasks interrupted by having to carefully unearth and examine bones, given that they were sometimes paid on the basis of the amount of earth they dug out and carried away (Varázséji 1880, 336). In more fortunate situations, animal remains were reburied and thus preserved for posteriority, when interest in them and progress in the analysis of animal bones found in archaeological contexts were thought to be more advanced. This is precisely the case of the animal bones excavated at the Tószeg tell in 1877, which were gathered and buried in the local parish churchyard:

> At Tószeg, the excavated animal remains form an immense quantity, but as they have not been properly identified yet, they have been set aside in one of the pits of the clergy house, for better times when our homeland's prehistoric sites will have a Rütimeyer who will establish the fauna of those times based on them (Csetneki 1877, 83).

Mixing and burying the bones in this way meant of course losing all the information about the context in which they were found. Despite this, the excavators' action indicates that they were aware of the importance of animal remains in reconstructing the past, as well as of the limitations existing in the research of the time. On other occasions, however, the animal remains were overlooked by the excavators themselves. One such example is that of Ferenc Kubinyi who, despite being a palaeontologist who had published an archaeozoological study in 1859, seems to have ignored the bone finds during his excavations at Várhegy in 1858:

A third similar site is that of Várhegy at Gomba, whose potsherds and antler objects are identical [to those found at the sites of Tószeg and Szihalom], but it is a pity that the bone tools bypassed the attention of the excavator, Ferenc Kubinyi (Csetneki 1876, 283).

Collectors and the analysis of faunal remains and bone artefacts

In this section the contribution of collectors to fostering the interdisciplinary study of archaeological finds, including animal remains and bone artefacts, in nineteenth-century Hungary will be examined. The collectors' work in this regard is best reflected in the journal *Archaeologiai Értesítő*, in their own publications and above all in their correspondence. Our discussion will focus on the examples of two Hungarian collectors and prehistoric archaeologists, Zsófia Torma and Jenő Nyáry, particularly the latter, given that more information has survived about his interdisciplinary pursuits.

Zsófia Torma (1832–1899) was a pioneering female archaeologist from nineteenth-century Transylvania, then part of Austria-Hungary. She made a significant contribution to the development of prehistoric archaeology in Transylvania through her research at various archaeological sites and particularly at the settlement of Turdaș-Luncă. With her finds she established an impressive archaeological collection that, towards the end of her life, comprised 10,387 objects (see Coltofean 2015; 2016; 2017). Zsófia Torma's research was interdisciplinary quite early on, but unfortunately there is little information in the archives about this aspect of her work. What is known, however, is that she sent various finds to different specialists during her preparations for the 1876 CIAAP Congress, where she exhibited part of the collection. For example, the human remains she unearthed at Turdaș-Luncă were examined by the doctor Antal Genersich (1842–1918). The animal remains and lithic materials were analysed by Antal Koch (1843–1927), a Hungarian geologist, petrographer, mineralogist and palaeontologist (OSzK Kézirattár, 1930/31, letters from Zsófia Torma to Flóris Rómer). Some of her stone artefacts were also identified by János Sándor, a local teacher in her hometown, Szászváros (Coltofean 2015, 1040; 2016, 83, 86; 94). Zsófia Torma continued to ask specialists from different fields to examine her finds after the CIAAP Congress of 1876, but information about her requests in this regard is hard to find. Nevertheless, she was certainly aware of the importance of animal remains in reconstructing the past. This is also shown by the fact that, besides her archaeological collection, she also had a paleontological collection. Very little is known about the latter, but it contained valuable specimens, including a previously unknown fossil shell species named after her (*Terebra (Myurella) sophiae* Hallavats, 1884) (Coltofean 2016, 68–70; 2017, 330–331).

One of the earliest examples of interdisciplinary collaboration in nineteenth-century Hungarian archaeology occurred in the processing of the finds from the Neolithic cave of Aggtelek. The excavations were conducted by Baron Jenő Nyáry (1836–1914), a prehistorian, speleologist and collector. He carried out several archaeological excavations in Hungary, but those at Aggtelek, undertaken over 'three continuous days' in August 1876 (Nyáry 1881, 1), are probably the best known from his work. The preliminary results of this research were first presented at the 1876 CIAAP Congress in Budapest (Nyáry 1877; Nyáry 1881, 6). In his talk on Stone Age people in the Aggtelek cave, Jenő Nyáry mentioned that the carbonised seeds he found had already been examined and identified by Imre Deininger, while thirteen human skulls had been 'measured' by Julius Kollmann (Nyáry 1877, 630–632). The latter also attended the congress but did not deliver a paper on his contribution at Aggtelek or his research in general (Compte-rendu 1877, II–IV, XI). The text of Jenő Nyáry's talk suggests that some animal bones were also studied, revealing the existence of *Ursus spelaeus* (cave bear) and rhinoceros in the cave, but the name of the specialist who identified them was not mentioned (Nyáry 1877, 630–634). Therefore, the interdisciplinary study of the archaeological finds excavated at Aggtelek had begun before the 1876 CIAAP Congress and Jenő Nyáry was in contact with those specialists before the event. However, as shown below, the congress may have contributed to broadening the interdisciplinary framework of his research. At the end of his talk, Jenő Nyáry promised that the results of his research would be published in a detailed publication (Nyáry 1877, 634). This was achieved a few years later, in 1881, when he published the monograph *Az aggteleki barlang mint őskori temető* (*The Aggtelek cave as a prehistoric cemetery*) under the auspices of the Archaeological Committee of the Hungarian Academy of Sciences (Nyáry 1881).

In the introduction to his monograph, Jenő Nyáry stated that he contacted 'researchers with acknowledged prestige inside and outside the country' in order to be able to offer proper answers to the questions raised by his discoveries (Nyáry 1881, V). Thus, the archaeological finds from his excavations were examined by a multidisciplinary team that included scholars from different fields who today are seen as the founders of their disciplines in Hungary. For example, the carbonised seed remains were examined by the Hungarian agronomist Imre Deininger (1844–1918), who undertook the first archaeobotanical analyses in Hungary and was particularly interested in prehistoric wheat. The chemical composition of seeds and human and animal bones was examined by the Hungarian agrochemist Tamás Kosutány (1848–1915). The analysis of lithic tools and the microscopic analysis of potsherds was undertaken by József Szabó (1822–1894), a Hungarian geologist, mineralogist and petrographer who is considered to have been the founder of the Hungarian school of geology. Human bones were examined by the well-known physician and polymath Rudolf Virchow (1821–1902), the anatomist and zoologist Julius Kollmann (1834–1918) and József Lenhossék (1818–1888) (Nyáry 1881, V). The last of these was a Hungarian doctor, anatomist and anthropologist who made an important contribution to the development of physical anthropology in Hungary. Human teeth were analysed by the Hungarian dentist József Iszlay (1840–1903) (Nyáry 1881, V), who is regarded as the founder of professional stomatology in Hungary. Animal bones were examined by László Örley (1856–1887) (Nyáry 1881, V), a promising young zoologist, as well as a future pioneer in nematological research and assistant curator of the Hungarian National Museum zoology collection (from 1882). He completed his graduate studies at the Science University in Budapest (Budapesti Tudományegyetem; today the 'Eötvös Lóránd' University) in the same year as the excavations at Aggtelek. He then became an assistant lecturer for five years at the same institution (for more information on his biography, see Szinnyei 1891–1914[4]; Andrássy 1976) and it was in this position that he examined the faunal remains from the excavations of Jenő Nyáry. With the exception of the Aggtelek excavations, László Örley's name does not appear in any other archaeological journals in relation to animal remains found in archaeological contexts. One reason for this might be that, beginning in 1880, he undertook several research stays abroad, devoting his time to his own investigative work. The second reason could be his sudden death in 1887, meaning that his academic career only lasted ten years. However, this does not exclude the possibility that he carried out analyses of faunal remains for other collectors of archaeological finds. Further research is needed to ascertain whether his analysis of the Aggtelek faunal remains was a one-off in his career or whether he carried out others. Finally, the subspecies of the faunal remains discovered by Jenő Nyáry were determined by the Swiss zoologist, anatomist and palaeontologist Ludwig Rütimeyer (1825–1895) (Nyáry 1881, V), who is considered one of the fathers of archaeozoology. Looking at the various specialisations of these scholars, we can indeed see that Jenő Nyáry aimed to gain a broad picture and a thorough understanding of the archaeological finds at the Aggtelek cave.

Jenő Nyáry met József Szabó, József Lenhossék and Rudolf Virchow at the CIAAP Congress in 1876, each presenting papers. József Szabó talked about prehistoric obsidian in Hungary and Greece (Szabó 1877), József Lenhossék about a deformed macrocephalous skull from Hungary (Lenhossék 1877), and Rudolf Virchow about 'The brown and blond races in Germany' (Virchow 1877). It is unclear whether they had been in contact before the event or whether they met there for the first time and that was also the starting point of their interdisciplinary collaboration. It is clear, however, that they met during the congress and probably also discussed processing the finds from the Aggtelek cave. Imre Deininger, Tamás Kosutány, József Iszlay, László Örley (Compte-rendu 1877, XXV–XXXIII) and Ludwig Rütimeyer (Compte-rendu 1877, XI–XXV) did not participate in the congress, which means their relationship with Jenő Nyáry cannot be linked to that event.

Jenő Nyáry included the analyses and conclusions of the scholars with whom he collaborated in his monograph. He did this thoroughly and carefully, by putting together and connecting the information he had received from them in interpreting the Aggelek site. The resulting work was a complex multidisciplinary endeavour. Jenő Nyáry was among the few archaeologists in nineteenth-century Hungary to recognise the importance of animal remains in reconstructing the past. That is why he believed their analysis to be important: 'I considered the identification of animal bones all the more important because it reveals the geographical location and climate of those times' (Nyáry 1881, 71).

Conclusions

This chapter explores the interest in faunal remains and bone artefacts and their analysis in nineteenth-century Hungarian archaeology. It does so by analysing a number of key publications that offer an overview of the Hungarian archaeological scene at the time. It shows that during the nineteenth century faunal remains and bone tools discovered in archaeological contexts were examined by zoologists, naturalists and palaeontologists. The specialists who carried out those studies included Ferenc Kubinyi, Nándor Báthory, Tivadar Margó, László Örley, Ludwig Rütimeyer and Antal Koch. Their work, however, was occasional and did not result in a continuous interest or tradition in the analysis of faunal remains. In this regard, the findings of this research confirm those of Eduardo Corona-M regarding Mexico, where 'the oldest works were part of naturalist practices but do not constitute a scientific tradition, because the effort did not produce a systematic interest in the issue or become an institutional process' (Corona-M 2008, 76). In the case of Hungary, the early death of László Örley, an assistant curator of the Hungarian National Museum zoological collection who analysed the animal remains discovered at the Aggtelek cave, may have prevented the establishment of such a tradition. Archaeozoological studies were initiated and requested in Hungary by archaeologists such as Flóris Rómer, Jenő Nyáry and Zsófia Torma. The last two also owned archaeological collections and were pioneers of prehistoric archaeology in the country. Nevertheless, their activity in this regard is not reflected in the important archaeological overviews of the time, such as *Magyarország archaeologiája* by Ferenc Pulszky, thus giving the impression that their efforts never existed. It is, however, mentioned in the archaeological journals and can be found above all in their own publications.

When published, faunal remains were usually enumerated with the names of the species they belonged to and sometimes even described. This indicates that identifications, at least on a basic level, were carried out quite often. They were in fact necessary, as for a certain time animal remains (*e.g.* mammoth, reindeer and cave bear bones) were also used for dating and establishing periods within prehistory. However, there is generally little or no information about those responsible for those identifications, the methods they used to make them or the contexts in which they were carried out. As shown in this chapter, apart from specialists from the natural sciences, animal remains were also identified by archaeologists and other individuals excavating sites, as well as by museum workers.

Animal remains and bone artefacts were common finds in nineteenth-century Hungarian archaeology and they were circulated widely. They were often donated to the Hungarian National Museum or kept in private collections. In many cases, they were sold, broken or thrown away by workers at archaeological sites. In other cases, they were reburied after the excavation and preserved for a time when they could be analysed. Despite this, faunal remains and bone artefacts were considered less important than other finds, such as tools and weapons made of stone and especially metal. Unless found in exceptionally important and interesting contexts (*e.g.* the domestic waste from Magyarád) or in private collections, unworked animal bones received less attention from archaeology practitioners than any other finds. Their value was utilitarian and they were therefore usually interpreted as domestic waste and seen as raw materials for producing tools, weapons and jewellery.

Faunal remains were not neglected due to a lack of resources and infrastructure, as there were several specialists who could examine them. In addition, many scholars had at least some basic knowledge of the natural sciences that equipped them to carry out elementary identifications. Their neglect may have been caused by the fact that their importance and potential for reconstructing the past and understanding human-environment interactions across time had not yet been realised. Faunal remains were usually found in a fragmented state that made their analysis difficult. They were also less visually appealing when compared to, for example, metal artefacts. Furthermore, with the exception of horse remains, their characteristics did not allow them to be used in nationalist discourses and for establishing ethnic roots. Nevertheless, the scientific attention paid to them gradually increased over the century and the discussions in the sessions of the 1876 CIAAP Congress organised in Budapest contributed to their acknowledgement.

This chapter also demonstrates that multidisciplinarity and interdisciplinarity were incorporated into nineteenth-century archaeological practice in Hungary in different ways and that there was no single model for this process. Some of these ways were congresses and other scientific meetings between scholars of different backgrounds (*e.g.* meetings of doctors and naturalists attended by archaeologists), archaeology exhibitions, reading and correspondence. Hungarian archaeologists were constantly reading about the advances in archaeology and other fields in Hungary, as well as in Europe and beyond. They were aware of what was happening on an international level and the archaeological journals, especially *Archaeologiai Értesítő* with its sections on the latest publications and scientific news from abroad, contributed to this knowledge in particular.

The encyclopaedic backgrounds and wide interests of the scholars who engaged in archaeology in the nineteenth century significantly contributed to fostering interactions between different disciplines. It seems that collectors, who were particularly motivated to find out more about the objects in their own collections, played an important role in this process. Future archival research, especially into the correspondence between collectors and the specialists who identified the faunal remains in their collections, will no doubt bring to light more information about early archaeozoological analyses in nineteenth-century Hungary. Nevertheless, the social and academic networks that the previously mentioned actors were part of facilitated the circulation of information about new methods, their gradual spread and later incorporation into archaeological practice. This was also enhanced by the fact that the boundaries of and between disciplines were not as clearly and strictly defined as today. Thanks to this flexibility, we could say that archaeology was in a way more open to multidisciplinarity and interdisciplinarity in the nineteenth century than later in the twentieth century.

Acknowledgements

This chapter was written within the framework of the InterArq research project (HAR2016-80271-P) (interarqweb.wordpress.com) subsidised by the State Research Agency (AEI) and the European Regional Development Fund (ERDF, EU). The author would like to thank archaeozoologist László Bartosiewicz for his valuable insights and comments that have significantly improved this article.

Notes

1 1899 is the year in which *Archaeologiai Közlemények* was published for the last time.
2 For their biographies see Szinnyei 1891–1914, http://mek.niif.hu/03600/03630/html/index.htm (accessed on 20 August 2020).
3 For more information on Ferenc Pulszky's first work on the Copper Age, see Pulszky 1883; for a recent analysis of the history of this concept on a global level, see Pearce 2019.
4 Text available at: http://mek.oszk.hu/03600/03630/html/oe/oe18619.htm (accessed on 15 July 2020).

References

Andrássy, I. (1976) A nematológiai kutatások hazai úttörői: Örley László és Daday Jenő. *Állattani Közlemények* 63 (1–4), 219–224.

Anonymous (1817) Elő szó. *Tudományos Gyűjtemény* 1, III–XII.

Bartosiewicz, L. (2001) Archaeozoology or zooarchaeology?: a problem from the last century. *Archaeologia Polona* 39, 75–86.

Bartosiewicz, L. (2017) Zooarchaeology in the Carpathian Basin and adjacent areas. In U. Albarella, M. Rizzetto, H. Russ, K. Vickers and S. Viner-Daniels (eds) *The Oxford Handbook of Zooarchaeology*, 99–112. New York, Oxford University Press.

Bartosiewicz, L. (2020) Zooarchaeology. In C. Smith (ed.) *Encyclopedia of Global Archaeology*, 1–11. Cham, Springer.

Bartosiewicz, L. and Choyke, A.M. (2002) Archaeozoology in Hungary. *Archaeofauna* 11, 117–129.

Bartosiewicz, L., Mérai, D. and Csippán, P. (2011) Dig up–dig in: practice and theory in Hungarian archaeology. In L. Lozny (ed.) *Comparative Archaeologies. A Sociological View of the Science of the Past*, 273–337. New York, Springer.

Báthory, N. (1868) Jelentés a Magyarád (Hont megye) helységében talált csontok összehasonlító boncztani vizsgálatáról. *Archaeologiai Közlemények* 7 (2), 73–75.

Becker, C. and Benecke, N. (2001) Archaeozoology in Germany. Its course of development. *Archaeofauna* 10, 163–182.

Çakirlar, C., van den Hurk, Y., van der Jagt, I., van Amerongen, Y., Bakker, J., Breider, R., van Dijk, J., Esser, K., Groot, M., de Jong, T., Kootker, L., Steenhuisen, F., Zeiler, J., van Kolfschoten, T., Prummel, W. and Lauwerier, R. (2019) Animals and people in the Netherlands' past: >50 years of archaeozoology in the Netherlands. *Open Quaternary* 5 (13), 1–30.

Capellini, G. (1877) Les traces de l'homme pliocène en Toscane. In *Congrès International d'Anthropologie et d'Archéologie Pré-historiques. Compte-rendu de la huitième session a Budapest*, vol. I, 46–63. Budapest, Imprimerie Franklin – Társulat.

Coltofean, L. (2015) Importanța ediției a opta a Congrès international d'anthropologie et d'archéologie préhistoriques în dezvoltarea arheologiei preistorice în Transilvania secolului al XIX-lea. In S. Forțiu and A. Stavilă (eds) *ArheoVest III: In Memoriam Florin Medeleț, Interdisciplinaritate în Arheologie și Istorie, Timișoara, 28 noiembrie 2015*, vol. 2: *Metode Interdisciplinare în Arheologie și Istorie*, 1035–1055. Szeged, JATEPress Kiadó.

Coltofean, L. (2016) *Zsófia Torma și așezarea de la Turdaș, punctul Luncă, județul Hunedoara*. Unpublished doctoral thesis, 'Lucian Blaga' University of Sibiu.

Coltofean, L. (2017) Zsófia Torma: a pioneer of prehistoric archaeology in nineteenth-century Transylvania. In Cs. Szabó, V. Rusu-Bolindeț, G.T. Rustoiu and M. Gligor (eds) *Adalbert Cserni and His Contemporaries. The Pioneers of Archaeology in Alba Iulia and Beyond*, 327–354. Cluj-Napoca, Mega Publishing House.

Congrès International d'Anthropologie et d'Archéologie Préhistoriques. Compte-rendu de la huitième session a Budapest, vol. I. (1877) Budapest, Imprimerie Franklin – Társulat.

Corona-M, E. (2002a) *Las Aves en la Historia Natural Novohispana*. México, Colección Científica, Instituto Nacional de Antropología e Historia.

Corona-M, E. (2002b) El pensamiento evolucionista y la paleontología de vertebrados en México (1790–1915). In M.A. Puig-Samper, R. Ruiz and A. Galera (eds) *Evolucionismo y cultura. Darwinismo en Europa e Iberoamérica*, 353–366. México, Ediciones Doce Calles.

Corona-M, E. (2008) The origin of archaeozoology in México: an overview. *Quaternary International* 185, 75–81.

Cosgrove, R. (2002) The role of zooarchaeology in archaeological interpretation: a view from Australia. *Archaeofauna* 11, 173–204.

Crader, D.C. (2002) Zooarchaeological literature in northeastern North American: The Gulf of Maine as a case study. *Archaeofauna* 11, 159–172.

Csetneki, J.E. (1876) Tószegi ásatások. *Archaeologiai Értesítő* 10 (9), 277–283.

Csetneki, J.E. (1877) A tószegi őstelep. *Archaeologiai Értesítő* 11 (3), 78–83.

Davis, S.J.M. (1987/1995) *The Archaeology of Animals*. London, Routledge.

Díaz-Andreu, M. (2007) *A World History of Nineteenth-Century Archaeology. Nationalism, Colonialism, and the Past*. Oxford, New York, Oxford University Press.

Driver, J.C. (1993) Zooarchaeology in British Columbia. *BC Studies* 99, 77–105.

Dudás, Gy. (1885) A zentai bronzleletről. *Archaeologiai Értesítő* (New series) 5 (5), 394.

Endre, Á. (1899) A nyitrai várhegy oldalában talált régi cserepek és csontok lelhelyéről. *Archaeologiai Értesítő* (New series) 19 (5), 404–408.

Gerecze, P. (1895a) A pécsi székesegyház régiségei, I. közlemény. Ember- és állat-alakokat ábrázoló szobormaradványok. *Archaeologiai Értesítő* 15 (1), 36–48.

Gerecze, P. (1895b) A pécsi székesegyház régiségei. Második közlemény. Ember- és állat-alakokat ábrázoló szobormaradványok. *Archaeologiai Értesítő* 15 (2), 129–146.

Gerecze, P. (1895c) A pécsi székesegyház régiségei. III. közlemény. Ember- és állat-alakokat ábrázoló szobormaradványok. *Archaeologiai Értesítő* 15 (4), 333–361.

Gifford-Gonzalez, D. (2018) *An Introduction to Zooarchaeology*. Cham, Springer.

Gräslund, B. (1987) *The Birth of Prehistoric Chronology. Dating Methods and Dating Systems in Nineteenth-century Scandinavian Archaeology*. Cambridge, New York, New Rochelle, Melbourne, Sydney, Cambridge University Press.

Grouard, S. (2010) Caribbean archaeozoology. In G. Mengoni Goñalons, J. Arroyo-Cabrales, Ó.J. Polaco y F.J. Aguilar (eds) *Estado Actual de la Arqueozoología Latinoamericana/Current Advances in Latin-American Archaeozoology*, 133–151. Mexico, Instituto Nacional de Antropología e Historia, Consejo Nacional para la Ciencia y la Tecnología, International Council for Archaeozoology and Universidad de Buenos Aires.

Hampel, J. (1876a) *Antiquités Préhistoriques de la Hongrie*. Esztergom, Alexandre Beszédes, Editeur.

Hampel, J. (1876b) *Catalogue de l'exposition préhistorique des musées de province et des collections particulières de la Hongrie, arrangée a l'occasion de la VIIIème session du Congrès International d'Archéologie et d'Anthropologie Préhistoriques a Budapest*. Budapest, Typographie Franklin – Társulat.

Hampel, J. (1886) *Trouvailles de l'Âge de Bronze en Hongrie* (also known as *Congrès International d'Anthropologie et d'Archéologie Préhistoriques. Compte-rendu de la huitième session a Budapest*, vol. II, part II). Budapest, Edition du Musée National Hongrois.

Hampel, J. (1886–1896) *A bronzkor emlékei Magyarhonban*, vol. I–III. Budapest, Az Országos Régészeti és Embertani Társulat Kiadványa.
Hampel, J. (1895) *Ujabb tanulmányok a rézkorról*. Budapest, Magyar Tudományos Akadémia.
Hampel, J. (1896) *A honfoglalási kor hazai emlékei*. Budapest, Magyar Tudományos Akadémia.
Hampel, J. (1902) Az érem- és régiségtár története. In *A Nemzeti Múzeum Érem- és Régiségosztálya*, Ismertetik az osztály tisztviselői, 6–18. Budapest, Hornyánszky Viktor Császári és Királyi Udvari Könyvnyomdája.
Henszlmann, I. (1866) *Régészeti kalauz különös tekintettel Magyarországra. II. rész. Középkori épitészet*. Pest, A Magyar Tudományos Akadémia Archaeologiai Bizottsága.
Horwitz, L.K. (2002) The development of archaeozoological research in Israel and the west bank. *Archaeofauna* 11, 131–145.
Jing, Y. (2002) The formation and development of Chinese zooarchaeology: A preliminary review. *Archaeofauna* 11, 205–212.
Kárász, L. (1894) Elefántcsont-nyergek a n. múzeumban. *Archaeologiai Értesítő* (New series) 14 (1), 53–60.
Kristiansen, K. (2002) The birth of ecological archaeology in Denmark: history and research environments 1850–2002. In A. Fischer and K. Kristiansen (eds) *The Neolithisation of Denmark. 150 Years of Debate*, 11–31. Poole, Orca Book.
Kršnjavi (1886) Két középkori elefántcsont dombormű. *Archaeologiai Értesítő* (New series) 6 (5), 398–405.
Kršnjavi (1887): Középkori elefántcsont dombormű a nemzeti muzeumban. *Archaeologiai Értesítő* (New series) 7 (1), 39–41.
Kubinyi, F. (1859) A teve és a ló, állat- és öslénytani s a Magyarok keletröl kijövetelére vonatkozólag történelmi tekintetben. *Akadémiai Értesítő* I/V, 397–446.
Lenhossék, J. (1877) Description d'un crane macrocéphale déformé et d'un crâne de l'époque barbare en Hongrie. In *Congrès International d'Anthropologie et d'Archéologie Préhistoriques. Compte-rendu de la huitième session a Budapest*, vol. I, 543–577. Budapest, Imprimerie Franklin – Társulat.
Lipp, V. (1876) A szombathelyi muzeum és a Vas-vármegyei legújabb leletek. *Archaeologiai Értesítő* 10 (3), 95–97.
Lyman, R.L. (2012) Lewis R. Binford's impact on zooarchaeology. *Ethnoarchaeology* 4 (1), 55–78.
Lyman, R.L. (2015) The history of 'laundry lists' in North American zooarchaeology. *Journal of Anthropological Archaeology* 39, 42–50.
Lyman, R.L. (2018) The history of MNI in North American zooarchaeology. In C.M. Giovas and M.J. LeFebvre (eds) *Zooarchaeology in Practice*, 13–33. Cham, Springer.
Majláth, B. (1873) Tanulmányok az ember eredetének történetéből. *Archaeologiai Közlemények* 9 (2), 1–34.
Melhárd, Gy. (1886) Somogymegyei ősleletekről. *Archaeologiai Értesítő* (New series) 6 (3), 231–233.
Mengoni Goñalons, G.L. (1988) Analisis de materiales faunisticos de sitios arqueologicos. *Xama* 1, 71–120.
Mengoni Goñalons, G.L. (2007) Archaeofaunal studies in Argentina: a historical overview. In M. Gutiérrez, L. Miotti, G. Barrientos, G.L. Mengoni Goñalons and M. Salemme (eds) *Taphonomy and Zooarchaeology in Argentina*, 13–35. BAR International Series. Oxford, Archaeopress.
Mengoni Goñalons, G.L. (2010) Advances in animal bone archaeology in Argentina: general trends and some prospects for the future. In G. Mengoni Goñalons, J. Arroyo Cabrales, Ó.J. Polaco and F.J. Aguilar (eds) *Estado Actual de la Arqueozoología Latinoamericana/Current Advances in Latin-American Archaeozoology*, 17–26. Mexico, Instituto Nacional de Antropología e Historia, Consejo Nacional para la Ciencia y la Tecnología, International Council for Archaeozoology and Universidad de Buenos Aires.
Mengoni Goñalons, G.L., Arroyo-Cabrales, J., Polaco, J.Ó. and Aguilar, F.J. (eds) (2010) *Estado Actual de la Arqueozoología Latinoamericana/Current Advances in Latin-American Archaeozoology*. Mexico, Instituto Nacional de Antropología e Historia, Consejo Nacional de Ciencia y Tecnología, International Council for Archaeozoology, and Universidad de Buenos Aires.

Morales Muñiz, A. (2002) 35 years of Archaeozoology in Spain: a critical review. *Archaeofauna* 11, 103–116.
Nyáry, J. (1877) Les hommes de l'âge de la pierre dans la caverne d'Aggtelek, comté de Gömör. In *Congrès International d'Anthropologie et d'Archéologie Préhistoriques. Compte-rendu de la huitième session a Budapest*, vol. I, 626–634. Budapest, Imprimerie Franklin – Társulat.
Nyáry, J. (1881) *Az aggteleki barlang mint őskori temető*. Budapest, A Magyar Tudományos Akadémia Könyvkiadó Hivatala.
Országos Széchényi Könyvtár, Kézirattár (Széchényi National Library, Collection of Manuscripts), 1930/31, letters from Zsófia Torma to Flóris Rómer.
Pearce, M. (2019) The 'Copper Age' – a history of the concept. *Journal of World Prehistory* 32, 229–250.
Pintér, S. (1886) Nógrádmegyei régiségekről. *Archaeologiai Értesítő* (New series) 6 (1), 44–47.
Pulszky, F. (1883) *A rézkor Magyarországban*. Budapest, A Magyar Tudományos Akadémia Archaeologiai Bizottsága.
Pulszky, F. (1897) *Magyarország archaeologiája*, vol. I–II. Budapest, Pallas Irodalmi és Nyomdai Részvénytársaság.
Reitz, E. and Wing, E. (2008) *Zooarchaeology*, 2nd Edition. New York, Cambridge University Press.
Rómer, F. (1860) *A Bakony, természetrajzi és régészeti vázlat*. Győr, Nymtatott Sauervein Gézánál.
Rómer, F. (1866) *Műrégészeti kalauz különös tekintettel Magyarországra. I. rész. Őskori műrégészet*. Pest, A Magyar Tudományos Akadémia Archaeologiai Bizottsága.
Rómer, F. (1873) A pilini Leshegyen talált csontvázakról. *Archaeologiai Közlemények* 9 (1), 16–25.
Rómer, F. (1878) *Congrès International d'Anthropologie et d'Archéologie Préhistoriques. Compte-rendu de la huitième session a Budapest*, vol. II, part I – *Resultats généraux du mouvement archéologique en Hongrie*. Budapest, Edition du Musée National Hongrois.
Sándorfi, N. (1890) A szomolányi őstelepröl. *Archaeologiai Értesítő* (New series) 10 (1), 66–71.
Semper, H. (1896) Kora-keresztény elefánt- és egyéb csontdomborművek a Magyar Nemzeti Muzeumban. *Archaeologiai Értesítő* (New series) 16 (3), 193–222.
Stewart, F.L. (1993) A history of zooarchaeology in Ontario. *Canadian Zooarchaeology/Zooarchéologie Canadienne* 4, 2–18.
Stewart, K.M. (2002) Past and present zooarchaeology in Canada. *Archaeofauna* 11, 147–157.
Strzygovszki, J. (1891) Domborműves elefántcsont-táblácska a salernoi székesegyház oltáráról. *Archaeologiai Értesítő* (New series) 11 (4), 338–340.
Szabó, J. (1877) L'obsidienne préhistorique en Hongrie et en Grèce. In *Congrès International d'Anthropologie et d'Archéologie Préhistoriques. Compte-rendu de la huitième session a Budapest*, vol. I, 96–100. Budapest, Imprimerie Franklin – Társulat.
Szendrei, J. (1889) Különfélék. *Archaeologiai Értesítő* (New series) 9 (4), 373–375.
Szinnyei, J. (1891–1914) *Magyar írók élete és munkái*, vol. I–XIV. Budapest, Hornyánszky.
Téglás, G. (1881) A bécsi csász. akadémia állandó ősrégészeti bizottságának munkálatai 1880-ról. *Archaeologiai Értesítő* (New series) 1 (2), 326–328.
Trantalidou, K. (2001) Archaeozoology in Greece: a brief historiography of the science. *Archaeofauna* 10, 183–199.
Trigger, B.G. (2006) *A History of Archaeological Thought*, 2nd Edition. Cambridge, New York, Melbourne, Madrid, Cape Town, Singapore, São Paulo, Delhi, Cambridge University Press.
Varázséji, G. (1880) A szeged-öthalmi őstelep és temető. *Archaeologiai Értesítő* 14, 323–336.
Vékony, G. (2003) A régészeti terepkutatás története Magyarországon. In Zs. Visy, *Magyar régészet az ezredfordulón*, 15–21. Budapest, Nemzeti Kulturális Örökség Minisztériuma, Teleki László Alapítvány.
Virchow, R. (1877) La race brune et la race blonde en Allemagne. In *Congrès International d'Anthropologie et d'Archéologie Préhistoriques. Compte-rendu de la huitième session a Budapest*, vol. I, 577–586. Budapest, Imprimerie Franklin – Társulat.
Živaljević, I. (2013) Životinje između Prirode i Kulture: priča o arheozoologiji. *Етноантропошки проблеми* 8 (4), 1137–1163.

Chapter 4

From plants to pollen, from Europe to Spain: looking at interdisciplinarity in archaeology

Margarita Díaz-Andreu

Abstract

This chapter examines the development of palynology in Spain as part of a wider European context. The first part of the article explores the first years of interest in palaeobotany and palynology in Northern Europe and its reception in other European countries. In south Europe it was only in the 1940s that the first professionals, most of them women, began to work in the field. In Spain there were both Spanish and foreign specialists working in the field in the early years. In the framework of a growing concern for the ecology, the 1970s saw the emergence of a new generation of specialists with a preoccupation for the context of prehistoric landscapes. The last four decades have seen a definitive move from a type of archaeology in which interdisciplinarity plays a key role and palynology has been established as a sub-specialisation. The chapter concludes with some thoughts about training, transmission of knowledge, personal circumstances, gender and the effect of a new, international belief in the benefits of interdisciplinarity.

Keywords: history of archaeology; palynology; interdisciplinarity; Spain; transmission of knowledge.

Introduction

Palynology, the study of vegetation based on the analysis of microscopic contemporary and fossil plant remains, was characterised by its marked interdisciplinary nature from its early years at the start of the twentieth century. Its methodology was created by a geologist but from the outset this new way of studying plants was received by other disciplines such as botany, geology and archaeology and soon became accepted as a subdiscipline within all those sciences. As this article will show, this did not take place at the same time everywhere. Several phases can be established, beginning with a preparatory period in the nineteenth century, its establishment as a methodology and dissemination across northern Europe, and finally its arrival in southern Europe. In the following pages these phases will be teased out in relation to archaeology. The article will first focus on northern Europe and the spread of the new methodology to central and western Europe. It will then centre its attention in Spain as a way of analysing the transmission of knowledge from the northern part of Europe to its southern neighbours after the Second World War. Issues under discussion will include the relationship between knowledge and reception in science; academic authority and gender; academic ambition in younger generations and progress in science; how new methodologies consolidate with academic maturity; and the power of networks. The elements needed for interdisciplinarity to become possible will all appear in the study: an effective collaboration by members of different disciplines in the same projects; the use of the same set of techniques; the establishment of meetings in which scientists based in diverse disciplines come together to discuss issues of common interest; and the organisation of joint publications.

From botany to palynology: from the nineteenth century to the 1940s

An interest in plants in prehistoric contexts first appeared in northern Europe. There are two reasons for this. On the one hand, the absence or scarcity of stone walls and pottery in excavations, in contrast to their overwhelming presence in southern European excavations, led archaeologists to pay attention to other types of remains overlooked in southern areas, such as those of plants. On the other hand, the better conservation of recognisable organic material in wet environments facilitated its identification. However, these two reasons would not have been enough if the knowledge of how to analyse ancient plants had not been developed in other sciences, particularly in botany. All this created a favourable context for the birth of what Kristian Kristiansen called ecological archaeology (Kristiansen 2002).

The Kitchen Midden Commissions

In today's overspecialised world, scientists need to make an effort to learn about sciences that are far from their own. Until the last decades of the nineteenth century, however, although university education was becoming more specialised, other scientific institutions were of a more general nature. This was particularly the case of learned societies, in which scientists from different disciplines were able to learn about each other's research and get together to discuss and attempt to resolve scholarly dilemmas. It was in one such society, the Danish Academy of Sciences and Letters, that scientists from different backgrounds became interested in the functional and chronological nature of shell middens. As a result of a presentation made to academics by Japetus Steenstrup (1813–1897) in 1848, in 1849 a commission was set up to study them within the framework of the Danish academy. Steenstrup was an acclaimed naturalist who had studied the Vidnesdam marshland where he had managed to distinguish five different phases of about two thousand years, each characterised by the presence of poplar, pine, oak (where he found an artifact), alder and beech (Gron and Rowley-Conwy 2018, 38). In his 1848 presentation Steenstrup spoke of his excavations in shell mounds and the debate emerging from his way of interpreting the results resulted in the formation of the *køkkenmøddingkommission* or Kitchen Midden Commission. Functioning between 1849 and 1869, it consisted of Steenstrup himself and Jens Jacob Asmussen Worsaae (1821–1885), an archaeologist with a strong commitment to science and its methodological principles, as opposed to historical myth. It was in this context that he considered it necessary to apply the principles of geology in order to understand archaeological stratigraphy (Kristiansen 2002, 12). It made sense, therefore, that a geologist, Johan Georg Forchhammer (1794–1865), was the third member of the commission.

This commission may well have been the first of an interdisciplinary nature. The new knowledge they constructed could have remained within the walls of the academy and thus have been diluted and forgotten over time. For new ideas and methods to be successful in science, the novel know-how and its results need to be transmitted. In the case of the *køkkenmøddingkommission* they were successful in effectively conveying their discoveries. The knowledge produced by the commission became widely known thanks to the contact networks of the time: correspondence, participation in conferences in other countries and publications. This is demonstrated, for example, by references to their work by the archaeologists Prosper Mérimée (1803–1870) and Édouard Lartet (1801–1871) (Kristiansen 2002, 13–15) and many others, as will be mentioned below in the case of Spain. However, in the latter case it will be seen that transmission is not enough, as reception also depends on what is going on in the country at the receiving end. This explains why on some occasions certain innovations do not become widespread in science, despite their apparently unproblematic transmission. The stronger the scientific networks between countries and the mobility between their scientists, the easier it becomes for knowledge, methodologies and techniques to be accepted in the other country.

Once favourable conditions are created in one country and those most closely connected to it, it becomes possible to create a tradition. This happened in the country where the *køkkenmøddingkommission* had been set up and in the neighbouring Scandinavian countries. The value added to archaeological knowledge from the interdisciplinary collaboration between archaeologists and other natural scientists led to a second commission in 1893. The key figures were archaeologists, not only from Denmark but also from Sweden: the Dane Sophus Müller (1846–1934) and the Swede Oscar Montelius (1843–1921). Both had been pushing in their own countries for more rigorous methodologies in the field, including the introduction of systematic excavation and recording techniques and the imposition of the typological method. The formation of this second commission would be linked to the criticism made by the naturalist Japetus Steenstrup and an amateur archaeologist Ludvig Zinck of the way archaeologists had divided the pre-metallurgical periods. In this commission, the Dane Emil Rostrup (1831–1907) and the Danish-Swedish Georg Sarauw (1862–1928) focused on botany (Kristiansen 2002, 19, fig. 2.3). The former identified the remains of charred plants and the latter plants based on the impressions they left on pottery and the grains found (Gron and Rowley-Conwy 2018, 39). However, this second commission allows us to see a different issue regarding the difficulties of establishing novel lines of research, *i.e.* the influence of extra-scientific factors such as personal issues. The forced departure of Georg Sarauw from the National Museum of Denmark due to the inflexible character of its director, Sophus Müller, markedly slowed down further developments in this line of work (Kristiansen 2002, 19). It was not until the 1940s that some of this research was taken up with new methodologies, in particular the study of plants through pollen analyses, which had been discovered thirty years earlier (Kristiansen 2002, 20).

Palynology in Scandinavia

Palynology was formalised as an analytical method by the Swedish geologist, Lennart von Post (1884–1951) in 1916 (Edwards 2018, 320). Von Post presented the first pollen diagrams at the 16th Scandinavian Meeting of Natural Sciences held in Christiania (today's Oslo) in that year (Manten 1966, 277). Although there are precedents in the nineteenth century (Manten 1966, 278–282), von Post not only identified pollens but also demonstrated the potential of such a study with his novel methodology. He presented the first modern analysis with percentages that allowed a direct quantitative description of the vegetation patterns of the past (Pearsall 1989, 256–257). Although the designation palynology would not appear until several decades later, specifically in 1944, interdisciplinarity was part and parcel of the new methodology from early on. This can be seen in archaeology, where it was soon adopted for environmental studies (Pearsall 1989, 257). In addition, palynology became useful to archaeologists as a way of deducing the chronology of sites where the vegetation had changed dramatically over time, for example with the appearance of cultivated plants (Gron and Rowley-Conwy 2018, 46).

A key element in the transmission of palynology as a new subdiscipline was for young scholars to learn about it. That became possible when a young professional, Gunnar Erdtman (1897–1973), joined the Geological Survey of Sweden's peat bog research team in which von Post worked. Like him, many of the very early pioneers of the study of ancient landscapes based on palynological studies were from Scandinavia: the Danish botanist Johannes Iversen (1904–1972), who would be part of a so-called Third Commission in 1939 (Kristiansen 2002, 20) (see also Troels-Smith, Jessen and Mortensen 2018), the botanist Knut Fagri (1909–2001) in Norway, Tage Nilsson (1933–) in Sweden and Knud Jessen (1884–1971) in Denmark. One of the oldest, Gunnar Erdtman, became one of the leading members of the new subdiscipline, regularly gathering and publishing bibliographies of literature on palynology from the mid-1920s (West 2014, 25). In doing this he created identity, ensuring that the members of the new subdiscipline were recognised as such by others and could feel themselves part of a community by seeing their names printed next to those of their peers. In his bibliographical lists he included the publications of geologists, ecologists, climatologists, botanists and archaeologists, thus reinforcing palynology's interdisciplinary nature (Nilsson and Praglowski 1978).

In addition to the bibliography lists, one of the other elements that consolidated palynology at that time was its members' sense of progress in the discipline. This is very marked in the early years of its development and can be observed in the words of one of Johannes Iversen's students, the head of the Danish National Museum's scientific department, Jørgen Troels-Smith (1916–1991). Explaining about the early years of palynology he noted that:

> When I [Troels-Smith] in 1934 began to learn pollen analysis with Iversen, it was very simple, one had to determine c. 10 different pollen grains, that is, the most common forest trees. During the 1930s more were added; Tage Nilsson in Lund demonstrated that pollen of ash could be determined, and Iversen added to the list grasses, half-grasses and tasselweed, but only as families. But later came the species of ribwort plantain (*Plantago lanceolata*, *Pl. major* and *Pl. maritima*). Together we determined ivy and mistletoe. At the same time Firbas in Gottingen had demonstrated that the domesticated cereals had big pollen grains. During the work with the Dyrholm site I succeeded in defining seaweed (*Ruppia*). It meant that by 1942 we were able to determine 22 different pollen grains from 10 species, *i.e.* double the number (Troels-Smith in Kristiansen 2002, 20–21).

Kristiansen argues that the article Iversen published with the discoveries he mentions in his quote (referring to Iversen 1942) was revolutionary in its nature (Kristiansen 2002, 20). According to him, Iversen identified not only pollen from trees but also from grasses and *Plantago lanceolata* (Kristiansen 2002, 20). He was able to demonstrate that the Neolithic had been characterised by a first phase of slash-and-burn agriculture (Gron and Rowley-Conwy 2018, 48).

Beyond Scandinavia: how the study of pollens spread to other central and western European countries

The network formed in southern Europe between Spain, France and Italy at the beginning of the twentieth century (for the case of prehistory see Díaz-Andreu 2014) contrasted with another established in the northern, north-western and central European countries. The latter allowed the developments in Scandinavian archaeology to reach the United Kingdom and Germany in the 1920s and 30s (for the Netherlands see Jonker 1967; Bakker 2001, 63; for Switzerland see Delley 2015, 49–50 and for beyond Europe see Bryant and Holloway 1996; Jha 2005). One of the factors in the international dissemination of palynology was the trips made by Gunnar Erdtman to undertake analytical research into pollen in several European countries. He was also awarded a Rockefeller scholarship that took him to Western Canada and the USA in 1930 and 1931 (Nilsson and Praglowski 1978, 1). It is impossible in a study such as this to provide a full account of the influence of Erdtman's trips on others, although comments in the literature seem to indicate that they did indeed have an impact. In England, for example, he sampled several peat bogs in the company of the botanist Thomas Woodhead (Smith 2009, 54). He also taught palynology to Oxford botany professor Arthur G. Tansley (Smith 1994, 28), who in turn taught it in 1931 to botanist Margaret Elizabeth Godwin. She then trained her husband, Harry Godwin, who would rapidly become an acclaimed botanist in England. In Cambridge, the creation of the Fenland Research Committee (FRC) in 1932, in which the Godwins collaborated with the archaeologist Grahame Clark, involved the application of this technique in the study of Peacock's Farm and Plantation Farm (Clark et al. 1935). Their research meant that for the first time in British archaeology, archaeologists were able to offer a relative climatological time scale for their findings. Their contribution to archaeological knowledge was of enormous importance (Smith 2009, 54). Harry Godwin wrote some methodological articles on palynology (Godwin 1934) and two decades later, his many studies became one of the main sources of data for his acclaimed work *The History of the British Flora* (Godwin 1956, see Clapham and Osborne 2004).

As in the United Kingdom, the earliest indication in Germany of palynological studies being applied to archaeology dates to the late 1920s and early 1930s. The first to adopt palynology was the botanist Karl Bertsch (1931) in his study of the Federsee basin. He provided key information on the changes in the environment of a 4,000-year-long prehistoric sequence unearthed by the archaeologists Rudolph Schmidt and Hans Reinerth. Between 1921 and 1923 Reinerth (1900–1990) had been an assistant to the geologist and prehistorian Robert Rudolph Schmidt (1882–1950) at the Prehistoric Research Institute of Tübingen. With Schmidt he had excavated several lake dwellings in the Federsee in the Baden-Württemberg area of southern Germany. The institute encouraged the examination of the sediments, pollen and fauna found during the excavations. In a letter to the Swiss botanist Ernst Neuweiler he mentioned that

> Until now, we had only one pollen diagram for the Mesolithic of South Germany, elaborated by Karl Bertsch, according to which our Tardenian coincides with the corylus peak (in Delley 2015, 55, see Bertsch 1928, 4)

From 1935 onwards, Bertsch's work would be overtaken by Franz Firbas and I. Müller, who refined the method in the Federsee area (Delley 2015, 49).

Also in Germany, this time the north of the country, the naturalist Rudolf Schütrumpf (1909–1986) analysed the palynological and geological profile of the Upper Palaeolithic reindeer hunting site of Meiendorf near Hamburg (Schütrumpf 1936). His early membership of the National Socialist Party from 1933 led him to join the Ahnenerbe (Ancestral Heritage), an association linked to the SS. He directed the Ahnenerbe Natural Science Prehistory Research Centre from April 1938. In its palynological laboratory in Berlin-Dahlem he analysed samples from the excavations undertaken by the Ahnenerbe and other museums and monument services (Kater 1974, 82; Meurers-Balke 1987).[1]

The establishment of a new line of research or a new discipline or subdiscipline implies, in the first place, its acceptance by the established institutions and, at a second stage, the creation of its own institutions. In Scandinavia, the United Kingdom and Germany all the researchers mentioned so far worked in long-established institutions. New institutions related to palynology appear to have been set up immediately before, during and soon after the Second World War. The palynological laboratory of the Ahnenerbe Natural Science Prehistory Research Centre in Berlin-Dahlem was established in April 1938 and was therefore probably the earliest to specialise in the subdiscipline. In 1943 the Danish National Museum set up a Bog-Geological Laboratory and in 1956 it became an independent department (Kristiansen 2002, 22). A palynological laboratory was founded at the Swedish Natural Science Research Council in 1948 with Gunnar Erdtman as its first director (Nilsson and Praglowski 1978). The creation of these institutions marked a further increase in the acceptance of palynology as a separate subdiscipline mainly linked to the natural sciences.

The influence of Scandinavia continued to be felt in the early post-war years, as the publications from those countries had a notable impact in the other countries. Thus, the aforementioned article published in Denmark by Iversen in 1942 had, according to Kristiansen (2002, 20), a considerable influence on prehistoric archaeology in Sweden, England (through Grahame Clark) and the Netherlands. It is significant that Kristiansen does not mention any of the southern European countries and indeed no immediate effect is observed in them.

From botany to palynology in Spain

In this section the reception of palynology in Spain will be investigated. In this country there were indeed botanists in the nineteenth century (Morales and Blanco 2013), but the focus seems to have been on cataloguing plants. Archaeologists, for their part, did not seem to be interested in the recovery of plant remains, although the dry climate may account for at least some of the differences with other European areas. It was mainly after the Spanish Civil War (1936–1939) that an interest in palynology emerged. As we see in other parts of Europe, the field was partly occupied, to begin with, by women (Jonker 1967, 33; Edwards 2018). However, in contrast to all the previous periods, Spain's firm commitment to interdisciplinarity in the last three decades has led to palynology becoming a fully developed subdiscipline with practitioners based in a series of faculties, departments, centres and laboratories related to geology, botany and archaeology. The personal, social, institutional and structural changes in the discipline will be the backbone of the account given below.

The long nineteenth century and the interwar period

The evolution of palaeobotany and the first palynological studies in northern and central Europe described in the previous section allows a better contextualisation of events in Spain. In comparison to northern Europe, in nineteenth-century Spain the interest in palaeobotany was extremely limited, even more so than in Italy (see Guidi, this volume). This was not related to a lack of knowledge of what was taking place in the north and it is a good example of how the reception of knowledge in science – of new methodologies and the emergence of a subdiscipline in this case – does not automatically mean its adoption. In 1872, for example, the theories regarding ancient vegetation found in peat bogs proposed by Steenstrup and Nilsson had been included in a book written by one of the pioneers of prehistoric studies in Spain, the Professor of Geology at the University of Madrid from 1852, Juan Vilanova y Piera (1821–1893) (Vilanova y Piera 1872, 264–266, 301–302). Despite this mention, most of the book focused on geology and used palaeofauna as a dating method, whereas vegetation was largely ignored, with the exception mentioned above. This was especially blatant in the last part of the book dedicated to Spanish prehistory where, although the term peat bog (*turbera*) was used, no concrete data were provided. He also talked about the origin of agriculture in 1880. His emphasis was on how the economy of production had arrived in Spain but he showed detailed knowledge of the types of plants that had been found in the lake-dwellings (Vilanova y Piera 1881). However, as Ayarzagüena mentions, 'the excavation methods in Spain prevented finding remains of seeds and therefore this knowledge did not have a practical application' (Ayarzagüena 1992, 310). The reason behind this apparent disinterest may have been, on the one hand, the different type of archaeology applied to dry lands, in which the much larger amount of material culture found tends to absorb the practitioner's attention; on the other, methods established for wet environments may be less applicable at most sites in dry lands. However, in addition to these two factors, a weak institutionalisation may also explain why there was not enough personnel to allow the appropriate development of specialisation, leading some scholars to specialise in palaeobotany.

In the final years of the nineteenth century and early decades of the twentieth century, Spanish prehistory went through a regeneration (Díaz-Andreu and Cortadella 2006). However, this did not include a greater consideration for palaeobotany or indeed palynology. The renewal was very much influenced by the research stays of young Spanish professionals in other countries of Europe, especially Germany (Díaz-Andreu 1995; 1996), although none of the grantees seem to have been in contact with the archaeologists mentioned in the previous section. Despite the fact that the academic networks had somehow moved on from those described above for the nineteenth century, as Germany was now considered to be a country to travel to and establish contacts, the network continued to avoid the Scandinavian countries. This means that the links we see between someone like the British archaeologist Grahame Clark and his Scandinavian peers were not established by any archaeologist in Spain. As occurred in the nineteenth century with scholars such as Vilanova y Piera (see above), in the early twentieth century geology and palaeontology continued to be the main concern of two of the key prehistorians of the time, Eduardo Hernández-Pacheco (1872–1965) and Hugo Obermaier (1877–1946). From 1927 the latter was deeply involved in the publication of *Investigación y Progreso* (Research and Progress), a journal designed to disseminate knowledge of German science in Spain as published by the journal *Forschungen und Fortschritte* (Research and Advancements). However, so far, no results about the excavations in the Federsee have come to light among its pages, an absence that is highly significant. The only note about the Federsee was published in a different journal, the *Anuario de Prehistoria Madrileña* (*Madrid Prehistory Yearbook*). Its author, the archaeologist Julio Martínez Santa-Olalla, had spent several years in Germany in the 1920s. In the 1931–1932 issue there was an article about the publications in the German journal *Führer zur Urgeschichte* (Guide to Prehistory) in which Martínez Santa-Olalla explained about the publication of Hans Reinerth's new book, *Die Wasserburg Buchau* (*The Water Castle at Buchau*). However, the note only highlighted the chronological periods identified (Martínez Santa-Olalla 1931–1932) and not the important palaeobotanical work undertaken at the site.

There is one exception to this lack of interest in palaeobotany. It is possible to find a later example of an echo of the interest in ancient plants, although in this case the knowledge was imported from Belgium. It can be found in the Siret brothers, Henri (1857–1933) and Louis (1860–1934), two Belgian engineers who arrived in Spain at the end of the nineteenth century, the youngest of them staying until his death in 1934. They followed closely European events in the field of prehistory and this meant, for the first time in Spain, that archaeologists were paying some attention to the discovery of carbonised seeds. The Siret brothers considered them important enough to be reproduced in their book *Las primeras edades del metal en el sudeste de España* (*The Early Metal Ages in Southeastern Spain*) (1890). The seeds and other charred remains excavated at the Spanish sites and deposited in Brussels were studied many years later by the botanists Friedrich (Fritz) Netolitzky (1875–1945) (1935) and Maria Hopf (1914–2008) (1990).

As can be seen, it is possible to argue that the interest in prehistoric environments did not arrive in Spain in the early and middle decades of the twentieth century due to the lack of personal relationships. However, another example will show that even where they existed, there was no automatic transmission of knowledge. We can see this in Professor Luis Pericot's knowledge of Grahame Clark's work and the British concern for issues relating to the economy and society (Pericot 1944; 1947–1948; 1968), an attention that in the 1930s had led, as seen above, to the creation of the Fenland Committee in Cambridge. Impervious to these influences, Pericot's interest continued to focus on the typological study of material culture, its geographical distribution and changes over time. He never thought of collaborating with botanists, as Clark had done from the early 1930s. Returning to Julio Martínez Santa-Olalla's case, he appeared to be more aware of research into ancient plants, judging by a note published in 1946 in the first issue of the *Cuadernos de Historia Primitiva* (a prehistory journal published in Madrid) under the title 'Cereals and plants of the Ibero-Saharan culture'. In it he alluded to the 'woeful state of backwardness of primitive history and its methods of work in Spain, almost fifty to sixty years in comparison with Germany, Sweden, etc.' (Martínez Santa-Olalla 1946, 35). Soon after he also commented:

> The search for an economic, social, authentically historical criterion in the Spanish bibliography of national authors is totally idle [...]; therefore we should not be surprised by the little or no attention paid among us to the collection of coals, seeds, bones, etc., which, on

the other hand, once carefully obtained, there is no way to use scientifically, due to the lack of collaborators duly prepared for their study (Martínez Santa-Olalla 1946, 35).

He then referred to the work of the botanist Friedrich Netolitzky, who, as mentioned above, had studied the plant remains deposited by Louis Siret at the Royal Museums of Art and History in Brussels (Netolitzky 1935). However, palynology was not mentioned in that article.

The pioneers (1940s–1960s)

In both France and Spain the study of palynology first appeared in the disciplines related to the natural sciences such as biology and geology. However, from the late 1940s and 1950s in France we see the first palynological studies appearing in archaeology, a development that was key for the introduction of palynology in Spain. As in other countries, this area of study was still considered an 'auxiliary science' of archaeology (see Delley, this volume) and its lesser status, together with the lack of interest shown in it by mainstream archaeology in both countries, may explain why women rather than men were the first to practice it. This has already been mentioned earlier in the article in relation to other countries. The first palynologist in France was Marie-Madeleine Paquereau (1922–2009) who, from 1952, worked at the Laboratoire d'Anthropologie et de Préhistoire (Laboratory of Anthropology and Prehistory) in the Faculty of Sciences at Bordeaux, an institution soon to be directed by the geologist and archaeologist François Bordes (Diot 2009–2010). She worked mainly in France and seems to have had little or no influence in Spain (she is not mentioned in the biographies that several interdisciplinary scholars recounted in a recent publication on the microhistories of interdisciplinarity in Spain (Díaz-Andreu and Portillo 2021)). This contrasts with the second woman to work as a palynologist in an archaeological institution, Arlette Leroi-Gourhan (1913–2005). Born Arlette Royer, while a student at the École du Louvre in 1934 she attended the classes given by the anthropologist Marcel Mauss at the École des hautes études en sciences sociales (EHESS). It was there that she met her future husband, André Leroi-Gourhan (1911–1986), whom she married in 1936, before going with him to Japan in 1937 to help him with his work (Leroi-Gourhan and Leroi-Gourhan 1989). International events obliged them to return to Europe, where the war and her small family of four prevented her from working (Emery-Barbier, Leroyer and Soulier 2006, 825). She returned to the professional world at the very end of the 1940s and in 1954 became interested in palynology. She learned the techniques from the biologist Madeleine Van Campo, who had recently presented a thesis on the subject (Van Campo 1950). From 1955 onwards Arlette Leroi-Gourhan worked in the laboratory of the Musée de l'Homme in Paris, writing her first articles (Leroi-Gourhan 1956a; 1956b) and publishing some of her earlier work with her mentor (van Campo and Leroi-Gourhan 1956a; 1956b). The latter, however, later only focused on natural rather than archaeological deposits.

In Spain there was a series of botanists who adopted palynology in those years, although some, such as Pedro Montserrat (1918–2017), were not interested in palaeosoils. Others, however, were, including Francisco Bellot Rodríguez (1911–1983) and his disciple

Ernesto Viéitez Cortizo (1921–2013). They began to publish on the pollen found in ancient Galician peat bogs in the 1940s (Bellot and Viéitez 1945), although they never collaborated with archaeologists.[2] This means that the role of bridging the two disciplines was left to other scholars, one of whom we have already introduced, Arlette Leroi-Gourhan, together with another woman, the Spanish geologist Josefina Menéndez Amor.

Arlette Leroi-Gourhan (1913–2005) and the excavations in Cantabria: El Pendo and Cueva de Otero

Martínez Santa-Olalla's (limited) knowledge of the results obtained from the studies by natural scientists led him to attempt the form an interdisciplinary team to excavate the Cave of El Pendo in Cantabria, northern Spain. His team was made up of several Spanish followers in 1955:

> He set up a specialised work team: a field excavation group with Santa-Olalla himself, Sáez Martín, Ruiz Argilés and [Joaquín] González Echegaray; the stratigraphy and excavation method by Albert Egges von Giffen from the University of Groningen and Peter Glazema from the State Archaeological Research Service of Amersfoort. The geological study was carried out by Jesús Carballo and Alfredo García Lorenzo, both from the Museum of Santander; the lithic industry was studied by François Bordes, from the CNRS, and Francisco Esteve Gálvez; the bone record was studied by Armand Donald Lacaille from the Wellcome Historical Medical Museum in London, Muzaffer Senyürek from the University of Ankara, and Moshe Stekelis from the Hebrew University of Jerusalem. The pieces of artistic value were established to be studied by Santa-Olalla and Alonso del Real. The C14 samples were to be analysed by Hallam L. Movius Jr., from the University of Chicago, Carl-Axel Althin from the University of Stockholm and Herman Schwabeidssen from the University of Cologne, through Karl Otto Münnich from the Institute of Physics at the University of Heidelberg. The chemical analyses and colour photography were carried out by Erich Pietsch of the Max Planck-Gessellschaft in Frankfurt and, finally, the palynological analyses by Arlette Leroi-Gourhan from the Musée de l'Homme in Paris (Mederos 2012, 75).

However, this multi-sided collaboration yielded very few results. In the last year of her collaboration, Arlette Leroi-Gourhan (Fig. 4.1) produced a report on her work at El Pendo between 1955 and 1957 (González Echegaray 1980, 11), but it was not published at the time. The results only became publicly known in 1980 when, at the request of the archaeologist Joaquín González Echegaray (1930–2013), she wrote a short contribution (Leroi-Gourhan 1980) to the publication about the excavation (González Echegaray 1980). In the meantime, she had mentioned some of her results in other publications (Leroi-Gourhan 1959; Leroi-Gourhan 1965; Leroi-Gourhan 1971), as had her husband André about his own work in Spain (Leroi-Gourhan 1970, 19). After El Pendo, Arlette only returned to Spain very occasionally to analyse pollens from a few sites, including the Palaeolithic caves of La Cueva de Otero and El Juyo, both also in Cantabria (Leroi-Gourhan 1966; Boyer-Klein and Leroi-Gourhan 1987). Her work in northern Spain was later continued by her disciple Anaïs Boyer-Klein, who published on Cantabria and the Basque Country (Boyer-Klein 1980; 1984; 1985; 1988; Boyer-Klein and Leroi-Gourhan 1987).

Figure 4.1. Arlette Leroi-Gourhan with Julio Martínez Santa-Olalla during the El Pendo excavation campaign. Source: private collection, all rights reserved.

Josefa [Josefina] Menéndez Amor (1916–1985)

At the same time as Arlette Leroi-Gourhan was becoming involved in palynology in Paris, in Madrid another female researcher, Josefina Menéndez Amor, was also beginning to publish on pollens found in archaeological contexts. Born in 1916, she graduated in Pharmacy in 1940 and in Natural Sciences in 1946, obtaining her doctorate in 1952. From the year of her degree she started to teach courses related to Pharmacy, Physical Geography and Palaeontology at the university. In 1954 she became an adjunct in Palaeontology and was promoted to Associate Professor of Invertebrate Palaeontology and Micropalaeontology in 1968. When she finally obtained a chair in 1984, she was already seriously ill and died just a few months later. Like many professionals in those years, she combined her university teaching with her work at the National Research Institute, the Consejo Superior de Investigaciones Científicas (CSIC). Her interest in palynological studies of quaternary peat sediments represented one of her main lines of research (Perejón 1988, 55). Her training in pollen analysis had taken place at the Palynological Laboratory of Leiden under Professor Frans Florschütz (1888–1965), who had learned it from von Post and Erdtman (Jonker 1967, 3; Anonymous 1988). He provided absolute dates from the radiocarbon laboratory at Groningen for many of the pollen sequences they took. Josefa Menéndez Amor was aware of the interdisciplinary nature of much of the work undertaken in palynology (Menéndez Amor 1957). Her relationship with archaeology, however, was intermittent and, according to one of her disciples, María Blanca Ruiz Zapata, she preferred to associate with geologists (personal comment, 27 May 2019).

Menéndez Amor and Florschütz worked together on archaeological pollens. Their first interdisciplinary work with archaeologists appears to have been the study of the Lower Palaeolithic sites of Torralba (Soria) and the terraces of Villaverde Bajo (Madrid) (Fig. 4.2). They commented on the similarity of the vegetation at those sites (Menéndez

Figure 4.2. Menéndez Amor and Florschütz at the Orcasitas site (Manzanares area, Madrid). Source: Archive of the Museum of San Isidro.

Amor and Florschütz 1959). Soon after they also worked on the prehistoric settlement of Ereta del Pedregal (Valencia), combining pollen results with carbon 14 dates, highlighting the alternation of *Pinus* and *Quercus* and the presence of cereals (Menéndez Amor and Florschütz 1961). Their article on the Cueva del Toll (Barcelona) was the result of the visit to the site made during the 5th International Congress for the Study of the Quaternary (INQUA) held in Madrid and Barcelona in 1957 (Menéndez Amor and Florschütz 1962). Two young Finns, Joakim Jalmar Donner (1926–) and Björn Kurtén (1924–1988), had visited the site before them and published on it (Donner and Kurtén 1958). In their publication Menéndez Amor and Florschütz were discreet about the differences between their proposal and that of the Finns. It was not until years later that the North American researchers Karl W. Butzer (born in Germany) (1934–2016) and Leslie Freeman (1935–2012) pointed out the contradictions in the two sets of results and agreed with those obtained by Menéndez Amor and Florschütz (Butzer and Freeman 1968).

The Chicago School in Torralba and Ambrona

The palynological study of the Lower Palaeolithic sites of Torralba (and Manzanares) that Menéndez Amor and Florschütz started in the late 1950s led to a resurgence of interest in that site, which had been extensively excavated several decades earlier (Santonja et al. 2005). One of those to become attracted to the sites was the American professor at the University of Chicago, Clark Howell (1925–2007). In a letter to the Barcelona professor, Luis Pericot, Howell explained that he wanted to go to Torralba and also to see the finds from the earlier excavations, now held in Madrid (Library of Catalonia, Fons Pericot, Howell file, letter dated 11-1-1959). His visit convinced the American of the potential of the site and he decided to excavate at Torralba and also at the nearby site of Ambrona, which he did between 1961 and 1963. Howell's work in Spain represented the first actual interdisciplinary team working in archaeology. The pioneering nature of his role in creating interdisciplinary teams was highlighted by one of his biographers (Cathy Willermet in Birx 2006, 1801–1802). In his excavations in Spain not only was he able to count on Josefa Menéndez Amor, her collaborator Frans Florschütz and her student Blanca Izquierdo as an assistant (Aguirre 2005, 8), but also on a whole set of specialists. This included the geologist and edaphologist Karl Butzer, whose mission was to study the geomorphology and stratigraphy of the excavation; the team also had Pierre Biberson from the Musée de l'Homme in Paris as deputy director, but especially in charge of the Ambrona site; Emiliano Aguirre acted as the specialist in vertebrate palaeontology and Leslie Gordon Freeman from the University of Chicago was responsible for records, assisted by Dolores Echaide who had been commissioned by the University of Zaragoza (Aguirre 2005).[3] The interdisciplinary team was different to that formed in the Fenland Research Committee in the 1930s. In this case it was not a collaboration between different scholars all at the same level, but a team formed by a leader who considered it essential for his excavation team to have an interdisciplinary nature and involve several specialists working on the site. This involves much more planning as well as greater stability in the team.

In addition to the transformation in the nature of excavation teams, we can observe another key change taking place from the period in which the first palynologists worked in isolation to the moment they started to form part of interdisciplinary teams. This relates to the status their work acquired. At first their reports were added as an attachment to the main, most important publication about a site excavation, in which the material culture – lithics and/or pottery, etc. – occupied the centre of attention. Such was the perceived lesser status of palynological reports that their authors were exclusively mentioned in the annex and not as part of the main writing team mentioned on the first page of the article. In a few cases their authorship was not even acknowledged, with the report being issued without their names (see, for example, Llanos *et al.* 1975, 205–206 and Hopf 1985). In truly interdisciplinary teams, such as that formed by the Chicago school, the work of palynologists received greater acknowledgement, although there was a transitional period during which their reports continued to be short and factual before they became more critical and detailed.

The last fifty years

Many changes have taken place in the last fifty years in Spain, to the extent that the situation today is radically different to that of the post-war years and throughout the Francoist dictatorship (1939–1975). In order to explain this transformation we will briefly go back in time to present the basis on which Spanish archaeology adjusted to a new type of practice with a strong interdisciplinary component.

A dying world

The First World War and especially the Second World War brought about a definitive rupture with the nineteenth-century belief in progress. A growing feeling of rejection of the socio-economic model generated by industrialism emerged, influencing all aspects of life and the sciences, including archaeology. An example of this in England is Eric Higgs (1908–1976), a trained economist who, dissatisfied with urban life, bought a farm in 1939. Having found it less idyllic than he had expected he decided to turn his life around and enrolled in the two-year Post-Graduate Diploma in Archaeology at Cambridge, where he was appointed a research assistant in 1956. Higgs argued that knowledge of the basic economy was essential for understanding prehistoric peoples. He proposed that human bones, the area he specialised in, were as good a source of information as more traditional archaeological finds such as pottery and lithics (Bailey 2004). Higgs' case may be exceptional but somehow reflects the personal experience of many scientists during those post-war years. These deepened with the Cold War conflicts in Korea and Vietnam and a series of ecological disasters and publications such as Rachel Carson's *Silent Spring* (Carson 1962) or, in the following decade, the article that raised the alarm about the disappearance of the ozone layer (Molina and Rowland 1974). In Spain this movement was received and was behind publications such as the book *A Dying World* written by the acclaimed novelist Miguel Delibes (1975). This was the framework in which the new generation of future professionals reaching the universities in the 1970s had grown up – a world against uncontrolled technological development. All over the world, and in Spain in particular, the young people of the 1970s were much more willing to learn about ancient landscapes than any of the previous generations and this had an effect on how the practice of archaeology developed. It led to the definitive breaking down of disciplinary barriers and it became common for archaeologists to specialise in bones, plants, palynology and the like. This meant a further step along the road to interdisciplinarity. The predominant presence of the archaeologist specialised in a particular period and type of material culture was giving way to a much more diverse composition of university departments and research centres.

Pilar López, Michèle Dupré and others

In Spain we can see the effect of this movement in the area of palynology with Pilar López in the 1970s. 'The day you do something different from others you will become essential,' her PhD supervisor, Martín Almagro, had told her when she graduated in the mid-1970s (personal communication, 16 February 2018). Influenced by those words, she decided to do something unusual at the time and this was to write her doctoral thesis on palynology, a topic that would make her unique. At first she turned to Josefa Menéndez Amor as a teacher, but the geologist did not believe in training someone with a background in archaeology.[4] This first setback did not deter Pilar, who kept on searching. Then an opportunity came her way; she met the archaeologist Joaquín González Echegaray at a congress and he told her that Arlette Leroi-Gourhan was eager to find someone to work with on all the material arriving from Spain that was stored on her laboratory shelves at the Musée de l'Homme. Pilar joined Arlette's team from 5 January 1976 for two years, getting to know the other researchers on the team, especially Michel Girard, and palynologists based at other institutions, including Josette Renault-Miskovsky (1938–2018) from the Institute of Human Palaeontology. In Paris she also coincided with another pioneer in palynological studies from a Spanish laboratory, the geographer Michèle Dupré. During her stay in Paris, Pilar analysed samples from the site of Verdelpino (López 1977). Her own PhD supervisor recognised the value of palynology in his *Introduction... a* university textbook that would be on the reading list of every single student at the time, at least in what was then the largest university in Spain, the Complutense of Madrid. In this text he said that:

> Palaeobotanical studies have also made great progress. It is also possible to determine the flora that lived in ancient times thanks to the analysis of pollen and other plant remains that can and should be studied and knowledge of which, at least in its possible application by specialists, all prehistorians should be informed as a methodological basis, not only because it helps establish the geographical environment generated in which man and his prehistoric cultures developed, but because it is a valuable aid to establishing a relative chronology (Almagro Basch 1978, 116).

Pilar López's first publications date from the end of the 1970s and the beginning of the 1980s. In some of them she attempted to explain what the study of pollens meant to archaeology on a more popular (López 1982b) as well as a scientific level (López 1984). She published on the results obtained in her doctoral thesis (López 1978) and also on new research (López 1981a; 1981b; 1982a; 1982b; 1983). Over the years the laboratory she set up, in which she worked throughout her time at the CSIC with her assistant Rosario Macías Rosado, was visited by a multitude of young trainees, including Maria Fernanda Sánchez Goñi, Fátima Franco and her successor in the post, José Antonio Lopez Sáez. They all began to publish in the 1990s. From 2006 onwards, her career took a turn away from active research to research administration.

Pilar López was not the only one to become interested in palynology in the late 1970s and early 1980s. She had two peers: the aforementioned Michèle Dupré and Riker Yll. The former studied geography in Valencia and wrote an undergraduate dissertation on a palynological analysis of the Cova de les Mallaetes in 1978. Her doctoral thesis, co-directed by the French palynologist Josette Renault-Miskovsky, dealt with sediments from excavations in the Valencian Country and was defended in 1986 (Dupré 1988). From 1980 onwards she published a large number of articles, the first of them on Mallaetes (Dupré 1980), El Puntal dels Llops (Dupré and Renault-Miskovsky 1981) and Les Calaveres (Dupré 1982b) and then others of a more general nature (Dupré 1979; 1982a; Fumanal and Dupré 1983; Anonymous 2001). The third archaeologist with an interest in palynology in Spain was Riker Yll. He first published at the Methodological Congress in Soria in 1981 (Yll 1984) but then did not reappear until a decade later (Yll 1995; Pantaleón-Cano, Yll and Roure 1999). López, Dupré and Yll were not alone in being trained in palynology at the time. There were other scholars with an education in the natural sciences, such as geology or biology, who occasionally worked with archaeologists over the years. One of them was the geologist Blanca Ruiz Zapata who, as mentioned, studied palynology with Josefa Menéndez Amor. After defending her doctoral thesis in 1980, she obtained a position at the University of Alcalá de Henares, where she set up her own palynology laboratory and supervised several PhD students. From there she would regularly collaborate with archaeologists, especially from the mid-1990s onwards (for example Ruiz Zapata 1995; Ruiz Zapata *et al.* 1997). Before her there had been another palynologist, the biologist María Victoria Jato Rodríguez (1974), although she later moved on to areas unrelated to palaeosoils.

All these young researchers went on to be supported by an increasing number of associations such as the Spanish Society for Quaternary Research (Asociación Española para el Estudio de Cuaternario, AEQUA) and, from 1978, the Association of Spanish-speaking Palynologists (APLE, Asociación de Palinólogos de Lengua Española) (set up as a mirror image of the sister institution in France that dated from 1967 (Riera in Díaz-Andreu and Portillo 2021)). The idea of establishing APLE came about at an international meeting of palynologists that the now defunct Instituto de Palinología de León had organised in 1976. The meeting, and then the association, became a key networking event for palynology in Spain (Ruiz Zapata, personal communication, 6 September 2018).

Developments in Catalonia and the Basque Country

In Catalonia, a key figure for the introduction of the formation of interdisciplinary teams in archaeology and of palynology as a field of study was the French archaeologist Henry de Lumley (1934–). His monograph on the Mousterian site of Grotte de l'Hortus (Valflaunès, France) included thirty-five specialists, among them Josette Renault-Miskovsky as a palynologist (Renault-Miskovsky 1972). Lumley accepted an invitation to collaborate with archaeologist Narcís Soler when he embarked on the excavation of the Cave of Arbreda in 1977. This excavation was very influential for later generations

> It was during the archaeological excavation campaign at the Cova de L'Arbreda (Serinyà, Girona) in 1977 (my first year of study, 1976–77), when, influenced by French prehistory (we had the help of the excavation team at the Cova de l'Aragó – Talteüll, Roselló, now a French territory, led by Henry de Lumley), decided in an assembly (in Spain we were in full transition to democracy) in which specialities we could be trained to carry out an investigation of Prehistory on a par with Europe. It was at this time that I opted for palynology, since botany had always attracted me (Francesc Burjachs, personal communication, February 2018).

At that meeting other students also decided for alternative specialisations:[5] M. Teresa Ros i Mora (anthracology), Ramon Buxó i Capdevila (carpology), Gabriel Alcalde i Gurt (micro-mammals), Joan Oller i Guinó (malacology), Núria Juan-Muns i Plans (ichthyofauna), Bibiana Agustí i Farjas (physical anthropology), Josep Manuel Rueda i Torres (bone tools) and Assumpció Toledo i Mur (ceramics) (Burjachs in Díaz-Andreu and Portillo 2021). Already as an undergraduate Burjachs had received a small grant from Lumley to learn about palynology at the Centre de Recherches Archéologiques (CRA) – Centre National de la Recherche Scientifique (CNRS) (Valbonne) with palynologists Michel Girard and his wife Bui Thi Mai. In his final undergraduate years he began to set up a laboratory[6] with the biologist and palynologist Joan Maria Roure i Nolla. Part of the group of students who attended the 1977 meeting, in 1981 they formed an interdisciplinary group that excavated in the Cova 120, naming themselves the 'Cent-Vint Group' after the cave (Fig. 4.3). They published a joint monograph (Agustí *et al.* 1987) and several articles (Burjachs in Díaz-Andreu and Portillo 2021). It is very interesting to note the feeling of being pioneers that transpires from the interviews given by the main actors in the project during those years.

Another group was formed in the Basque country where the Aranzadi Science Society (Sociedad de Ciencias Aranzadi) had been able to set up a laboratory thanks to a donation from the artist Eduardo Chillida in 1979 (Iriarte in Díaz-Andreu and Portillo 2021). That was where Cristina Peñalba (1987; 1988a; 1988b), María José Isturiz and María Fernanda Sánchez Goñi (1988) started. Peñalba and Sánchez-Goñi moved to France to write their PhDs, one in Aix-en-Provence (1989) and the other under Josette Renault-Miskovsky's supervision at the Institut de Paléontologie Humaine (1991). Both remained in that country. A latter addition to the laboratory was María José Iriarte, who would learn palynology by travelling to Valencia to work with Michèle Dupré (Iriarte in Díaz-Andreu and Portillo 2021).

Figure 4.3. Members of the 'Cent-Vint Group' during one of the excavation campaigns at Cova 120 (Sales de Llierca, Alta Garrotxa, Girona). In the top row, from left to right: Gabriel Alcalde i Gurt, Francesc Burjachs i Casas, Josep Manuel Rueda i Torres, Ramon Buxó i Capdevila, Joan Oller i Guinó. In the bottom row, from left to right: Maria Teresa Ros i Mora, Núria Juan-Muns i Plans, Assumpció Toledo i Mur and Bibiana Agustí i Farjas (Source: Francesc Burjachs).

At a different university – the University of Barcelona – the new professor from 1985, Josep M. Fullola Pericot, became part of the movement towards interdisciplinarity. He encouraged students to specialise in different scientific areas (Fullola *et al.* 2015). One of those who graduated from that university was Santi Riera, who decided to focus on palynology. He benefited from the creation, at the end of the 1980s, of a laboratory by the Centre for Landscape Research in the Department of Geography of the same university in collaboration with the prehistorians. Thanks to small grants he was able to undertake research stays in Montpellier with Nadine Planchais and the Università degli Studi di Roma La Sapienza with Maria Follieri (Riera Mora in Díaz-Andreu and Portillo 2021).

Establishing a career path

With the exception of Pilar López, who had no problem in finding a permanent job, access to permanent research or university positions for this group of young palynologists turned out to be not easy at all. Burjachs remembers how during his undergraduate years he had explicitly been discouraged by one of the most important professors at the time who had told him that there would be no jobs for him (Burjachs in Díaz-Andreu and Portillo 2021). Among the different disciplines with which archaeology was establishing bridges, palynology does not seem to have attracted sufficient attention. In recent interviews, one of the comments made by some members of this group of then young palynologists-to-be is that they usually suffered from a lack of proper training during their PhD years. This led them to take longer to be in the position to defend their PhDs (usually about 8 or 9 years from graduation). They also had to wait for many years, normally working in commercial archaeology, until they were successful in obtaining a permanent position (more than a decade after having defended their PhDs) (Burjachs, Iriarte-Chiapusso and Riera in Díaz-Andreu and Portillo 2021). Their situation was not that unusual in the 1990s and 2000s. Like many others, they were victims of a situation that had burdened Spanish archaeology since the late 1980s, when most available positions were filled by young people with some experience who were not due to retire until the 2010s. In the early 2000s, the apparent good health of the country's economy led to an expansion in the staff of universities and research centres and many finally obtained regular jobs.

In the new framework of growing acceptance of interdisciplinarity there are two aspects that can be highlighted. The first refers to the university curriculum. In the 1990s it had already undergone significant changes in the case of a few archaeology degrees around the country. These took place especially in the universities in which a certain degree of interdisciplinarity had already been put in place among the staff. The case of the University of Barcelona has already been commented on in the previous section and similar situations existed in Valencia and Granada, where some of the new appointees were specialists in different techniques (Contreras 2017; Badal in Díaz-Andreu and Portillo 2021). The second aspect to be highlighted relates to the final disappearance of the term 'auxiliary sciences' to designate the different interdisciplinary areas of study. Still employed in the 1980s (Ros Mora 1981; López 1982b; Gutiérrez, Burillo and Peña 1983), at the end of the decade there were voices asking for the end of its use for this undermined the value of interdisciplinary work, whereas the information coming from the analyses of soils, bones, plants, pollens and so on were, in fact, crucial for archaeological interpretation (Vila and Estévez 1989). By the early 2010s, the term 'auxiliary sciences' was talked about as something of the past (Iriarte and Zapata 2013).

Conclusions

This chapter has presented a historical overview of the academic context and development of palynology, initially in northern Europe, then in other countries in the central and western parts of the continent and finally explaining how and when it arrived in Spain. Palynology has been chosen as a case study because of its truly interdisciplinary nature as a subdiscipline of several long-established disciplines including geology, botany and archaeology. The account provided shows how the creation of knowledge – of a new discipline, subdiscipline or methodology – does not necessarily lead to its reception in other countries. For this to take place, a series of conditions has to be present: the existence of previous academic networks that allow the circulation of people and bibliographies and even the establishment of common projects. As academic contacts between Scandinavia and Spain were extremely limited (mainly constrained to the encounters of scholars of both areas at international congresses), the transference of knowledge produced in the first area mainly took place through intermediate countries such as Belgium (in the case of the Siret brothers), Germany (Julio Martínez Santa-Olalla), France (Arlette Leroi-Gourhan, Pilar López and others) and the Netherlands (Josefa Menéndez Amor). Another condition needed for a good reception is the capacity of the other country to absorb innovations. As a negative example, the small scholarly community in Spain in the nineteenth and early twentieth centuries is given as another factor that prevented the country taking on board developments in the north.

The historical analysis undertaken in these pages has also highlighted how even within the same country the consolidation of a new discipline also requires a series of provisions for it to be successful. To ensure its future, it is essential that the younger generations are taught it. At the same time, however, they need to see the advantages of being trained in it. The benefits can be professional – being in possession of the new knowledge will facilitate their entry into the profession – or psychological – the self-esteem they obtain from feeling that they are actually making a positive difference to the profession. Of course, the latter on its own can only last so many years as, sooner or later, the young need to consolidate their positions. Once they manage to do this it is not only their future careers but indeed the future of the new knowledge that is guaranteed. Several examples of this are provided in the article and of them two are highlighted here: how von Post's method became well established and indeed grew to be a subdiscipline thanks to his followers' efforts (Erdtman and Iversen), and how Pilar López learned from Arlette Leroi-Gourhan to then train others younger than her. However, the transmission from specialist to newcomer is not sufficient for the discipline's survival, as personal issues may hinder it or even bring it to a halt. This happened, for example, when Georg Sarauw had to leave the National Museum of Denmark, thus delaying research into ancient plants in that country. Finally, as discussed in the article, for a new discipline or subdiscipline to properly unfold, a key element is institutionalisation. Laboratories, associations and journals offer extremely useful infrastructure for practitioners. They provide space for training and research, are a means for exchanging information, and also provide the work context in which professional identity is formed. This may be further reinforced by personal initiatives including, as explained in the article, the bibliographical lists published by Erdtman, as well as the textbooks he produced.

This chapter has also drawn attention to the changes interdisciplinarity has gone through over the years. For the study of ancient plants, the collaboration between archaeologists, botanists and geologists established common ground in the nineteenth century and the first decades of the twentieth century. This took the form of a commission in the case of Denmark and a committee in the case of Cambridge. These allowed members of different disciplines to work together on common projects and exchange ideas among themselves. However, the creation of these interdisciplinary groups was sporadic and died out after a few years. In contrast, the interdisciplinary groups that emerged in the 1960s were of a very different nature: it was at that time, at least in the case of Spain, although thanks to American initiative, that projects were organised by a researcher who formed an interdisciplinary team composed of specialists in different sciences. This allowed the combination of alternative perspectives to better interpret an archaeological site or problem. As is usually the case, this innovation took several decades to become common practice in the profession. Nevertheless, admiration of the model thus created led other scholars to become more open to expanding the specialisations expected to be offered in university departments. This in turn opened up the way for including some palynologists in archaeological institutions.

As mentioned in one of the overviews of the development of palynology that precede this one, 'if I had attempted to continue my history of palynology [in such detail] from 1970 to the present, this paper would have been at least thrice its present length' (Sarjeant 2002, 304). A much wider context of the last few years can be found elsewhere thanks to the articles written by many specialists who formed part of the revolution that has marked the transformation of archaeology into a fully interdisciplinary field over the last few years (Díaz-Andreu and Portillo 2021). Palynology has been part and parcel of such a revolution and today there is a healthy number of specialists in it who are in regular contact with their international peers. Many of the problems that slowed down the introduction of scientific innovations in Spain have been resolved and it should be noted that a firm commitment to post-doctoral international training has been partially responsible for this change. Disciplines and subdisciplines, however, are in continuous transformation and there will no doubt be unexpected developments in the future that will have to be analysed in years to come.

Notes

1 During the Second World War, Rudolf Schütrumpf worked at the Entomological Institute of the Dachau concentration camp. However, after a spell in prison after the war, he headed up the 'Travelling Museum' in Schleswig-Holstein and in 1958 he set up the Laboratory for the History of Vegetation and Pollen Analysis at the Institute for Prehistory and Early History of the University of Cologne and was its director for many years. He retired in 1974 (see Kater 1974).
2 Between 1955 and 1980 the only academic archaeologist in that region was Carlos Alonso del Real y Ramos (1911–1993), whose interests lay elsewhere (Martínez Navarrete in Díaz-Andreu, Mora and Cortadella 2009).
3 The other major project that brought foreign archaeologists to Spain was the Early History of Agriculture project led by Cambridge. Palynology, however, did not seem to be one of the approaches favoured. These two projects influenced the young Spanish archaeologists who had been sent to act as inspectors, Dolores Echaide and Francisco Burillo, the latter being one of the drivers behind the introduction of spatial archaeology in Spain (see Díaz-Andreu 2012).

4 In those years Josefa Menéndez Amor was supervising the geologist Blanca Ruiz Zapata, who would finally defend her thesis in 1980: Ruiz Zapata, M.B. (1980) *Estudio palinológico de las turberas superficiales del delta del Ebro*. Madrid, Universidad Complutense de Madrid. Tesis Doctoral.
5 At the same time as Francesc Burjachs he mentions that other young researchers had opted for palynology: Riker Yll Aguirre (1992 PhD UAB), Igor Parra i Vergara (1994, doctoral thesis at the École Pratique des Hautes Etudes, France), Agustí Esteban and Amat (1995 PhD UB) and Artur Cebrià i Escuer (who then moved onto other topics), together with the ill-fated Enric Pleguezuelos (Burjachs i Casas 2021 in Díaz-Andreu and Portillo).
6 Burjachs has set up three laboratories, the first at the Unitat de Botànica de la Universitat Autònoma de Barcelona, then at the Instituto de Ciencias de la Tierra Jaume Almera (ICTJA-CSIC), together with geologist Ramon Julià i Brugués, and then in Tarragona, first at the university and then at the IPHES.

References

Aguirre, E. (2005) Torralba y Ambrona. Un siglo de encuentros. *Zona Arqueológica* [In M. Santonja Gómez and A. Pérez González (eds) *Los yacimientos paleolíticos de Ambrona y Torralba (Soria). Un siglo de investigaciones arqueológicas*] 5, 3–39.

Agustí, B., Alcalde, G., F., B., Buxó, R., Juan-Muns, N., Oller, J., Ros, M.T., Rueda, J.M. and Toledo, A. (1987) *Dinàmica de la utilització de la Cova 120 per l'home en els darrers 6000 anys*. Sèrie Monogràfica 7. Girona, Centre d'Investigacions Arqueològiques de Girona.

Almagro Basch, M. (1978) *Introducción al estudio de la prehistoria y de la arqueología de campo*. Cultura Antigua 162. Barcelona, Labor.

Anonymous (1988) The development of palaeobotany and palynology in Utrecht. *Commission Internationale de Microflore du Paleozoique Newsletter* 37, 8–10.

Anonymous (2001) Michèle Dupré, palinòloga. *Cuadernos de Geografía* 69–70, 1–6.

Ayarzagüena, M. (1992) *La arqueología prehistórica y protohistórica española en el siglo XIX*. Madrid, UNED.

Bailey, G. (2004) Higgs, Eric Sidney (1908–1976) In *Oxford Dictionary of National Biography*, online. Oxford, Oxford University Press.

Bakker, J.A. (2001) Childe, van Giffen, and Dutch Archaeology until 1970. In W.H. Metz, B.L. van Beek and H. Steegstra (eds) *Patina, Essays presented to Jay Jordan Butler on the occasion of his 80th birthday*, 49–74. Groningen & Amsterdam, Metz, Van Beek & Steegstra.

Bellot, F. and Vieitez, E. (1945) Primeros resultados del análisis polínico de las turbas galaicas. *Anales del Instituto Español de Edafología, Ecología y Fisiología Vegetal* 4, 280–307.

Bertsch, K. (1928) Klima, Pflanzendecke und Besiedlung Mitteleuropas in vor- und frühgeschichtlicher Zeit nach den Ergebnissen der pollenanalytischen Forschung. *Bericht der Römisch-Germanischen Kommission* 18, 1–67.

Bertsch, K. (1931) Paläobotanische Monographie des Federseerieds (mit Pollendiagrammen). *Bibliotheca Botanica* 103, 1–127.

Birx, H.J., ed. (2006) *Encyclopedia of Anthropology*. London, Sage.

Boyer-Klein, A. (1980) Nouveaux résultats palynologiques de sites Solutréns et Magdaléniens cantabriques. *Bulletin de la Société Préhistorique Française* 77, 4.

Boyer-Klein, A. (1984) *Nouveaux résultats palynologiques dans les Cantabres au Tardiglaciaire*. Centre de Recherches Archéologiques. Notes et monographies techniques 17. Paris, CNRS.

Boyer-Klein, A. (1985) Analyse pollinique de la grotte d'Erralla. *Munibe* (dossier: J. Altuna, A. Baldeón, & K. Mariezkurrena (eds) *Cazadores Magdalenienses en la cueva de Erralla (Cestona-País Vasco)* 37, 45–48.

Boyer-Klein, A. (1988) Analyses polliniques au Tardiglaciaire dans le Nord de l'Espagne: au sujet du Dryas I, II, III. In J. Civis Llovera and M.F. Valle (eds) *Actas de palinología: actas del VI Simposio de Palinología, A.P.L.E.*, 227–285. Salamanca, Universidad de Salamanca.

Boyer-Klein, A. and Leroi-Gourhan, A. (1987) Análisis palinológico de la cueva del Juyo. In I. Barandiarán, L.G. Freeman, J. González Echegaray and R.G. Klein (eds) *Excavaciones en la cueva del Juyo*, 57–61. Madrid, Ministerio de Cultura.

Bryant, V.M. and Holloway, R.G. (1996) Archaeological palynology. In J. Jansonius and D.C. Mcgregor (eds) *Palynology: Principles and Practice, Vol. 3*, 913–918. College Station, American Association of Stratigraphic Palynologists Foundation.

Butzer, K.W. and Freeman, L.G. (1968) Pollen analysis at the Cueva del Toll, Catalonia: a critical re-appraisal. *Geologie en Mijboww* 47 (2), 116–120.

Carson, R. (1962) *Silent spring*. Boston, Houghton Mifflin.

Clapham, A.R. and Osborne, P. (2004) Godwin, Sir Harry (1901–1985), botanist. In *Oxford Dictionary of National Biography*, online. Oxford, Oxford University Press.

Clark, J.G.D., Godwin, H., Godwin, M.E. and Clifford, M.H. (1935) Report on Recent Excavations at Peacock's Farm, Shippea Hill, Cambridgeshire. *The Antiquaries Journal* 15 (3), 284–319.

Contreras, F. (2017) La Arqueología en la Universidad de Granada. In M.I. Mancilla Cabello, A. Moreno, D. García and P. Sánchez (eds) *El patrimonio arqueológico. De las trincheras a la sociedad. Catálogo de la Exposición*, 95–109. Granada, Colegio Oficial de Doctores y Licenciados en Filosofía y Letras y en Ciencias de Granada, Almería y Jaén.

Delibes, M. (1975) *Un mundo que agoniza*. Barcelona, Plaza & Janés.

Delley, G. (2015) *Au-delà des chronologies. Des origines du radiocarbone et de la dendrochronologie à leur intégration dans les recherches lacustres suisses*. Archéologie Neuchâteloise 53. Neuchâtel, Office du patrimoine et de l'archéologie.

Díaz-Andreu, M. (1995) Arqueólogos españoles en Alemania en el primer tercio del siglo XX. Los becarios de la Junta para la Ampliación Estudios (I) Pedro Bosch Gimpera. *Madrider Mitteilungen* 36, 79–89.

Díaz-Andreu, M. (1996) Arqueólogos españoles en Alemania en el primer tercio del siglo XX. Los becarios de la Junta para la Ampliación Estudios e Investigaciones Científicas. *Madrider Mitteilungen* 37, 205–224.

Díaz-Andreu, M. (2012) *Archaeological encounters. Building networks of Spanish and British archaeologists in the 20th century*. Newcastle, Cambridge Scholars.

Díaz-Andreu, M. (2014) Transnationalism and archaeology. The connecting origins of the main institutions dealing with prehistoric archaeology in Western Europe: the IPH, the CIPP and the CRPU (1910–1914). In A. Guidi (ed.) *150 anni di preistoria e protostoria in Italia*, 163–177. Studi di Preistoria e Protostoria I. Firenze, Istituto Italiano di Preistoria e Protostoria.

Díaz-Andreu, M. and Cortadella, J. (2006) Success and failure: alternatives in the Institutionalisation of pre- and proto-history in Spain (Hernández-Pacheco, Obermaier, Bosch Gimpera). In J. Callmer, M. Meyer, R. Struwe and C. Theune-Vogt (eds) *The beginnings of academic pre- and protohistoric archaeology (1830-1930) in a European perspective*, 295–305. Berliner Archäologische Forschungen 2. Berlin, Verlag Marie Leidorf.

Díaz-Andreu, M. and Portillo, M., eds (2021) *Arqueología e interdisciplinaridad: la microhistoria de una revolución en la arqueología española (1970-2020)*. Barcelona, Universitat de Barcelona.

Díaz-Andreu, M., Mora, G. and Cortadella, J., eds (2009) *Diccionario Histórico de la Arqueología en España (siglos XV-XX)*. Madrid, Marcial Pons.

Diot, M.-F. (2009–10) Marie-Madeleine Paquereau (1922–2009) *Paleo. Revue d'archéologie préhistorique* 21, 12–16.

Donner, J.J. and Kurtén, B. (1958) The floral and faunal succession of 'Cueva del Toll', Spain. *Eiszeitalter und Gegenwart* 9, 72–82.

Dupré, M. (1979) *Breve manual de análisis polínico*. Madrid, Valencia, CSIC, Universidad de Valencia.

Dupré, M. (1980) Análisis polínico de sedimentos arqueológicos de la cueva de Les Malladetes (Barx, Valencia). *Cuadernos de geografía* 26, 1–22.

Dupré, M. (1982a) Aportación al conocimiento de la vegetación valenciana en época ibérica. *Cuadernos de Geografía* 31, 180–181.

Dupré, M. (1982b) Vll-Palinología. In J. Aparicio Pérez, M. Pérez Ripoll, E. Vives Balmañá, M.P. Fumanal García and M. Dupré (eds) *La cova de les Calaveras*, 77–86. Trabajos Varios 75. Valencia, Diputación Provincial de Valencia, S.I.P.

Dupré, M. (1988) *Palinología y paleoambiente. Nuevos datos españoles. Referencias.* Serie de Trabajos Varios del SIP 84. Valencia, Diputación Provincial de Valencia.

Dupré, M. and Renault-Miskovsky, J. (1981) Análisis polínico. In H. Bonet Rosado, C. Mata Parreño, I. Sarrión Montañana, M. Dupré and J. Renault-Miskovski (eds) *El poblado ibérico del Puntal dels Llops (El Colmenar) (Olocau-Valencia)*, 181–188. Trabajos Varios 71. Valencia, Diputación Provincial de Valencia, SIP.

Edwards, K.J. (2018) Pollen, women, war and other things: reflections on the history of palynology. *Vegetation History and Archaeobotany* 27 (2), 319–335.

Emery-Barbier, A., Leroyer, C. and Soulier, P. (2006) Arlette Leroi-Gourhan (1913–2005). *Bulletin de la Société préhistorique française* 103 (4), 821–831.

Fullola, J.M., Albizuri, S., Álvarez, R., Bergadà, M.M., Cebrià, A., Daura, J., Domingo, I., Ejarque, A., García-Argüelles, P., López Cachero, F.J., Lloveras, L., Mangado, X., Nadal, J., Oms, X., Petit, M.À., Rey-Solé, M., Riera, S., Román, D., Sánchez de la Torre, M., Sanz, M., Tejero, J.M., Tresserras, J. and Zilhão, J. (2015) Seminari d'Estudis i Recerques Prehistòriques (SERP). Núcleo de cohesión en formación e investigación en Prehistoria de la Universitat de Barcelona desde 1987 *Pyrenae* Número Especial 50è Aniversari, 9–90.

Fumanal, M.P. and Dupré, M. (1983) Schéma paléoclimatique et chrono-stratigraphique d'une séquence du Paléolithique Supérieur de la région de Valence (Espagne). *Bulletin de l'Association française pour l'étude du quaternnaire* 1, 39–46.

Godwin, H. (1934) Pollen Analysis. An Outline of the Problems and Potentialities of the Method. *New Phytologist* 33, 278–358.

Godwin, H. (1956) *The history of the British flora: a factual basis for phytogeography. Cambridge*, Cambridge University Press.

González Echegaray, J. (1980) *El yacimiento de la cueva de 'El Pendo': (excavaciones 1953-57). Bibliotheca Praehistorica Hispana* 17. Madrid, CSIC, Instituto Español de Prehistoria; Departamento de Prehistoria de la Universidad Complutense.

Gron, K.J. and Rowley-Conwy, P. (2018) Environmental Archaeology in Southern Scandinavia. In E. Pişkin, A. Marciniak and M. Bartkowiak (eds) *Environmental Archaeology. Current Theoretical and Methodological Approaches*, 35–74. Interdisciplinary Contributions to Archaeology. New York, Springer.

Gutiérrez, M., Burillo, F. and Peña, J.L. (1983) La geoarqueología como ciencia auxiliar: aplicación en la Cordillera Ibérica turolense. *Revista de arqueología* 4 (26), 6–13.

Hopf, M. (1985) Restos vegetales de la Cueva de Don Gaspar. Icod (Tenerife). *Noticiario Arqueológico Hispánico* 20, 363–364.

Hopf, M. (1990) Kulturpflanzenreste aus der Sammlung Siret in Brüssel. In H. Schubart and H. Ulreich (eds) *Die Funde der südostspanischen Bronzezeit aus der Sammlung Siret*, 397–413. Madrider Beiträge 17. Mainz am Rhein, Verlag Phillipp von Zabern.

Iriarte, M.J. and Zapata, L. (2013) Por un paisaje con figuras. *Revista Arkeogazte* [Dossier: *Arqueología y medio ambiente, una historia de una ida y una vuelta*] 3, 23–25.

Iversen, J. (1942) *Landnam i Danmarks Stenalder: en pollen-analytisk Undersøgelse over det første Landbrugs Indvirkning på Vegetationsudviklingen*. Danmarks Geologiske Undersøgelse, Series 2/66. Copenhagen, Reitzel.

Jato Rodríguez, M.V. (1974) *Contribución a la cronología de suelos por análisis de polen*. Santiago de Compostela, Universidade de Santiago de Compostela.

Jha, N. (2005) Permian palynology in India – Past, present and future. In *Challenges in Indian Palaeobiology. Current Status, Recent Developments and Future Directions. Abstract book*, 48–49. Lucknow, Birbal Sahni Institute of Palaeobotany.

Jonker, F.P. (1967) Palynology and The Netherlands. *Review of Palaeobotany and Palynology* 1 (1–4), 31–35.

Kater, M. (1974) *Das Ahnenerbe der SS 1935-1945. Ein Beitrag zur Kulturpolitik des Dritten Reiches*. Studien zur Zeitgeschichte 6. Stuttgart, Oldenbourg Verlag.

Kristiansen, K. (2002) The Birth of Ecological Archaeology in Denmark: history and research environments 1850–2002. In A. Fischer and K. Kristiansen (eds) *The Neolithisation of Denmark. 150 years of debate*, 11–31. Poole, Orca Book.

Leroi-Gourhan, A. (1956a) Analyse pollinique et Carbone 14. *Bulletin de la Société préhistorique française* 53, 291–301.

Leroi-Gourhan, A. (1956b) Notes sur l'analyse pollinique des sédiments quaternaires des grottes. In *XXIIe Congrès préhistorique de France, Poitiers*, 671–675. Paris, Société préhistorique française.

Leroi-Gourhan, A. (1959) Résultats de l'analyse pollinique de la grotte d'Isturitz. *Bulletin de la Société préhistorique de France* 56 (9), 619–624.

Leroi-Gourhan, A. (1965) Flores et climats du Paléolithique Récent. In *Congrès préhistorique de France, XVIe Session, Monaco 1959*, 808–813. Paris, Société préhistorique française.

Leroi-Gourhan, A. (1966) Analyse pollinique de la Cueva del Otero. In J. González Echegaray, M.Á. García Guinea and A. Begines (eds) *Cueva del Otero*, 83–85. Excavaciones Arqueológicas en España 53. Madrid, Servicio Nacional de Excavaciones Arqueológicas.

Leroi-Gourhan, A. (1970) *Collège de France, Chaire de Préhistoire. Leçon inaugúrale fait le Vendredi 5 Décembre 1969*. Paris, Collège de France.

Leroi-Gourhan, A. (1971) La fin du Tardiglaciare et les industries préhistoriques (Pyrénées-Cantabres). *Munibe* XXIII (2/3), 249–254.

Leroi-Gourhan, A. (1980) Análisis polínico de El Pendo. In J. González Echegaray (ed.) *El yacimiento de la cueva de 'El Pendo': (excavaciones 1953-57)*, Bibliotheca Praehistorica Hispana 17. Madrid, CSIC, Instituto Español de Prehistoria; Departamento de Prehistoria de la Universidad Complutense.

Leroi-Gourhan, A. and Leroi-Gourhan, A. (1989) *Un voyage chez les Aïnous, Hokkaido, 1938*. Paris, Albin Michel.

Llanos, A., Apellániz, J.M., Agorreta, J.A. and Fariña, J. (1975) El castro del Castillo de Henayo (Alegria - Alava). Memoria de excavaciones. Campañas de 1969-1970. *Estudios De Arqueologia Alavesa* 8, 87–212.

López, P. (1977) Estudio Polínico del yacimiento de Verdelpino (Cuenca). *Trabajos de Prehistoria* 34, 31–83.

López, P. (1978) Resultados polínicos del Holoceno en la Península Ibérica. *Trabajos de Prehistoria* 35, 9–45.

López, P. (1981a) Análisis polínico del yacimiento de los Azules (Cangas de Onís, Oviedo). *Botánica Macaronésica (Dossier: Palinología: Sistemática y filogenia)* Extra 8–9, 243–248.

López, P. (1981b) Los pólenes de la Cueva de El Salitre. *Trabajos de Prehistoria* 38 (1), 93–96.

López, P. (1982a) Estudio palinológico del yacimiento de Lavapés. *El Museo de Pontevedra* 36, 83–90.

López, P. (1982b) Polen para arqueólogos: palinología, ciencias auxiliares. *Revista de arqueología* 21, 8–13.

López, P. (1983) Análisis polínicos de cinco Fondos de Cabaña del kilómetro 7 derecha de la carretera. *Estudios de Prehistoria y Arqueología Madrileñas* 2, 265–270.

López, P. (1984) Aplicaciones de la Palinología a la Prehistoria: metodos utilizados y resultados In *Primeras jornadas de metodología de la investigación prehistórica. Soria 1981*, 309–317. Madrid, Ministerio de Cultura, Instituto de Conservación y Restauración de Bienes Culturales.

Manten, A.A. (1966) Half a century of modern palynology. *Earth-Sciences Review* 2, 277–316.

Martínez Santa-Olalla, J. (1931-32) Führer zur Urgeschichte. *Anuario de Prehistoria Madrileña* 2-3, 270–272.

Martínez Santa-Olalla, J. (1946) Cereales y plantas de la cultura ibero-sahariana. *Cuadernos de Historia Primitiva* 1, 35–45.

Mederos, A. (2012) El periplo académico de Julio Martínez Santa-Olalla en la década de los cincuenta. In L. Roldán and J. Blánquez (eds) *Julio Martínez Santa-Olalla y el descubrimiento arqueológico de Carteia (1953-1961)*, 69–82. Madrid, Universidad Autonoma de Madrid.

Menéndez Amor, J. (1957) *La Palinología en relación con otras Ciencias y en especial con la Paleoclimatología*. Publicaciones de la Real Sociedad Geográfica Serie B. Madrid, Real Sociedad Geográfica.

Menéndez Amor, J. and Florschütz, F. (1959) Algunas noticias sobre el ambiente en que vivió el hombre en dos zonas de ambas Castillas durante el Gran Interglaciar. *Estudios Geológicos* 15, 277–282.

Menéndez Amor, J. and Florschütz, F. (1961) Resultado del análisis polínico de una serie de muestras de turba recogidas en la Ereta del Pedregal (Navarrés, Valencia). *Archivo de Prehistoria Levantina* 9, 97–99.

Menéndez Amor, J. and Florschütz, F. (1962) Análisis polínico de sedimentos tardiglaciares en la Cueva de Toll (Moyá, Barcelona). *Estudios Geológicos* XVIII (1–2), 93–95.

Meurers-Balke, J. (1987) Rudolf Schütrumpf. *Eiszeitalter und Gegenwart* 37, 149–150.

Molina, M. and Rowland, F. (1974) Stratospheric sink for chlorofluoromethanes: chlorine atom-catalysed destruction of ozone. *Nature* 249, 810–812.

Morales, R. and Blanco, P. (2013) Breve historia de la investigación botánica en España. In R. Morales (ed.) *Las plantas silvestres en España*, 55–68. Madrid, CSIC.

Netolitzky, F. (1935) Kulturpflanzen und Holzreste aus dem Prähistorischen Spanien und Portugal. *Buletinul Facultăţii de Ştiinţe din Cernăuţi* IX, 4–8.

Nilsson, S. and Praglowski, J. (1978) Professor Gunnar Erdtman 1897–1973. *Grana* 17 (1), 1–4.

Pantaleón-Cano, J., Yll, R. and Roure, J.M. (1999) Evolución del paisaje vegetal en el sudeste de la Península Ibérica durante el Holoceno a partir del análisis polínico. *Saguntum (Dossier: II Congrés del Neolític a la Península Ibèrica, 7-9 d'Abril, 1999)* Extra 2, 17–24.

Pearsall, D.M. (1989) *Paleoethnobotany. A Handbook of Procedures*. San Diego, Academic Press.

Peñalba, M.C. (1987) Mulisko gaineko indusketa arkeologikoa. Urnieta-Hernani (Gipuzkoa). Analisi polinikoaren emaitzak. *Munibe* 39, 107–108.

Peñalba, M.C. (1988a) Análisis polínicos de dos turberas holocenas de Navarra, España. In *Actas de palinologia, Salamanca, 1986*, 327–331. Acta Salmanticensia. Salamanca, Universidad de Salamanca.

Peñalba, M.C. (1988b) Analyse pollinique de quatre tourbières du Pays Basque espagnol. *Inst. fr. Pondichéry, trav. sec. sci. tech.* 25, 65–71.

Peñalba, M.C. (1989) *Dynamique de végétation Tardiglaciaire et Holocene du Centre-Nord de l'Espagne d'apres l'analyse pollinique*. Aix-Marseille, Unpublished thesis, Aix-Marseille III.

Perejón, A. (1988) Josefa Menéndez Amor (1916–1985). *Boletín Real Sociedad Española de Historia Natural* 84, 53–60.

Pericot, L. (1944) Nuevas hipótesis sobre el mesolítico Norteeuropeo. *Ampurias* VI, 290–291.

Pericot, L. (1947-48) Grahame Clark, From savagery to Civilization (Londres, 1946). *Ampurias* IX–X, 401–402.

Pericot, L. (1968) Grahame Clark, World Prehistory (A new Outline, Cambridge, 1969). *Pyrenae* IV, 188–189.

Renault-Miskovsky, J. (1972) La végétation pendant le Würmien II, aux environs de la grotte de l'Hortus (Valflaunès, Hérault) d'après l'étude des pollens. In H.d. Lumley (ed.) *La Grotte de l'Hortus (Valflaunès, Hérault): les chasseurs néandertaliens et leur milieu de vie: elaboration d'une chronologie du Wümien II dans le Midi méditerranéen*, 313–324. Études quaternaires 1. Marseille, Laboratoire de paléontologie humaine et de préhistoire.

Ros Mora, M.T. (1981) Una nova ciència auxiliar de l'arqueologia: La Paleoantracologia. *Revista de Girona* 97, 263–265.

Ruiz Zapata, M.B. (1980) *Estudio palinológico de las turberas superficiales del delta del Ebro*. Madrid, Universidad Complutense de Madrid. Tesis Doctoral.

Ruiz Zapata, M.B. (1995) Análisis polínico del yacimiento de 'Soto de Medinilla': campaña de 1986-87 en el poblado vacceo. In G. Delibes, Z. Escudero, F. Romero and A. Morales (eds) *Arqueología y Medio ambiente: el primer milenio a. C. en el Duero medio*, 351–356. Valladolid, Junta de Castilla y León.

Ruiz Zapata, M.B., Andrade, A., Dorado, M., Gil, M.J., Franco, F., López, P., López Sáez, J.A., Macías, R., Arnanz, A.M. and Uzquiano, P. (1997) Las transformaciones del ecosistema en la Comunidad de Madrid. *Arqueología, paleontología y etnografía (Dossier: El paisaje vegetal de la Comunidad de Madrid durante el Holoceno Final)* 5, 95–164.

Sanchez-Goñi, M.-F. (1988) A propos de la présence du pollen de Castanea et de Juglans dans les sédiments archéologiques würmiens anciens du Pays Basque espagnol. *Inst. fr. Pondichéry, trav. sec. sci. tech.* 25, 73–82.

Sanchez-Goñi, M.-F. (1991) *Analyses palynologiques des remplissages de grotte de Lezetxiki, Labeko et Urtiaga (Pays Basque Espagnol). Leur place dans le cadre des séquences polliniques de la côte Cantabrique et des Pyrénées Occidentales*. Paris, Thèse, Institut de Paléontologie Humaine, Paris.

Santonja, M., Pérez González, A., Ruiz Zapata, B., Sesé, C. and Soto, E. (2005) *Esperando el Diluvio. Ambrona y Torralba hace 400.000 años*. Alcalá de Henares, Museo Arqueológico Regional.

Sarjeant, W.A.S. (2002) 'As chimney-sweepers, come to dust': a history of palynology to 1970. *Geological Society, London, Special Publications* 192, 273-327.

Schütrumpf, R. (1936) Pollenanalytische Untersuchungen der Magdalenien- und Lyngby-Kulturschichten der Grabung Stellmoor. *Nachrichtenblatt für deutsche Vorzeit 2*.

Siret, H. and Siret, L. (1890) *Las primeras edades del metal en el sudeste de España*. Barcelona, Imprenta de Henrich.

Smith, P.J. (1994) *Grahame Clark, the Fenland Research Committee and prehistory at Cambridge*. Cambridge, MPhil Thesis, University of Cambridge.

Smith, P.J. (2009) *A Splendid Idiosyncrasy: Prehistory at Cambridge 1915-50*. British Archaeological Reports 485, Oxford, Archaeopress.

Troels-Smith, J., Jessen, C. and Mortensen, M.F. (2018) Modern pollen analysis and prehistoric beer – A lecture by Jørgen Troels-Smith, March 1977. *Review of Palaeobotany and Palynology* 259, 10–20.

van Campo, M. (1950) *Recherches sur la phylogénie des Abiétinées d'après leurs grains de pollen*. Travaux du Laboratoire forestier de Toulouse 2-I (4). Toulouse, Université de Toulouse.

van Campo, M. and Leroi-Gourhan, A. (1956a) Note préliminaire à l'étude des pollens fossiles de différents niveaux des grottes d'Arcy-sur-Cure. *Bulletin du Museum* XXVIII (3), 326–330.

van Campo, M. and Leroi-Gourhan, A. (1956b) Un paysage forestier rissien dans l'Yonne. *Bulletin de la Société botanique de France* 103 (5–6), 285–286.

Vila, A. and Estévez, J. (1989) «Sola ante el peligro»: la arqueología ante las ciencias auxiliares. *Archivo Español de Arqueología* 62, 272–278.

Vilanova y Piera, J. (1872) *Origen, Naturaleza y Antigüedad del hombre*. Madrid, Imprenta de la Compañía de Impresores y Libreros del Reino.

Vilanova y Piera, J. (1881) *Agricultura prehistórica: conferencias*. Madrid, R.Moreno y R.Rojas.

West, R. (2014) *Quaternary research in Britain and Ireland. A history based on the activities of the Subdepartment of Quaternary Research*, University of Cambridge, 1948–1994. Leiden, Sidestone Press.

Yll, R. (1984) Problemas de interpretación del análisis polínico en la reconstrucción paleoeconómica. In *Primeras jornadas de metodología de la investigación prehistórica. Soria 1981*, 319–322. Madrid, Ministerio de Cultura.

Yll, R. (1995) Análisis polínico de los yacimientos de la Edad del Hierro de Soto de Medinilla, La Era Alta y La Mota (Valladolid). In G. Delibes, Z. Escudero, F. Romero and A. Morales (eds) *Arqueología y Medio ambiente: el primer milenio a. C. en el Duero medio*, 357–370. Valladolid, Junta de Castilla y León.

Chapter 5

Archaeology and interdisciplinarity in the Irish Free State in the 1930s: the role of the Committee for Quaternary Research

Mairéad Carew

Abstract

The Committee for Quaternary Research (CQR) was a key organisation in the evolution of interdisciplinarity in archaeological practice in the 1930s in the Irish Free State. The founding of this organisation, its aims and the role of the scientists included in its membership on the discipline of archaeology was influential. Its work on bogs had important implications for archaeology, a particularly rich resource in terms of the preservation of archaeological material. This focus on wetland archaeology presaged the coming of age of archaeology in the Irish Free State as an interdisciplinary science.

Keywords: history of archaeology; quaternary science; interdisciplinarity; botany; pollen analysis; geology; bogs; crannógs; artefacts.

Introduction

In 1934, Adolf Mahr, Director of the National Museum of Ireland (NMI), wrote that 'it is no fantastic vision to foresee the day, distant as it may be, when archaeology and natural science combined will draw up the settlement maps of prehistoric Ireland for all consecutive periods' (Mahr 1934b, 140). In the interwar period in the Irish Free State the gradual process of transitioning from antiquarianism to scientific archaeology was taking place. There was a new focus on the incorporation of scientific reports including geology, botany, pollen analysis, dendrochronology, zoology and physical anthropology to corroborate archaeological data resulting in a more complex picture of the past (Carew 2018, 162–187). This process was influenced by international ideas and new methodologies from Denmark, Germany and the United States. There was a drive for international expertise in the newly independent state. Adolf Mahr was

Austrian and an expert in European Celtic archaeology. American academics from the Harvard Archaeological Mission undertook a five-year project between 1932 and 1936, using a three-stranded approach including physical anthropology, social anthropology and archaeology. They sought to determine who the Celts were, their racial type and who their descendants were. Social and physical sciences during this period were 'strategic instruments vital to the bio-political ambitions of the state' (Brannigan 2009, 84).

During the 1930s Irish archaeologists tended to have other professions entirely or were engaged in archaeology as part of their interdisciplinary studies of science. The National Museum was at the hub of archaeology and interdisciplinarity during this decade. In 1934, Mahr's ambition was to have all work of an archaeological character, carried out under the authority of the State, to be centred in the National Museum. He played a prominent role in the selection of sites for excavation by the Harvard Archaeological Mission, the Unemployment Schemes for Archaeological Research, instigated by Éamonn de Valera, President of the Executive Council in 1934, and the sites for examination by the Committee for Quaternary Research (CQR), set up in 1933. It was stated in the *Report of the Department of Education* (shortened as DOE) *1933–1934* that 'the two most important events of the year' were the commencement of systematic excavations on a large scale under the auspices of the Free State Government and the formation of the Committee for Quaternary Research in Ireland' (DOE 1933–1934, 93).

Founding the Committee for Quaternary Research

Anthony Farrington, engineer, geologist and Assistant Secretary of the Royal Irish Academy (RIA) invited some eminent scientists, including botanists, geologists and archaeologists to a meeting on 25 January 1933 to discuss the possibilities of quaternary research in Ireland (Farrington 1934, 128–130; Watts 1988, 61–67). One of the main objects of the research was 'the establishment of a general chronological sequence for archaeological and biological purposes' (RIA 1933–1953, 1). At that meeting the Committee for Post Pliocene Research in Ireland was set up. At a subsequent meeting on 20 March 1933, the name was changed to the Committee for Quaternary Research (RIA 1933–1953, 4, 7). There were representatives of many scientific bodies and universities in Ireland on the CQR including the NMI, the RIA, the National Library (NL), University College Dublin (UCD), Trinity College Dublin (TCD), the Geological Survey of Ireland (GSI) and Queens University Belfast (QUB). The first chair of the CQR was Robert Lloyd Praeger, 'an engineer by graduation, a librarian by profession and a botanist by inclination' who was also recognised for his contributions to ecology, history, quaternary geology, phytogeography, zoology and Irish archaeology (Dalton and McGlynn 2019, 44–47). Praeger had identified the need for quaternary research as early as 1902. He came to the conclusion in his paper 'On types of distribution in the Irish flora', published in *Proceedings of the Royal Irish Academy* (PRIA), that records lying buried in peat bogs would yield very important evidence to the discipline of botany (Praeger 1902, 60).

There was a strong representation of archaeologists and scientists from the National Museum of Ireland and those closely associated with the museum's work on the CQR. Chief among them was Adolf Mahr, Keeper of Irish Antiquities from 1927 to 1934 and Director of the National Museum of Ireland from 1934 to 1939 (Stephan and Gosling 2004, 105–119). Another important member was Claude Blake Whelan, a talented amateur prehistorian, who was influential in the work of the CQR on the Harvard Archaeological Mission sites in Northern Ireland (Carew 2018, 106–133). Seán P. Ó Ríordáin, Mahr's protegée at the museum, did not become a member of the CQR but he participated in the collection of scientific samples for analysis from archaeological sites. He was later to become Professor of Celtic Archaeology at UCD in 1943 (Cooney 1997, 30–31). Scientists from the National Museum on the CQR included Dr Patrick O'Connor, Keeper of the Natural History Division between 1930 and 1954 and an expert on the physiology of pollen tube development, who completed the *Handlist of Irish plants* (1934), an important work begun by the botanist Matilda Cullen Knowles (Desmond 1994, 2281); Robert Francis Scharff, a leading member of the RIA, a specialist in Irish fauna and 'one of Ireland's foremost zoologists' (Anonymous 1934, 487); and Arthur Wilson Stelfox, a 'great entomologist' and naturalist who was an authority on Irish plants, molluscs and geology. In his obituary, Stelfox was described as knowledgeable in conchology, genetics, botany and archaeology. He worked with the Harvard Archaeological Mission on cave sites, crannógs (prehistoric and medieval lake dwellings) and Mesolithic sites. In Stelfox's obituary in 1973 it was stated that: 'It will be many years before a true assessment of Stelfox's work can be made for he stood so far above his contemporaries that they are not able to assess more than a fragment of his achievements, due to their own specialisation' (Graham and Heal 1973, 289). Another prominent Irish archaeologist, Robert Alexander Stewart Macalister, Professor of Celtic Archaeology at UCD between 1909 and 1943 (O'Sullivan 2009, 521–530), also became a member.

Scientific archaeology in the 1930s emerged from a nascent scientific antiquarianism which also involved a cursory knowledge of a variety of disciplines within a historical framework (Carew 2018, 162–174). Other scholars involved in the CQR included Jesse Austin Sidney Stendall, described in his obituary as a naturalist 'with a good working knowledge of a wide variety of disciplines' (C.D.D. and A.W. 1974, 8–9). He served as Assistant Curator and later Curator (1942) of the Belfast Museum and Art Gallery. He founded the *Irish Naturalists' Journal* in 1924 and served as its editor between 1925 and 1950. He was also a very active member of the Belfast Naturalists Field Club. Stendall liaised with Mahr in the work of the Harvard Archaeological Mission in Northern Ireland. Other scientists working on the CQR included botanists such as Henry Horatio Dixon of TCD and Professor Joseph Doyle, appointed to the Chair of Botany at UCD in 1924. Geologists included Timothy Hallissy of the GSI; Henry J. Seymour of UCD; Louis Bouvier Smyth, professor of geology and minerology at TCD from 1934; and John Kaye Charlesworth of QUB, a member of the RIA and 'one of the most significant figures in Irish glacial geology in the first half of the 20th century' (Dalton and McGlynn 2019, 52).

At the first meeting of the CQR on 25 January 1933 a draft statement for transmission to the council of the RIA was prepared and the importance of the proposed research was emphasised:

> Recent work in biology and archaeology has proved the necessity of obtaining further information relative to glacial and post-glacial history in order that it may be possible to trace and date the migrations of our plants and animals and to establish a sound basis for the chronology of early human history (RIA 1933–1953, 2).

At a subsequent meeting a three-year research programme was proposed, and it was anticipated that £300 per annum was needed to fund it. It was agreed that the CQR should act as the Irish sub-commission of the International Commission for the Study of Fossil Man which was founded at the Geological Congress in Pretoria in 1929. A sub-committee consisting of Praeger, Macalister, Mahr, Whelan and Hallissy was appointed to prepare annual reports to the International Commission (RIA 1933–1953, 4, 6). The work of the CQR involved the study of botany, palaeobotany, geology, history of climate and the environment. As human habitation is influenced by these factors, they provide much information about human history. The archaeological implications of this research were therefore promising. Many hundreds of samples of peat and other soils were sent to Copenhagen for analysis (RIA 1933–1953, 18).

An invitation to the Maestro

Danish Professor Knud Jessen (1884–1971), described in 1934 by Adolf Mahr as 'one of the greatest living experts in palaeobotany' (Mahr 1934b, 137–138), was invited to Ireland to lead the research for the CQR (Edwards and Warren 1985, 155). Jessen had been appointed to the Chair of Botany at the University of Copenhagen and as Director of the Botanical Gardens and the Botanical Museum in 1931. The prominent English botanist, ecologist and peatland scientist, Harry Godwin, praised Jessen's interdisciplinary work in the field of plant sciences and described him as a 'maestro' (Godwin 1973, 1248). In 1932, Godwin had been involved with the prehistorian John Grahame Douglas (Grahame) Clark in the Fenland Research Committee, a new departure in environmentally-informed archaeology (Smith 1997, 11–30).

Knud Jessen was taught by Nils Gustaf Lagerheim (1860–1926), a botanist and early pioneer of pollen analytical studies, to identify pollen (Edwards 2018, 319, 326). Lagerheim was a 'seminal influence' on the Swedish naturalist and geologist Lennart von Post (1884–1951), a geologist at University College Stockholm, who drew the first pollen diagrams and defined distinctive tree pollen horizons in 1909 (Edwards 2018, 319). In 1916, von Post presented a paper with many pollen diagrams at the Sixteenth Meeting of Scandinavian Naturalists in Oslo, examining the pollen of forest trees in bogs in Southern Sweden. His presentation is regarded as 'the realization of pollen analysis as a science' (Kneller 2009, 816). At the time von Post received his training, the natural sciences of geology, botany and zoology were often studied together (Edwards 2018, 322). Pollen analysis developed from this interdisciplinary perspective. The quantifying of pollen in the stratigraphic position of a peat sample meant that a time dimension was added to the study of vegetation (Vincent 1990). Jessen, in his work in the Irish Free State in the 1930s, hoped to be able 'to localize the very horizon in which prehistoric implements had been found' in several sections (RIA, 1933–1953). The preservative environment of bogs provided good conditions for the survival of pollen as well as archaeological material. Dr Gunnar Erdtman of Stockholm University was the first botanist to include Irish sites in a palaeo-ecological survey using the method of pollen statistics regarded by Mahr as 'highly creditable pioneer work' (Erdtman 1928, 123–192). His pioneering work was described as 'highly creditable' by Mahr (Mahr 1934–1935, 12). Erdtman wrote an early history of pollen analysis in his book *An Introduction to Pollen Analysis* in 1943.

Jessen obtained a grant from the Rask-Orsted Foundation in Denmark and arrived in Dublin with his assistant Hagbard Jonassen on 5 July 1934 (RIA 1933–1953, 14). Between 1934 and 1938, the work of the CQR was funded by the Government of the Irish Free State, the Rask-Orsted Foundation, the RIA, the Royal Dublin Society (RDS), the Belfast Natural History and Philosophical Society, UCD, TCD, University College Cork (UCC) and QUB (RIA 1933–1953, 51). Under the Unemployment Schemes a grant was made available to the Danish scientists for excavations. Also, the Harvard Archaeological Mission agreed to pay money to the CQR on condition that Professor Jessen should visit some of their sites and report on the sections (RIA 1933–1953, 18; Whelan 1934, 134–137; Jessen 1936, 31–37). The Office of Public Works (OPW) and private subscriptions also funded the research for 1934 (RIA 1933–1953).

Central to the CQR programme of research was the training of students in collection and laboratory methods. Students were instructed in methods of surveying, sampling and classifying peat, and trained in laboratory work including washing and treating of samples, identification of macroscopical and microscopical remains and pollen analysis (RIA 1933–1953, 32). Six students were selected for participation, including Frank George Francis (Frank) Mitchell who later went on to have a career as a multi-talented Quaternary scientist and to become a leading Irish palynologist (Plunkett 2007, 224). It was Mahr's intention to train museum staff in the methods developed in northern Europe for this research. His ambition was for important archaeological and palaeobotanical finds to be dealt with independently by the National Museum in the future without the necessity for outside help (DOE 1935–1936, 114). Training in the field and in the laboratory under Jessen was provided in Copenhagen for two people selected by the NMI. One of these was Frank Mitchell and the other was Mollie O'Leary, an assistant in the Botanical section who was given leave of absence and paid some travelling expenses by the NMI (DOE 1935–1936, 114).

Twenty-one artefacts

CQR research, according to Mahr, was very important to international archaeology and natural history because of Ireland's unique archaeological importance and its implications for Atlantic Europe (Mahr 1934b, 142). In 1937, he listed sixty sites examined by the CQR (Mahr 1937, 424–425) of which at least thirty-eight were archaeological. Without this stimulus from Scandinavia and the Fenland Research Committee in Cambridge, he believed that they would probably never have made any headway in Ireland (Mahr 1937, 273). Grahame Clark, secretary of the Fenland Research Committee, founded in 1932, explained the multidisciplinary nature of its work:

> To achieve the intimate correlation of the events of natural and of human history made possible by the peculiar constitution of the fenland it is necessary both to pursue highly specialised lines of enquiry and to secure that research workers in subjects so various should co-operate to achieve the synthesis desired (Clark 1934, 147).

The basis of Jessen's CQR Survey was a list of twenty-one archaeological finds from bogs, prepared by Adolf Mahr. Mahr was convinced of the importance that the Irish peat-bogs had for botanical, geological and other scientific problems, as well as for archaeology (Mahr 1937, 272). It was already established by botanists that pollen was best preserved in waterlogged and unaerated deposits of mineral and organic origin (Godwin 1934, 289; Jessen 1934, 130–134).

About half of all the new important archaeological objects reported yearly to the National Museum were being discovered during turf-cutting. Jessen believed that without Mahr's list 'it would have been impossible to attempt such an extensive preliminary survey' (RIA 1933–1953). He explained that:

> If we know the exact place and layer in a bog where an implement of a fixed archaeological period has been found, we can determine by pollen-analysis the exact composition of the surrounding forest at that particular period. It will then be possible, by the application of the same method to other bogs, to find which layers in them are of the same age (Mahr 1934b, 138–139).

Adolf Mahr was satisfied that pollen analysis could be used to date artefacts that did not lend themselves to chronological studies (Mahr 1934b, 139). Jessen published the results of the examination of the Irish post-arctic deposits carried out in the summers of 1934 and 1935 in an extensive paper published in the *PRIA* in 1949 (Jessen 1949, 85–290). He was able to do this thanks to a grant that the semi-state company Bord na Móna gave to pay for the cost of publication. Jessen was ably assisted by his assistant Hagbard Jonassen who carried out most of the extensive examination of the pollen analysis. Frank Mitchell, who was also in attendance for fieldwork throughout, described how he accompanied Jessen 'in the dual capacity of courier and brain-picker' (Mitchell 1976, 12). His training under Jessen was the beginning of an illustrious career (Cooney 1989, 91–95). Mitchell later succeeded in establishing Trinity College Dublin's reputation in the field of quaternary science (Edwards 2018, 326).

Jessen divided the Irish post-glacial period into a series of numbered zones and identified which trees were the most important producers of pollen in each zone. Mitchell then explained how this was correlated with archaeological objects:

> If the level at which an archaeological object has been found in a pollen-containing deposit such as a mud or a peat is known, and a series of samples is taken above and below this level, a diagram may be constructed at which the object occurred to a particular phase of forest development. The succession of archaeological cultures may thus be related to the sequence of forest development (Mitchell 1944–1945, 3).

In 1937, Lennart von Post commented in his article 'The Geographical Survey of Irish Bogs' that the establishment of pollen diagrams and peat stratification by Jessen was 'an excellent basis for deciphering Irish bog evolution and chronology' (von Post 1937, 226).

Jessen's and Mahr's academic relationship was a symbiotic one between an archaeologist and a botanist in the 1930s, with possible benefits to both disciplines. Mahr was hopeful that a more coherent picture of the Bronze Age in Ireland could be obtained by the study of palaeobotany than it had been possible with the isolated finds at the disposal of the archaeologist in museums and in the field (Mahr 1934b, 140). Bronze implements on his list included a socketed axe, flat axes, axes with stopridges, a spearhead, a halberd, palstaves, daggers, rapiers and leaf-shaped swords. Wooden artefacts comprised a shield, a cauldron and a statue of a 'Bronze Age God' (RIA 1933–1953). The finds were recent and had come from bogs in Counties Mayo, Roscommon, Cork, Kerry, Tipperary, Armagh, Monaghan and Cavan. Their find locations were examined in detail and samples of the peat taken from the find locations. Recent find locations were more likely to be accurate than ancient ones.

One of the recent finds was a set of fragments of a wooden cauldron recovered from a bog in Altartate Glebe, near Clones, County Monaghan in 1933. This artefact was examined by Jessen who carried out a pollen-analytical examination of the samples of peat from the find spot. Adolf Mahr was satisfied that:

> This is the first time that an important archaeological object from a peat-bog in Ireland has been made subject to pollen-analytical examination of the conditions of its discovery, and it is gratifying that the results obtained by purely archaeological reasoning have been corroborated, as far as could be expected at the present moment, by the expert in pollen-analysis (Mahr 1934–1935, 11–12).

The wood from which the cauldron was made was examined by Dr Patrick O'Connor (NMI). The species was found to be poplar (*genus Populus*) with the only remaining handle to be made of yew. Mahr believed this cauldron with its skilfully made handle and ornamentation of the upper portion of the vessel was 'a translation in wood of Bronze Age cauldrons' (Mahr 1934–1935, 17). He described it as a blending of Bronze Age tradition and La Tène style with an ornamentation in which La Tène influence was obvious (Mahr 1934–1935, 23, 26). He concluded that the results of Professor Jessen's investigation of the samples of peat are that the cauldron most probably belongs to the older part of the Early Iron Age (Mahr 1934–1935, 28). Jessen was more circumspect.

In his letter to Seán P. Ó Ríordáin on 14 January 1934 about the Altartate cauldron he gave his opinion that the peat samples were from the sub-Atlantic time, which in Ireland must have been contemporary with the Iron Age. However, he also inserted a note of caution in respect of his views:

> These remarks can of course only be rather uncertain. If we had had a wider range of pollen-analysed sections from Irish peat bogs, and if an experienced peat-botanist had had the opportunity to survey the whole section in question and to work out the stratigraphy of the bog, it would perhaps have been possible to reach a more definite conclusion as to the age of the cauldron (Mahr 1934–1935, 29).

Later, in 1937, Mahr asserted that the Altartate cauldron could be assigned to the Early Iron Age on stylistic and palaeobotanical evidence (Mahr 1937, 273). Mitchell, however, believed that it was unlikely that this vessel could have survived unless it had been deliberately buried, and it was, therefore, possible that it was much younger than the peat by which it was surrounded (Mitchell 1944–1945, 9).

While wooden objects were often recovered from bogs because of their preservative properties, sometimes information surrounding the find-spot was lacking. One example was a large anthropomorphic figure, carved from yew, from Ralaghan Bog in County Cavan (Mahr 1934b, 142; Coles 1990, 315–333; O'Sullivan 2007, 106–107). It was described by Adolf Mahr in 1930 as a wooden idol (Mahr 1930, 487) and later included in a similar group of artefacts interpreted as representations of deities or human effigies ritually deposited in lieu of actual human sacrifices (Stanley 2012, 36–37). Jessen, in his 1949 paper, wrote that:

> Archaeologically, this site where a wooden idol, presumably of the Bronze Age or Early Iron Age had been found was disappointing; it was not possible to establish the exact stratum whence this very important object came, as it had been found prior to the reorganisation of the National Museum (Jessen 1949, 277).

From a palaeobotanical viewpoint, however, Jessen believed Ralaghan to be very instructive as a series of late glacial deposits, similar to those at Ballybetagh, County Dublin (discussed below), were discovered (Jessen and Farrington 1938; Jessen 1949, 149). The pollen diagrams as well as the macroscopic plant remains assigned these lake deposits to the late glacial time (Jessen and Farrington 1938, 243). This was considered particularly important as it was possible to compare the late glacial deposits in Ireland with those in Denmark (Jessen and Farrington 1938, 245).

A bone of contention about the dating of the beginning of the Late Bronze Age in Ireland arose between archaeologists and botanists from the CQR as a result of the palaeobotanical analyses. Jessen interpreted it to be much later in date than postulated by Irish archaeologists. In his contribution to Mahr's presidential address in 1937, Jessen explained that the Irish bogs showed a change in the moisture influencing the growth of plants on what is now bog-land. This increase in rainfall indicated a change in climate. A 'border-horizon', an important level in Irish bogs, was the evidence for this change in climate. Jessen wished to date this 'border-horizon' in absolute terms. He argued that a climatic change of such magnitude, as revealed by the Irish peat-bogs, could not have been a purely local phenomenon and must have extended over a much larger region (Mahr 1937, 277). He compared the 'border-horizon' in the Irish bogs with the 'border-horizon' of the Danish-Scandinavian bogs. There was a similar rise in rainfall levels in Denmark and Scandinavia generally at a time when the Bronze Age came to an end and the Iron Age began, around 400 BC. He concluded that the Late Bronze Age in Ireland should be contemporaneous with the earliest Iron Age of Denmark (Mahr 1937, 278).

It was Jessen's view that 'it should be possible to fix the border-horizon between such chronological landmarks' as he wanted to form an opinion as to its absolute dating (Mahr 1937, 277). He did this by the examination of four artefacts from Mahr's list found in bogs. These included a wooden shield from Cloonlara, County Mayo, a bronze leaf-shaped sword with an ancient repair to the hilt from Canbo, County Roscommon, a bronze dagger from Glannalappa East, County Kerry, and a bronze rapier from Togherbane, County Kerry. The dagger and the rapier 'would indicate the relevant Middle Bronze Age layers' and the wooden shield and leaf-shaped sword were 'indicative of the Late Bronze Age'. He based this assessment on the relative depth at which the four archaeological objects coming from these sites were said to have been discovered (Jessen in Mahr 1937, 277). The wooden shield from Cloonlara was found in April 1934. Seán P. Ó Ríordáin visited the site, established the exact location with the help of the finder, and took samples for pollen analysis in the peat-cutting where the shield was found. Jessen visited Cloonlara also in 1934. He suggested that the shield, on preliminary examination of the samples, 'might be dated to the sub-Boreal/sub-Atlantic transition'. He believed that it had been placed on the surface of the bog at the beginning of the moist sub-Atlantic period and must have been covered by peat almost immediately after its deposition because of its preservation (Jessen 1949, 161–162). In addition, Dr Patrick O'Connor established that the artefact was made of alder-wood (Mahr 1937, 278, 383). The shield, together with a similar one found in Annandale, County Leitrim, in 1863, were, according to Mahr the only wooden shields of Bronze Age date in European museums (Mahr 1934b, 143).

Mahr referred to the real difficulty Irish prehistorians would have in accepting such a late date, 400 BC, for the inception of the Late Bronze Age in Ireland, as postulated by Jessen. His own belief was that the Late Bronze Age began approximately 900 BC. According to Mahr, Jessen's new date would be 'quite inadmissible and be tantamount to a wholesale crash of our chronological structure' (Mahr 1937, 278). Later, the American archaeologist and member of the Harvard Archaeological Mission to Ireland, Hugh Hencken, wrote in his paper 'Palaeobotany and the Bronze Age', published in 1951, that Jessen's date of 400 BC was a 'rather startling conclusion' (Hencken 1951, 53). However, a note from Jessen was included in the paper reiterating his previous claims that:

the sub-Boreal deposits in the Irish bogs reflecting a dry warm climate are separated from the sub-Atlantic ones indicating a colder wetter climate by what is called Recurrence Surface C. In the southern Baltic countries Denmark, Southern Sweden and Northern Germany, there is a similar phenomenon called Recurrence surface III by Granlund (1932) and this also separates the sub-Boreal and sub-Atlantic deposits (Hencken 1951, 53).

Recurrence surface III was dated to about 400 BC in Denmark. Jessen dated Recurrence Surface C in Ireland also to 400 BC on the grounds that both were caused by the same natural phenomenon. However, his use of such a limited number of Bronze Age artefacts for absolute dating was not acceptable to archaeologists. This debate has still not been satisfactorily resolved.

Bogs, archaeology and interdisciplinarity: innovations and issues

Jessen and Jonassen's survey of the peat-bogs in the Irish Free State in the summers of 1934 and 1935 was ambitious. The formation, depth and varying strata of bogs were examined scientifically. Ballybetagh Bog was the first to be fully excavated. Praeger referred to it as 'the classical site for finds of remains of the Irish Elk' (Praeger 1934, 131). The investigation was carried out under the direction of Anthony Farrington on behalf of the CQR for five weeks, between 9 July and 11 August 1934. Labour costs were defrayed under the Unemployment Schemes (Carew 2018, 134–161). The deposits of the bog were studied in eleven pits and by a number of borings with samples being sent to Denmark for analysis. Geological, botanical and climatological evidence was gathered in the process. The purpose of the excavation for archaeologists was to find stratified evidence for the giant deer (*Megaloceros giganteus*) and to throw light on its co-existence with early humans in Ireland. The importance to archaeology in allocating the remains of giant deer to late glacial times at Ballybetagh was described by Mahr as follows:

> Work in progress shows that this bed, with its characteristic flora of arctic willow and associated plants, may be traced from bog to bog right across Ireland from Galway to Wexford. It forms a certain base for all dating of post-glacial deposits, and gives point to studies of the retreat of the ice-sheets. This, and the dating of the giant deer, which will always be an important indicator fossil, are most essential particularly for future work in cave excavation (Mahr 1937, 275).

Previous excavators at Ballybetagh Bog were generally only interested in the recovery of elk bones, with little interest in any other animal or plant remains, in planning the site, in examining the deposits in which the bones were discovered or in the layers above or below the find spot (Jessen and Farrington 1938, 209). The exceptions to this were the Swede Gunnar Erdtman, who visited the site in 1924 and took samples for pollen analysis, and Arthur Wilson Stelfox who recorded his discovery of arctic willow (*salix herbacea*) in beds associated with those in which elk bones were found (Stelfox 1927, 781; Erdtman 1928). The purpose of their investigation, according to Jessen and Farrington of the CQR was to collect the macroscopic plant remains from the bog deposits and undertake pollen analysis to establish the conditions under which the elk flourished. This would in turn throw light on the climate changes of late and post-glacial times in the area (Jessen and Farrington 1938, 216). The results of this work were recognised by the Office of Public Works (Department of Finance) in its annual report for 1938. It was established that the Irish elk lived on in Ireland to a much later period than had previously been believed. This meant essentially that the contemporaneity of humans with the elk would no longer be a sufficient argument for a great antiquity of human occupation in Ireland (Commissioners of Public Works Annual Report 1938, 47).

In 1935, Jessen and Jonassen received funding to continue their work in Ireland from 5 July to 3 September. Jessen gave a three-week course in laboratory work concerning peat investigations in the Botanical Department of UCD. The material for the laboratory studies was collected at Lagore during the fourth and fifth Harvard Archaeological Missions (RIA 1933–1953, 34–35). The course content was described as follows:

> The laboratory work in which training was given consisted specially of washing analysis of different kinds of peat and mud, with collecting and determining of seeds and other macroscopical plant remains found in the stuff, and of the commonly used methods for microscopical investigation of peat, mud and clay especially such concerning the pollen analytic method (RIA 1933–1953, 34–35).

The Lagore excavations were funded by the Irish Free State, the American Council of Learned Societies, the Milton Fund of Harvard University and the American Philosophical Society and The Penrose Fund paid for the illustrations. Lagore was excavated under the auspices of the Harvard Archaeological Mission for three seasons, from 1934 to 1936. Hugh O'Neill Hencken, the excavator of Lagore, regarded it as one of the classic sites of Irish archaeology as well as the most important of the many hundreds of existing crannógs. It was one of eighteen sites excavated in the Irish Free State and Northern Ireland during a five-year project by the Harvard Mission (Carew 2018, 211, appendix 1). The bulk of the work undertaken and money spent was on three crannóg sites in the Irish Free State: Lagore, County Meath, Ballinderry 1, County Westmeath and Ballinderry 2, County Offaly (Hencken 1935–1937, 103–237; 1942, 1–76; Hencken, Price and Start 1950–1951, 1–247). This decision was directly influenced by Adolf Mahr, the chief adviser and sponsor for the Harvard Mission, who played a prominent role in the selection of sites for excavation. His reasons for choosing crannógs were practical, ideological and academic. Bogs, because of their preservative properties, guaranteed a high yield of artefacts. It was Mahr's belief at the time that the Celts invaded Ireland in the Late Bronze Age and brought the idea of crannóg construction with them. His hope was that the Harvard team would discover a crannóg dating to the Bronze Age and that 'one of the most important problems of Irish archaeology will have been solved' (Mahr 1934a). Ballinderry 2 was to yield Bronze Age dates and so was Knocknalappa,

County Clare, excavated under the Unemployment Schemes (Hencken 1942; Raftery 1942). Lagore, in particular, was suggested for excavation for the pragmatic reason it would yield many finds for comparatively little expenditure. This turned out to be the case and a vast array of objects was recovered from the crannóg. There was evidence for grazing and farming, bronze working, iron working, hunting, fowling and trade. Hencken deemed that the culture of Lagore was 'wholly self-supporting', the centre of an agricultural community with a variety of craftsmen employed (Hencken, Price and Start 1950–1951, 12).

Labour costs were defrayed under the Unemployment Schemes for Archaeological Research, despite the fact that these funds were initially directed towards prehistoric sites only. Prior to this it was believed that there was no need to excavate sites dating to the historic period because evidence for the past was already contained in the historical sources. Harold Graham (H.G.) Leask, Inspector of Ancient Monuments at the Office of Public Works, who administered the schemes, commented in his memo on 'the applicability of the term *archaeological*' that 'in effect archaeology ceases to exist only where well and fully documented history begins' (Leask 1938). Leask accepted Mahr's argument that 'a site which yielded objects of the Christian Period from its upper strata might well prove on examination, to belong to the Bronze Age or an even earlier period' (Leask 1938). Lagore's inclusion was important because it opened the door to further state-sponsored excavations of archaeological sites dating to historical times.

Various scholars and experts contributed to Hencken's study, including Dr Patrick O'Connor, who examined the wooden objects and identified the wood used in building the crannóg at Lagore to be from native trees with one single example of sycamore which was not native. His Deputy Keeper, Arthur Wilson Stelfox, identified the bones of animals. At Lagore, 47,976.25 pounds of animal bones were found, which included skulls of ox, pig, sheep, horse, dog, red deer, fox, hare, otter and heron (Hencken, Price and Start 1950–1951, 225). Farrington examined the stone objects and reported that rolled flint pebbles sufficient for the flints from Lagore were found locally.

Insects from Lagore were identified by Dr Robert Neil Chrystal, an entomologist at the Imperial Forestry Institute, Oxford. Joseph Cecil Maby, a British biophysicist, examined the charcoal, which revealed that it consisted mainly of common oak, hazel with smaller amounts of ash, hawthorn and willow. He also analysed numerous samples of slag and material from hearths. Dr Dorothy Jordan Lloyd, a pioneering British woman chemist from the British Leather Manufacturers Research Association, was invited to examine the shoes and reported that they were probably made of the skins of cattle. M.S.D Westropp, an expert in Irish glass and silver, identified the coins. Horace C. Beck, a Fellow of the Society of Antiquaries and author of *Classification and Nomenclature of Beads and Pendants* (1926) examined the beads. Thomas Davies Pryce, a surgeon and a Fellow of the Society of Antiquaries, who co-authored *An Introduction to the Study of Terra Sigillata* (1920), gave Hencken advice on the Samian pottery found at Lagore. Two hundred human bones were sent to the University of Wisconsin in the

United States to be studied by the physical anthropologist William White Howells. Laura Emily Start's study of the textiles was incorporated as an individual report into Hencken's paper. An ethnographic textile historian from Victoria University of Manchester, Start explained how she worked:

> The tender state of many of the specimens and their tendency to disintegrate if dried has necessitated great care in the examination of them. They were stored as little bundles fastened with very fine copper wire in air-tight bottles in a weak solution of formaldehyde (Hencken, Price and Start 1950–1951, 203).

A report from William George (Liam) Price, a graduate in Classics from TCD, a judge and amateur archaeologist on 'The History of Lagore, from the annals and other sources', was also included in Hencken's paper. Hencken acknowledged assistance received from an international cohort of museums based in England, Scotland, France, Belgium, Holland, Germany, Denmark, Norway, Sweden, Switzerland, Austria and Hungary (Hencken, Price and Start 1950–1951, 2).

The work of the CQR was hampered by problems with flooding at Lagore. In 1936 it was impossible to excavate the crannóg fully because even by pumping by night as well as by day it was no longer possible to keep the site from flooding (Hencken, Price and Start 1950–1951, 37–38). The final excavation produced some stratified areas and a large body of finds but a considerable part of the site was dug over, so dates were suggested from historical sources (Hencken, Price and Start 1950–1951, 3). Correlating pollen analysis with finds in these circumstances was very difficult. This may be the reason why Hencken, despite referring to Jessen's examination and description of the crannóg, did not include a separate appendix from Jessen in his final report. However, Frank Mitchell, who assisted Jessen on the work of the CQR in 1934 and 1935, authored separate papers which included some references to Lagore on archaeology and pollen analysis. These included 'Studies in Irish quaternary deposits: some lacustrine deposits near Dunshaughlin, County Meath' and 'The relative ages of archaeological objects recently found in bogs in Ireland' in *Proceedings of the Royal Irish Academy*, published in 1940–1941 and 1944–1945 respectively. Mitchell suggested that 'Zone VII should begin at 500 BC' (Mitchell 1944–1945, 5). He explained that the many archaeological objects of Late Bronze Age types including socketed axes, socketed spearheads and a leaf-shaped sword examined in Ireland 'were embedded in peat formed after the beginning of Zone VII, and in Ireland the transition from Zone VI to Zone VII appears to separate Late Bronze Age from the earlier Bronze cultures' (Mitchell 1944–1945, 5).

At Lagore, the skull of an ox killed by a pole axe and also a few bones of ox and pig and many bones of a deer's skeleton, found in the same layer of mud as a bronze spearhead, were attributed by Mitchell to Pollen Zone VII (1940–41, 29–30; 1945, 14). While Hencken posed the question about the spear having possibly sunk into an earlier pollen zone, he accepted Mitchell's placing of the spearhead in Zone VII with 'reservations' (Hencken, Price and Start 1950–1951, 228). Hencken also suggested that the bones of the domestic animals may have sunk down from the crannóg through the soft mud (Hencken, Price and Start 1950–1951, 228). This possibility arose because the layers of lake mud were firm when dry, but were very soft in their natural state, when anything might sink into them. Most of the finds from the lower layers, such as human bones, some of the flints, a piece of a lignite bracelet and bits of leather could have come from the crannóg just as well as from some earlier culture. Hencken regarded the bronze spearhead, however, to be an exception (Hencken 1949, 228).

Mitchell accepted, unquestioningly, Hencken's dating of Lagore crannóg between the latter part of the eighth and the latter part of the tenth centuries AD and placed the crannóg firmly in pollen Zone VIII. It was his view that the beginning of Zone VIII corresponded with the opening of the historic period in England (Mitchell 1944–1945, 10). In his report, Hencken wrote that 'to the question, when was the first artificial island made in the lake history gives no answer' (Hencken, Price and Start 1950–1951, 34). Since the publication of the report, Hencken's dates have been challenged by several archaeologists (Raftery 1972, 53; 1994, 84; Caulfield 1994, 210).

Conclusions

In 1934, Adolf Mahr referred to the ongoing work of the CQR as a 'fine scientific achievement, linking up, as it does, different branches of learning which normally follow very different lines' (Mahr 1934a, 138). In his opinion it would result in 'a vastly improved conception of the appearance of the country in the past' (Mahr 1934b, 138). While Mahr may be overstating the possibilities for archaeology in this interdisciplinary research at that time, his desire to integrate the natural sciences into archaeology in the 1930s was an innovative one. While Lagore crannóg may have been the poster site in terms of a burgeoning interdisciplinarity and a case study in the developing complexity of archaeological practice in the Irish Free State in the 1930s, Hencken himself was ill-equipped to integrate the diverse information accumulated and to provide a holistic interpretation based on the data. The Lagore report is reminiscent of a nineteenth-century museum catalogue, whereby artefacts are grouped together according to the material from which they were made. When Hencken's paper was published, the American anthropologist William Duncan Strong described it as 'a fascinating subject with a rich content' but was critical of it because 'the paper under review had no outline of subject matter, no list of figures or plates, no index, nor general conclusions'. He praised the maps and diagrams Hencken presented 'despite the fact that water, human detritus, and clear delineations do not go well together' (Strong 1953, 732–733). In a general comment on the crannóg excavations, Fredengren suggests that 'the rich excavations imposed such a burden of information that an understanding of the nature of the sites was nearly impossible to reach' (Fredengren 2002, 50). Brian Fagan (2005, 161) also criticised this tendency to be descriptive because it meant that there was little attempt to explain the meaning of the archaeological record. During the 1930s the focus of American archaeology was continued improvements of field methods and excavations and the careful recovery of artefacts and features. The period between 1914 and 1940 in American archaeology is described as the 'Classificatory-Historical Period' (Willey and Sabloff 1980, 83–84). The structure and descriptive nature of the Lagore report reflects the fact that the excavator was an American archaeologist. Lagore, as well as Ballinderry 1 and Ballinderry 2 crannógs, served as templates for future work on wetland sites in the Irish Free State. These reports are still very important to modern archaeologists and their dating, structure and artefactual assemblages are still discussed and reinterpreted (Lynn 1985–1986, 69–73; Johnson 1999, 23–71; Newman 2002, 99–123; Guglielmi 2014, 12–19). This can only happen because of the accurate recording of information and the clear presentation of the data contained in the Harvard Mission crannóg reports which have stood the testament of time. Chris Lynn (1985–1986, 73) paid tribute to the excavators, expressing his optimism that in the future 'more plausible interpretations can be offered without encountering any logical impasse in the data'. In its theoretical approaches, wetland archaeology in general 'retains a strong empirical, functionalist core' (Van de Noort and O'Sullivan 2006, 10). This was the legacy of the American archaeologists in Ireland.

Jessen (1949, 278) was satisfied that the work undertaken by the CQR corresponded well with the results which Praeger had reached, but with some modifications. However, he explained that the limitations of the survey carried out in the limited time available could give only 'an orientation as to the general development of the post-arctic flora in relation to changes of climate, to changes of sea-level and to cultural periods' (Jessen 1949, 89). In 1973, Godwin described Jessen's paper on 'Studies in Late Quaternary deposits and flora history of Ireland', published in 1949, as 'monumental' as it 'placed Ireland at a stroke in the forefront of European Quaternary research' (Godwin 1973, 1248). A few years ago, Gill Plunkett described the research conducted by Jessen and Mitchell as, not surprisingly, 'rudimentary' in comparison to modern studies. She praised, however, the fact that they succeeded in outlining the major post-glacial vegetation history for the greater part of Ireland (Plunkett 2007, 224).

The CQR's work was very beneficial to Irish archaeology but, unfortunately, many factors were working against it in the Lagore excavations. Interpretations were both hampered and enhanced by the historical narrative. There were also practical considerations to grapple with such as continual flooding of the site. Lagore had been dug over many times, which meant that most of the finds were not stratified. Hencken pointed out that, because of the makeup of the crannóg site the physical depth meant little as to age, because in deeper water the layers were much thicker than in shallow water (Hencken, Price and Start 1950–1951, 229). The pollen analysis conducted in the 1930s by the CQR was based on the assumption that the deposits surrounding the objects were the same age.

Interdisciplinary science has problems of integration and bias. The more specialised each respective science becomes the more accurate the information provided. However, it can be extremely difficult to resolve problems as the interpreter may not have the skills needed to read information from a cognate discipline. Sometimes, as in the case of Mahr's list of twenty-one artefacts, each respective scientist viewed the other's science as absolute or fool-proof, when in reality each had its limitations. This interdisciplinary approach to establish dating did not work out as Jessen depended on dateable artefacts if they were to be incorporated into a pollen diagram, and Mahr had provided a list hoping that pollen analysis would date the artefacts. When conflict arose such as in the case of Jessen's postulated date for the beginning of the Late Bronze Age in Ireland, his theory was roundly rejected by archaeologists. Pollen analysis continued from its tentative beginnings under the auspices of the CQR in the 1930s to be an important tool in interpreting human interference with the natural environment. Problems remained, however, and included the movement of pollen grains through a soil profile by faunal activity and the over-representation of more resistant types of pollen (Plunkett 2007, 223, 226). It was possible for a pollen analysis study to be slanted toward botanical, ecological or geological research questions depending on the sedimentary deposits analysed and the researcher's background (Kneller 2009, 815).

Despite the problems and limitations, however, the pioneering work of the CQR deserves acknowledgement. Its interdisciplinary approach to understanding archaeology in the context of the environment was not emulated, however, until the 1980s when systematic surveys and excavations were carried out on archaeological sites in Irish bogs. The discovery of the road extending across Corlea Bog, in County Longford, in 1984, resulted in the significance of wetland archaeology being 'truly realised' (Raftery 1996; Reilly 1996; Plunkett and McDermott 2007, 277). The Irish Archaeological Wetland Unit (IAWU) was subsequently set up in 1990 as a joint venture between the Office of Public Works and University College Dublin. Its work has been described as 'heroic and successful' (Coles 2001, 9). The work of the CQR also influenced the acceptance of the importance of archaeological sites dating to the historical period. Ultimately, it helped to shape archaeology as a modern interdisciplinary science in Ireland.

Acknowledgements

This chapter was written within the framework of the InterArq research project (HAR2016-80271-P) (interarqweb.wordpress.com) subsidised by the State Research Agency (AEI) and the European Regional Development Fund (ERDF, EU).

References

Anonymous (1934) Dr. Robert Francis Scharff. *Nature* 134 (3387), 487.
Brannigan, J. (2009) *Race in Modern Irish Literature and Culture.* Edinburgh, Edinburgh University Press.
Carew, M. (2018) *The Quest for the Irish Celt: The Harvard Archaeological Mission to Ireland, 1932–1936.* County Kildare, Irish Academic Press.
Caulfield, S. (1994) Some Celtic problems in the Irish Iron Age. In D. Ó Corráin. (ed.) *Irish Antiquity: Essays and Studies Presented to Professor M.J. O'Kelly.* Dublin, Four Courts Press Ltd.

C.D.D. and A.W. (1974) J.A.S. Stendall (1887–1973). *Irish Naturalists Journal* 18 (1), 8–9.
Clark, J.G.D. (1934) Recent researches on the post-glacial deposits of the English Fenland. In R.Ll. Praeger, A. Farrington, K. Jessen, C.B. Whelan, A. Mahr and J.G.D. Clark (eds) The Committee for Quaternary Research in Ireland and its work. *Irish Naturalists' Journal* 5 (6), 144–152.
Coles, B. (1990) Anthropomorphic wooden figures from Britain and Ireland. *Proceedings of the Prehistoric Society* 56, 315–333.
Coles, J. (2001) Irish wetland archaeology: from opprobrium to opportunity. In B. Raftery and J. Hickey (eds) *Recent Developments in Wetland Research. Wetland Archaeology Research Project Occasional Paper 14*, 7–35. Dublin, Seandálaíocht, Department of Archaeology, University College Dublin.
Commissioners of Public Works (1938) *Annual Report* 106. Dublin, Office of Public Works.
Cooney, G. (1989) Frank Mitchell: a man and the landscape. *Archaeology Ireland* 3 (3), 91–95.
Cooney, G. (1997) The legacy of Seán P.Ó. Ríordáin. *Archaeology Ireland* 11 (4), 30–31.
Dalton, C. and McGlynn, G. (2019) *Giants of the Irish Quaternary*. Dublin, Irish Quaternary Association.
Desmond, R. (1994) *Dictionary of British and Irish Botanists and Horticulturalists including Plant Collectors, Flower Painters and Garden Designers*. London, Taylor and Francis.
Edwards, K. (2018) Pollen, women, war and other things: reflections on the history of palynology. *Vegetation History and Archaeobotany* 27, 319–335.
Edwards, K. and Warren, W.P. (1985) *The Quaternary History of Ireland*. Cambridge, MA, Academic Press Inc.
Erdtman, G. (1928) Studies in the post-arctic history of the forests of Northwestern Europe 1. Investigations in the British Isles. *Geologiska Foreningens i Stockholm Forhandlingar* 50, 123–192.
Erdtman, G. (1943) *An Introduction to Pollen Analysis*. Waltham, MA, Chronica Botanica.
Fagan, B.M. (2005) *A Brief History of Archaeology Classical Times to the Twenty-First Century*. New Jersey, Pearson, Prentice Hall.
Farrington, A. (1934) The organisation of the Committee for Quaternary Research in Ireland. In R.Ll. Praeger, A. Farrington, K. Jessen, C.B. Whelan, A. Mahr and J.G.D. Clark (eds) The Committee for Quaternary Research in Ireland and its work. *Irish Naturalists' Journal* 5 (6), 128–130.
Fredengren, C. (2002) *Crannógs: A Study of People's Interaction with Lakes with Particular Reference to Lough Gara in the North-west of Ireland*. Dublin, Wordwell.
Godwin, H. (1934) Pollen analysis. An outline of the problems and potentialities of the method, part 1, technique and interpretation. *The New Phytologist* 33 (4), 278–305.
Godwin, H. (1973) Tribute to four Botanists. *The New Phytologist* 72 (5), 1245–1250.
Graham, M. and Heal, H.G. (1973) Arthur Wilson Stelfox, 1883–1972. *Irish Naturalists Journal* 17 (9), 285–295.
Guglielmi, A. (2014) My kingdom for a pot! A reassessment of the Iron Age and Roman material from Lagore crannóg, Co. Meath. In G.J.R. Erskine, P. Jacobsson, P. Miller and S. Statkiewicz (eds) *Proceedings of the 17th Iron Age Research Student Symposium*, 12–19. Edinburgh, Archaeopress Access Archaeology.
Hencken, H. (1935–1937) Ballinderry Crannóg No. 1. *Proceedings of the Royal Irish Academy* 43, 103–237.
Hencken, H. (1942) Ballinderry Crannóg No. 2. *Proceedings of the Royal Irish Academy* 47C, 1–76.
Hencken, H. (1951) Palaeobotany and the Bronze Age. *Journal of the Royal Society of Antiquaries of Ireland* 81, 53–64.
Hencken, H., Price, L. and Start, L.E. (1950–1951) Lagore Crannóg: an Irish Royal Residence of the 7th to 10th centuries AD. *Proceedings of the Royal Irish Academy* 53, 1–247.
Jessen, K. (1934) Preliminary report on bog investigations in Ireland, 1934. In R.Ll. Praeger, A. Farrington, K. Jessen, C.B. Whelan, A. Mahr and J.G.D. Clark (eds) The Committee for Quaternary Research in Ireland and its work *Irish Naturalists' Journal* 5 (6), 130–134.
Jessen, K. (1936) Palæobotanical report on the Stone Age site at Newferry, County Londonderry. Appendix 1. In H.L. Movius, A Neolithic site on the River Bann. *Proceedings of the Royal Irish Academy* 43C, 31–37.

Jessen, K. (1949) Studies in late quaternary deposits and flora–history of Ireland. *Proceedings of the Royal Irish Academy* 52B, 85–290.

Jessen, K. and Farrington, A. (1938) The bogs at Ballybetagh, near Dublin with remarks on late-glacial conditions in Ireland. *Proceedings of the Royal Irish Academy* 44B, 205–260.

Johnson, R. (1999) Ballinderry Crannóg No. 1: a reinterpretation. *Proceedings of the Royal Irish Academy* 99, 23–71.

Kneller, M. (2009) Pollen analysis. In V. Gornitz (ed.) *Encyclopedia of Palaeoclimatology and Ancient Environments. Encyclopedia of Earth Sciences Series*, 815–823. Dordrecht, Springer.

Leask, H.G. (1938) Memo on 'Applicability of term *archaeological*', NMI Topographical file E29, 1–260.

Lynn, C.J. (1985–1986) Lagore, County Meath and Ballinderry No. 1, County Westmeath crannógs: some possible structural reinterpretations. *Journal of Irish Archaeology* 3, 69–73.

Mahr, A. (1930) A wooden idol from Ireland. *Antiquity* 4, 487.

Mahr, A. (1934a) Cloonfinlough, Co. Roscommon, report dated 13 August 1934, NAI D/Taois S10940.

Mahr, A. (1934b) Quaternary research in Ireland, 1934, from the archaeological viewpoint. In R.Ll. Praeger, A. Farrington, K. Jessen, C.B. Whelan, A. Mahr, and J.G.D. Clark (eds) The Committee for Quaternary Research in Ireland and its work *Irish Naturalists' Journal* 5 (6), 144–152.

Mahr, A. (1934–1935) A wooden cauldron from Altartate, Co. Monaghan. *Proceedings of the Royal Irish Academy* 42, 11–29.

Mahr, A. (1937) New aspects and problems in Irish prehistory, presidential address for 1937. *Proceedings of the Prehistoric Society* 11, 262–436.

Mitchell, G.F. (1940–1941) Studies in Irish quaternary deposits: some lacustrine deposits near Dunshaughlin, County Meath. *Proceedings of the Royal Irish Academy* 46B, 13–37.

Mitchell, G.F. (1944–1945) The relative ages of archaeological objects recently found in bogs in Ireland. *Proceedings of the Royal Irish Academy* 50, 1–19.

Mitchell, G.F. (1976) *The Irish Landscape*. London, Collins.

Newman, C. (2002) Ballinderry Crannóg No. 2, Co. Offaly: Pre-Crannóg Early Medieval Horizon. *Journal of Irish Archaeology* 11, 99–123.

O'Sullivan, A. (2007) Exploring past people's interactions with wetland environments in Ireland. *Proceedings of the Royal Irish Academy* 107C, 147–203.

O'Sullivan, M. (2009) The life and legacy of R.A.S. Macalister: a century of archaeology at UCD. In G. Cooney, K. Becker, J. Coles, M. Ryan, and S. Sievers (eds) *Relics of Old Decency: Archaeological Studies in Later Prehistory Festschrift for Barry Raftery*, 521–3. Dublin, Wordwell.

Plunkett, G. (2007) Pollen analysis and archaeology in Ireland. In E.M. Murphy and N.J. Whitehouse (eds) *Environmental Archaeology in Ireland*, 221–240. Oxford, Oxbow Books.

Plunkett, G. and McDermott, C. (2007) Exploring the role of environment in wetland archaeological contexts in Ireland. In E.M. Murphy and N.J. Whitehouse (eds) *Environmental Archaeology in Ireland*, 277–295. Oxford, Oxbow Books.

Praeger, R.Ll. (1902) On types of distribution in the Irish flora. *Proceedings of the Royal Irish Academy* 24B, 1–60.

Praeger, R.Ll. (1934) The Botanical importance of the work and the inception of the present scheme. In R.Ll. Praeger, A. Farrington, K. Jessen, C.B. Whelan, A. Mahr and J.G.D. Clark (eds) The Committee for Quaternary Research in Ireland and its work *Irish Naturalists' Journal* 5 (6), 126–128.

Raftery, B. (1972) Irish hill-forts. In C. Thomas (ed.) *The Iron Age in the Irish Sea Province*. Papers given at a C.B.A. conference held at Cardiff, Jan 3–5, 1969 (Research Report 9). London, Council for British Archaeology.

Raftery, B. (1996) *Trackway Excavations in the Mountdillon Bogs, Co. Longford 1985–1991* (IAWU Transactions 3). Dublin, Crannóg Publications.

Raftery, J. (1942) Knocknalappa, Crannóg, Co. Clare. *North Munster Antiquarian Journal* 3, 53–72.

Raftery, J. (1994) Concerning chronology. In D. Ó Corráin (ed.) *Irish Antiquity: Essays and Studies Presented to Professor M.J. O'Kelly*, 82–90. Dublin, Four Courts Press Ltd.

Reilly, E. (1996) The Insect fauna (Coleoptera) from the Neolithic trackways Corlea 9 and 10: the environmental implications. In B. Raftery (ed.) *Trackway Excavations in the Mountdillon Bogs, Co. Longford 1985–1991* (IAWU Transactions 3), 403–410. Dublin, Crannóg Publications.

DOE *Report of the Department of Education, 1935–1936*. Dublin, Stationery Office.

RIA Minutes of the Committee for Quaternary Research in Ireland, Jan 1933–Oct 1953, Archive MSS No. SR/Bay 16/1/B.

Smith, P.J. (1997) Grahame Clark's new archaeology; the Fenland Research Committee and Cambridge prehistory in the 1930s. *Antiquity* 71 (271), 11–30.

Stanley, M. (2012) The 'Red Man' of war and death? *Archaeology Ireland* 26 (2), 34–37.

Stelfox, A.W. (1927) An arctic peat in Ireland. *Nature* 119, 781.

Stephan, A. and Gosling, P. (2004). Adolf Mahr (1887–1951): his contribution to archaeological research and practice in Austria and Ireland. In G. Holfter, M. Krajenbrinke and E. Moxon-Browne (eds) *Connections and Identities: Austria, Ireland and Switzerland*. Wechselwirkungen 6, 105–119. Bern, Peter Lang.

Strong, W.D. (1953) Lagore crannóg: an Irish royal residence of the 7th to 10th centuries AD by Hugh Hencken, review article. *American Anthropologist* 55 (5), 732–733.

Van der Noort, R. and O'Sullivan, A. (2006). *Rethinking Wetland Archaeology*. London, Bristol Classical Press.

Vincent, P. (1990) *The Biogeography of the British Isles: An Introduction*. London, Routledge.

Von Post, L. (1937) The geographical survey of Irish bogs. *Irish Naturalists Journal* 6 (9), 210–227.

Watts, W.A. (1988) The role of the Academy in the field of natural sciences and in conservation: presidential address to the Royal Irish Academy. *Proceedings of the Royal Irish Academy* 88B, 61–67.

Whelan, C.B. (1934) Pollen-analysis and Irish prehistory. In R.Ll. Praeger, A. Farrington, K. Jessen, C.B. Whelan, A. Mahr and J.G.D. Clark (eds) The Committee for Quaternary Research in Ireland and its work *Irish Naturalists' Journal* 5 (6), 134–137.

Willey, G.R and Sabloff, J.A. (1980) *A History of American Archaeology*. New York, W.H. Freeman and Co.

Chapter 6

Interdisciplinarity? The word and the practice in the history of Swiss wetland archaeology

Géraldine Delley

Abstract

Since the middle of the nineteenth century, research into Swiss wetlands has favoured collaborations between archaeology and the natural sciences. While the term 'interdisciplinarity' as it is used today could define such practices, this word did not appear in the language of Swiss researchers and science administrators until around the 1970s. Moreover, between the 1970s and the 2000s, a science funding agency like the Swiss National Science Foundation (SNSF) did not use the term 'interdisciplinary' to describe collaborative prehistoric research in its reports. This obliges us to treat the question of interdisciplinarity in the history of archaeology as a complex issue, distinguishing the use of the word and the practice over time.

Keywords: interdisciplinary; wetland archaeology; politics of science; history of archaeological practice.

Introduction

The emergence of a word and a practice are not necessarily contemporary. Since the 1860s, prehistory has borrowed as much from the imperatives of collecting, describing and classifying the natural sciences as it has from the comparative imperatives of art history and ethnography (Blanckaert 2017). Thus, prehistorians have long been practising what we now call interdisciplinarity. However, the expression did not appear in the European scientific field until the 1960s–70s (Feuerhahn and Reubi forthcoming). Until the 1960s, Swiss prehistorians and science administrators used other words such as *Hilfswissenschaften, Naturwissenschaften* and *Nachbarwissenschaften* in German and *annex-* and *auxiliary sciences* in French to qualify collaborations between archaeology and other disciplines. Moreover, these expressions continued to be used after the 1960s and were complemented by other terms such as *archaeometry*, *archaeobotany* and *ethnoarchaeology*, which described particular collaborations and knowledge production events between archaeology and other disciplines. This contribution describes and attempts to interpret the scope of these varied expressions, which converge towards the same idea of 'interdisciplinarity'. It is based on observations drawn from the history of an emblematic case study, wetland archaeology in Switzerland, which has been particularly active in spanning different approaches, thanks to the exceptional conservation of organic remains in humid contexts. Despite this long scientific tradition, which has involved practitioners, institutions and tools in transversal approaches for epistemic and heuristic purposes, the word 'interdisciplinarity' was mobilised very late in the twentieth century by Swiss administrators of science to characterise these scientific productions. Between words and practices, this historical analysis of interdisciplinarity[1] reveals the role played by the politics of science and the power of its arbitration when it comes to saying what is interdisciplinary and what is not. This article is not a historical review of the exemplary practice of prehistorians who have adopted transversal perspectives in their research. Rather, it proposes a historical reflexion on the inventiveness of archaeologists when they talk about their practices and reveals the political uses of the expression 'interdisciplinarity' over time – during a period in which it has become commonplace to talk about interdisciplinarity when practising science.

Wetland archaeology and the coexistence of different forms of collaboration

Since the middle of the nineteenth century, the archaeology of pile-dwellings has been the driving force behind the institutional and epistemological development of prehistoric research in Switzerland. In these wetlands, organic remains – such as wood, seeds, plants, fibres and textiles – are exceptionally well preserved and their huge diversity has led to the development of approaches and tools to exploit them heuristically. Botanists including Oswald Heer (1809–1883), Carl Schröter (1855–1939), Ernst Neuweiler (1875–1951), Werner Lüdi (1888–1968) and Max Welten (1904–1984) played a significant role in the study of these wetlands, which they explored from the twin natural- and cultural-historical perspective (Heer 1866; 1872; Neuweiler 1905; 1908; 1910; Lüdi 1935; 1955; 1956; Welten 1955; Troels-Smith 1956; see also Delley 2015a, 46–51). Between 1920 and 1950, archaeologists and botanists in Switzerland, Germany, Austria and France regularly stressed the heuristic contribution of palynology to archaeology (Bertsch 1928; Stokar and Zotz 1938; Vaufrey 1941; Guyan 1946).[2] In those years, the history of vegetation and landscape – *Paläoökologie* in German – was a novel tool used by natural scientists and prehistorians to make observations and produce new results. In 1938, the German prehistorians Lothar Zotz and Walter von Stokar placed palynology on the frontier between geology and botany, noting that palynologists investigated clusters of climatic and sedimentological clues through the detailed analysis of the sediments around the specimens they studied. Following Stokar and

Zotz's explanations, these palaeoecological observations were complemented by those of the prehistorians through the typological attribution of objects and the analysis of the stratigraphic arrangement of the remains, which then made it possible to date the natural scientists' data (Stokar and Zotz 1938, 9–10). Once dated through stratigraphy and typology, the changes in the vegetation landscape that botanists reconstructed through pollen diagrams became, in turn, available for use by prehistorians. The latter then tried to explain the changes in the landscape attributable to human action and the lifestyles of the populations they studied (Guyan 1946, 99).

Initially, research into the history of vegetation and the landscape was intended for the development of local knowledge, based on the study of plant remains and the reconstruction of the landscape at a given place and time. However, these approaches also provided a broader vision through which the correlation of representative data from different spatial and temporal scales was supposed to allow the reconstruction of a global history of climate and landscape (see for instance De Geer 1934; Hult 1936). When interpreting these environmental changes, the role played by humans was a question that natural scientists asked and that archaeologists were likely to answer by highlighting, describing and dating the material traces left on the landscape by human activities, particularly in relation to agriculture and cattle farming. While these collaborations raised the two issues of nature and culture, the measurement of time constituted a third major factor, in the first instance because dating made it possible to inscribe the observations and measurements made by natural scientists into a historical narrative (Delley 2015b, 106–107). Thus, around the 1940s–50s, pile dwelling research offered possible conditions for the stabilisation of dendrochronology as a dating method for European archaeologists, while it was also on such settlements that the first successful attempts to calibrate 14C with dendrochronology took place in the 1960s, in a prehistoric context (Delley 2015a, 85–103, 166–169). While archaeologists faced difficulties with the interpretation of 14C time, which was cast probabilistically, dendrochronological and archaeological time could easily be compared, given that the unity of time – one tree ring produced annually – corresponded directly to the rhythm of an annual calendar. Dendrochronology became the most expedient way of transforming 14C dates into real calendar years and facilitated the recognition of 14C dating among the archaeological community (see Delley 2015b, 106–107). Once again, whereas the implementation of these practices and collaborations first took place on a local level, in which interpersonal relationships played an important role, the institutional recognition of the results and the epistemic impact of these cross-approaches took place on an international scale (Ferguson, Huber and Suess 1966; Suess and Strahm 1970).

Which words for which practice?

As early as the first decades of the twentieth century, Swiss German-speaking prehistorians (Bandi 1945; Guyan 1946) who played an important role in wetland research were using the terms *Hilfsmitteln, Hilfswissenschaften, Hilfsdisziplinen* or *Nachbarwissenschaften* to refer to the collaborations between the natural sciences and prehistory. In French, these were translated as *sciences annexes* and *sciences auxiliaires*, or by other terms such as *recherches convergentes*.[3] For prehistorians, these terms corresponded to a set of disciplines, techniques and tools that originated from and encompassed, for the most part, the natural sciences or laboratory sciences. It must be pointed out that in most European countries, prehistory developed during the first decades of the twentieth century as an independent discipline (Callmer *et al.* 2006) and many of its practitioners, although there were exceptions,[4] considered it a discipline of the humanities, a *Geisteswissenschaft* that borrowed many of its research methods from the natural sciences.[5] Considered as external to the field of prehistory, these methods and sciences were thus defined as 'annexes' or 'auxiliary' to it.

The visibility given to these tools and methods from the natural sciences does not mean, however, that all prehistorians used them. What seemed to play an important role in the chosen methodological approaches and the use that prehistorians made of what they called auxiliary sciences or disciplines, depended, on the one hand, to a great extent on their personal background, and on the other, on the different types of archaeological field in which they were active. Emil Vogt (1906–1974), for instance, one of the first prehistorians to pursue an academic career in Switzerland, illustrates this complexity. He was appointed extraordinary professor to teach pre- and protohistory at the Faculty of Philosophy of the University of Zurich in 1945. He also held a position as curator of the prehistoric collections at the Swiss National Museum in Zurich (1930), where he became vice-director (1953) and then director (1961–1971). Vogt was a specialist in Bronze Age typology. His initial training at the universities of Paris, Breslau (Wrocław), Berlin and Vienna prepared him above all for the morphological and stylistic study of archaeological artefacts. In 1928, he defended his doctoral thesis on the chronology of Late Bronze Age ceramics in Switzerland at the University of Basel, where he proposed a classification of pottery from the lakeshore settlements of Switzerland.

Although his typo-chronological questions led him to think more in terms of style and forms, thus closer to art history and ethnography than the natural sciences, to a certain extent Vogt was also interested in these naturalist approaches. In 1937, he started collaborating with the botanist Ernst Neuweiler, then working for the Swiss Federal Institute of Agriculture.[6] Vogt wanted Neuweiler to determine whether the plant species he had discovered on the pile dwellings of Uerlikon were domesticated or wild. In 1939, he also sent Neuweiler wood samples from the palisades of the settlement of Baldegg and he did the same for the Egolzwil site he excavated in the early 1950s (Vogt 1951; Delley 2015a, 48, 85–88). The first question he asked was whether the wood species used in the construction of prehistoric pile dwellings corresponded to cultural and technical choices. He also hoped to be able to use the results of the wood analysis for dating purposes (Delley 2015a, 105–107). Of course, Vogt's use of auxiliary sciences depended largely on the possibilities he had at his disposal. For example, the issues he raised and the methodological tools he used were not the same when excavating in wetlands – where the heuristic potential for naturalist studies was widely recognised – as they would have been if he had been excavating a terrestrial site where the chances of exploiting organic remains were reputedly limited. While in both cases questions of site function and dating were crucial, the typology of objects was almost self-sufficient in dryland areas. In contrast, in wetlands, environmental issues (landscape and climate change), as well as the cultural and technological aspects of habitat construction, were added to questions of chronology and site function.

In parallel to Vogt's example, Walter Guyan (1911–1999) is also an interesting case regarding collaborations between archaeology and other disciplines. In 1946, he authored an article in the *Yearbook of the Swiss Prehistory Society* in which he gave an account of the diversity of sciences considered to be useful for prehistory (Guyan 1946). Guyan listed tools, methods and techniques, borrowing his examples from the natural sciences, as the title of his article ('Naturwissenchaft und Urgeschichte'[7]) indicates. However, unlike most of his prehistorian colleagues, who primarily envisaged collaborations with auxiliary sciences among the natural sciences, Guyan also stressed the importance of the humanities and social sciences (Guyan 1946, 100). Trained in geography, history and prehistory, he was interested in the cultural history of landscapes. In his book *Mensch und Urlandschaft der Schweiz* (*Man and Primal Landscape in Switzerland*), he explained that, like geographers, he too took sociological, economic and ethnographic aspects into account in his analysis of the transformative processes of landscape over time and their impact on society (Guyan 1954, 13). The cultural history of landscapes therefore constituted for Guyan a study subject in its own right, bringing together prehistory, the natural sciences and the human sciences around the question of man and his environment. However, Guyan's approach remained an exception and, generally speaking, when prehistorians listed collaborations with other disciplines around the 1950s, natural sciences, rather than human sciences, were cited first. Logically, prehistorians first sought collaborations with disciplines outside their own wide field of the humanities.

Teamwork set up as an absolute model

In fact, these practices were not only well thought of by archaeologists, to the point that the procedures were seen by many scholars as inevitable, but teamwork and the exchange of skills were also in line with a modern vision of science defended by the politics of science, the SNSF in this case. In his 1946 article, Walter Guyan explained that, 'in the future', collaborations between prehistory and the natural sciences would have to take place within a more general framework that would begin in the field and continue in the laboratory. He used the term 'teamwork' to refer to these new ways of undertaking archaeological research (Guyan 1946, 110). For his part, Hans-Georg Bandi (1920–2016), professor of prehistory at the University of Bern and curator of the prehistoric collections at the Historical Museum of Bern, considered that not allowing a regular exchange with the natural sciences would constitute a form of negligence on the part of archaeologists with regard to a heritage that they irremediably destroyed. For Bandi, 'the smallest section taken from a pile dwelling settlement contains a multitude of information for the excavator. [...] Only the meticulous work of prehistorians and natural scientists in the field and in the laboratories will enable us to make progress on the pile dwelling question [...] everything that is not resolved at the moment will be lost forever [...] any other way of proceeding today on a lakeshore settlement would be completely irresponsible' (Bandi 1954, 192). It should be noted that in those same years, the French prehistorian André Leroi-Gourhan (1911–1986) was making observations similar to those of Bandi. He too stressed that the natural scientists' tools had become indispensable to prehistorians, reporting that 'In twenty years we have come to tell the prehistorian that he could no longer understand anything without pollen, without small molluscs, without the orientation of grains of sand, without the radioactivity of carbon 14. Today, the smallest grain of earth hides a trap: it requires many people to remember what the geologist, chemist or physicist will ask for'[8] (Leroi-Gourhan 1952, 5).

These remarks by the prehistorians Walter Guyan, Hans-Georg Bandi and André Leroi-Gourhan are in line with the science policy discourse formulated in the same period, which emphasised the importance of sharing methods and circulating knowledge between different areas of research. This model retained the intention of the founder of the Swiss National Science Foundation (SNSF), the physiologist Alexander von Muralt (1903–1990), who first came to know about this model of science during a trip to the United States a few years before setting up the SNSF. Muralt explained in 1948 that 'The scientific team spirit reigns there [in the United States] in a very different way [to Switzerland] and the disinterested and frank collaboration on a scientific problem is one of the refreshing characteristics of the younger generation'.[9] While this interest spread indirectly in the fields of astronomy, mathematics and sociology, Muralt explained that it would finally, as always, also reach the human sciences (as quoted in Fleury and Joye 2002, 131). Two years later, while preparing the project that would take the form and name of the SNSF in 1952, Muralt further explained that: 'Nowadays, the zoologist works with the physicist's electron microscope, the botanist determines amino acids and vitamins for the biochemist, the geneticist [sic] talks to the organic chemist about nucleic acids, the physicist builds mass spectrographs that allow the physiologist to penetrate the complicated workings of metabolism'[10] (as quoted in Fleury and Joye 2002, 142).

Regarding the human sciences, these forms of collaboration would only begin to be noticed by Swiss science policy makers in the first half of the 1970s (see below). Before that, prehistory remained an exception in terms of collaboration between scientific fields that were, after all, quite distant from each other.

Collaborations with the natural sciences as a means of distinction for prehistorians

There are many ways to measure the role of the natural sciences in Swiss lake-dwelling research from the 1950s onwards. Books and articles, as well as exchanges of correspondence between researchers, give an account of the collaborations between natural scientists and archaeologists. In the following chapter, we focus on a particular period in the development of wetland archaeology – the 1950s – which marks a turning point in the way Swiss prehistorians see themselves in the modernity of science. In this regard, among the numerous publications, in addition to those already mentioned, the book *Das Pfahlbauproblem* (Guyan et al. 1955) stands out. It is a commemorative volume published one hundred years after the discovery of the first prehistoric wetland settlements with the aim of renewing knowledge in this field. Emil Vogt, the archaeologist who orchestrated this publication project, specified that it is not a 'book of memories', but rather a 'collection of scientific works concerning the problems of lake dwellings'[11] (Letter from Vogt to Guyan, 14.7.1954, Correspondence Vogt. National Museum Zurich).

Das Pfahlbauproblem[12] refers to the debate that emerged in the 1920s in Germany concerning the positioning of prehistoric pile-dwellings. As a result of research carried out in the Federsee (Germany) by the archaeologists Robert Rudolf Schmidt (1882–1950) and Hans Reinerth (1900–1990), the position of these villages on platforms, as imagined in the second half of the nineteenth century by Ferdinand Keller, president of the Zurich Antiquarian Society, was questioned for the first time. Using sedimentology, geology, botany and climatology, German scientists came to the conclusion that they were originally located on the shores of lakes that were flooded periodically by lake transgressions or in marshes (Reinerth 1922, 61). However, until the 1950s, the observations made by German archaeologists were not enough to convince the Swiss archaeological community. Rather, this interpretation was perceived as a provocation on the part of German scholars and especially by Reinerth, who openly defended a pan-Germanist and then Nazi position (Rückert 1998, 87–88; Kaeser 2004, 107–108).

In 1950, a small group of Swiss prehistorians reconsidered the issue of the lake- versus pile-dwelling settlements. They excavated several emblematic sites and presented the results in *Das Pfahlbauproblem*. The emphasis on the natural sciences made this work a collection of observation procedures that reflected what the authors of the time claimed to be a renewal of lake-dwelling research (Delley 2015a, 78–81). The book's table of contents gives an account of the multiplicity of methods used stemming from the natural sciences. Some of the chapters were written by prehistorians. These included Emil Vogt (on the Egolzwil 3 site), Walter Guyan (on Thayngen-Weier) and Josef Speck (on Zug-Sumpf), who described their own observations and those of the natural sciences (*e.g.* sedimentology, dendrochronology, malacology, etc.) on the issue of wetland habitats. Others were assigned directly to natural scientists. Thus, one chapter written by the Danish palaeobotanist Jens Troels-Smith reported the results of pollen analyses carried out on several Swiss wetland settlements. Another chapter authored by the physicists Hilde Levi and Henrik Tauber, both working in the brand-new C14 laboratory installed at the National Museum in Copenhagen, presented the results of radiocarbon analyses carried out on organic material from Egolzwil 3.

Two of the chapters were written by botanists: Max Welten dealt with the results of the Burgäschisee pollen analysis and Werner Lüdi the history of vegetation in the Alpine region during the Bronze Age (Guyan et al. 1955, 5–6).

By selecting a research topic that for one hundred years had revealed the scientific potential of Swiss archaeology, the publication of *Das Pfahlbauproblem* in 1955 enabled researchers to eloquently illustrate the methodological innovations taking place in their fields and to inscribe them within the modernist discourse of the time. Teamwork, through the cross-fertilisation of approaches and tools, was reflected in the following quotation from Marc-Rodolphe Sauter (1914–1983), professor of anthropology and prehistory in Geneva and president of the scientific commission of the Swiss Prehistory Society (SSP), under whose aegis *Das Pfahlbauproblem* appeared in 1955:

> The solution to the problem of pile-dwelling will not only be found in a critical reading of ancient excavation reports or in ethnographic comparison; it will emerge after numerous excavations have been carried out in the various types of settlements and lakes by teams of specialists who will no longer devote themselves so much to the collection of archaeological material as to the careful examination of the remains of constructions in relation to the conditions of the geological and biological environment in which they were made [13] (Sauter 1954, 116).

In our opinion, this quotation sums up well the virtues that the researchers of the time wanted to account for through these practices in which intersecting approaches and methods were a sign of both scientificity and modernity.

Another indicator to measure the place of these collaborations in the scientific field, on the one hand, and the perception that the actors of the time may have had of them, on the other, is the amount of funding allocated by the SNSF to prehistorians' research projects. Compared to other disciplines in the humanities, the involvement of natural sciences specialists is clearly visible in the applications submitted to the SNSF. From the time the institution was established in 1952, prehistorians obtained large amounts of funding for their investigations, ranging from 20,000 to 50,000 Swiss francs in the 1950s and 1960s (equivalent to between 70,000 and 170,000 euros today) for a three-year study campaign (Delley 2015a, 83–84). Since 1957, the SNSF has also been committed to funding equipment and some of the staff to run a radiocarbon dating laboratory at the University of Bern (Delley 2016, 207–210). The latter project corresponded perfectly to the expectations of the SNSF: set up by a prehistorian who joined forces with a botanist and a nuclear physicist, the C14 laboratory in Bern was also intended to obtain absolute dating in a variety of fields including botany, geology, archaeology, glaciology and sedimentology. The multiple skills and scientific profiles brought together in this laboratory project was underlined by the experts responsible for evaluating the first funding application.[14] In addition to funding the equipment and development of this method, the SNSF was also committed to funding the C14 dating requests submitted by researchers supported by the SNSF as part of their research, in order to encourage Swiss scientists to use this innovative tool.

Until the beginning of the 1970s, prehistory was considered to be a discipline whose modernity the SNSF was pleased to mention, due to the collaborations and exchanges that took place between archaeologists and natural scientists. The following quotation gives an idea of the perception of innovation as seen by the SNSF regarding archaeological practice at the beginning of the 1960s:

> In recent decades, a new 'style' of research has been affirming itself in many areas of science. Major projects can no longer even 'get off the ground' without cooperative work from veritable groups of scientists: a result of ever-increasing specialisation. The business of an excavation, for example, was in the last century the work of someone such as Schliemann, assisted by his wife and a few faithful handlers of the pick and shovel; today it is necessary that the archaeologist and the prehistorian collaborate with the physicist (in physical procedures to determine dates), with the botanist (in pollen analysis), with the specialist in dendrochronology (in the determination of annual layers in the trunks of trees), with the parasitologist (in the determination of the internal parasites of the inhabitants), with the entomologist–archaeologist (in the determination of insects for prior periods), with the palaeontologist and with the chemist[15] (von Muralt 1963, 13).

The modernity of archaeology was thus revealed by collaborations with other disciplines and by exchanges of tools and methods. In other words archaeologists reproduced in an exemplary manner the scientific model of teamwork that the SNSF had been promoting since its foundation in 1952.

Interdisciplinarity as a label?

A detailed analysis of the evolution of the perception of prehistory in the SNSF annual reports (see Delley forthcoming) reveals that prehistory was recognised as a model of collaboration as long as the word 'interdisciplinary' remained absent from the SNSF jargon. As a matter of fact, when the term 'interdisciplinary' appeared in Switzerland, at the beginning of the 1970s, the word began to be used to designate new scientific configurations in the domains of physics (Baumann 1972, 59), as well as in the educational sciences, psychology and sociology (Biaudet 1973, 42–44; 1974, 49–50; 1975, 50–51), although not in prehistory. This would remain the case until the 2000s. It seems therefore that from the 1970s onwards, the 'team spirit' and the 'auxiliary sciences' model adopted by prehistorians from the first decades of the twentieth century was no longer seen as innovative and modern by the SNSF. Moreover, we understand by this detour that the word 'interdisciplinary' and then 'interdisciplinarity' as used by the SNSF, before referring to a scientific practice that privileged collaborations between fields of research, was employed as a label by science administrators – first in the USA and then in Europe (see Feuerhahn and Reubi forthcoming) – to brand and give visibility to practices judged modern and innovative. Why the collaborations implemented by prehistorians during the first half of the twentieth century were no longer considered as modern in the 1970s needs to be clarified. This is a vast issue that we will not deal with here.[16]

Swiss prehistorians, for their part, have been using the words 'interdisciplinary' and 'pluridisciplinary' at their convenience since the 1970s to describe their well-established ways of carrying out research between archaeology and other scientific domains. Some early occurrences of the term include that of 1969 by the French prehistorian Annette Laming-Emperaire, who used the word several times in an article devoted to the relations between prehistory, the humanities and the natural sciences, while the question arose within the CNRS of bringing together prehistory and Quaternary studies (Laming-Emperaire 1969). In 1975, Swiss archaeologist Christine Osterwalder, who was the secretary of C14 commission of the Bern 14C Laboratory, used 'interdisziplär' to speak of collaborations between archaeology and physics in the definition of the next 14C dating programme (Osterwalder 1975, 63–64). The same year, Swiss prehistorian Michel Egloff used 'pluridisciplinary' to talk about the methods chosen in the Auvernier excavations in the 1960s and 70s.[17] Many other examples would certainly be revealed if specific research were undertaken into the occurrences of the term in correspondence, reports, articles and monographs produced by European prehistorians from the 1960s on. At the same time, the last of these developed other designations that revealed the considerable interweaving and intersections between archaeology and other disciplines in their daily practices. Thus the term archaeometry, invented in the 1960s, reflected new institutional and editorial situations (see Delley and Plutniak 2018, 1). It was followed by archaeobotany, archaeozoology, ethnoarchaeology and bioarchaeology over the following decades. Alongside the realities imposed by the politics of science, it appears therefore that archaeologists have defined their own concepts, configurations and designations that report on what science administrators have designated as 'interdisciplinary'.

One of the specificities of modernity is the possibility of being reinvented at any time. This is particularly evident when one looks at the history of interdisciplinarity. We observe for example different moments in which interdisciplinarity was particularly present in the SNSF discourse. We have spoken of the 1970s, but the 1990s and 2000s correspond to a second important period. In terms of prehistory, research laboratories, where collaborations between archaeology and different fields of the natural sciences had been a tradition for several decades, suddenly labelled the interdisciplinary dimension of their practice. This is the case for instance of the *Integrative Prähistorische und Naturwissenschaftliche Archäologie* (IPNA), which, at the beginning of 2000s, established collaborations between prehistory and other sciences as a new scientific model labelled as 'interdisciplinary', whereas the institutionalisation of collaborations between prehistory and the natural sciences at the University of Basel dates back to the 1950s (Jagher, Röder and Schibler 2012). To take measure of this phenomenon, it is worth remembering that already in the 1920s such hybrid research centres considered as innovative began to combine prehistory and the natural sciences. This is the case of the Urgeschichtliches Forschungsinstitut in Tübingen founded in 1921 by the geologist Robert Rudolph Schmidt, which promoted the use of natural sciences such as geology, sedimentology, botany and palynology in the study of preserved wetland habitats in southern Germany (Strobel 2003; Schöbel 2011). We should also mention the Biologisch–Archeologisch Instituut established around the same time by Albert Egges van Giffen (1884–1973) at the University of Groningen. This institute brought together archaeologists, botanists and sedimentologists to study archaeological sites preserved in the peat bogs of the Netherlands (Eickhoff 2005).

Finally, at the beginning of the 2000s, the SNSF adopted new funding tools explicitly designed to support 'interdisciplinary' projects, whereas until then funding applications had to be submitted in sections that corresponded to strict disciplinary subdivisions. By means of 'interdisciplinary' or 'ERC' grants, archaeologists, like all other categories of researchers, have been encouraged to tag and demonstrate their inter- or transdisciplinarity. In these recent configurations, prehistorians have managed to gain a new visibility in the SNSF annual reports. This can be measured by the titles given to the research projects, where the words 'inter-' or 'transdisciplinary', which were rarely present before, are now clearly visible as a label that gives more credibility to the research.

Conclusions

Many questions remain regarding interdisciplinarity in the history of Swiss prehistoric research; in this analysis, we have shed light on a few of them. Firstly, as we have seen, it is crucial to distinguish between the analysis of the word, on the one hand, and that of the practice, on the other. In the case of wetland archaeology, we showed that the emergence of the words 'interdisciplinary' and then 'interdisciplinarity' occurred in a context in which transversal or combined approaches between archaeologists and other scientists had become a tradition. To that extent, we were able to establish that as long as the word 'interdisciplinarity' was absent from the vocabulary of the SNSF reports, it was relatively easy for prehistorians to be recognised for the originality of their approach. Indeed, until the 1970s, crossing the boundaries of disciplines was not common, especially within the humanities, and as such, prehistory was something exceptional.

As has been shown, a change was taking place in the 1970s, when the word 'interdisciplinary' made its first appearance in the SNSF reports. Strangely enough, from that moment and until the beginning of the 2000s, the word was not mobilised to define the transversal approaches that continue to be developed in prehistory. Other disciplines and projects were cited as examples of interdisciplinary practices in the domains of physics, psychology, sociology and the educational sciences. As we pointed out, this change in configuration is intimately linked to the role of the politics of science, which is defining what is innovation and scientific modernity. Expressions such as 'groundbreaking', which is now currently used in funding offers, summarise this idea of modernity, as did 'teamwork' between the 1950s and 1960s. These expressions, together with 'interdisciplinarity', have been used at different times to label innovation and modernity in science. What was at stake around the 1970s, from the perspective of science administrators, was that prehistory was not as innovative as it had been 20 years before. This was despite the fact that the prehistorians' practice would have fitted in perfectly with the idea of interdisciplinarity introduced in those years with the aim of combining different kinds of sciences. To put it simply, it seems that the *tradition* of transversality in the prehistorians' practice – which had reflected the intersection between archaeology and other disciplines for a century – was somehow incompatible with the idea of *modernity* and *innovation* conveyed by interdisciplinarity in the 1970s.

At the same time, prehistorians who were then very well trained in the practice of these transversal approaches, since the 1960s–70s have developed other terms and configurations of science – *i.e.* archaeometry, archaeobotanic, archaeozoology, etc. – that have progressively stabilised their long tradition of collaboration with other sciences. If these developments revealed the considerable experience of prehistorians in a configuration of science that they considered to be part of a long practice, they also probably contributed to disconnecting them from the formal expectations of the science policy makers, for whom the important thing was not tradition but innovation and modernity.

To conclude, it appears that prehistory constitutes an interesting case study for reflecting on the history of interdisciplinarity in science. This is not because prehistorians appear to have always been interdisciplinary in their approaches, but rather because the history of prehistory offers long-term perspectives for reflections on the question of interdisciplinarity and its multiple significations and uses.

Notes

1 This contribution summarises the argumentation of a paper written as part of the *Politics and Practices of Interdisciplinarity* research programme supervised by Wolf Feuerhahn and Rafael Mandressi between 2015–2018 at the Centre Koyré in Paris. The article will be published under the title 'Des sciences auxiliaires à l'interdisciplinarité: les recherches préhistoriques en Suisse et la création du Fonds national de la recherche scientifique' in a volume entitled *L'interdisciplinarité: une histoire* to be published by Les Editions de l'EHESS.
2 In Great Britain and Scandinavia, several scholars also considered these approaches as relevant (see Smith 1997 and Kristiansen 2002).
3 Marc-Rodolphe Sauter used this term in a research proposal submitted in 1966 to the Swiss National Science Foundation for the analysis of the results from the excavation of the settlement of Auvernier. Archives of the Swiss Society of Prehistory, Basel – Commission of the motorway excavations (see Delley 2015a, 155–157).
4 In Geneva, for example, the Institute of Prehistory established in 1949 by the anthropologist and prehistorian Marc-Rodolphe Sauter belongs to the Faculty of Science.
5 In this regard, Swiss prehistorian Walter Guyan explains that, for a long time, prehistorians had been naturalists (*Naturforscher*). But gradually, reports Guyan, it was recognised that these scientific approaches did not provide sufficient answers to prehistoric questions. Thus the historical orientation of research emerged with its comparative formal science and stylistic analysis (Guyan 1946, 100). In order to distinguish an approach based on the humanities from a naturalistic approach, Guyan used the term *Geschichtswissenschaft* or *geschichtliche Forschungsrichtungen, i.e.* historical science or directions on historical research (Guyan 1946, 99–100). For Guyan, it was the intersection of the

study of soil types (geology, hence naturalistic), and that of cultural groups (form and style, hence historical), that characterised the work of the prehistorian (Guyan 1946, 102).

6 It should be noted here that ten years before, the German archaeologist Hans Reinerth had also called on the expertise of Neuweiler to determine wood samples from the pile dwellings of Germany and Switzerland. Vogt, who took over the lake-dwelling dossier in the 1950s, therefore followed forms of collaboration initiated before the Second World War by the German *Pfahlbauforschung* (Delley 2015a, 54–56).
7 'Natural science and prehistory'.
8 Translation G. Delley.
9 Translation G. Delley.
10 Translation G. Delley.
11 Translation G. Delley.
12 'the pile-dwelling problem or debate'.
13 Translation G. Delley.
14 An expert report dated May 23, 1956 talks about a partnership between disciplines, which 'guarantees the success of the research', File No. 962, Division I, Archives of the Swiss National Science Foundation, Bern.
15 Translation Y. Overfield Shaw.
16 Elements of explanation in relation to the political and economic situation of Swiss archaeology in the decades between the 1970s and the 2000s are proposed in Delley forthcoming.
17 Egloff complains about the absence of publication of these spectacular discoveries. He says: 'These excavations [...] must be followed by high-quality publications, which alone will justify the investment made as well as the choice of methods employed – otherwise the house will remain roofless and modern archaeology, a pluridisciplinary science, will not have provided better results than those of the 19th century' (Minutes of the Archaeological Commission for the construction of the N5 [motorway section], 16.5.1975. Archives Laténium. Translation G. Delley).

References

Bandi, H.-G. (1945) Archäologische Erforschung des zukünftiges Stauseegebietes Rossens-Broc. *Annuaire de la Société suisse de préhistoire* 36, 100–107.

Bandi, H.-G. (1954) Hundert Jahre Pfahlbauforschung in der Schweiz. *Revue universitaire suisse* XXVII, 185–194.

Baumann, E. (1972) *Fonds national suisse de la recherche scientifique. Rapport (1e janvier–31 décembre 1972)*. Berne, OFES.

Bertsch, K. (1928) Klima, Pflanzendecke und Besiedlung Mitteleuropas in vor- und frühgeschichtlicher Zeit nach den Ergebnissen der pollenanalytischen Forschung. *Bericht der Römisch-Germanischen Kommission* 18, 1–67.

Biaudet, J.-C. (1973) *Fonds national suisse de la recherche scientifique. Rapport (1e janvier–31 décembre 1973)*. Berne, OFES.

Biaudet, J.-C. (1974) *Fonds national suisse de la recherche scientifique. Rapport (1e janvier–31 décembre 1974)*. Berne, OFES.

Biaudet, J.-C. (1975) *Fonds national suisse de la recherche scientifique. Rapport (1e janvier–31 décembre 1975)*. Berne, OFES.

Blanckaert, C. (2017) Nommer le préhistorique au XIXe siècle. Linguistique et transferts lexicaux. *Organon* 49, 57–103.

Callmer, J., Meyer, M., Struwe, R. and Theune-Vogt, C., eds (2006) *The Beginnings of Academic Pre- and Protohistoric Archaeology (1830–1930) in a European Perspective*. Berlin, Verlag Marie Leidorf (Berliner Archäologische Forschungen 2).

De Geer, G. (1934) Geology and geochronology. *Geografiska Annaler* 16, 1–52.
Delley, G. (2015a) Au-delà des chronologies. Des origines du radiocarbone et de la dendrochronologie à leur intégration dans les recherches lacustres suisses. *Archéologie Neuchâteloise 53*. Neuchâtel, Office du patrimoine et de l'archéologie.
Delley, G. (2015b) The long revolution of radiocarbon as seen through the history of Swiss lake-dwelling research. In G. Eberhardt and F. Link (eds) *Historiographical Approaches to Past Archaeological Research*, 95–114. Berlin, Edition Topoi.
Delley, G. (2016) Radiocarbon and archaeology: an innovative alliance in the post-WWII scientific field. In G. Delley, M. Díaz-Andreu, F. Djindjian, V. Fernández, A. Guidi and M.A. Kaeser (eds) *History of Archaeology - International Perspectives*, 207–211. British Archaeological Reports. Oxford, Archaeopress.
Delley, G. (forthcoming) Des sciences auxiliaires à l'interdisciplinarité: les recherches préhistoriques en Suisse et la création du Fonds national de la recherche scientifique. In W. Feuerhahn and R. Mandressi (eds) *L'interdisciplinarité: une histoire*. Paris, Éditions EHESS.
Delley, G. and Plutniak, S. (2018) History and sociology of science. In S.L. López Varela (ed.) *The Encyclopedia of Archaeological Sciences*. Oxford, John Wiley & Son.
Eickhoff, M. (2005) German Archaeology and National Socialism. Some historiographical remarks. *Archaeological Dialogues* 12 (1), 73–90.
Ferguson, C.W., Huber, B. and Suess, H.E. (1966) Determination of the age of Swiss lake dwellings as an example of dendrochronologically-calibrated radiocarbon dating. *Zeitschrift für Naturforschung* 21, 1173–1177.
Feuerhahn, W. and Reubi, S. (forthcoming) Interdisciplinarité, pluridisciplinarité...: émergence, dissémination et resémantisations d'un vocable et de pratiques. In W. Feuerhahn and R. Mandressi (eds) *L'interdisciplinarité: une histoire*. Paris, Éditions EHESS.
Fleury, A. and Joye, F. (2002) *Les débuts de la politique de la recherche en Suisse. Histoire de la création du Fonds national suisse de la recherche scientifique 1934-1952*. Genève, Librairie Droz.
Guyan, W.U. (1946) Naturwissenschaft und Urgeschichte. *Annuaire de la Société suisse de préhistoire* 37, 99–110.
Guyan, W.U., ed. (1954) *Mensch und Urlandschaft der Schweiz*. Zurich, Büchergilde Gutenberg.
Guyan, W.U., Levi, H., Ludi, W., Speck, J., Tauber, H., Troels-Smith, J., Vogt, E. and Welten, M., eds (1955) *Das Pfahlbauproblem*. Basel, Birkhäuser Verlag.
Heer, O. (1866) *Die Pflanzen der Pfahlbauten*. Zürich, Zürcher und Furrer.
Heer, O. (1872) *Flachs und Flachskultur im Althertum. Eine kulturhistorische Skizze*. Zürich, Zürcher und Furrer.
Hult, E. (1936) Jahresringe und Jahrestemperatur. *Geografiska Annaler* 18, 277–297.
Jagher, R., Röder, B. and Schibler, J. (2012) Geschichte der Ur- und Fruhgeschichtlichen - und Provinzial römischen sowie der Naturwissenschaftlichen Archäologie an der - Universität Basel. In A. Laschinger and A. Kaufmann-Heinimann (eds) *Knochen, Scherben und Skulpturen. 100 Jahre Archäologie an der Universität Basel*, 25–33. Bale, Département des sciences de l'Antiquité de l'Universite de Bâle.
Kaeser, M.-A. (2004) *Les Lacustres. Archéologie et mythe national*. Lausanne, Presses polytechniques et universitaires romandes.
Kristiansen, K. (2002) The birth of ecological archaeology in Denmark: history and research environments 1850–2002. In A. Fischer and K. Kristiansen (eds) *The Neolithisation of Denmark. 150 Years of Debate*, 11–31. Poole, Orca Book.
Laming-Emperaire, A. (1969) Préhistoire, sciences humaines et sciences de la nature. *Bulletin de la Société préhistorique française. Comptes rendus des séances mensuelles* 66 (6), 166–171.
Leroi-Gourhan, A. (1952) Discours de M.A. Leroi-Gourhan, Président entrant. *Bulletin de la Société préhistorique française* 1952 (1), 5–8.

Lüdi, W. (1935) *Das Grosse Moos im westschweizerischen Seeland und die Geschichte seiner – Entstehung.* Bern, Verlag Hans Huber.
Lüdi, W. (1955) Beitrag zur Kenntnis der Vegetationsverhaltnisse im Schweizerischen Alpenvorland wahrend der Bronzezeit. In W. Guyan (ed.) *Das Pfahlbauproblem*, 92–109. Monographien zur Ur- und Früh-geschichte der Schweiz 11. Basel, Birkhäuser Verlag.
Lüdi, W. (1956) Die vorgeschichtlichen Pfahlbauten als naturwissenschaftliches Problem. *Bericht über das Geobotanische Forschungsinstitut Rübel in Zürich für das Jahr 1955* 1955, 108–136.
Neuweiler, E. (1905) Die prähistorischen Pflanzenreste Mitteleuropas: mit besonderer – Berücksichtigung der Schweizerischen Funde. *Vierteljahrsschrift der Naturforschenden Gesellschaft in Zürich* 50, 23–134.
Neuweiler, E. (1908) Pflanzenreste aus der römischen Niederlassung Vindonissa. *Vierteljahrsschrift der Naturforschenden Gesellschaft in Zürich* 53, 398–407.
Neuweiler, E. (1910) Untersuchungen über die Verbreitung prähistorischer Hölzer in der – Schweiz: Beitrag zur Geschichte unseres Waldes. *Vierteljahrsschrift der Naturforschenden Gesellschaft in Zürich* 55, 156–202.
Osterwalder, C. (1975) *14C Kommission. Rapport de gestion de la Société suisse des sciences humaines.* Bern, Société suisse des sciences humaines.
Reinerth, H. (1922) Die Pfahlbauten des Bodensees im Lichte der neuesten Forschung. *Schriften des Vereins für Geschichte des Bodensees und seiner Umgebung* 50, 56–72.
Rückert, A.M. (1998) Pfahlbauleute und Nationalismus 1920–1945. In U. Altermatt, C. Bosshart-Pfluger and A. Tanner (eds) *Die Konstruktion einer Nation. Nation und Nationalisierung in der Schweiz, 18.–20. Jahrhundert*, 87–100. Zurich, Cronos.
Sauter, M.R. (1954) Un jubilé: 1854–1954. Centenaire de la découverte des palafittes. *Archives suisses d'anthropologie générale* 19, 115–116.
Schöbel, G. (2011) Von der Steinzeitsiedlung zum Furstengrabhugel – herausragende archäologische Forschungen der 1920er und 1930er Jahre am Federsee und an der Heuneburg in Sudwestdeutschland. In E. Schallmayer (ed.) *Archäologie und Politik. Archäologische Ausgrabungen der 30er und 40er Jahre des 20. Jahrhunderts im zeitgeschichtlichen Kontext*, 75–120. Bonn, Selbstverl. des Landesamtes für Denkmalpflege Hessen.
Smith, P.J. (1997) Grahame Clark's new archaeology: the Fenland Research Committee and Cambridge Prehistory in the 1930s. *Antiquity* 71, 11–30.
Stokar, W. and Zotz, L. (1938) Die Beziehungen der Vorgeschichtskunde zur Naturwissenschaft. *Wiener Prähistorische Zeitschrift* 25, 4–19.
Strobel, M. (2003) Hans Reinerth und Gustav Riek- Modernitätsflüchtlinge in einer ungewissen Wissenschaft. *Arbeits- und Forschungsberichte zur Sächsischen Bodendenkmalpflege* 43, 443–461.
Suess, H. and Strahm, C. (1970) The Neolithic of Auvernier, Switzerland. *Antiquity* 44, 91–99.
Troels-Smith, J. (1956) Neolithic period in Switzerland and Denmark. *Science* 124 (3237), 876–879.
Vaufrey, R. (1941) L'organisation des recherches et des études préhistoriques en France. *La Revue scientifique* 10, 483–518.
Vogt, E. (1951) Das steinzeitliche Uferdorf Egolzwil 3 (Kt. Luzern). Bericht über die Ausgrabung 1950 *Zeitschrift für Schweizerische Archäologie und Kunstgeschichte* 12, 193–215.
Welten, M. (1955) Pollenanalytische Untersuchungen uiber die neolithischen Siedlungsverhaltnisse am Burgaschisee. In W. Guyan (ed.) *Das Pfahlbauproblem*, 61–88. Monographien zur Ur- und Frühgeschichte der Schweiz 11. Zurich, Archéologie Suisse.

Chapter 7

In search of interdisciplinarity in Portuguese archaeology: notes on the 1960s

Ana Cristina Martins

> *Archaeology is no longer a hobby*;
> it became a domain with rigorous methodology.
> Archaeology *requires a long learning with experts.* [...].
> The *archaeologist working alone is outdated*
>
> (III Curso... 1970, 313. Our italics)

Abstract

Beginning with the question of whether there had been any kind of interdisciplinarity in Portuguese archaeology during the 1960s, this chapter examines some of the situations of that decade through the analysis of certain episodes and the pages of the journal O Arqueólogo Português *(The Portuguese Archaeologist), published by the Museu Nacional de Arqueologia (National Museum of Archaeology) in Lisbon since 1895. It aims to assess the extent to which the older generation of Portuguese archaeologists understood and applied the new theories and methods arriving from abroad, including interdisciplinarity. It also analyses the role played by the 'Transition Generation'/'Three Pillars' in training the succeeding generation in new theories and methods, with special focus on interdisciplinarity. Finally, the chapter reflects on whether the presumed interdisciplinarity claimed by many actors from these three generations was really an interdisciplinary approach or, in contrast, a multidisciplinary one.*

Keywords: interdisciplinarity; archaeology; *O Arqueólogo Português*; 1960s; 'Transition Generation'/'Three Pillars'; Portugal.

Introduction

In this article we follow the historian and philosopher of science Olga Pombo in her understanding of 'interdisciplinarity' as the combination of various academic disciplines working in an 'intradisciplinary' way on one activity in order to establish an organisational unit crossing traditional scientific boundaries (Pombo 2008). As she herself states, 'it is extremely difficult to talk about interdisciplinarity nowadays [...] [since] it seems that no one knows exactly what it is' (2008, 9-10). Moreover, other authors have drawn 'attention to the "comedy" of pretending to be interdisciplinary when almost everyone understands that this is an unattainable goal – at least in the framework of the traditional scientific paradigm characterised by hyper specialisation and fragmentation of human knowledge about the world' (Heintz, Origgi and Sperber 2004, 9). However, Pombo's definition clearly marks the distinction between 'interdisciplinarity' and 'collaboration' (Pombo 2004, 31-32). 'Collaboration' refers to the pre-existence of a hierarchical way of producing science, although encompassing some negotiation. It means that there is a project led by the representatives of one academic discipline, who ask for 'collaboration' to clarify certain issues. Nothing is unexpected in archaeology, since it is a vast multi- and interdisciplinary academic field.

The need for 'interdisciplinarity' results from the long modern road to scientific specialisation. A long way filled with various narratives of crises and resistance and consisting of a permanent search for relationships and articulation between sciences revealed in multiple prefixes: *pluri*, *multi* (both denoting multiplicity) and *inter* and *trans* (indicating homogeneity) (Pombo 2008, 15). All these are prefixes (*i.e.* semiotics) that can clarify much about each concept (*i.e.* semantics). *Pluridisciplinarity* (or *multidisciplinarity*) means the 'collaboration' between two or more disciplines in order to analyse one problem together. This 'collaboration' is coordinated by one of the involved disciplines, often without real communication between them. *Interdisciplinarity* involves the search for convergent points of view (Pombo 2008, 14-15), *i.e.* for a synthesis demanding continuous teamwork and the reorganisation of research processes (Pombo 2004, 37-38), often in a context of hybridisation and intersection, understood by some authors as a *notion trompeuse* (Dogan and Pahre 1991, 155-160). Finally, *transdisciplinarity* implies the unification of disciplines and the building of a common language. This is the ultimate but less often attained goal in a scientific world that is still very segmented into its own specialisations with well-defined territories. Even so, it is stated that 'nobody knows exactly where is the frontier from which a certain practice – scientific or educational – becomes *interdisciplinary and not multidisciplinary, pluridisciplinary or transdisciplinary*' (Pombo 2004, 3). That is also why it is possible to state that the concept of 'interdisciplinarity' is – as are all the others – polysemic, illustrating the complex path from specialisation to the unity of science. In this context, 'interdisciplinarity' means *interspace*, *i.e.* an in-between position (Pombo 2004, 5). Moreover, as stated by Pombo (2008, 22-24), *interdisciplinarity* enriches science thanks to the transfer of concepts, questions and methods, as well as through an in-depth, stratigraphic analysis of realities. This transfer and analysis allow the emergence of new (post-modern) challenges to be studied, thus fulfilling the French philosopher Etienne Durand's (1921-2012) 'poetics of interdisciplinarity' (Durand in Pombo 2008, 21-24).

This chapter aims to provide an understanding of whether the archaeology practiced in Portugal during the 1960s assumed a clearly collaborative (*i.e.* pluridisciplinary) approach, or whether it began to take on some interdisciplinary insights. It was a crucial decade for this science in general, as archaeologists attempted to implement databases, new field and laboratory methodologies and conceptual frameworks such as 'interdisciplinarity' (Klein 1990, 56). It was then that certain theoretical and practical changes took place in Portuguese archaeology, mainly due to the presence of the German Archaeological Institute (Deutsches Archäologisches Institut, operating in Portugal from Madrid) at the excavation of the Chalcolithic hillfort of Zambujal (Parreira 1995, 227–211) and that of the Luso-French mission at the Roman site of Conimbriga (1964–1971) (Alarcão and Étienne 1974–1977). Cultural and scientific journals were crucial in this context, along with conferences, exhibitions and university courses. *O Arqueólogo Português* (*OAP*; *The Portuguese Archaeologist*) was one of those journals. Launched in 1895 by the Museu Etnológico Português (MEP/MNA; National Ethnologic Museum),[1] this journal is one of the oldest in the country devoted to the study, safeguarding and dissemination of knowledge, especially that of archaeology. More than that, it was one of the first journals to publish innovative approaches in archaeology written by young Portuguese archaeologists. In the framework of the analysis of interdisciplinarity, we will explore how 'interdisciplinarity' worked in Portuguese archaeology in the 1960s or whether, in contrast, 'collaboration' in the sense of *pluridisciplinarity* continued to prevail.

Previous practices in a nutshell

'Collaboration' is a substantial component of archaeology's DNA. Rooted deeply in philological, literary, architectural and artistic traditions, archaeology was genealogically entangled with antiquarian practices from the fifteenth to the eighteenth centuries, especially with Johann Joachim Winckelmann (1717–1768) (Harloe 2013, 14–29). The end of the eighteenth and the beginning of the nineteenth century opened the way to the birth of archaeology as an academic discipline (Díaz-Andreu 2007). This was especially possible due to the emergence of prehistoric studies methodologically connected to numismatics (Schlanger 2010; 2011), geology and zoology. These fields helped 'free archaeology from its [...] status as an auxiliary discipline to history [...] contributing to the emerging acceptance of the evolution of mankind' (Kristiansen 2009, 24). In the nineteenth and twentieth centuries, humanistic disciplines (*e.g.* history, ethnography, ethnology and anthropology), natural sciences (*e.g.* biology and medicine) and certain techniques (*e.g.* photography) also contributed to the establishment and development of archaeology. Additionally, the Three Age System gradually became standard practice in prehistoric studies and museum exhibitions after its publication (Rowley-Conwy 2007).

The contacts between archaeology and other disciplines were more collaboration exercises than interdisciplinary work. It stayed that way for most of the time until the 1940s and 1950s, when the new form of absolute dating and the *-isms* brought new theoretical and practical frameworks into archaeology. The time had come for a new 'revolution' in archaeology and the use of computer technology. It was during this period that archaeology became an innovative and inventive scientific discipline, if we look back at some of the coeval multidisciplinary approaches and attempts at interdisciplinarity (Born and Barry 2013, 6–8). Since then, archaeology has been transformed into a growing intersection of scientific fields that collaborate in order to solve archaeological questions, beginning with the understanding of original landscapes and ecosystems. However, it appears that it was necessary to wait until the end of the 1970s and the early 1980s to finally open up the way to a truly interdisciplinary approach that transcended collaborations. This was possible once the concept of 'interdisciplinarity' – the idea appeared in the 1920s and gained prominence in the 1960s – was coined in 1972 by the Organisation for Economic Cooperation and Development (Miller 2010, 2). This is perhaps the reason why some authors tend to root the concept in the labour economy: 'the hierarchical division of labour that characterises many kinds of interdisciplinarity is an arrangement that may favour the stability and boundedness of component disciplines and inhibit epistemic change. In this mode the service discipline(s) is commonly understood to be making up for or filling in for an absence or lack in the other, (master) discipline(s)' (Barry, Born and Weszkalnys 2008, 28–29). This period was followed by an almost simultaneous spread of scientific need for 'interdisciplinarity', despite the arrival, for example, of post-processual, interpretive approaches in archaeology (Thomas 2000, 3–4; Repko 2008, 17; Kluiving and Guttmann-Bond 2012, 14): 'The concept [...] gained prominence [...] to solve the problem of how knowledge can be unified and what the implications of such unity are for teaching and research in the universities' (Miller 2010, 1).

Interdisciplinarity in Portuguese archaeology: a brief overview

In 1958, a National Congress of Archaeology (CNA after its name in Portuguese) was organised for the first time in Portugal (Martins 2016, 92–95). Reading its proceedings, it is possible to find papers dealing with the relevance of an interdisciplinary approach in archaeology. Nonetheless, it was only at the end of the 1960s, as a result of the presence of the DAI Madrid (see introduction) and the efforts of the (mostly) Lisbon-based 'Transition Generation' – in a very positive, productive and challenging sense – that a new group of young archaeologists began to search for other models to follow. They were aware of the latest literature in the field, attended conferences and congresses, even if mainly in Portugal due to political and financial obstacles and restrictions. The 'Transition Generation' was composed of the so-called (by us) 'Three Pillars', *i.e.* those who played important roles in Portuguese archaeology, such as the physician, archaeologist, museum director and university professor Fernando de Almeida (1903–1979); the archaeologist, university professor, museologist and heritage manager João Manuel Bairrão Oleiro (1923–2000); and the economist and archaeologist Eduardo da Cunha Serrão (1906–1991).

Contrary to what could have been expected, considering their somewhat leading roles in Portuguese archaeology, it was not the Faculty of Letters of the University of Coimbra or that of Lisbon (FL-UL)[2] or even the prestigious journal *OAP* that led the process towards interdisciplinarity. This role was fulfilled by the journal of the Sociedade Martins Sarmento (Martins Sarmento Society), a nineteenth-century private erudite society established in 1881 in Guimarães, in the northern part of the country. The journal was directed by the society's president, Colonel Mário Cardozo (1889–1982), who was an open-minded person with a concern for heritage. It was he who published the first articles signed by the young University of Coimbra (UC) professor Jorge de Alarcão (1934–) and the young University of Lisbon student Vítor Oliveira Jorge (1948–). Both were subsequently to introduce new archaeological specialities, make significant inputs and set up innovative working groups in the country: Jorge Alarcão in classical archaeology and Vítor Oliveira Jorge in prehistoric and protohistoric archaeology. Through their activity, they placed the Universities of Coimbra and Porto at the forefront of their specialties in the country (Martins 2016).

Although it did not stand out on its own in this field, this chapter will mainly focus on the *OAP* and on how it influenced the introduction and dissemination of 'interdisciplinarity' in Portuguese archaeology. It was (and still is) the major reference journal in Portuguese archaeology and is published by the MNA, whose director was always the full professor of archaeology at the FL-UL. This means that in the 1960s and 1970s, Fernando de Almeida played one of the core roles in Portuguese archaeology, as he was the head of archaeology at the FL-UL and director of the MNA. He was also the president of the country's oldest and most prestigious private society for heritage safeguarding, the Associação dos Arqueólogos Portugueses (AAP; Association of Portuguese Archaeologists), based in Lisbon since 1863. During de Almeida's presidency, the AAP was revitalised and opened its doors to new generations of archaeologists. Together with the Serviços Geológicos de Portugal (SGP; Geological Survey of Portugal) (1918) and the Archaeology Section of the Sociedade de Geografa de Lisboa (SGL; Geographical Society of Lisbon) (1895), the FL-UL, MNA and AAP were the main places where a group of young archaeologists connected to Fernando de Almeida and Eduardo da Cunha Serrão began to grow intellectually and professionally, at least as far as Lisbon was concerned. Therefore, a thorough analysis of the OAP's content shows that, despite it not having played the leading role, it did in fact contribute to the development of this science according to international theoretical and methodological standards. This was because the young scholars at the time used it as a means of publishing their first articles, in this way contributing to the introduction, assertion and development of interdisciplinarity in Portuguese archaeology. The decision to focus on the OAP also makes it possible to contextualise this process from different institutional points of view.

Collaboration

An analysis of the content of the OAP volumes published between the mid-1950s and the end of the 1970s, a period that coincides with the origin of interdisciplinarity in science (Hoffmann-Riem 2008; Schmidt 2008), allows us to reach some conclusions regarding the evolution of interdisciplinarity in Portugal. Firstly, there are no references to 'interdisciplinarity' as a term in the *OAP*, as it was not established in an academic context until 1972. However, it may have been known, as the idea of 'interdisciplinarity' was already being referred to in the 1920s (see above), although it was not generally included in the Portuguese language dictionaries published during the decades discussed in this section. This means that the term was still officially ignored by academics and unknown to most of society. At the same time, these dictionaries (including those published early in the twentieth century) included the concept of *collaboration* as a synonym for *cooperation*, *i.e.* 'working together with one or more persons, especially on a literary or scientific monograph' (Séguier 1910, 293). However, in order to explain the absence of 'interdisciplinarity' from later dictionaries (even in the 1970s) and the *OAP*, it is important to know whether it was being introduced and systematically applied in other countries or at least in the main western archaeological schools. It would also be interesting to see whether the concept was somehow already present in the Portuguese academic milieu, even if unofficially.

The concept of 'interdisciplinarity' was known in economic and social science circles where it seems to have emerged in the 1920s (Sills 1986/2016, 17–18). Furthermore, the Portuguese journal *Análise Social* (*Social Analysis*) was to be founded in 1963 by the then recently established Gabinete de Investigações Sociais (Cabinet for Social Research). The journal's title might seem unexpected in the context of Portugal's internal political agenda, which was dominated by a totalitarian regime that was generally unfavourable to social analysis, as it could not be controlled by the government. However, its publication was possible as universities maintained a considerable degree of autonomy and many professors encouraged the adoption of new scientific approaches, especially those that were being generated in the French and Anglo-Saxon historical and sociological schools (Cruz 2000, 466–468). Even so, there is no reference to 'interdisciplinarity' in the first issue of *Análise Social*. Conversely, the word 'collaboration' (understood as *pluridisciplinarity*) did appear, being used in the sense of *interrelation*, *interconnection* and *interaction*. The presence of the prefix 'inter' in the journal would suggest the existence of a common ground of analysis, *i.e.* the search for the practice of 'interdisciplinarity', although this was still uncommon at the time. The same is true for the *OAP*, in which it is possible to observe an increasing number of papers dealing with 'collaboration' research work, mainly in the areas of prehistoric studies, conservation and restoration.

Despite the growing interest of academics and students in specialising abroad, the main actors of this process in archaeology in the country were foreign scholars, especially German archaeologists. Nevertheless, the first interesting idea to be found in the *OAP* is the emphasis placed on one of the oldest, although subsequently almost forgotten, interactive practices: 'collaboration' with local actors such as priests, schoolmasters, doctors, lawyers, landlords, journalists, photographers, employees of museums and other institutions, etc. (Almeida 1956, 111–116). The importance of collaboration was underlined by the MNA's future director (1967–1973), Fernando de Almeida, who, thanks to his personal and professional power and influence, opened up the way for a new generation of Portuguese archaeologists, motivating and enabling them in the accomplishment of their projects. He considered collaboration especially valuable, particularly in classical archaeology, which encompassed the 'collaboration' of numismatists, epigraphists, philologists, historians, architects and museologists (Coelho 1971, 167–180). This situation could explain the existence of different forms of 'collaboration' and an inherent (unofficial) hierarchy, neither of which was acknowledged as such by their actors.

The excavation of the Escoural cave (near Évora city, Alentejo region, Portugal) is an example of collaboration in Portuguese archaeology. The anthropological finds from the first excavations were examined at the Anthropological Institute of the University of Oporto (UP). The drawings were executed by Virgílio dos Reis Cadete, a proficient book translator from Verbo publishers (Lisbon), who is much less known for his drawings, and Francelina Gonçalves Rodrigues (Santos and Ferreira 1969, 62), who studied painting at the Escola Superior de Belas-Artes de Lisboa (High School for Fine Arts of Lisbon) between 1940 and 1950.

Pluridisciplinary collaboration

Another form of 'collaboration' consisted of the participation of Portuguese and foreign professors, young scholars and students in archaeological excavations. This demonstrates that, despite being totalitarian, the 'Estado Novo' (New State) regime did not completely obstruct scientific, technological and cultural contacts with other countries (Lopes 2018). Apart from these irregular episodes, there was a cumulative number of systematic types of 'pluridisciplinary' collaborations aimed at understanding certain archaeological questions and finding new research topics. However, the results enriched mostly foreign research projects. From this point of view, there was no real and systematic 'collaboration'. Looking at the several volumes of the *OAP* published between the mid-1950s and the mid-1970s, we note the prevalence of 'collaborations' with fields such as geology and zoology in articles related to prehistoric research (twenty-five examples). This can be compared to those in the archaeology of later periods (eight examples), in particular ancient Rome in which there were 'collaborations' with epigraphy and numismatics. This is not surprising considering the genealogical links between prehistory and geology, in contrast to those of classical archaeology, which arose from philology, epigraphy, numismatics, architecture and the history of art. In addition, this suggests that archaeology gained much from the continuous proximity of prehistorians to other human, social, natural and technological academic disciplines. However, this does not mean that all Portuguese archaeologists fully understood the inferences and consequences of the new theoretical approaches such as structuralism and functionalism or even processualism when applied to archaeology. On the contrary, most archaeologists in Portugal showed little interest in theoretical approaches to their discipline before the 1970s.

The majority of the 25 examples of collaboration in prehistoric studies were related to the need to learn about palaeoenvironments and improve understanding of the ways of life in ancestral human communities. This is clearly the case of the first examples of 'collaboration' identified in the mid-1950s that were linked to geology. Archaeologists' collaborations with geologists, geographers and geomorphologists were strengthened from the 1940s, thanks to the presence in Portugal of foreign researchers and professors such as Henri Breuil (1877–1961), Pierre Birot (1909–1984) and Georges Zbyzewski (1909–1999). The latter was a Russian-born French geologist and prehistorian who lived and worked in Portugal for many years right up until his death. Between 1952 and 1976, he was invited to collaborate by Ernâni Barbosa, a research fellow from the governmental Instituto de Alta Cultura (Institute for High Culture). He 'kindly classified the shell debris from the site of "castro da Pedra de Ouro" as belonging to different species' (Barbosa 1956, 83), while working on the Geological Map of the country. A logical request since archaeologists should be leaving

> to our colleagues specialised in typology the concern to review and clarify this question [debris of biface use] whose importance cannot be underestimated. Being the purpose of Prehistory to reconstruct the evolution of the human civilisations which preceded us, we believe we should not neglect any observation and interpretation brought from all (not that many) the available sources (Oliver 1956, 109. Our italics).

Gradually, other concerns were also included in the complex academic 'collaboration'. As director of the MNA, Manuel Heleno[3] (1894–1970) was well aware of the need to achieve a solid and permanent 'collaboration' in the conservation and restoration of museum artefacts. The museum did not have enough experts in those fields. Therefore, he sought them outside the museum. This was the case with the consolidation and restoration of the mosaics from the Roman site of Conimbriga, near the university city of Coimbra, or the ruins of the Roman villa of Torre de Palma (Monforte) with the team from the *Opificio delle Pietre Dure* of Florence to survey the discovered mosaics and transport them to the museum. With a nationalistic approach specific to those times, Manuel Heleno stated that it would be possible to

> introduce to Portugal new methods of conservation and restoration, whose success will determine the safeguarding of a significant part of the *national archaeological heritage.//* [...] being the first attempt in Portugal to consolidate and restore in situ Lusitanian-Roman mosaics and release them from the mask of sand that obscures and damages their beauty (Heleno 1956, 253–255. Our italics).

The First National Congress of Archaeology in Portugal

There was a long gap in the publication of the *OAP* between 1956 and 1962. There were several reasons for this. The fact that its director, Manuel Heleno, was intensely involved in the long and intricate process of transferring the MNA to its new site (which never took place), while ingloriously fighting against ceding a part of the museum's building to the Ministry of Maritime Affairs, were surely not the least of them. Another was that he also became deeply involved in the organisation of the First CNA, whose global aim – *i.e.* the diffusion of new archaeological theories, methods and techniques and the establishment of personal contacts between Portuguese and foreign researchers – was to be achieved in the near future (Martins 2017, 87–98).

After a break of half a decade, the newest edition of *OAP* (now in its second series) appeared in 1962, the same year the First Archaeological Colloquium of Oporto (ACP) was held in Porto and Guimarães. This colloquium was organised in the absence of the Second National Archaeology Conference, which would take place in 1969 (Anonymous 1970a). The first volume of the third *OAP* series (1967–1977) is the most relevant for the topic of this chapter, as it includes three articles covering scientific 'collaboration', two in prehistoric archaeology and one in classical studies. This confirms that collaborations were becoming more frequent in Portuguese archaeology, mainly due to a scientific policy and strategy established in the MNA by its new director, Fernando de Almeida, who was appointed after Manuel Heleno's retirement. Additionally, a growing number of enthusiastic young scholars was demanding the study, debate and application of new theoretical understandings and field methods.

The 1967 *OAP* volume shows that something was really changing in Portuguese archaeology, perhaps as a delayed echo of the first CNA final resolutions (Actas e Memórias 1970, 367–368). The academic milieu was beginning to witness an increasing number of projects, papers and monographs jointly signed by Portuguese and foreign experts from fields such as epigraphy, geology and zooarchaeology. Nevertheless, there had also been some attempts to collaborate with other disciplines. This is suggested by the narrative of two of the authors, the archaeologist Jean Roche (1913–2008),[4] a researcher at the Centre National de la Recherche Scientifique (CNRS) and the Laboratoire de Paléontologie des Vertébrés et de Paléontologie Humaine in the Sorbonne, and the geologist and prehistorian Octávio da Veiga Ferreira (1917–1997) from the SGP. Both mentioned that the physician, anthropologist, prehistorian and UP professor, António A.E. Mendes Correia (1888–1960),

> wishing to obtain more solid data to establish an *absolute chronology* of shell mounds asked us to date the coals by the *Carbon 14 method*. This work was done by the *Laboratoire l'Électronique Physique du Centre d'Études Nucléaires de Saclay*[5], in France. […]//2 - *analysis of fauna and its paleoclimatic effects*//3 – *anthropological study*[6] carried out by *Mademoiselle D. Ferembach*[7] (Roche and Ferreira 1967, 32 34. Our italics).

In addition to clarifying how Portuguese archaeology followed the news concerning absolute chronology, the excerpt above also informs us of the international institutional and individual networks established by some Portuguese researchers. It also shows what types of analyses were requested in the 1960s and their aims, in this case to gain an insight into the palaeoclimate in order to understand the initial environment of humankind.

The importance of absolute dating and physical anthropology analyses was also highlighted by the requests from other Portuguese scholars. This was the case of the prehistorian Manuel Farinha dos Santos (1921–2001), who mentioned that the anthropologic finds from the Escoural cave were to be studied by the Anthropological Institute of the University of Oporto and the carbonised material sent to the laboratory for absolute dating (Santos 1967, 108). Together with Fernando de Almeida, Octávio da Veiga Ferreira also pointed out the relevance of similar analyses, reporting that 'The *seeds* found [in a Lusitanian-Roman well] were *identified by the expert from the National Agronomic Station*, A.R. Pinto da Silva' (Almeida and Ferreira 1967, 59. Our italics). However, it is interesting to note that, in contrast to these last two examples, the radiocarbon dating of the finds from shell mounds (see above) requested by Mendes Correia was only carried out by foreign (*i.e.* French) institutions and individuals. It has not been possible to find an ultimate explanation for this. Even so, it is likely that the closeness of Mendes Correia to European scientific institutes, laboratories and university departments could have enabled such requests. On the other hand, it is important to note that some of the better equipped research units were located abroad. Moreover, it was still not possible to carry out some of the analyses in Portugal, simply because the human or material resources did not exist at that time. Nevertheless, it is unclear how Mendes Correia was able to pay for the analyses he requested from outside the country. Perhaps it was thanks to the financial capacity of the institutions he was leading or other funding obtained from the IAC or the Fundação Calouste Gulbenkian (FCG; Calouste Gulbenkian Foundation).

Deutsches Archäologisches Institut

The volume of the *OAP* published in 1968 brought some novelties. One of them was related to a brief report on the excavation of the site of Zambujal (Torres Vedras municipality, Centro region, Portugal) that would open the way for a large number of articles to be published on the subject of 'collaboration' (Sangmeister, Schubart and Trindade 1968, 35–38). Although the paper was co-authored by Portuguese and foreign researchers, the leading scientific role had been assumed by Germans, albeit only unofficially, as the site was in Portugal. In addition, the actors and the results were to be shared by both the Portuguese and German teams. Moreover, it is important to note that the Zambujal site had already been transformed into a non-official archaeological field and laboratory working school. Excavated between 1964 and 1973, mainly thanks to a joint venture established between the DAI and the Institute of Prehistory of the University of Fribourg (IPUF), the site was able count on the collaboration of

> U. Heinberg, P. Kalb, E. Klemm, G. Lindemann, [...] H. Pereja, B. Sielmann, K. Spindler, Y. Vuilleumier, R. Wolf [...] and Miguel Requena and Fermin Garcia from the German Archaeological Institute of Madrid. E. Soergel studied the *animal bones* from the excavations of 1964 and 1966. As our guests for several weeks we had Dr. A. Dauber and his wife, Dr. P. Harbison, Mr. Herberg and his wife, Mrs. Françoise Treines, as well as several Portuguese students who visited us for some days (Sangmeister, Schubart and Trindade 1969, 71–114).

More than the International Archaeological Camps co-organised by the Mocidade Portuguesa (Portuguese Youth, the Portuguese version of the fascist and totalitarian

Italian, German and Spanish youth organisations) at the northern Portuguese Iron Age hillforts, the Zambujal site was considered by the youngest Portuguese archaeologists as *the* school. It was also the first example of an organised, long-term 'collaboration' in Portuguese archaeology based on a win-win approach. All its members contributed something and obtained something in return; either theoretical and practical archaeological knowledge or even data essential to the building of a new narrative of the country's past. In summer 1968, counting workers and scientific collaborators, 61 Portuguese, English, French, Irish and German researchers visited Zambujal (Sangmeister, Schubart and Trindade 1968, 36–37). In 1970, in the *OAP*'s fourth volume, the excavation's scientific directors described the 1968 campaign at Zambujal in detail, mentioning the name of each specialised collaborator, including two colleagues from the Central Institute for Conservation and Restoration in Madrid, an expert on animal bones from Freiburg, and a photographer (Sangmeistser, Schubart and Trindade 1970, 65–113), as if it were a truly pluridisciplinary effort of teamwork.[8] Thus, it seems that scientific research in archaeology was especially accepted when it involved the collaboration of experts from the natural sciences, as scientificity was still very closely related to the idea of 'measure(ment)'. Therefore, in the 1960s, archaeology in Portugal could be seen more as an ample ground for scientific 'collaboration' than an autonomous scientific discipline.

The second news item reported in the 1968 *OAP* dealt with the growing importance of underwater 'activities' in archaeology (Escavações 1968, 193–194). These 'activities' were undertaken by certified members of the Portuguese Youth Group Escola de Brigadas Especiais (School for Special Brigades) and the Centro Português de Actividades Submarinas (Portuguese Centre for Submarine Activities). The idea of 'underwater archaeology' was gradually being conceptualised and introduced into the Portuguese scientific lexicon (Notícias 1959, 12).[9]

1969: a turning point

This was a particularly important year for Portuguese culture, science and university life. Following the 'May 68' movement in France, Portuguese students requested that universities update their course programmes and that the material associated with them include their recommended bibliographies. They also requested the renewal of the lecturing staff and better classrooms. These demands emerged from a new democratic and liberal spirit nourished by a strong need for freethinking and a country without intellectual and cultural boundaries. These voices increased at the same pace as the disillusion that came with the failure of the Primavera Marcelista (Marcelo's Spring) between 1968 and 1970, a period characterised by political openness, economic liberalisation and social policy improvements (Rato 2000, 421–427). At the same time, thousands of people were being murdered in the colonial wars in Africa, compromising the future of new generations and discrediting Portuguese policy and the country's image abroad (Pélissier 2000, 159–163).

Subsequent to the student manifestation that took place at the University of Lisbon in 1962, and following the Parisian 'May 68', the University of Coimbra witnessed a general student strike on 17 April 1969 (Ferreira 2000, 553–555). This strike symbolised the profound disenchantment with national policy and the people's yearning for freedom of thought. However, only a completely new ideology and political agenda could accomplish that aim. The success of archaeology in Portugal also depended on this. Much had already been done and, although slowly, new theories (mainly structuralism and functionalism) and field and laboratory work were being introduced into the Portuguese archaeological milieu (Raposo 2011, 6). Gradually, a growing number of international collaborations was established. The FCG was increasingly sponsoring archaeological projects; young Portuguese students and scholars were travelling abroad and spending time at internationally reputed archaeological institutions. More frequently than ever, future Portuguese archaeologists were gaining access to specialist foreign archaeological literature, *i.e.* that published mainly by Anglo-Saxon and French authors. This meant that even though the country was still dominated by a totalitarian regime, Portuguese institutions such as the AAP were welcoming and promoting debates on the most varied archaeological topics.

The above described internal scenario seemed to appeal to and justify the organisation of a new kind of archaeological meeting: not a congress, not a colloquium, but a several-day seminar called 'Jornada(s)' in Portuguese. This term is possibly more than a change of name or the literal translation of the French *journée*; it could also suggest a conceptual and intellectual change in behaviour. Open to all those interested in archaeology, including students, the 'Jornadas' implied a permanent dialogue between speakers and attendees on a specific subject, regardless of their age and academic status. In addition, these 'Jornadas' were meant to 'analyse the latest scientific research, and prepare for that to come, both collectively and individually' (Jorge 1970, 15). This was somewhat unexpected, as Portugal was still under an authoritarian regime. Even more unusual was the fact that the First Archaeological 'Jornadas' took place not at a university, a state academy or a national or municipal museum, but at a civilian, private, scientific, cultural society. Of course, this was not an ordinary society, it was the AAP. However, looking at the venues of the first CNA and the several ACPs, one could have expected the 'Jornadas' to take place at a university, for example the UL, given the status and influence of Fernando de Almeida. Perhaps this was the best solution considering the country's political regime and the students' general strike in April 1969 (see above). At the AAP, Fernando de Almeida could easily decide to organise such a 'Jornada', as it was somehow considered to be neutral scientific and cultural territory (Martins 2016, 183–184).

Taking place between 3 and 5 November 1969, *i.e.* about half a year after the student movement at the University of Coimbra (see above), the 'Jornadas' were reported in different newspapers, emphasising the valuable collaboration between Portuguese archaeologists and their Spanish, French, German and English counterparts. These foreign colleagues included Antonio García y Bellido (1903–1972), Miquel Tarradell

(1920–1995), Hubert Newman Savory (1911–2001), Jean Roche, Jean Guilaine (1936–), Konrad Spindler (1939–2005) and Ignacio Barandiarán (1937–) (Primeiras Jornadas 1969, 304). The importance of most papers presented at the 'Jornadas' was such that the proceedings were published the following year. As expected from such an innovative scientific meeting, the first novelty in the proceedings of the 'Jornadas' was the presence, albeit minor, of papers written by both senior and junior scholars in the same publication. Despite this, most of the texts continued to follow the strongly descriptive and now outdated cultural-historical approach. Nevertheless, there was a significant improvement in the quality and number of illustrations, including drawings, photographs, maps and detailed stratigraphic profiles.

One of the papers in the proceedings of the 'Jornadas' emphasised the importance of rigorous stratigraphic analysis. Apart from debating the need for an objective and uniform descriptive archaeological vocabulary, the article, 'Estratigrafia' ('Stratigraphy'), written by the archaeologists Octávio da Veiga Ferreira and Carlos Tavares da Silva (1970), may have been, together with that published by Vítor Oliveira Jorge (1970), the first to include the concept of *interdisciplinarity*. Octávio da Veiga Ferreira's position should not surprise us, as he was one of the first in Portugal to understand and attempt to apply what could be considered 'interdisciplinarity' in archaeology. This was an objective he demonstrated, for instance, during his presentation of the fauna from a Mesolithic site at the IV International Congress of Pre- and Proto-Historic Sciences (Zaragoza, Spain, 1954) (Cardoso 1997). In these two articles, *interdisciplinarity* was needed to understand the daily life of ancient communities, which is why it should be jointly analysed by several academic disciplines. The article 'Estratigrafia' also mentioned the concept of social life, which was not particularly welcomed by the dominant political regime in the country, as it was always apprehensive about (almost) everything related to 'social' topics if it was not controlled by its own ideological agenda (Cruz 2000, 466–468):

> it is *urgent* [...] *to make archaeology interdisciplinary*, as already happens in other countries.// At every archaeological site *everything can talk* about the ancestral *social life* that took place there. From simple grains of sand to elaborately decorated vases, everything must be collected and *studied simultaneously*, not only by archaeologists, but also by geologists, zoologists, palaeobotanists, physicians, chemists, etc. In our case, there is a group of finds awaiting more detailed study by experts. We have fauna and flora, ceramic pastes, metals (spectrograph), lithics (mineralogic and petrographic analysis) and charcoal (C14 analysis) (Ferreira and Silva 1970, 4. Our italics).

Pluridisciplinarity (as 'collaboration'), together with laborious fieldwork, was essential for comprehending ancestral 'social' life. The past then began to be analysed by Portuguese archaeologists more focused on the relevance of permanent contacts and interinfluences than on diffusions and migrations. Statistics were fundamental in this research process as they could guarantee the 'scientisation' (in the sense of quantification) of archaeology:

prehistoric archaeology being a way of doing *social history* [...] we [paper authors] are committed to establishing general tendencies *statistically translated* based on which it can be possible to reach chronological conclusions and search for *contacts* and *interinfluences* between differentiated cultures (Arnaud and Gamito 1972, 143. Our italics).

'Collaboration' in Portuguese archaeology strengthened in 1969. This was the case with the analyses carried out by Manuel Trabucho from the Chemical Laboratory of the Portuguese Geological Services on a metal ring (Ferreira 1969, 115); the radiography applied to the reconstitution of bronze manufacturing techniques (Secção 1970, 309); the 'collaboration' of palaeobotanists from the Copenhagen High Institute of Agronomy (Secção 1970, 322); the possibility of using two EDXRF (Energy dispersive X-ray fluorescence) instruments, one in the Centre for Atomic Physics at the UL and the other at the Laboratory for Nuclear Physics and Engineering at the Technical University of Lisbon (Araújo *et al.* 2013, 69–70). This collaboration was enhanced in the following year during the Second CNA held at the UC with the participation of 43 Spanish, French, English, German, Italian and Brazilian archaeologists, as well as 104 from Portugal (O II Congresso Nacional 1970, 301–303). It appeared that the road was being definitively opened up to an increasing *pluridisciplinarity*. However, as pointed out by Vítor Oliveira Jorge, one of the main problems of archaeology in general and particularly in Portugal was,

> the lack, insufficiency or ineffectiveness of institutes that could *gather together* experts from different scientific branches with the aim of an indispensable *collaboration*, and in this way to extend university classes in order to more efficiently prepare the researchers; the inexistence or scarcity of true laboratories, the need for non-mausoleum museums; and for the non-separation of activities still performed by one only person – the archaeologist (Jorge 1970, 14. Our italics).

This situation was perhaps the reason why Vítor Oliveira Jorge and other archaeologists frequently requested 'collaboration' and not 'interdisciplinarity', as the latter demanded more expertise and equipment (Arnaud, Oliveira and Oliveira 1971, 112).

Another pioneering paper in the proceedings of the 'Jornadas' was written by Eduardo da Cunha Serrão, one of the aforementioned 'Three Pillars' of the future generation of archaeologists, along with João Manuel Bairrão Oleiro and Fernando de Almeida. Being theoretically up to date and reflecting – as did Vítor Oliveira Jorge[10] – on concepts such as *type*, *artefact-type*[11] and *archaeological culture*, Eduardo da Cunha Serrão underlined the need for 'collaboration' in gathering data as essential for comprehending ancient phenomena, that was 'only possible in *well-equipped laboratories* and thanks to the intervention of very well-trained experts' (Serrão 1970, 7. Our italics). In addition, he was perfectly conscious that, 'only a close *collaboration* between those *experts and archaeologists* makes truly profound knowledge of the past possible' (Serrão 1970, 7. Our italics).

Supported by the IAC and the FCG, some young archaeologists, *e.g.* María de los Ángeles Querol (1948–), Susana Lopes (1953–), Vítor Oliveira Jorge, Jorge Pinheiro

Monteiro and Francisco Sande Lemos, travelled to France in the spring of 1972 to learn about recent methods in archaeology such as those applied by the French prehistorian Michel Brézillon (1924–1993) to engravings in the Sahara desert (Serrão *et al.* 1972; Lemos 2011, 9). However, on their return to Portugal they seem to have failed in implementing a truly interdisciplinary approach based on the French experience. Instead, they tried to apply the methods learned abroad, perhaps because they did not have sufficient means to carry out a collaborative and even less an interdisciplinary project. Moreover, there was perhaps an individual (albeit unconscious) effort to be encyclopaedical or even scientifically hybrid, as in the case of some geologists who were still becoming archaeologists (Dogan and Pahre 1991, 155–160).[12]

The reflections, demands and experiences of the new generation of archaeologists resulted from (and motivated) a profound theoretical and methodological renewal of archaeological practice in Portugal. This transformation was also made possible by the influence of foreign archaeologies and archaeologists in the country, and of young Portuguese archaeologists studying abroad. This renovation was urgent in order to overcome many scientific problems and was needed to change the negative ideas foreign colleagues had about the way archaeology was practiced in the country:

> In recent years, Portugal has observed a discontinuous, but very plain movement, aiming to achieve not the renovation of fieldwork and cabinet methods, but a complete restructuring of all the archaeological *processus*. A perfectly understandable attitude, considering the European hostility to Portuguese research that was responsible for a long period of isolation with extremely negative consequences[13] (Gonçalves 1970, 390).

Conclusions

The examples from the *OAP* journal discussed in this article indicate that 'interdisciplinarity' was still a mirage in Portuguese archaeology, at least between the end of the 1950s and the beginning of the 1970s, the period chosen for analysis. This was a time of political, social, economic and cultural challenges and transformations in the country. However, at the same time considerable effort was put into strengthening *pluridisciplinarity* in archaeology as a way of attempting to fill the gap of 'interdisciplinarity', which was impossible to achieve due to the absence of the necessary human and material resources. Even so, interdisciplinarity was frequently referred to by young students and scholars, not only as something to attain in a near future, but as a deeper, vaster and scientifically more challenging approach than *pluridisciplinarity*. In any case, it was not only the lack of resources that had to be solved to achieve 'interdisciplinarity', a concept that was changing in full during the 'Big Science', *i.e.* the period in which complex and holistic scientific progress was demanded, incentivised and funded by national and transnational governments or groups of governments, and *subjected to overflow* [in the sense of being improved] *in the 1950s and 1960s* (Frank 1988, 139–140). There was an epistemological and – what was more urgent – a mental scheme that had to be transformed in Portugal for interdisciplinarity to be achieved. This change could only be brought about by a new democratic Portuguese regime. Until then, 'collaboration/interrelation/interconnection' remained the predominant research form in Portuguese archaeology, even if the prefix *inter-* could point to *inter*disciplinarity (see introduction) (Frank 1988, 73–77).

Due to the indifference of the Estado Novo's propaganda machine, which was more focused on the monumental vestiges of the past, Portugal did not yet have a body of professional archaeologists; the discipline was mainly practised by amateurs, except for those who came from abroad, as was the case of German and French colleagues.[14] Nonetheless, in the 1960s and 1970s, archaeology in the country was between two phases: the disciplinary (Klein 1990, 59), from 1969 to roughly 1973, and that corresponding to the so-called *group work* (Klein 1990, 56), which lasted from circa 1973 until 'interdisciplinarity' began to be established between the late 1980s and early 1990s. During this period of transition to 'interdisciplinarity', archaeology in Portugal seemed to be more 'additive'[15] than 'integrative' and more 'cumulative' than 'interactive' (Klein 1990, 56). Although motivated and inspired towards interdisciplinarity by the most productive and challenging 'transition generation', it was the new generation of archaeologists influenced by French culture, the importance of French Palaeolithic research, and some German and French archaeological projects, that adopted and accomplished it. The fact that these young archaeologists became aware of the need to learn English also enabled them to stay abreast with the latest archaeological theories and practices in Anglo-Saxon archaeology.

In the same period, the 'Three Pillars' enabled the foundation of an archaeological circle at the FL-UL. Additionally, they facilitated the integration of some circle members, including Vítor Oliveira Jorge and José M. Arnaud, into prestigious Lisbon archaeological societies (*i.e.* the AAP and the SGL). They also authorised the recently established informal Grupo para o Estudo do Paleolítico Português (GEPP; Group for the Study of the Portuguese Palaeolithic) to establish its headquarters at the Museu Etnológico Português and invited its members to work on projects, receive institutional support to travel abroad, and present and publish papers. It was that state of mind that offered this new generation the possibility of advancing in their scientific intents and aspirations. Moreover, it was the international experience of this new generation that allowed its members to speak and write about 'interdisciplinarity'. However, it is debatable whether this was true 'interdisciplinarity'.

We could assume that the new generation of Portuguese archaeologists was perfectly aware of what 'interdisciplinarity' implied and did not use the term only to describe various kinds of research activity (Frank 1988, 139–140). It might be that 'interdisciplinarity' was a way of highlighting the need for a deeper and (almost) permanent 'collaboration'. Perhaps a different strength was given (even if unconsciously) to 'pluridisciplinarity' and 'interdisciplinarity' in science and especially in political life; for example, with innovative resolutions such as the educational reform drawn up in 1973 by the Minister for National Education, Professor José Veiga

Simão (1929–2014) in an attempt to modernise and 'pre'-democratise the political regime (Vicente 2000, 430–431). In this area, it would also be interesting to look at the difference between 'collaboration' and 'cooperation', 'collaboration' being a sort of middle of the way between cooperation – in which leadership is unquestionable – and 'interdisciplinarity', which implies a certain degree of negotiation.[16] The prefix *inter-* was perhaps more suitable for this modern appeal and to people anxiously awaiting the political renewal or change, as opposed to the prefix *pluri-*, which always demands a strong – although informal and perhaps subconscious – hierarchical 'collaboration' and a leading academic discipline. *Interdisciplinarity* could give the idea (if not the illusion) of equality in the contributions of each discipline to the solution of a certain problem. It would be a kind of hierarchy versus equality, a vertical/pyramidal versus a horizontal system. It would almost be an analogy of a totalitarian regime versus a democratic regime. These reflexions notwithstanding, the fact is that it was an approach incentivised by the 'transition generation', at least within the same research group, as appears to have happened with the GEPP. Nonetheless, on further analysis of the word, we could ask if there was a true 'interdisciplinarity' or if the quoted examples were of *pluridisciplinarity*. This is an understandable hesitation when one of the first papers analysing ceramics based on new technology and a natural scientific approach was written solely by a chemical engineer, João Manuel Peixoto Cabral (1928–), despite the fact that it aimed to increase 'collaboration' between Portuguese archaeologists and experts from other academic disciplines (Cabral 1977, 103–137).

Pluridisciplinary was (almost) largely impossible to achieve in Portugal, due to several constraints. The statement by Octávio da Veiga Ferreira is relevant in this respect:

> [it would be important] to know if the mineral came from the same source. But of course, we cannot know this since it is impossible to obtain *spectrographic analyses* in our country, not only because there are *no specialists*, but also because of the *high cost* of such an analysis (Ferreira 1971, 143. Our italics).

This was not new. In 1958, the First CNA resulted in several important conclusions and requests. One of them was to encourage 'the application of modern techniques to archaeological research through the establishment of appropriate laboratories at the main Institutes of Archaeology or by requesting assistance from specialist Portuguese and foreign laboratories' (Actas e Memórias 1970, 367–368). Despite this, there appeared to be a clear – albeit unofficial – notion that archaeology was an academic discipline to be undertaken with extensive teamwork (Pereira 1971, 145) by *an expert team* (Arnaud 1970, 312).

Another question that can (and must) be asked is whether 'pluridisciplinarity' reflects on 'periphery', one of the paradigms that is being reanalysed in this chapter from a history of science perspective. If the concept implies the existence of a centre (or several centres) and institutional and individual hierarchies, then it is possible to examine the case study discussed in the chapter from that point of view. The *OAP* includes numerous examples confirming that Portuguese archaeology was peripheral to the main archaeological theories and practices or that perhaps it was only relevant when it could confirm ideas or was essential for establishing certain archaeological agendas and hypotheses.

Centrality and periphery regarding institutions, people and artefacts depend on the perspective from which the subject is being analysed. With regard to *interdisciplinarity* in archaeology it is possible to say that Portugal was peripheral. It was peripheral from the point of view of *pluridisciplinarity* and even from that of *interdisciplinarity*, the former being a sophisticated version of *collaboration* (as is *multidisciplinarity*). It was also peripheral in terms of new field and laboratory methods. However, it was not peripheral when it contributed to the consolidation of theories, even when these were drawn up abroad by foreign experts, or when they helped reinforce institutional and/or individual scientific *statuses*, in this case archaeological.

The concept of 'periphery' (not only geographic) in the history of science can (and perhaps should) be related to one of the 'invisibilities' of the history of science, as it deals with topics such as the relevance of couples, main and (presumed) secondary actors (individual and collective, public and private) in the establishment and development of different academic disciplines. Therefore, recovering invisibilities from the history of archaeology contributes to rebuilding forgotten trajectories, as well as to following the construction of scientific memories, individual and collective personalism, and the process of forgetting. This is also the case for the introduction, implementation and development of collaboration and interdisciplinarity in Portuguese archaeology, the building of bridges between disciplines. It is a topic that will continue to be studied and will examine, among other issues, the reason(s) why some of the first treatises on the need for an interdisciplinary approach in Portuguese archaeology were published in the *Revista Guimarães* (*RG*; *Guimarães Journal*). This was a peripheral journal from the point of view of national political and cultural geography, but not from the point of view of archaeological practice in the country. To understand this phenomenon, it will be necessary to contextualise it in many ways and from very different intertwined points of view, comparing it to the one we have analysed in this chapter: the *OAP*; a journal that played an important role in the introduction and dissemination of collaboration and interdisciplinarity in archaeology, as well as in the development of science according to international theoretical and methodological standards.

The topic of interdisciplinarity in Portuguese archaeology has not been exhausted in this chapter. In fact, this is merely a first approach to it. There are aspects that still require in-depth analysis and that need to be linked to the events discussed here. Among the aspects that merit further exploration is the collaboration between archaeologists and epigraphers, art historians, museum curators, conservators, restorers and, finally, science communicators who worked in both Portuguese and foreign teams.

Acknowledgements

This article is an outcome of the research project entitled InterArq – Archaeology and Interdisciplinarity: archaeological and historical research on interdisciplinarity in the history of archaeology (19th and 20th centuries), MINECO-Ministerio de Economía y Competitividad, Ref. HAR2016-80271-P. I would like to thank Paul Turner for the language editing funded by National Funds through the FCT – Foundation for Science and Technology within the project: UID/HIS/04209/2020. I would also like to thank Margarita Díaz-Andreu and Laura Coltofean-Arizancu for all their support, suggestions and understanding regarding the writing of this text.

Notes

1. Today the Museu Nacional de Arqueologia (MNA; National Museum of Archaeology).
2. The full professor of archaeology at the Faculty was by law (1913) also director of the National Museum of Archaeology, i.e. the OAP publisher.
3. Manuel Heleno was the Museum's second director following José Leite de Vasconcelos (1858–1941).
4. Invited for the first time to travel to Portugal at the end of the 1940s, J. Roche returned several times, including in 1959 to lecture at the Faculty of Letters of the University of Coimbra on methodology in prehistoric archaeology, fieldwork techniques and typology.
5. Inaugurated in 1952, meaning that Mendes Correia was attentive to recent scientific news.
6. These two analyses were carried out after 1952.
7. Physical anthropologist Denise Ferembach (1924–1994) from the *Centre National de la Recherche Scientifique* (CNRS) 1939, whose 'collaboration' should also be analysed from the point of view of the history of women in science.
8. In the meantime, towards the end of the 1960s, as the person responsible for archaeological studies at FL-UL, the MNAE and the AAP, Fernando de Almeida reinitiated research into the Roman period. This opened the way to pre-medieval archaeology while reinforcing prehistoric studies in 'collaboration' with several institutions and experts: 'it is being explored [Lapa da Rainha] by an *archaeological mission* coordinated by the [Portuguese] National Museum of Archaeology under direction of Professor Fernando de Almeida with the *collaboration* of the *General-Board for Mines and Geology*//[…] and the French scientist Professor *Ab. Jean Roche* from the «*Centre National de la Recherche Scientifique de Paris*» […]//From 1968 we began to undertake *scientific research* there […] in order to *understand the nature of the identified archaeologic deposit*' (Segunda campanha 1969, 295–96. Our italics).
9. The first attempt had been at the end of the 1930s (Southern Portugal) and was taken up again by Fernando Bandeira Ferreira (1921–2002) and Fernando Russel Cortez (1913–1994) in the 1950s.
10. In 1971, Vítor Oliveira Jorge presented *Languedocense in the light of proposals from statistical typology and cultural paleo-anthropology – concepts of «industry», «culture» and «cultural ensemble»* (O problema do Languedocense… 1971).
11. Eduardo da Cunha Serrão reproduced the concept established by David L. Clarke in Analytical Archaeology, the relevance of which was then underlined by Vítor de Oliveira (Jorge 1970, 497).
12. This is the case of the geologist Miguel Ramos (1932–1991) who became a prehistorian specialising in African archaeology after attending the *Sorbonne* in the 1960s (Coelho, Pinto and Martins 2015, 145–160; Martins 2015, 129–143).

13 This was especially worrying considering the recommendations approved by the General Conference of UNESCO on the international principles to be applied in archaeological excavations (New Delhi, 1956), as mentioned by Manuel Bairrão Oleiro during the III CNA (Porto, 5-8 de Novembro de 1973) (Oleiro 1974, 18), already as Director General for Cultural Affairs.
14 It is important to remember here that the degree in archaeology only began to be taught in the late 1980s, and even then as a variant of the history course.
15 However, some authors defend the idea that 'interdisciplinarity should not necessarily be understood as the sum of two or more disciplinary components or as being achieved through a synthesis of different approaches' (Barry, Born and Weszkalnys 2008, 28).
16 This is perhaps the reason why, although published much later, some papers written up to the end of the 1950s continued to use the term 'cooperation' (Viana 1970, 329).

References

Actas e Memórias (1970) *Actas e Memórias do I Congresso Nacional de Arqueologia* Lisboa, Instituto para a Alta Cultura.

Alarcão, J. de and Étienne, R., dirs. (1974–1979) *Fouilles de Conimbriga*. 7 vols. Paris, Boccard.

Almeida, F. de (1956) Marcos miliários da via romana «Aeminium Cale». *O Arqueólogo Português* 3 (2a série), 111–116.

Almeida, F. de and Ferreira, O. da V. (1967) Um poço lusitano-romano encontrado em Idanha-a-Velha. *O Arqueólogo Português* 4, 57–63.

Anonymous (1959) Notícias *Conimbriga* I, 146–163.

Anonymous (1970a) II Congresso Nacional de Arqueologia *O Arqueólogo Português* 5, 301–303.

Anonymous (1970b) O Musteriense da Gruta Nova da Columbeira (Bombarral). *O Arqueólogo Português* 5, 51–96.

Araújo, M. de F. et al. (2013) Investigação em arqueometalurgia em Portugal. Resultados recentes e perspetivas futuras de uma equipa multidisciplinar. *Al-madan* 17 (2) (2ª Série), 69–78.

Arnaud, J.M. (1970) O «Castelo Velho» de Veiros (Estremoz). Campanha preliminar de escavações de 1969. In *Actas das I Jornadas de Arqueologia II,* 311–328. Lisboa, Associação dos Arqueólogos Portugueses.

Arnaud, J.M. and Gamito, T.J. (1972) O povoado fortificado neo- e eneolítico da Serra das Baútas (Carenque, Belas). *O Arqueólogo Português* 6, 119–161.

Arnaud, J.M., Oliveira, V.S. de and Oliveira, J.V. (1971) O povoado fortificado neo- e eneolítico do Penedo de Lexim (Mafra): campanha preliminar de escavações – 1970. *O Arqueólogo Português* 5, 97–132.

Barbosa, E. (1956) O castro da Pedra de Ouro (Alenquer). *O Arqueólogo Português* 3, 75–85.

Barry, A., Born, G. and Weszkalnys, G. (2008) Logics of interdisciplinarity. *Economy and Society* 37(1), 20–49.

Born, G. and Barry A., eds (2013) *Interdisciplinarity: reconfigurations of the social and natural sciences.* London, Routledge.

Cabral, J.M.P. (1977) Caracterização de cerâmicas arqueológicas mediante análise por activação com neutrões térmicos. Classificação das cerâmicas por métodos de taxonomia numérica. *Conimbriga* XVI, 103–137.

Cardoso, J.L. (1997) *Biografia de Octávio Reinaldo da Veiga Ferreira (1917-1997)*.

Coelho, A.G., Pinto, I. and Martins, A.C. (2015) Percursos de Miguel Ramos (1932–1991) na arqueologia: síntese e perspetivas. *Africana Studia* 24, 145–160.

Coelho, L. (1971) Inscrições da necrópole proto-histórica da Herdade do Pêgo – Ourique. *O Arqueólogo Português* 5, 167–180.

Cruz, M.B. da (2000) Sociologia. In A. Barreto and M.F. Mónica (eds) *Dicionário de História de Portugal* IX, sup. P/Z, 66–68. Porto, Figueirinhas.

Díaz-Andreu, M. (2007) *A World History of Nineteenth-Century Archaeology: Nationalism, Colonialism, and the Past*. Oxford, Oxford University Press.

Dogan, M. and Pahre, R. (1991) *L'innovation dans les sciences sociales. La marginalité créatrice*. Paris, Presses Universitaires de France.

Escavações (1968) Escavações na gruta do Bugio (Sesimbra) *O Arqueólogo Português* 4, 193–194.

Ferreira, J.M. (2000) Movimento estudantil. In A. Barreto and M.F. Mónica (eds) *Dicionário de História de Portugal* VIII, sup. F/O, 552–555. Porto, Figueirinhas.

Ferreira, O. da V. and Silva, C.T. da (1970) A estratigrafia do povoado pré-histórico da Rotura (Setúbal). Nota preliminar. In *Actas das I Jornadas Arqueológicas*, vol. II, 203–225. Lisboa, Associação dos Arqueólogos Portugueses.

Ferreira, O. da V. (1969) Nota acerca de um fragmento de um diadema ou adorno? dourado. *O Arqueólogo Português* 3, 115–117.

Ferreira, O. da V. (1971) Um esconderijo de fundidor no Castro de S. Bernardo (Moura). *O Arqueólogo Português* 5, 139–143.

Frank, R. (1988) Interdisciplinarity: the first half century. *Items* 40, 73–77.

Gonçalves, V. dos S. (1970) A propósito de um elemento decorativo da cerâmica campaniforme. In *Actas das I Jornadas Arqueológicas* V(I), 388–400. Lisboa, Associação dos Arqueólogos Portugueses.

Harloe, K. (2013) *Winckelmann and the Invention of Antiquity. History and Aesthetics in the Age of Altertumswissenschaft*. Oxford, Oxford University Press.

Heintz, Ch., Origgi, G. and Sperber, D., eds (2004) *Rethinking Interdisciplinarity. Emergent Issues* (online conference).

Heleno, M. (1956) Consolidação e restauro dos mosaicos de Conimbriga. *O Arqueólogo Português* 2, 253–255.

Hoffmann-Riem, H. (2008) Idea of the handbook. In G. Hadorn, H. Hoffmann-Riem, S. Biber-Klemm, W. Grossenbacher-Mansuy, D. Joye, C. Pohl, U. Wiesmann and E. Zemp (eds) *Handbook of Transdisciplinary Research*, 3–17. Suíça, Springer.

III Curso (1970) III Curso de iniciação à Arqueologia. *O Arqueólogo Português* 5, 314–316.

Jorge, V. de O. (1970) *A arqueologia no contexto da actual metodologia científica: uma perspectiva*. Lisboa, Associação dos Arqueólogos Portugueses.

Klein, J.Th. (1990) *Interdisciplinarity: History, Theory & Practice*. Detroit, Wayne State University Press.

Kluiving, S. and Guttmann-Bond, E. (2012) LAC2010: First International Landscape Archaeology Conference. In S. Kluving and E. Guttmann-Bond (eds) *Landscape Archaeology Between Art and Science. From a Multi- to an Interdisciplinary Approach*. Amsterdam, Amsterdam University Press.

Kristiansen, K. (2009) The Discipline of Archaeology. In B. Cunliffe, Ch. Gosden and R.A. Joyce (eds), *The Oxford Handbook of Archaeology*. Oxford, Oxford University Press.

Lemos, F.S. (2011) Vale do Tejo – a Aventura da Arte Rupestre. In P. Bueno, R. de Balbín and R. Barroso (eds) *Nos 40 anos do início da descoberta da Arte Rupestre do Tejo. Balance de um modelo integrador de Megalitos y Grafías Rupestres em el Tajo Internacional [AÇAFA 4]*. Vila Velha de Rodão, Associação do Estudos do Alto Tejo.

Lopes, Q.M.J. (2018) *A europeização de Portugal entre guerras. A Junta de Educação Nacional e a investigação científica*. Vale de Cambra, Caleidoscópio.

Martins, A.C. (2015) Arqueologia portuguesa em solo africano durante o Estado Novo: (alguns) autores, espaços e projectos – o caso de Moçambique. *Africana Studia* 24, 129–143.

Martins, A.C. (2016) 'Mission': modernize! Portuguese archaeology in the 1960s (a preamble). In G. Delley, M. Díaz-Andreu, F. Djindjian, V.M. Fernández, A. Guidi and M.-A. Kaeser (eds) *History of Archaeology: International Perspectives Proceedings of the XVII UISPP World Congress* (1–7 September 2014, Burgos, Spain) 11, 179–185. Oxford, Archaeopress.

Martins, A.C. (2017) «Porque havemos de deixar nas mãos de especialistas estrangeiros perspectivas que tanto nos dizem respeito?». A colaboração arqueológica internacional no Portugal dos anos 50–60 do século XX: tradições, inovações e contradições. In J.M. Arnaud and A. Martins (eds) *Arqueologia em Portugal: 2017 - Estado da Questão*, 87-98. Lisboa, Associação dos Arqueólogos Portugueses.

Miller, R.C. (2010) Interdisciplinarity: its meaning and consequences. In *Oxford Research Encyclopedias*. International Studies Association and Oxford University Press. [https://doi.org/10.1093/acrefore/9780190846626.013.92].

Oleiro, J.M.B. (1974) *Palavras de Abertura*. In *Actas do III Congresso Nacional de Arqueologia*. Porto, Junta Nacional de Educação.

Oliver, J. (1956) Galets-racloirs de quartzite. Contribution à l'étude du Paléolithique d'Amadora. *O Arqueólogo Português* 3, 107-109.

O problema do Languedocense em Portugal: notas para a sua revisão. 1971. *O Arqueólogo Português* 5, 264.

Parreira, R. (1995) Zambujal: Die Grabungen 1964 bis 1973. *O Arqueólogo Português* IV (3), 227-211.

Pélissier, R. (2000) Guerras Coloniais. In A. Barreto and M.F. Mónica (eds) *Dicionário de História de Portugal* VIII, sup. F/O, 159-163. Porto, Figueirinhas.

Pereira, M.A.G. (1971) Fragmento de vaso vidrado a verde, da estação romana de Tróia. *O Arqueólogo Português* 5, 145-154.

Pombo, O. (2004) *Interdisciplinaridade: ambições e limites*. Lisboa, Relógio D'Água.

Pombo, O. (2008) Epistemologia da Interdisciplinaridade. *Ideação. Revista do Centro de Educação e Letras da Unioeste* 10 (1), 9-40.

Primeiras Jornadas Arqueológicas da Associação dos Arqueólogos Portugueses (1969) *O Arqueólogo Português* 3, 300-304.

Raposo, L. (2011) Ródão, há quatro décadas – um eixo vertebrador do 'meu mundo'. In P. Bueno, R. de Balbín and R. Barroso (eds) *Nos 40 anos do início da descoberta da Arte Rupestre do Tejo. Balance de um modelo integrador de Megalitos y Grafías Rupestres em el Tajo Internacional [AÇAFA 4]* [https://www.altotejo.org/acafa/docsn4/Rodao_ha_quatro_decadas_Luis_Raposo.pdf]. Vila Velha de Rodão, Associação do Estudos do Alto Tejo.

Rato, V. (2000) Marcelismo. In A. Barreto and M.F. Mónica (eds) *Dicionário de História de Portugal* VIII, sup. F/O, 421-427. Porto, Figueirinhas.

Repko, A.F. (2008) *Interdisciplinarity in Research. Process and Theory*. Los Angeles, Sage.

Roche, J. and Ferreira, O.V. (1967) Les fouilles récentes dans les amas coquillers Mésolithiques de Muge (1952-1965). *O Arqueólogo Português* 3, 19-41.

Rowley-Conwy, P. (2007) *From Genesis to Prehistory: The Archaeological Three Age System and its Contested Reception in Denmark, Britain, and Ireland*. Oxford, Oxford University Press.

Sangmeister, E., Schubart, H. and Trindade, L. (1968) Zambujal – 1968. *O Arqueólogo Português* 2, 35-38.

Sangmeister, E., Schubart, H. and Trindade, L. (1969) Escavações no castro eneolítico do Zambujal, 1966. *O Arqueólogo Português* 3, 71-114.

Sangmeister, E., Schubart, H. and Trindade, L. (1970) Escavações na fortificação eneolítica do Zambujal, 1968. *O Arqueólogo Português* 4, 65-113.

Santos, M.F. dos (1967) A necrópole de tipo 'tholos' de Santiago do Escoural. *O Arqueólogo Português* 3 (1), 107-113.

Santos, M.F. dos and Ferreira, O. da V. (1969) O monumento eneolítico de Santiago do Escoural. *O Arqueólogo Português*. 3, 37-62.

Schlanger, N. (2010) Series in progress: antiquities of nature, numismatics and stone implements in the emergence of Prehistoric Archaeology. *History of Science* 48 (3/4 (161)), 343-369.

Schlanger, N. (2011) Coins to flint. John Evans and the numismatic moment in the history of archaeology. *European Journal of Archaeology* 14, 465-479.

Schmidt, J. (2008) Towards a philosophy of interdisciplinarity: an attempt to provide a classification and clarification. *Poiesis Prax* 5, 53-69.

Secção de Pré-História da Associação dos Arqueólogos Portugueses (1970) *O Arqueólogo Português* 4, 310–311, 321–322, 324.
Séguier, J. de, dir. (1910) *Diccionário prático illustrado*. Lisboa, Empresa do Diccionário Prático Illustrado.
Segunda campanha de escavações na Lapa da Rainha (Vimeiro) (1969) *O Arqueólogo Português* 3, 295–297.
Serrão, E. da C. (1970) As cerâmicas de «retícula bruñida» das estações arqueológicas espanholas e com «ornatos brunidos» da Lapa do Fumo. In *Actas das I Jornadas Arqueológicas* I, 273–308. Lisboa, Associação dos Arqueólogos Portugueses.
Serrão, E. da C., Lemos, F. and Monteiro, J.P. (1972) O complexo de arte rupestre do vale do Tejo (V.ª V.ª de Ródão- Nisa): primeiras hipóteses e programa de trabalhos. *O Arqueólogo Português* 6, 63–72.
Sills, D.L. (1986/2016) A note on the origin of 'interdisciplinary'. *Items* 40 (1), 17-18.
Thomas, J. (2000) Introduction: the polarities of post-processual archaeology. In J. Thomas (ed.) *Interpretive Archaeology. A Reader* 1–18. Leicester, Leicester University Press.
Viana, A. (1970) Arqueologia, arqueólogos e escavações arqueológicas: monumentos, achados, espólios e museus. In *Actas e Memórias do I Congresso Nacional de Arqueologia* II, 319–329. Lisboa, Instituto de Alta Cultura.
Vicente, A P. (2000) José Veiga Simão. In A. Barreto and M.F. Mónica (eds) *Dicionário de História de Portugal* VIII, sup. F/O, 430–431. Porto, Figueirinhas.

Chapter 8

Science and archaeology in Italy: a difficult marriage

Alessandro Guidi

Abstract

In this chapter some periods of the difficult relationship between scientific disciplines in Italy will be reconstructed. In addition to archaeology, the main scientific disciplines analysed will be zoology, botany, geology and physical anthropology. A comparison will be made with the contemporary development of interdisciplinary methods in France and the United Kingdom. The main Italian, French and English prehistory and archaeology journals will be used as sources. To this end, three periods will be examined in detail, the first being the nineteenth century when evolutionist prehistory was developed. The second is the interwar period, characterised by the cultural hegemony of idealism, a philosophy openly hostile to the application of experimental methods in the human sciences and the cause of an increasingly wide rift between the Italian and European experiences. The last of the examined periods spans from the end of the Second World War to the present day and was witness to an exponential growth in interdisciplinary studies, in both prehistoric and classical archaeology.

Keywords. archaeology; interdisciplinarity; prehistory; classical archaeology; Italy; France; United Kingdom.

Introduction

Multidisciplinarity is one of the main characteristics of prehistoric archaeology. Articles about archaeological sites often include listings and observations of anthropological or archaeozoological finds, as well as on seeds, pottery, tools or geology. In order to measure the importance of these scientific disciplines in archaeology and to understand their progressive integration into our field in terms of true interdisciplinarity, this chapter examines articles devoted exclusively to zoology, botany, geology and physical anthropology. They are taken from a selection of the most important Italian and foreign journals published in two sample periods corresponding to seminal historical events in Italy: 1870–1900 (the years following the unification of Italian states in 1861) and 1919–1939 (the years of the Fascist regime). This will be the occasion to compare different intellectual environments. The first case looked at will be Italy and France, which are closely linked due to a common intellectual milieu in the two countries. On the other hand, for the years between the two World Wars it seemed interesting to add a selection from British journals (for recent reviews of the history of archaeology in different European countries see Biehl, Gramsch and Marciniak 2002; Moro Abadía and Huth 2013). Given the disparity between Italy and France in the first analysed period, England was a further decisive test for highlighting the systematic delay of Italian archaeology in incorporating interdisciplinary practices during the second period, in comparison to other European countries. A further section of the chapter is dedicated to a survey of the current situation of multidisciplinarity in archaeology in Italian and English universities; the comparison is considered here as a motivation for an increase in the qualitative standards of Italian archaeology.

The period between 1870 and 1900

In Italy, this phase begins with the conquest of Rome as the capital of the new united state (1870) and ends with a period of unrest marked by numerous social riots that culminated in General Bava Beccaris' bloody repression of the social uprising in Milan in 1898. The latter event was the background to the assassination, two years later, of King Umberto I by the anarchist Gaetano Bresci (Petacco 2000). This was a particularly fervent period for Italian archaeology, mainly due to the birth, development and consolidation of prehistory. It was characterised by the enthusiastic activity of many scholars (Tarantini 2012; for a complete panorama of the history of Italian pre- and protohistory studies see Guidi 2014a). To examine the situation in this period we must, however, provide an overview of the first developments of prehistoric studies in Italy.

From its beginnings, Italian prehistory was deeply influenced if not shaped by the natural sciences. In fact, the first Italian prehistorians were naturalists based in Tuscany. The first Congress of Italian scientists was held in Pisa in 1839. Four years later, at the Fifth Congress held in Lucca, Antonio Salvagnoli Marchetti, a doctor and natural science scholar, gave a lecture on the arrowheads and lithic tools found in a cave (Grotta dei Santi, at Mount Argentario). This gave birth to a local tradition of researching in caves, for example, Igino Cocchi's excavations (Tarantini 1998–2000, 11–16). In the same years, the Turin lawyer, Bartolomeo Gastaldi (1818–1879), decided to follow his true passion, devoting himself to geology and palaeontology, as well as to his developing interest in prehistory. In 1850, the geologist Giuseppe Scarabelli (1820–1905), the first scholar in Italy to use the term 'geoarchaeology' (Vai 2014, 39), published a report on Palaeolithic tools found in association with an extinct faunal assemblage near Imola (Scarabelli 1850), considered by many historians of archaeology to be the first Italian paper on prehistory.

Around 1860 a second group of scholars emerged in northern Italy (especially in the Emilia region). Although they all came from the field of traditional historical research (except Strobel, who taught zoology) and were open to positivism, they were aware of the importance of the natural sciences. This group was made up of liberal intellectuals (often Catholic and in some cases priests), many of whom were involved in the political struggle for independence (the Risorgimento). Politically, however, they were not a homogeneous group, as can be seen from the presence of Pellegrino Strobel (1821–1895), a freemason sympathetic to socialist movements and involved in an anti-clerical intellectual climate that was also shared by many patriots (Guidi 2014b). Almost isolated from this group, but equally important, was another scholar, born in Genua, the naturalist Arturo Issel (1842–1922). His first paper, published in 1864, was on the palaeontological finds from a cave that later, thanks to his excavations, became a key site for Italian prehistory, the Arene Candide cave (De Pascale 2008).

Pellegrino Strobel was certainly the scholar most aware of the importance of integrating the natural sciences into historical research. This can be seen from his studies of the animal remains from pre- and protohistoric sites, in some cases the documentation of single animal species. However, we should also remember the peculiar 'archaeozoological' observations of animal remains in lake dwellings by the archaeologist and naturalist Camillo Marinoni (1845–1882) and the naturalist Paolo Lioy (1834–1911). Their observations were not only related to the identification of bones, but also to the part they played in the human diet (see De Grossi Mazzorin 2014). Strobel was also interested in palaeoethnobotanical remains. In this field, the pioneers in Italy were Gastaldi and Antonio Stoppani (1824–1891), a priest, intellectual and patriot from Milan. Specialists in botany, such as Ferdinando Sordelli (1837–1916), Giovanni Passerini (1816–1893) and Agostino Goiran (1835–1909), were among the first scholars to study this type of material (Castelletti and Martinelli 2014). It is possible to perceive an easier integration between archaeology and the natural sciences in the field of physical anthropology. Two interesting figures in this sphere were the physician and naturalist Leopoldo Maggi (1840–1905) with his studies of prehistoric skulls and, in a later phase, Giuseppe Sergi (1841–1936), founder of the Roman anthropological school and a scholar of international relevance (on Sergi see Pizzato 2015).

Despite a diversity in their intellectual milieu and interests, the pioneers of Italian prehistoric archaeology formed a lively scientific community that had frequent contacts with foreign specialists, including the geologist and naturalist Édouard Desor (1811–1882) and the archaeologist Gabriel de Mortillet (1821–1899). It is therefore not strange that as early as 1865, during a meeting of the Società Italiana di Scienze Naturali, founded in 1856 in Milan, Italian and foreign pioneers of prehistory (encouraged by De Mortillet) decided to call the discipline 'paleoetnologia', which translated as 'ethnology of ancient peoples'. This name is preserved in the Italian academic tradition as 'Paletnologia'. Furthermore, the presence among the scholars of many naturalists based in Tuscany makes it understandable that many important articles were published between 1870 and 1900 in the *Archivio per l'Antropologia e l'Etnologia*, a scientific journal founded in Florence by the anthropologist Paolo Mantegazza

(1831–1910) in 1871. For a while, none of these intellectuals emerged as a leader of the 'new' science. However, from the mid-1870s, Italian prehistory was completely hegemonised by the tireless activity of Luigi Pigorini (1842–1925), a scholar who often integrated the natural sciences into his fieldwork and scientific activity. However, he never prioritised this approach in his activity, as for example in his long-lasting and aprioristic polemic against the scholars who demonstrated the existence of Upper Palaeolithic cultures in Italy (Tarantini 1998–2000, 25–28). Luigi Pigorini initially specialised in numismatics, as did the 'father' of prehistory, Christian Jurgensen Thomsen. Aware of the work of Pellegrino Strobel and Bartolomeo Gastaldi, who first excavated lake dwellings in Italy, Luigi Pigorini soon became interested in prehistory. He and Pellegrino Strobel (later with the help of another priest interested in palaeoethnology, Gaetano Chierici (1816–1886)), began to discover the fortified prehistoric settlements of the Po Plain ('terramare') and wrote reports about their findings in several foreign languages, thus entering the wider European intellectual environment.

In 1865, Luigi Pigorini took a degree in administration (not natural sciences!) and two years later he became director of the Parma Museum. There he initiated an astute policy of exchanging prehistoric finds with foreign museums. In 1870 he was appointed an official of the newly established State Antiquity Office (Guidi 1988, 27) that had been founded by Giuseppe Fiorelli (1823–1896), an archaeologist from Naples who received his training in the excavations of Pompeii (Kannes 1997). Thanks to this new post and his ability to create a true Italian 'network' of prehistorians, Luigi Pigorini was the leading figure at the International Congress of Prehistory and Anthropology held in Bologna in 1871, stealing the show from the well-known geologist Giovanni Capellini (1833–1922), a member of the congress organising committee. Four years later, together with Gaetano Chierici and Pellegrino Strobel, Pigorini founded the first journal devoted entirely to prehistory, the *Bullettino di Paletnologia Italiana* (published in Rome). In 1876, he inaugurated, as its director, the Rome Museum of Prehistory and Ethnography, built thanks to an intensive and extraordinary task of persuasion he had undertaken with the Minister of Public Education, Ruggero Bonghi (1826–1895); the politician had been fascinated by Pigorini while he was director of the Parma Museum and had taken him to see the newly discovered terramare. Finally, in 1877, he was appointed Professor of Prehistory at Rome University. This was the only chair of its type in Italy until his death in 1925.

In selecting the articles for this chapter, it was essential to include those devoted to the scientific disciplines linked to archaeology published by the *Bullettino*, the journal of reference for Italian prehistory all over Europe. At the same time, given the existence of the aforementioned tradition in Italy of prehistoric studies conducted with a more pronounced naturalistic approach (for this 'divide' in Italian prehistory see Tarantini 1998–2000 and Guidi 2000), not only was the *Archivio per l'Antropologia e l'Etnologia* analysed, but also the *Atti della Società Italiana di Scienze Naturali*, a journal founded in 1859 in Milan, another centre of interest for the new discipline.

In terms of statistics for this period between 1870 and 1900, the *Archivio per l'Antropologia e l'Etnologia* was definitely a favourite for articles (41) devoted to the scientific disciplines, even though many research projects were published in the *Bullettino* (26). Only a few (9) appeared in the pages of *Atti della Società Italiana di Scienze Naturali* (Fig. 8.1a). There is a first peak of articles published in the Archivio between 1881 and 1883, although most were published in the *Archivio* and the *Bollettino* at the beginning of the 1890s. This was followed by a drastic decrease from 1892 onwards (from that year up to 1897 there is often one article from one or the other reviews, in some cases two or three), with a complete absence of articles in 1898 and 1899. A similar situation had only occurred two decades before, in 1870 and 1874.

Regarding the single disciplines of anthropology, archaeozoology and palaeoethnobotany (Fig. 8.1b), 37 (almost 50%) of the 76 articles published in this period were devoted to anthropology and 32 (42%) to archaeozoology (for the first impressive development in this field of study, linked above all to the need to study the numerous animal bones found in the terramare, see De Grossi Mazzorin 2014). More than half of the articles relating to archaeozoology were written by Pellegrino Strobel (see, for example, Strobel 1877; 1880; 1886). Six (8%) of these papers dealt with palaeoethnobotany (the best example is Sordelli 1880; Castelletti and Martinelli 2014) and there is only one article devoted to human and animal remains found together in a Ligurian cave (Issel 1884). The latter is in a category labelled here as 'mixed disciplines', consisting of papers in which anthropology and geology[1] or anthropology and archaeozoology are taken into consideration in equal measure. Only 5 of the 76 articles were written by foreign scholars (two from Great Britain, one from France and one from Argentina). They were all published in the *Archivio per l'Antropologia e l'Etnologia* and on the subject of Pleistocene human fossils (for a general review of the relationships between Italian and foreign scholars see Guidi 2008; 2018; for a recent enquiry into the progressive growth of internationalisation in Italian prehistoric research, see Plutniak 2018).

In contrast to Italy, in France, prehistory was acknowledged sooner as an autonomous and important discipline (for more details about the delay of Italy as compared to France, see Schnapp 2014; a different point of view in Hurel 2007; on the relationships between archaeology and geology in France, see Hurel and Coye 2011). This is demonstrated by the outstanding discoveries of Palaeolithic tools by the archaeologist and antiquarian Boucher de Perthes (1788–1868), which were recognised as authentic in 1859. Boucher also played an important role in the establishment of the prehistoric section of the Paris National Antiquities Museum. Consequently, journals devoted to prehistory were established earlier in France than in Italy. For an analysis of the French situation, three journals comparable to those of Italy were chosen (even though they were established earlier). The first two are the *Bulletin de la Société d'anthropologie*, founded in Paris in 1859 by the anthropologist Paul Broca (1824–1880), and *Matériaux pour l'Histoire Primitive et Naturelle de l'Homme*, established in 1865 by Gabriel de Mortillet. The latter changed its name to

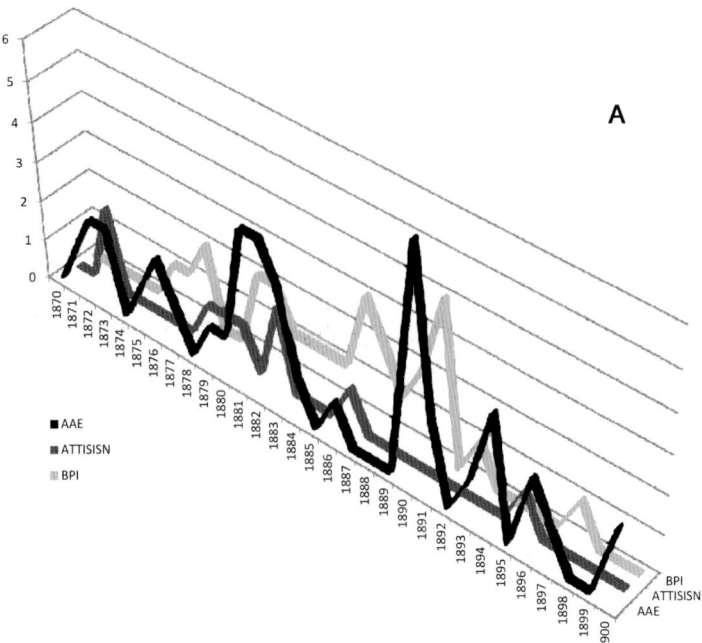

Figure 8.1a. Articles in Italian journals (1870-1900). AAE, Archivio per l'Antropologia e l'Etnologia; *BPI,* Bullettino di Paletnologia Italiana; *AttiSISN,* Atti Società Italiana di Scienze Naturali.

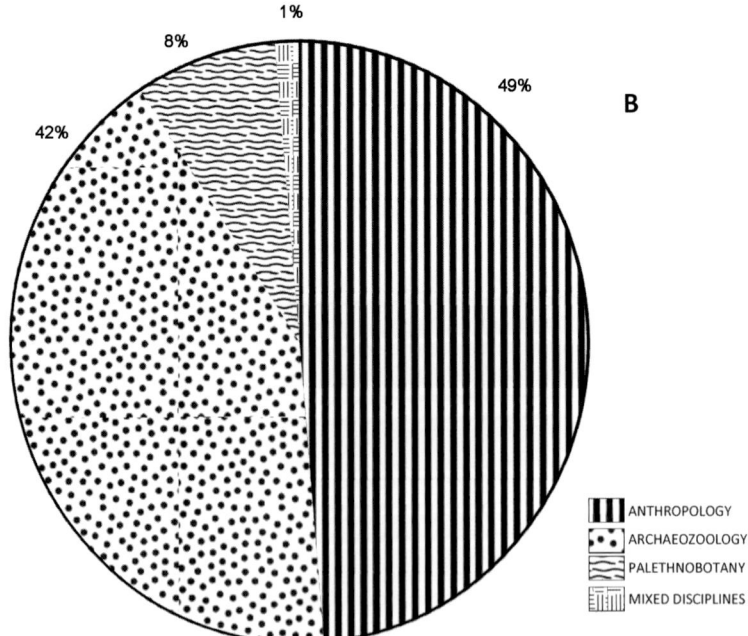

Figure 8.1b. Chart representing the different disciplines dealt with in Italian journals (1870-1900).

L'Anthropologie in 1890, as well as its director to Émile Cartailhac (1845–1921). The third French publication used for statistical purposes is the *Revue Archéologique*, a more traditional journal mainly devoted to classical archaeology founded in 1844, a period still dominated by antiquarianism. Of the 101 articles concerning the disciplines examined in this chapter, the majority (50) (Fig. 8.2a) were published in the *Bulletin de la Société d'anthropologie*, although the issues of *Matériaux/L'anthropologie* also include a similar number of papers (49). Only 12 such articles were published in the *Revue Archéologique*. A climax of articles can be easily seen in the 1870s, the golden age of positivism. In the 1890s, there was also an obvious decrease in the number of articles in France, which was probably also caused by a generalised loss of interest in the instances of positivism, although not a 'collapse', as is demonstrated by the quantitative data regarding Italy. During that decade, there were only two years, 1885 and 1895, in which no articles were published.

As in the Italian journals, anthropology, whose origins in France date back to the end of the eighteenth century,[2] played an important role, accounting for 52% of papers, a fact that can explain the imbalance with the archaeozoology papers (only 28% of the total). Apart from these, however, there is also a good percentage of articles on other disciplines (17%), as well as a clear difference between single fields of study (archaeometallurgy 8%, archaeometry 5.5%, palaeoethnobotany 4%, geology 2.2%) (Fig. 8.2b). It is interesting to note that many articles on anthropology were written by one of the best scholars in the field, Paul Broca (see for example Broca 1873; 1876). At the same time, we must note that De Mortillet was able to write about different fields, including geology (1874), anthropology (1877) and archaeozoology (1879). The number of articles written by foreign scholars in French journals is more or less the same as in those of Italy (7 out of 101). However, there is a difference in the number and variety of the countries those authors came from, which ranged from Italy, Switzerland and Great Britain to Germany, Denmark and Poland. In addition, they did not only deal with anthropology, but also with archaeozoology and palaeoethnobotany.

The period between 1919 and 1939

A totally different situation can be perceived in Italy during this period. From a historical point of view, these are the years, after a long period of social riots, of the birth and development of the Fascist regime. Its cultural policy was characterised from the beginning by the exaltation (with clear propagandistic aims) of classical antiquity, especially the Roman period (Canfora 1980). This led to the creation of numerous academic chairs of Classical Archaeology. As a consequence of these lines of cultural policy, the 'traditional' narrative in this period was aimed at ignoring Italian prehistory.

In fact, in the early twentieth century, it was already possible to perceive a decline in the standards of field methods and the degree to which the natural sciences were integrated into archaeology. Italian scholars, who had been fully immersed in the European intellectual climate of the nineteenth century, were now increasingly

164 Alessandro Guidi

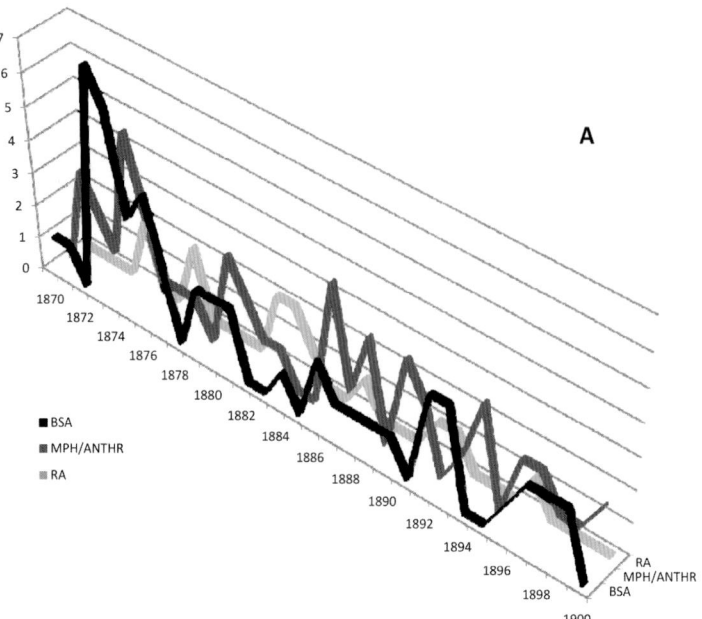

Figure 8.2a. Articles in French journals (1870–1900). BSA, Bulletin de la Société d'anthropologie; *MPH/ANTHR*, Matériaux pour l'Histoire Primitive et Naturelle de l'Homme/L'Anthropologie; *RA*, Revue Archéologique.

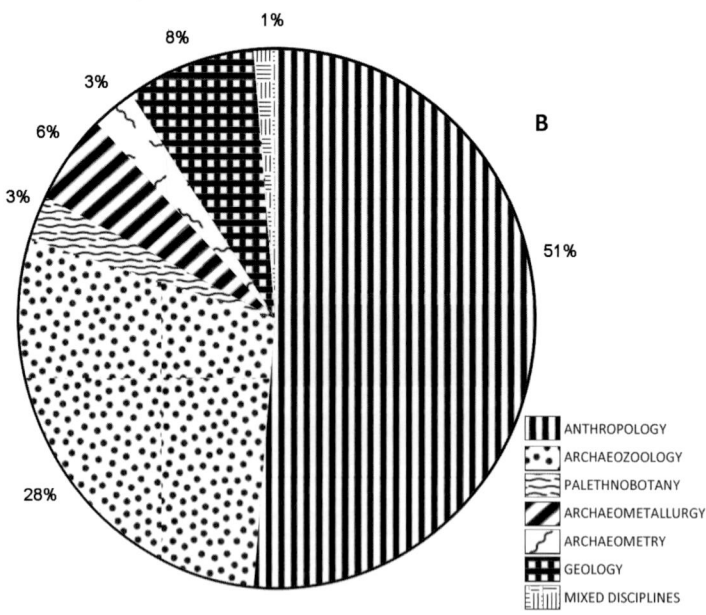

Figure 8.2b. Disciplines that are dealt with in French journals (1870–1900).

isolated from the international milieu of prehistoric studies, except for the aforementioned naturalist school based in Tuscany (Peroni 1992, 56–58). In this school, many distinguished scholars continued to explore prehistoric (especially Palaeolithic) sites using advanced multidisciplinary methods, while remaining immune to the isolation and provincialism that affected Italian palaeoethnological research during that period. The origin of this decline can be found in the progressive predominance in Italian culture of an idealistic ideology championed by the philosopher, historian and politician Benedetto Croce (1866–1952). He was against the introduction of experimental methods in historical disciplines and preferred to carry on with a robust separation between humanistic and scientific disciplines, a choice whose negative consequences can still be felt today (for the influence of this philosopher in archaeology, see Guidi 1988, 78–79). Within the 'Roman school' of archaeology, the most interesting figure, although he had his ups and downs (especially with regard to his very low interest in multidisciplinarity), was Ugo Alberto Rellini (1870–1943), a scholar trained in the field of the natural sciences. He was the successor to Pigorini's chair and, in that role, he exerted a strong control over almost all the issues (*i.e.* editorials, reviews, articles, etc.) in the *Bullettino* during the Fascist period. His activity was marked by a cautious willingness to renew Italian prehistoric studies.

In the choice of journals, together with the *Bullettino di Paletnologia Italiana* and the *Archivio per l'Antropologia e l'Etnologia*, it is possible to take into account from the first year of its publication (1927) *Studi Etruschi*. The journal of the new discipline of Etruscology (that held its first national and international congresses in the 1920s) was founded (not by chance) in Florence by the head of the State Antiquity Office, Antonio Minto (1880–1954), with the enthusiastic support of many naturalists, some of whom came from the cultural tradition of the nineteenth century (Tarantini 2002, 152–154). This could explain the large number of published articles (33 of a total of 51) related to the natural sciences, compared to very few that appeared in the *Archivio* and even fewer in the *Bullettino* (Fig. 8.3a). In contrast to the previous period, there are many years (1919, 1920, 1923, 1925, 1926) with no articles devoted to the use of scientific methods in archaeology. Thus, in addition to the persisting predominance of anthropological research, due above all to the finds from the Palaeolithic period or from the Etruscan tombs (27%; see for example Puccioni 1932), a very high percentage of articles (*e.g.* D'Achiardi 1929; Badii 1931; Tongiorgi 1937) dealt with archaeometallurgy (23%) (Fig. 8.3b), due to the importance of Tuscan mining resources in the history of the middle Thyrrenian area. Other contributions were devoted to archaeometry (16%), while only 34% to archaeozoology (11.7%), paleoethnobotany (11.7%), geology (5.8%) and mixed disciplines (4%), the latter on Palaeolithic archaeology by Blanc (1938) and Mochi (1927). Only two articles about archaeometallurgy were written by foreign scholars, from Belgium and Germany.

Again, France reveals a clearly different situation to that of Italy. In the years between the two World Wars there were many intellectual 'outbursts', not only in the arts and literature, but also in the anthropological and archaeological disciplines. All

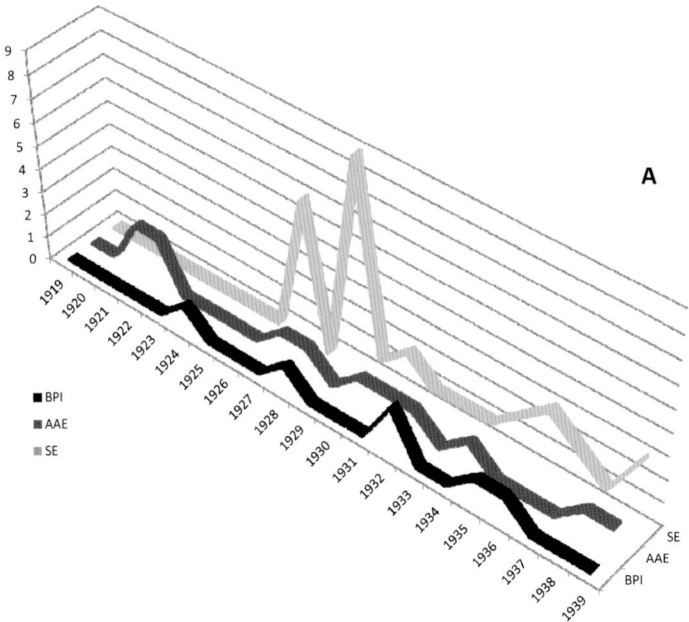

Figure 8.3a. Articles in Italian journals (1919-1939). AAE, Archivio per l'Antropologia e l'Etnologia; *BPI*, Bullettino di Paletnologia Italiana; *SE*, Studi Etruschi.

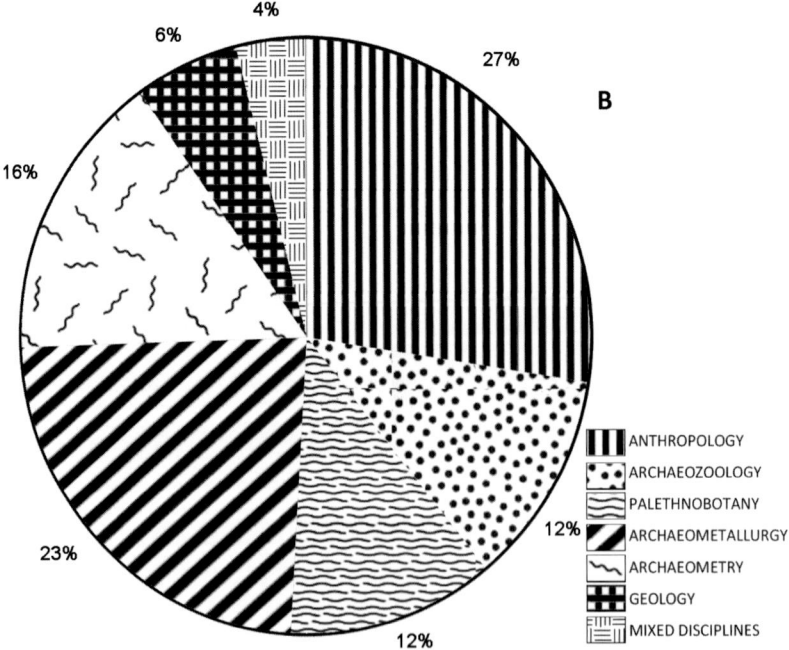

Figure 8.3b. Disciplines that are dealt with in Italian journals (1919-1939).

these 'outbursts' consisted of an increasing integration of scientific disciplines into their methodologies. Examples include the sociological school of Durkheim, Marcel Mauss' 'gift' theory, the birth of the Annales historical school and, in prehistory, the work of Abbé Breuil (1877–1961) on Palaeolithic rock art. From this perspective, the French situation is remarkable, not only due to the large number of articles, mostly devoted to Palaeolithic sites (74), but also because of a continuous interest in scientific methods that could be applied to archaeology. There was no year without contributions on this topic. Journals such as *L'Anthropologie* and *Revue Archéologique* were examined for this chapter, along with the volumes of the *Bulletin de la Société préhistorique française*. The latter, published for the first time in 1904 in Paris, was the first journal explicitly addressed at prehistorians and soon acquired an important role, as demonstrated by the large number of articles (53) (Fig. 8.4a) published between 1919 and 1939 about scientific methods in archaeology. In comparison, only 14 articles appeared in *L'Anthropologie* and even fewer (7) in *Revue Archéologique* than in the preceding period.

Confirmation of a solid scientific environment can be seen in the chart that presents the disciplines dealt with in these articles (Fig. 8.4b). This chart can be easily superimposed on the graph of the preceding period (Fig. 8.2b). Pontier's articles on archaeozoology (1922; 1933) and the anthropological research published by Montandon (1926) and Vallois (1927; 1936) merits special mention. The articles devoted to the Neanderthal skulls found in Rome and Mount Circeo (Blanc and Breuil 1936; Lantier 1936; 1939) are also interesting, while again the considerable interest in Palaeolithic archaeology could explain the high percentage (8%) of geology articles. International contributions (5) can be observed in the fields of anthropology, archaeozoology, archaeometallurgy and geology, with authors from countries including Italy, Germany, Russia, Czechoslovakia and Turkey.

It is important to assess the situation in another European country during the same period. With this aim, a further comparison will be made with the United Kingdom, which was an even more stimulating intellectual milieu for archaeology. In that country, the interwar period witnessed much outstanding progress in field methods, archaeological theory and the integration of scientific disciplines into archaeological research. These advances included, for example, the first formalisation and practical application in Great Britain and the Near East of a modern stratigraphic practice (also based on geological principles!), the so-called 'Wheeler method'; the development of surveys and, at the same time, the use of aerial photography in archaeology, techniques developed by the archaeologists O.G.S. Crawford (1886–1957) and Cyril Fox (1882–1967); a real interest in the relationship between the environment and archaeological sites, which developed in Cambridge with the creation of an interdisciplinary group of archaeologists, palaeontologists and palaeoethnobotanists led by J.G.D. Clark; the diffusion of large-area open-air excavations.

Three journals were used for the comparison with the United Kingdom. *Man*, the journal of the Royal Anthropological Institute founded in 1901; *Proceedings of the Prehistoric Society of East Anglia*, started in 1911 (the journal changed its name to

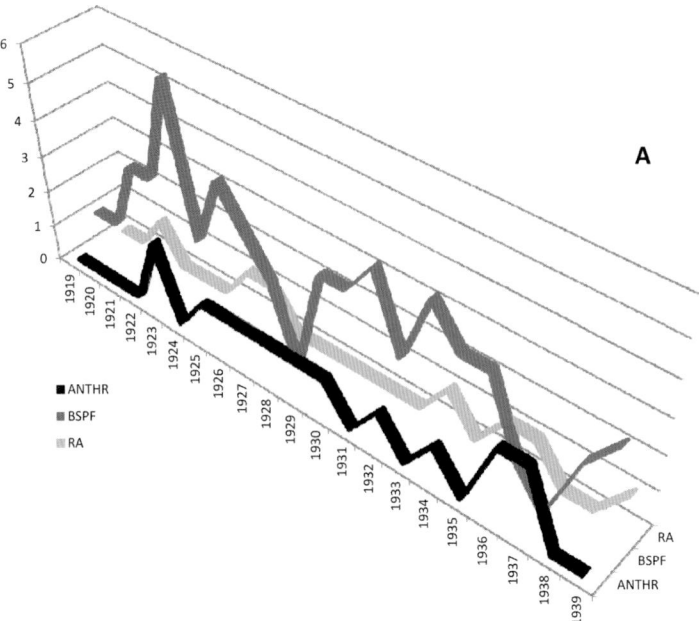

Figure 8.4a. Articles in French journals (1919–1939). ANTHR, L'Anthropologie; RA, Revue Archéologique; BSPF, Bulletin de la Société préhistorique française.

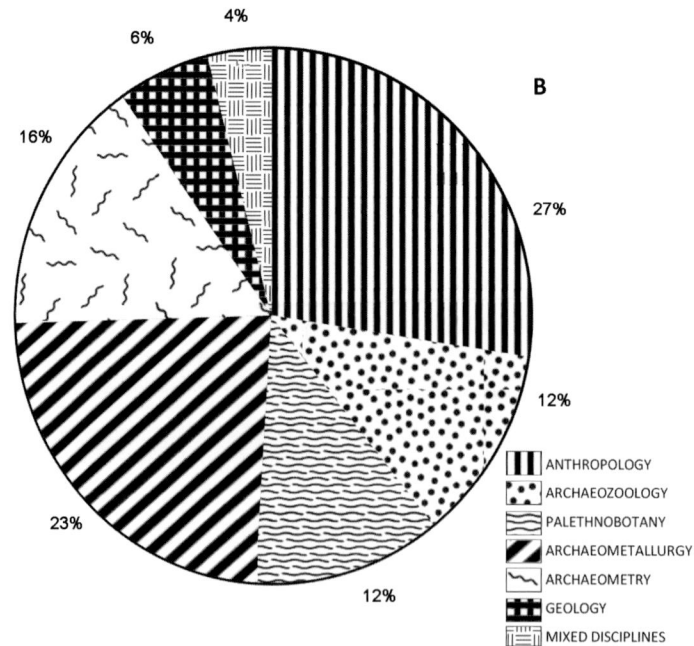

Figure 8.4b. Disciplines that are dealt with in French journals (1919–1939).

Proceedings of the Prehistoric Society in 1935); and *Antiquity*, a more modern archaeological journal founded in 1927 by O.G.S. Crawford. In spite of the major role played by *Man*, with 63 articles published between 1919 and 1939 (Fig. 8.5a), a good number of papers (32) appeared in *Antiquity* from its beginnings. Finally, a few articles (11) were published in *Proceedings of the East Anglia Society/Proceedings of the Prehistoric Society*. There were only two years, 1920 and 1922, when no such articles were published. In fact, England turned out to be a further good test and decisive in underlining Italy's systematic delay compared to other European countries in this field, also in the second period.

In contrast to Italy and France, in the 1930s there was an evident quantitative growth. Of the 102 articles published in the three journals (Fig. 8.5b), the majority (34%) – often consisting of only a few pages – dealt with anthropology, followed, as in Italy, by archaeometallurgy (20%; *e.g.* Wainwright 1936). A consistent number of articles was devoted to geology (18%; *e.g.* that by Swedish scientist De Geer (1928)) and archaeozoology (13%; of which four were by a German scientist, Max Hilzheimer (1932; 1935; 1936a; 1936b)). The percentage of articles on palaeoethnobotany (11%; *e.g.* Huntingford 1932; Curwen 1938a; 1938b) was similar to that of Italy in the same period. The large number of foreign scientists (9) publishing in these journals demonstrates the openness of the British academic environment in the interwar period. If we compare the number of articles in the historical phases taken into consideration here (Fig. 8.6), the imbalance between the results obtained for Italy and France are evident and this difference becomes even more striking in comparison to the United Kingdom.

From the end of the Second World War to the present

In the 1950s, the botanist Ezio Tongiorgi (1912–1987) founded the first Italian laboratory for radiometric dating chronology in Pisa (Ferrara, Reinhard and Tongiorgi 1959). In the same period, an engineer from Milan, Carlo Maurilio Lerici (1890–1981), began undertaking the first geophysical prospections in Italy, mainly at Etruscan burial sites (Lerici 1959). Between the end of the 1950s and the beginning of the 1960s, the use of quantitative graphs (*e.g.* chronological, block and cumulative diagrams) also began in Italian archaeology (Guidi 2015, 45–47). Despite the pioneering work of these scholars, anthropology, archaeozoology, paleoethnobotany, chemistry and physics have been labelled for many years as 'subsidiary sciences for archaeology' (*scienze sussidiarie dell'archeologia*) in Italy. This shows the consideration that many scholars (especially in the field of the Classics) had for these now indispensable disciplines. Researchers specialising in these disciplines worked during many years for the National Research Council (CNR). A Service for the Subsidiary Sciences in Archaeology was established in 1970 and specialised in archaeometry (particularly geophysical prospections and dating methods), geology and chemistry. In 1981, this service was transformed into the Institute for Technologies applied to Cultural Heritage (Istituto per le Tecnologie

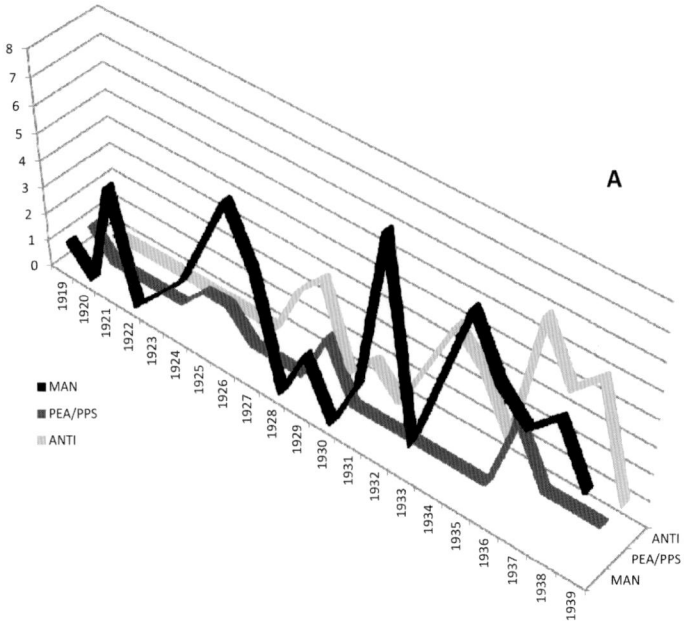

Figure 8.5a. Articles in English journals (1919-1939). PEA/PPS, Proceedings of the East Anglia Society/Proceedings of the Prehistoric Society; ANTI, Antiquity.

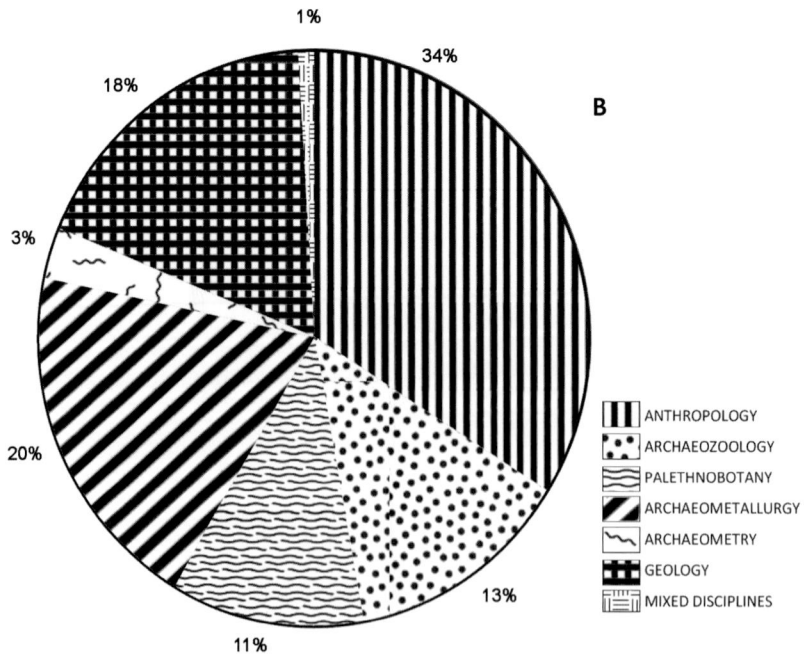

Figure 8.5b. Disciplines that are dealt with in English journals (1919-1939).

8. Science and archaeology in Italy: a difficult marriage

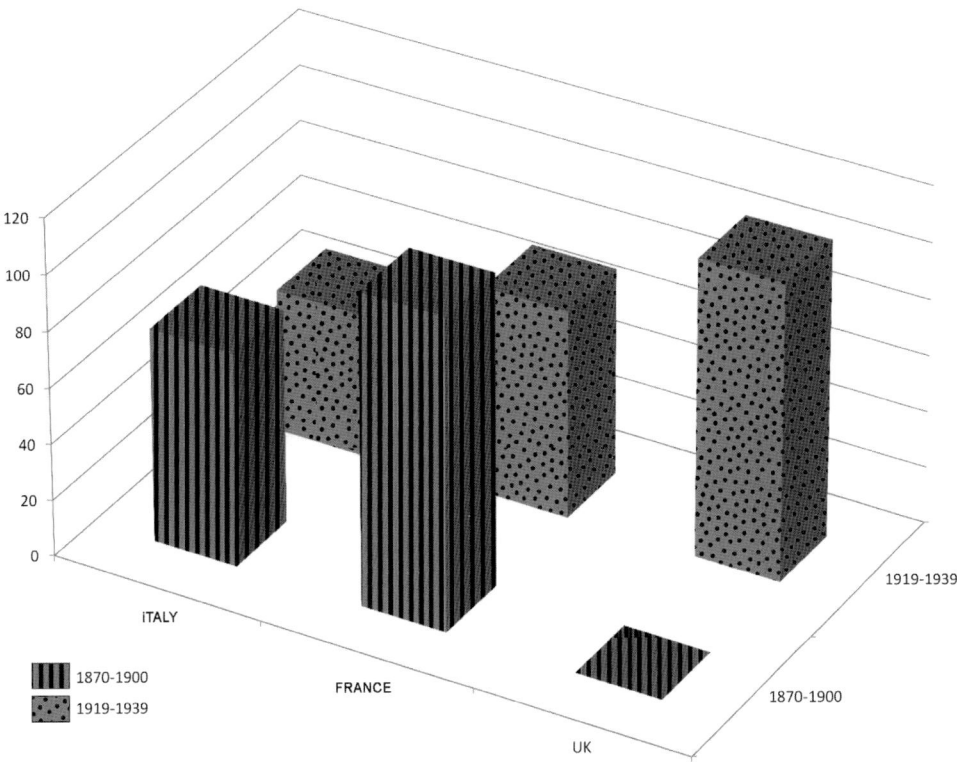

Figure 8.6. Italy, France, United Kingdom: comparison of the total number of articles in the two periods.

applicate ai Beni Culturali, ITABC). This institute still exists today and participates in many research projects in Italy and abroad.

Six years earlier, in 1975, the Ministry for Cultural and Environmental Heritage (Ministero per i Beni Culturali e Ambientali) had been founded. The members of the Ministry were architects, archaeologists and historians of art. It is only since the 1980s that anthropologists, archaeozoologists, geologists, biologists and chemists have been hired in the State Antiquity Offices (Soprintendenze), thanks to the passing of new legislation for the creation of youth cooperative societies in the wider field of Cultural Heritage (Guidi 2016, 217). In recent years, the employees of these institutions have no longer been required to be civil servants as previously and some work for societies or as freelance archaeologists. In contrast to common practice in other European countries, in Italy there are only a few cases in which archaeozoologists or palaeoethnobotanists work for museums. Different again (and critical especially for the recruitment of new professors) is the situation in universities. Aware of the fundamental differences in the development and present situation of the archaeological disciplines in Italy and Great Britain, I have attempted to make a comparison between the universities of those two countries. For my purposes, the Italian and English situations have been assessed by *only* focusing on people working part-time or full-time.

In Italy these are the Ordinary Professors, Associate Professors, part-time or full-time Researchers, while in England they are the Ordinary Professors, Readers, Associate Professors and Lecturers.[3] Regarding Italy, in 27 universities (which make up more or less one third of the 75 existing in our country) 84 persons teach these disciplines (Fig. 8.7a). There are some universities that operate as true 'centres of excellence' in the field of multidisciplinarity, including Lecce with 12 chairs, Roma-Sapienza with 10 and Padua with 6. Most universities, however, have only four or five courses in scientific disciplines related to archaeology and many only one or two. At the same time, it is important to underline that in Rome-Sapienza there are full-time chairs of anthropology, archaeometry, paleoethnobotany and geology, while in Padua only of archaeometry. If we look at the representativeness of each discipline (Fig. 8.7b), nearly 60% of the courses analysed in Italian universities are of archaeometry, 15% of anthropology, 10% of paleoethnobotany, 8% of geology, and only very few of archaeozoology (5%) or archaeometallurgy (4%). The academic affiliations of the persons who teach those courses (Fig. 8.7c) are even more impressive. 55% of them work in geology or physics departments, 14% in biology departments, 10% in botany departments, 7% in chemistry departments and *only* 18% (less than a fifth of the total) in archaeology departments.

This system obviously calls for an ever-growing need for part-time contracts for professors or, more often, freelance specialists in the disciplines not taught at every

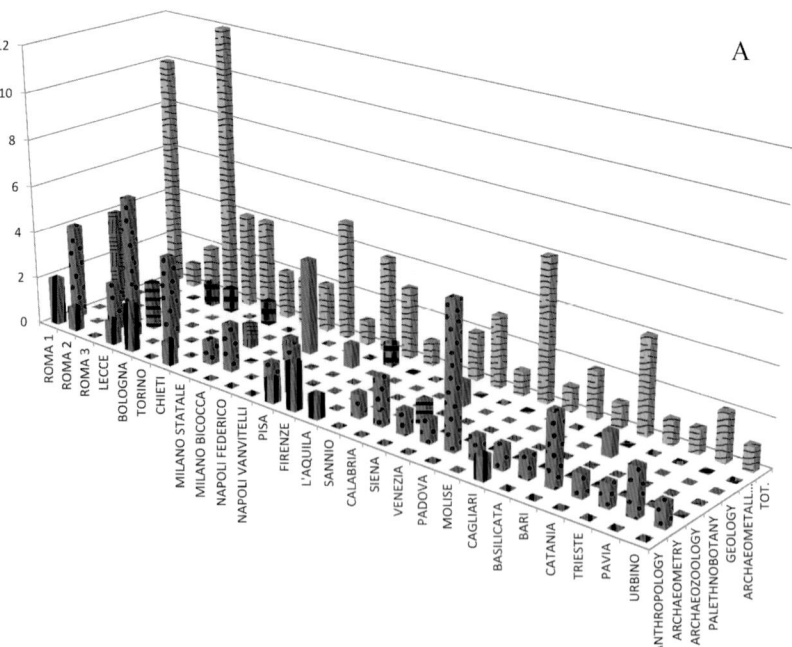

Figure 8.7a. Number of disciplines officially taught in Italian universities.

8. Science and archaeology in Italy: a difficult marriage 173

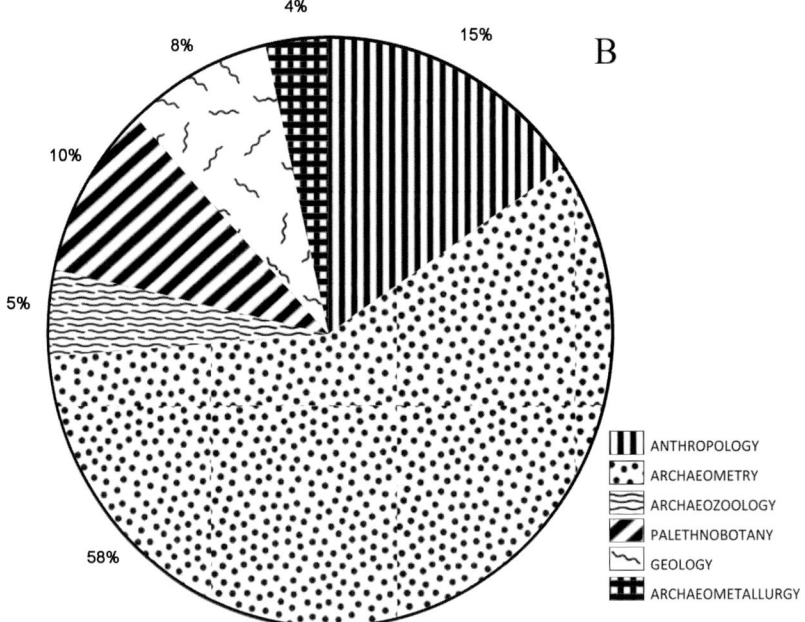

Figure 8.7b. Types of disciplines taught in Italian universities.

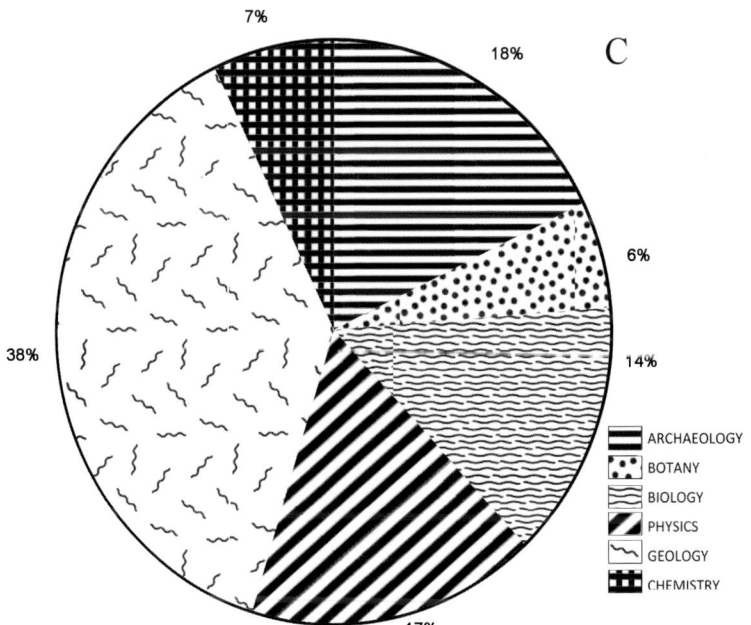

Figure 8.7c. Academic affiliations. Data source. http://www.miur.it/0002Univer/0030Profes/index_cf2.htm (official data of the Italian Ministry for University and Research).

174   Alessandro Guidi

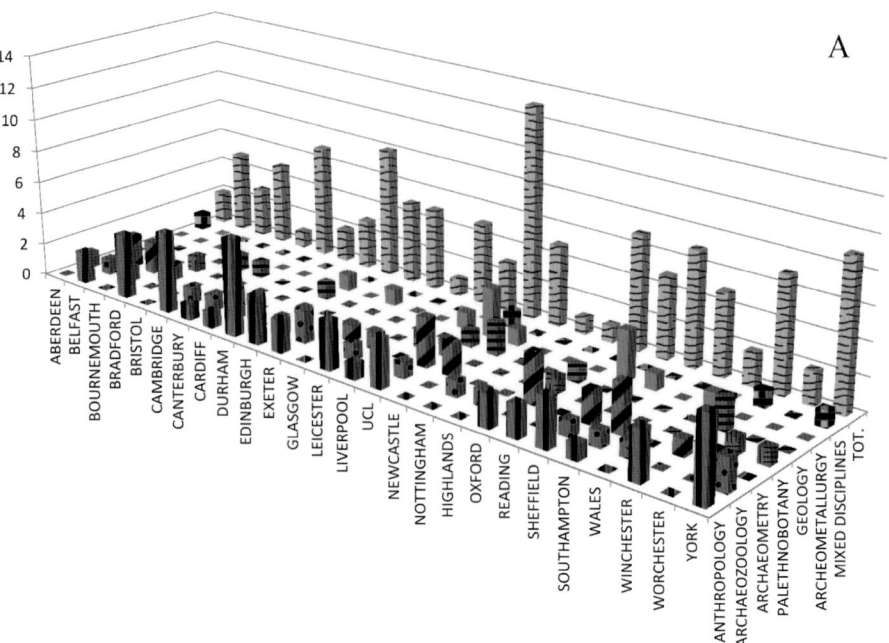

Figure 8.8a. Number of disciplines officially taught in English universities.

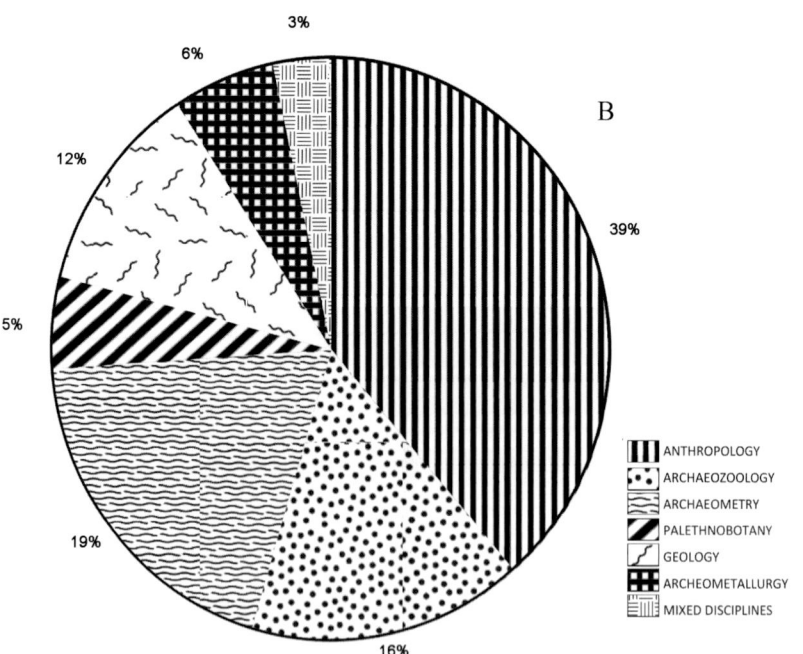

Figure 8.8b. Types of disciplines taught in English universities. Data source. https://www.universityarchaeology.co.uk/members (links to the websites of 26 university archaeology departments).

single university. At the same time, there are many associations that bring together all those who work in those disciplines in universities, museums, state antiquity offices and the National Research Council. Such associations include, for example, the Italian Society of Anthropology and Ethnology, the Italian Society of Archaeozoology (AIAZ) and the Italian Society of Archaeometry (AIAR). The latter is the most influential of these bodies, given the economic interests linked to the chemical and physical study of objects of art or even simple bricks or slag from all the periods studied by archaeologists and especially by classical archaeology scholars.

The data gathered on the web about English universities allows us to identify, as in Italy, some universities that privilege the practice of multidisciplinarity in their archaeology courses (Fig. 8.8a), such as Durham University, University College London and the University of York. The first important difference between Italy and the United Kingdom is that in the latter the majority of teaching is given in the archaeology departments. The second is a less pronounced imbalance between the disciplines taught (Fig. 8.8b). Anthropology plays a major role, with 39% of the teaching, while archaeometry (19%) and archaeozoology (16%) have more or less equal weight. Twelve per cent of the teaching focuses on geology, 6% on archaeometallurgy, 5% on palaeoethnobotany and the remaining 3% is represented by mixed disciplines, such as 'archaeological sciences' (Aberdeen, University College London and Winchester). The third, although no less important difference is the degree of internationalisation. In the United Kingdom a good percentage of those teaching those disciplines are foreign scholars (*e.g.* 5 are Italian), while on the list of Italian scholars it is impossible to find a foreigner.

Conclusions

The metaphor of the 'difficult marriage' seems to be the most useful for describing the complicated history of relationships between archaeology and sciences in Italy. It all looked easy in the nineteenth century (especially in the period analysed here, between 1871 and 1900). This was thanks to the general framework of positivism (accepted by the entire scientific community), although a comparison with a country such as France reveals substantial difficulty in having new ideas accepted, mainly due to the reactionary and conservative intellectual contexts (*e.g.* the Catholic church). Following a long decline in the first decades of the twentieth century, the period between the two World Wars was characterised by a substantial indifference to the application of natural sciences in interpreting the archaeological record, except for the intellectual environment of the Tuscan school, which generally focused on Palaeolithic archaeology and the newly founded journal of Etruscan studies. The post-war years were characterised by a sudden 'rebirth' of interest in these lines of research, coinciding with the beginning of many new university courses in prehistory and, at the same time, with the activity of other 'protagonists' in archaeological research, such as the foreign schools or volunteers.

The situation today appears to have changed. At the same time, despite the work of many excellent Italian specialists from the scientific disciplines in high-ranking international projects (*e.g.* Stefano Campana in ground penetrating radar prospections or Cristina Lemorini in functional analyses at Çatalhöyük),[4] the growing imbalance with some of the most important European countries in this field of interdisciplinary studies in archaeology is worrying. As this chapter has attempted to demonstrate, this gap was first determined by a persistent separation of humanistic and scientific disciplines in Italian culture. This is one of the consequences of the already discussed idealistic philosophy that was present in Italy from the beginning of twentieth century. There are several other causes as well. The first is an imbalance between the academic power of classical archaeology and the other 'archaeologies' (starting with prehistory), which have been more interested in introducing methods borrowed from the natural sciences in archaeological research since their emergence. Secondly, in Italy there is a substantial distrust in the application of experimental methods in historical disciplines, something that can be observed at all levels of the education system, from primary school to university. Thirdly, there is the damaging effect of the peculiar organisation of the State Antiquity Offices, which often compete (and do not cooperate) with universities and/or local museums or volunteers. Finally, Italian politicians are not interested in many of the subjects discussed in this chapter, such as creating a truly functional university system, which has been subjected over the years to much poorly-thought-out reforming legislation.

Acknowledgements

This chapter was written within the framework of the InterArq research project (HAR2016-80271-P) (interarqweb.wordpress.com) subsidised by the State Research Agency (AEI) and the European Regional Development Fund (ERDF, EU). The author is grateful to the anonymous reviewers and the two editors of the volume for their help in improving the first version of this chapter.

Notes

1 Strangely enough, in these journals there are no papers on geology applied to prehistoric archaeology, notwithstanding a great tradition of studies in this field since the first half of nineteenth century (Vai 2014).
2 The *Société des observateurs de l'homme*, an association of scholars interested in medical and anthropological questions, was founded in Paris in 1799.
3 The data for Italy were compiled from http.//Www.Miur.It/0002univer/0030profes/Index_Cf2.Htm and for Great Britain from https://Www.Universityarchaeology.Co.Uk/Members.
4 For more information on the work of Cristina Lemorini, see http.//www.catalhoyuk.com/.

References

Badii, G. (1931) Le antiche miniere del Massetano (Massa metallorum). *Studi Etruschi* 5, 455–474.
Biehl, P.F., Gramsch, A. and Marciniak, A., eds (2002) *Archäologien Europas. Geschichte, Methoden und Theorien/Archaeologies of Europe. History, Methods and Theories*. Münster. New York, München, Berlin, Waxman (Tübinger Archäologische Taschenbücher 3).

Blanc, A.C. (1938) Testimonianze paletnologiche e biogeografiche sulla via percorsa dai Grimaldiani nella loro immigrazione in Europa e in Italia. *Archivio per l'Antropologia e l'Etnologia* 68, 17–28.

Blanc, A.C. and Breuil, H. (1936) Le nouveau crâne neanderthalienne de Saccopastore (Rome). *L'Anthropologie* 46, 1–16.

Broca, P. (1873) Sur les crânes de Solutré. *Bulletin de la Société d'anthropologie* 8, 819–836.

Broca, P. (1876) Sur les trépanations préhistoriques. *Bulletin de la Société d'anthropologie* 11, 236–256, 431–440.

Canfora, L. (1980) *Ideologie del Classicismo*. Torino, Giulio Einaudi.

Castelletti, L. and Martinelli, N. (2014) Il difficile cammino dell'Archeobotanica nel periodo pre- e postunitario. In A. Guidi (ed.) *150 anni di preistoria e protostoria in Italia*, 203–212. Firenze, Istituto Italiano di Preistoria e Protostoria.

Curwen, E.C. (1938a) Early agriculture in Denmark. *Antiquity* 12, 135–153.

Curwen, E.C. (1938b) The early development of agriculture in Britain. *Proceedings of the Prehistoric Society* 2 (4), 27–51.

D'Achiardi, G. (1929) L'industria metallurgica a Populonia. *Studi Etruschi* 3, 397–404.

De Geer, G. (1928) Geochronology. *Antiquity* 2, 308–318.

De Grossi Mazzorin, J. (2014) Le prime ricerche sulle faune nei siti dell'età del Bronzo in Italia. In A. Guidi (ed.) *150 anni di preistoria e protostoria in Italia*, 73–78. Firenze, Istituto Italiano di Preistoria e Protostoria.

De Pascale, A. (2008) Le prime esplorazioni nelle caverne ossifere del Finalese. tracce, ipotesi e scoperte ad opera di Issel, Perrando, Morelli, Rovereto, Rossi, Amerano.... In *La nascita della Paletnologia in Liguria. personaggi, scoperte e collezioni tra XIX e XX secolo. Atti del Convegno (Finale Ligure Borgo, 22–23 settembre 2006)*, 233–248. Bordighera, Istituto Internazionale di Studi Liguri.

Ferrara, G., Reinhard, M. and Tongiorgi, E. (1959) Carbon-14 dating in Pisa. *American Journal of Sciences. Radiocarbon Supplement* V (1), 103–110.

Guidi, A. (1988) *Storia della paletnologia*. Roma, Laterza.

Guidi, A. (2000) La storia dell'archeologia preistorica italiana nel contesto europeo. In N. Terrenato (ed.) *Archeologia Teorica*, 23–37. Firenze, Insegna del Giglio.

Guidi, A. (2008) Italian prehistoric archaeology in the international context. *Fragmenta* 2, 109–120.

Guidi, A., ed. (2014a) *150 anni di preistoria e protostoria in Italia*. Firenze, Istituto Italiano di Preistoria e Protostoria.

Guidi, A. (2014b) Preistoria, politica e potere dal 1861 al 1871. In A. Guidi (ed.) *150 anni di preistoria e protostoria in Italia*, 25–30. Firenze, Istituto Italiano di Preistoria e Protostoria.

Guidi, A. (2015) Quantitative methods in Italian archaeology. a review. *Archeologia e Calcolatori* 26, 45–58.

Guidi, A. (2016) Lobbying for archaeology in the Italian 'First Republic'. In G. Delley, M. Díaz-Andreu, F. Djindjian, V. Fernández, A. Guidi and M.A. Kaeser (eds) *History of Archaeology - International Perspectives*, 213–220. British Archaeological Reports. Oxford, Archaeopress.

Guidi, A. (2018) Italian prehistorians and their relationships with foreign colleagues. *UISPP Journal* 1 (1), 73–85.

Hilzheimer, M. (1932) Dogs. *Antiquity* 6, 411–419.

Hilzheimer, M. (1935) The evolution of the domestic horse. *Antiquity* 9, 133–139.

Hilzheimer, M. (1936a) The Inca Bull-Dog. *Antiquity* 10, 358–359.

Hilzheimer, M. (1936b) Sheep. Antiquity. *Antiquity* 10, 195–206.

Huntingford, G.W.B. (1932) Ancient agriculture. *Antiquity* 6, 327–337.

Hurel, A. (2007) *La France préhistorienne de 1789 à 1941*. Paris, CNRS Éditions.

Hurel, A. and Coye, N., eds (2011) *Dans l'épaisseur du temps. Archéologues et géologues inventent la préhistoire*. Paris, Muséum national d'Histoire naturelle (Publications scientifiques du muséum).

Issel, A. (1884) Esame sommario d'avanzi d'uomo e di animali raccolti nella grotta degli Orreri in Sardegna. *Bullettino di Paletnologia Italiana* 10, 9–12.

Kannes, G. (1997) Fiorelli, Giuseppe. In *Dizionario Biografico degli Italiani XLVIII*, 137–142. Roma, Istituto dell'Enciclopedia Italiana.
Lantier, R. (1936) Le nouveau crâne de Saccopastore (Italie). *Revue Archeologique serie 3* 7, 115.
Lantier, R. (1939) L'Homme fossile du Monte Circeo. *Anthropologie Paris* 49 (3/4), 253–264.
Lerici, C.M. (1959) Periscope on the Etruscan Past. *National Geographic* 116 (3), 336–350.
Mochi, A. (1927) I sincronismi tra glaciazioni faune e industrie quaternarie in Europa e le concordanze italiane. *Archivio per l'Antropologia e l'Etnologia* 57, 137–186.
Montandon, G. (1926) Craniologie paléosiberienne (néolithiques, mongoloïdes, tchouktchi, eskimo, aléoutes, kamtchadales, aïnou, ghiliak, négroïdes du Nord). *L'Anthropologie* 36, 209–296, 447–543.
Moro Abadía, O. and Huth, C. (2013) Speaking materials. Sources for the history of archaeology. *Complutum* 24 (2), 1–212.
Mortillet, G.d.e. (1874) Climat de l'époque quaternaire. *Bulletin de la Société d'anthropologie* 9, 391–393.
Mortillet, G.d.e. (1877) Races humaines et chirurgie de l'époque des dolmens. *Matériaux pour l'Histoire Primitive et Naturelle de l'Homme* XII, 153–166.
Mortillet, G.d.e. (1879) Sur l'origine des animaux domestiques. *Bulletin de la Société d'anthropologie* 3 (2), 232–252.
Peroni, R. (1992) Preistoria e protostoria. La vicenda degli studi in Italia. In *Le vie della preistoria*, 9–70. Rome Manifesto Libri.
Petacco, A. (2000) *L'anarchico che venne dall'America. Storia di Gaetano Bresci e del complotto per uccidere Umberto I*. Milan, Mondadori.
Pizzato, F.A. (2015) Per una storia antropologica della nazione. Giuseppe Sergi e il mito della razza mediterranea nella costruzione culturale dello stato unitario italiano e nella competizione politica europea (1880–1919). *Storia del Pensiero Politico* 2015 (1), 25–51.
Plutniak, S. (2018) A co-authorship network analysis of national and international growth in prehistoric archaeology, Italy (1875–2000). Combining bibliometric and qualitative data in the history of science. *MEFRIM* 130, 417–430.
Pontier, G. (1922) A propos de l'existence à Arques (Pas-de-Calais) d'un Mammouth nain. Elephas Primigenius, variété Leith Adamsi. *Bulletin de la Société préhistorique française* 19, 7–9, 169–174.
Pontier, G. (1933) Nouvelle contribution à l'étude des Eléphants quaternaires de la Charente. *Bulletin de la Société préhistorique française* 30 (1), 68–80.
Puccioni, N. (1932) Appunti sui resti scheletrici umani del giacimento di Belverde (Cetona). *Archivio per l'Antropologia e l'Etnologia* 62, 26–64.
Scarabelli, G. (1850) Intorno alle armi antiche di pietra dura che sono state raccolte nell'Imolese. *Nuovi Annali delleScienze Naturali [Bologna]* 3 (2), 258–266.
Schnapp, A. (2014) I prodromi della Preistoria nella tradizione erudita italiana. In A. Guidi (ed.) *150 anni di preistoria e protostoria in Italia*, 41–48. Firenze, Istituto Italiano di Preistoria e Protostoria.
Sordelli, F. (1880) Sulle piante della torbiera e della stazione preistorica della Lagozza. *Atti della Società Italiana di Scienze Naturali* 23, 219–243.
Strobel, P. (1877) Avanzi animali dei fondi di capanne nel Reggiano. *Bullettino di Paletnologia Italiana* 3, 45–57, 65–79.
Strobel, P. (1880) Le razze del cane delle Terramare. *Bullettino di Paletnologia Italiana* 6, 13–53, 110–130, 140–154, 169–178.
Strobel, P. (1886) Avanzi di vertebrati preistorici nella Valle della Vibrata. *Bullettino di Paletnologia Italiana* 12, 162–179.
Tarantini, M. (1998–2000) Tradizioni e tensioni disciplinari nell'archeologia prehistorica italiana tra ottocento e novecento. *Origini* XXII, 7–43.
Tarantini, M. (2002) Archeologia e scienze naturali in Italia. Il caso dell'organizzazione degli studi etruschi (1925–1932). *Rassegna di Archeologia, s. B* 19, 321–351.

Tarantini, M. (2012) *La nascita della Paletnologia in Italia (1860–1877)*. Quaderni del Dipartimento di Archaeologia e Storia dell' Arti. Sezione Archaeologia. Siena, Universitá degli Studi di Siena.

Tongiorgi, E. (1937) Esame dei carboni provenienti dallo scavo dell' impianto metallurgico – Ricerche archeologico-minerarie in Val Fucinaia. *Studi Etruschi* 11, 331–334.

Vai, G.B. (2014) Geologia e Archeologia Preistorica. I pionieri europei prima del 1860. In A. Guidi (ed.) *150 anni di preistoria e protostoria in Italia*, 31–40. Firenze, Istituto Italiano di Preistoria e Protostoria.

Vallois, H.V. (1927) Les ossements énéolithiques de l'Ombrive (Ariège). *L'Anthropologie* 37, 277–305, 473–490.

Vallois, H.V. (1936) Les ossements natoufiens d'Erq-el-Hahmar (Palestine). *L'Anthropologie* 46, 529–540.

Wainwright, G.A. (1936) The coming of iron. *Antiquity* 10, 5–24.

Chapter 9

Archaeology and the Armed Forces in Spain from the nineteenth to the twenty-first century

Francisco Gracia Alonso

Abstract

Relations between the Armed Forces and civil society in Spain between the nineteenth and twentieth centuries have been difficult due to the succession of civil wars and military dictatorships. Unlike other European countries, the Spanish Armed Forces developed ballooning and aerial observation units late, delaying the impact of aerial photography on archaeological research. After the Spanish Civil War (1936-1939), the collaboration of the Armed Forces focused on the transfer of prisoners of war as forced labour, especially in the Greek colony and Roman city of Ampurias. At the same time, several archaeological schools, headed by Martín Almagro and Julio Martínez Santa-Olalla, competed for the support of the Air Force in the initial development of aerial archaeology. The end of the Franco regime in 1975 and the restoration of democracy favoured the interest of the Armed Forces to improve their image before the civilians. Their support in archaeological research, especially in underwater archaeology, has been essential in achieving this.

Keywords: Spain; Armed Forces; archaeology; society; research; interdisciplinarity; cultural heritage.

Introduction

This chapter examines the relations between the Armed Forces and archaeology in Spain from the nineteenth to the twenty-first century. In the second half of the nineteenth century, archaeological research in Spain was organised out of the need to build a historical account that would serve as support for consolidating the restoration of the monarchy (1874), in which the army would have a prominent role. However, unlike in other European countries, the predominance of Greek and Latin texts in research and the disregard of interdisciplinarity impeded the development of collaboration with the Armed Forces, except for works in archaeological sites such as Numancia, where heroisation was an essential factor. Aerial photography, developed before the Spanish Civil War, allowed the identification and study of some sites, but not extensive research projects despite the advance in the organisational structuring of Spanish archaeology after the Heritage Act of 1911. During the Francoist dictatorship (1936–1975), the collaboration of the Armed Forces in archaeology focused on the assignment of prisoners of war as forced labour for the development of research in sites such as Ampurias. It also served the interests of some military, such as Admiral Bastarreche, who was the protector and collaborator of the main archaeologists of the period 1940–1960 (*e.g.* Antonio Beltrán, Martín Almagro Basch and Lluís Pericot), achieving progress in some fields such as underwater archaeology. Since 1977, the Armed Forces have become increasingly involved in supporting archaeological investigation as a way of expanding their social presence and prestige, but not in the development of the main contemporary lines of research in Conflict Archaeology, such as the mass graves of the Civil War and the concentration camps of the first phase of Francoism.

Ideology and research (from the nineteenth century to 1939)

During the second half of the nineteenth century and the beginning of the twentieth, scientific archaeology was beginning to take shape in Europe. States were beginning to promote the construction of knowledge of the past as a way to support their social and ideological cohesion. In Spain, however, archaeological research still lacked the political and administrative recognition necessary for its development. Archaeology as a science was only valued as a source of evidence to support the historical account based on written documentation and on the works of the fathers of Spanish history, Juan de Mariana (1536–1624) and Modesto Lafuente Zamalloa (1806–1866). As a result, the Spanish Army played no practical or technical role in archaeological research. Interest in the past among the military was channelled into the creation of an ideological narrative that upheld the defining features of the interpretation of the past of the Spanish nation: the indissoluble unity and independence of the *patria*, its ancestral values, and the defence of Christianity. In the strictly military domain, the reaffirmation of the stories of heroism, sacrifice and the contribution to a rather simplistic and uncritical account of Spanish history kept alive the Army's influence in Spanish society in the turbulent second half of the nineteenth century. Indeed, the linking of this heroic memory to Antiquity was reflected in the names given to military units like the infantry regiments *Mérida* 44 (1856) and *Iberia* 63 (1846), and the cavalry regiments *Sagunto* (1718) and *Numancia* (1703). The name of the *Numancia* regiment was particularly poignant, recalling the site of the doomed resistance of the Celtiberians against the Romans in the second century BC; in fact, several patriotic celebrations were held there, including the inaugurations of the site memorials in 1842, 1886 and 1905 (Jimeno and Torre 2005, 153–157; Gómez-Barrera 2014, 129–135).

Figure 9.1. King Alfonso XIII's visit in Guadalajara at the barracks of the Military Aerostat Service in 1922. Source: Wikimedia Commons.

The first instances of the Armed Forces' limited contributions to archaeological research were the result of technological advances. Aerial photography had become popular in Spain after photographer Antoni Esplugas Puig (1852–1929) took pictures from an air balloon during the Universal Exhibition of 1888 in Barcelona, but its development in military circles would have to wait until the creation of the Military Aerostat Service by Royal Order in 1896 (Fig. 9.1), which was led by military engineer Pedro Vives Vich (1858–1938) (Fig. 9.2) (Fernández García 2015). In 1913 this unit became part of the Military Aeronautics Service. Its main objective was to map the Spanish Protectorate in Morocco (especially the areas around the military headquarters in Ceuta and Melilla) so as to increase the Army's knowledge of the territory and to facilitate military operations against the native insurgents. But in the early 1910s the proper documentation of the main cities and towns in Spain was started with oblique photographs that made it possible to take photographic measurements (Quirós Linares and Fernández García 1996). These flights were able to document historical monuments and archaeological sites that could be excavated in the future, and they helped to put together the first sets of reference photographs which would be used for many years to come, such as the ones included in the report of the 1917 campaign carried out by the Spanish Commission in Numancia. This report contained what is probably the first explicit photograph of an archaeological site in Spain, the enclave of

Loma de Garay outside the city of Soria. The photographs were taken by military aviators Joaquín González-Gallarza (1887–1961) and Luis Gonzalo Victoria (1883–1975), the latter of whom was to become one of the theorists of aerial observation in Spain. Other examples were the photographs taken of Ampurias in 1922, and those of the Mérida excavations, which archaeologists José Ramón Mélida y Alinari (1856–1933) and Maximiliano Macías Liáñez (1867–1934) included in the reports delivered to the Higher Council for Excavations and Antiquities (Junta Superior de Excavaciones y Antigüedades, JSEA) in 1932, 1934 and 1936. Nevertheless, these are the only instances of the participation of the Armed Forces in archaeological research in Spain from the nineteenth century until 1939. A number of historical and archaeological materials were preserved in military museums or other military premises because of their representativeness or typological interest, but in general the Army played a very minor role in the development of archaeology.

Figure 9.2. Major and military engineer, later general and minister, Pedro Vives Vich (1858–1938) (left) next to Henri Deutsch de la Meurthe (circa 1909). Source: Wikimedia Commons.

The Civil War, the postwar period and Francoism (1939–1977)

The military uprising of July 1936, the revolution and the three years of war that ensued caused serious damage to the archaeological heritage, both sites and artefacts, due to hostilities themselves, looting and the lack of maintenance. The protective measures taken by the Republican government at the beginning of the war, and later by the Burgos government with the creation of the Service for the Defence of the National Artistic Heritage (Servicio de Defensa del Patrimonio Artístico Nacional, SDPAN), managed to locate artefacts (sometimes through espionage), gathered them together in protected warehouses, and in some cases sent them abroad (Colorado Castellary 2010, 13–28; 2018, 53–62). In Catalonia the autonomous government of the Generalitat, applying the legislation approved in 1934 by the Catalan Parliament, secured private deposits and collections by confiscating and storing them under the protection of technical staff and armed guards (Gracia Alonso and Munilla 2011, 62–78). These stocks, commandeered by the Museum of Archaeology of Catalonia as an integral part of the Catalan Artistic Treasury, were sent to Geneva in February 1939, where they were placed under the protection of the League of Nations. The organisation and execution of this process were exemplary. In fact, they were later used as a reference point for the protection of works of art in the event of war by the Office International des Musées (OIM), and also in the evacuation of public collections during the Second World War.

The collections evacuated during the Civil War came back to Spain between May and September of 1939. They were returned to their museums of origin, where they were used to reshape the mission and the philosophy of these institutions in tune with the changing times (Colorado Castellary 2018, 65–72). However, some collections of great historical importance had been lost. For example, the coin collection of the National Archaeological Museum had been melted down by the Republican government in order to finance the war effort (Gracia Alonso and Munilla 2013, 153–202); other items were condemned to the same fate by the Generalitat between 1936 and 1937 (Gracia Alonso and Munilla 2018). The pre-eminence of military considerations over archaeological heritage during the war was also reflected in the installation of a coastal artillery battery by the Anarchist militias from the Buenaventura Durruti barracks in Barcelona on the site of the Roman city of Ampurias. The purpose of this action was to protect the southern sector of the Gulf of Rosas in the presence of vessels of Franco's navy and the Italian Regia Marina. This practice was repeated at other sites such as the necropolis and settlement of Coll del Moro (Gandesa, Tarragona) in 1938, where Franco's headquarters were set up during the battle of the Ebro. Most of these acts were left unrecorded after the war, so as not to incriminate those responsible for the neglect of heritage. On a more positive note, the military operations provided new resources for the analysis of the territory, like the repeated series of observation flights made by the Condor Legion during the fighting in the Ebro, which revealed the alterations made to the landscape in earlier times in an essentially agricultural area, were demonstrated in the record photographic series at the Spanish Civil War Archives in Salamanca.

The outcome of the Civil War meant that Franco's Army was obliged to take control of the museums and material deposits located in the Republican zone, ensuring their transfer to centres of classification, organisation and return, under the supervision of the staff of the SDPAN. Many of the staff were graduates in history or history of art or archaeologists who had been called up, like Martín Almagro Basch (1911–1984), Blas Taracena Aguirre (1895–1951) and Luís Monreal Tejada (1912–2005). Their work was always driven more by a concern for propaganda than for heritage, and this situation governed the economic, human and material resources available for the execution of the task at hand. The same propagandistic purpose underpinned the return of the Iberian sculptures preserved in the Louvre – including the Lady of Elche and artefacts from the sites of Osuna (Seville) and Cerro de los Santos (Albacete) – in 1941, in application of the agreements between Franco and Marshal Philippe Pétain (the Chief of State of Vichy France, 1940–1944) after the French defeat by Germany in 1940. In all cases, the Spanish government and the security forces in charge attributed the success of these operations exclusively to the sterling work of the new regime (Colorado Castellary 2018, 195–218).

After the Civil War, the Army held a large number of prisoners of war who had been arrested or returned to Spain by friendly powers. These prisoners were used as slave labour by public and private companies under the supervision of the military authorities. It so happened that archaeologist Martín Almagro Basch (Gracia Alonso 2012, 165–175; Mederos 2017) had been appointed director of the Provincial Archaeological Museum of Barcelona on 15 April 1939, and of the Archaeological Research Service of the Provincial Delegation of Barcelona on 26 June. Lacking any resources to resume the work at Ampurias, which had been at a standstill since December 1936, Almagro Basch enlisted the help of the Captain-General of the Fourth Military Region, Luis Orgaz Yoldi (1881–1946), in obtaining forced manual labour to work at the site, thus obviating the expense that would have been entailed by the hiring of civilian workers (Fig. 9.3). Thus, between September 1940 and May 1941, the members of the Fourth Company of the Workers' Battalion *Figueras 71* worked at the archaeological site under armed guard, and under the technical management of the staff members of the Ampurias museum, a certain Ramos and assistant Juan Bautista Escrivá Pons (1872/1877–1960). Archaeologists Josep Colominas Roca (1883–1958), Alberto del Castillo Yurrita (1899–1976), José de Calasanç Serra Ràfols (1902–1971) and Juan Maluquer de Motes (1915–1988) also took part in the excavations. The assignment of worker soldiers to the excavations was part of the Army's policy of using the manpower at its disposal in the tasks of reconstruction, essentially public works and productive structures. Nevertheless, Captain-General Orgaz's decision to deploy this labour force in Ampurias can be regarded as exceptional, given that in other military regions no support at all was given for archaeological interventions. In any case, Almagro was merely reviving an idea that the archaeologist Blas Taracena Aguirre (1895–1951) had already submitted to the Ministry of National Education in 1938, in which he proposed the use of captive labour in tasks of protection of the historical heritage under the supervision of SDPAN.

The work carried out by this forced labour enabled Almagro Basch to present the first results of the excavations to the leaders of the Feminine Section (the women's branch of the Falange political movement in Spain), headed by Pilar Primo de Rivera (1907–1991) and the Minister of the Party, Pedro Gamero del Castillo (1910–1984), during their visit to the site in January 1941. Their presence was turned into an important propaganda exercise by the press, which celebrated the Army's involvement in the study of a site presented as the point of entry into Spain of Roman civilisation and Christianity, two of the essential components of the ideological construction of the regime. The connection between the Provincial Archaeological Museum of Barcelona and the Army was repeatedly praised in the press and received financial support from the Diputación (the Provincial Council). However, it came to an end when Lieutenant General Orgaz was transferred to Morocco as High Commissioner of the Spanish Protectorate on 12 May 1941. The decision to assign prisoners to Ampurias had been a personal one, rather than a structural policy regarding the division of duties implemented by the Construction Command of the Fourth Military Region.

Figure 9.3. Republican Prisoners of War (POW) employees in the field, during the survey of Greek colony and Roman city of Ampurias, 1940–1942. Source: Museu d'Arqueologia de Catalunya.

In addition, the workers were needed to form defensive lines in the Pyrenees due to the military activity of the Second World War. Nevertheless, Almagro obtained the support of the new Captain-General, Alfredo Kindelán Duany (1879–1962), who used his contacts to obtain a new contingent of forced labour, the Disciplinary Battalion of Worker Soldiers (Batallón Disciplinario de Soldados Trabajadores, BDST) 46, to work in the excavations at Ampurias (Gracia Alonso 2003; 2009, 335–354; 2012, 165–175).

Formed in the military camp of Punta Palomera (Cádiz) from the earlier contingent of BDST 1, the soldiers arrived in Ampurias on 5 December 1941. In extremely difficult sanitary, hygiene and food conditions, they worked on the sector of the wall, the amphitheatre and the Roman city, supervised by an armed escort and under the inspection of the Fortifications and Construction Command of the Fourth Military Region. Technical aspects of the work were overseen once again by Ramos and Escrivá, along with Del Castillo, August Panyella Gómez (1921–1999) and Miquel Tarradell Mateu (1920–1995), at that time students of Almagro Basch at the University of Barcelona. However, after an inspection of the Fourth Military Region's disciplinary units, the visiting inspector complained directly to the Captain General about the harsh working conditions, and Kindelán decided to end the presence of the BDST 46 in May 1942. However, the unit would not leave Ampurias until 7 August, when the remaining troops were sent to work at the coastal fortifications of the island of Mallorca. Determined to maintain the collaboration of the Army as a source of cheap labour, Almagro Basch multiplied his contacts with military structures, visiting the Captaincy General, praising the work of the Army in the press, and even giving lectures at the Centre for Military Culture of Barcelona to bolster confidence in his management of the troops and of the resources allocated to the excavations (Gracia Alonso 2012, 173–174).

The new military officer of the Fourth Region, Lieutenant General José Moscardó Ituarte (1878–1956), granted the requests of Almagro Basch due to his ideological and political links and assigned reserve troops from the Fortifications Regiment No. 3 in Figueras to work at the site in March 1943. Confrontations immediately arose between the members of military and the directors of the site with regard to the troops' accommodation, which in principle was going to be the same as those endured previously by the members of the Workers' Battalion – the difference being that now the workers were reservists rather than forced labourers, Spanish Army soldiers and not republican prisoners, so their importance for the army officers was different. After receiving funds from the Provincial Council and the City Council of Barcelona to improve the living conditions and solving the problems, a new unit, the Sappers' Regiment No. 4 (the structural arm of the engineers of the Fourth Military Region until the mid-1950s) was sent to the site. Assigning specialised troops to the site was an indication of how seriously the Army took the work. The soldiers dug mainly in the sector of the Roman city, contributing to the study of the Roman houses and the forum, and also deconstructed other sectors. For the next fifteen years, the manpower contributed by the Army was essential in the development of the research. Almagro Basch continued to cultivate his relations with the Army leaders in Catalonia, such as Lieutenant General Juan Bautista Sánchez González (1893–1957), whom he visited frequently at the Captaincy General. Over time, Almagro Basch had relations with the region's five military commanders: Orgaz, Kindelán, Moscardó, José Solchaga Zala (1881–1953) and Sánchez González. He also organised repeated visits to the site for the Army leadership. Such a visit is, for example, the inspection made by the general chief engineer of the Fourth Military Region, Joaquín Coll Fuster (1881–1969), accompanied by more than thirty chiefs and officers, on 15 April 1943 and again on 3 August of the same year (Gracia Alonso 2009, 351).

In 1946, the Second Section of the First Battalion of the Sappers' Regiment was moved and replaced by the First Company of the First Battalion, which was stationed in the nearby town of L'Escala. Its main mission was to help in the preparation of the site's museum, which was inaugurated on 5 September 1947. Almagro also persuaded the Army to provide a workforce for the excavations of the Hallstatt necropolis of Can Bech de Baix (Agullana, Girona), led by archaeologists Joaquín Tomás and Pere de Palol Salellas (1923–2005) between 1943 and 1945. The work was carried out by a detachment of the Fourth Company of the First Battalion of the Fortifications Regiment No. 3, a unit that also worked for a time in the excavations of the Visigothic town of Puig Rom (Roses, Girona) (Gracia Alonso 2009, 352–353).

Archaeology was used by the military dictatorship in the construction of its historiographic project. Speeches by propagandists such as historian, philologist and linguist Antonio Tovar Llorente (1911–1985) made efforts to equate Spain's ancient history with the Francoist *caudillismo* – the political, military and social leadership exercised by Franco. Researchers prioritised the need to mould the interpretation of historical documentation to the political reality of their time, neglecting the strict requirements of scientific research. The aim of this was to celebrate the three essential elements of Francoist thought: the Army, the Empire and Christianity. These ideas were developed by, among others, archaeologist Julio Martínez Santa-Olalla (1905–1972), appointed General Commissioner of Archaeological Excavations in 1939 (Díaz-Andreu and Ramírez Sánchez 2004; Gracia Alonso 2009, 213–290). In his speeches at the end of the Second World War, Martínez Santa-Olalla not only defended this ideology but supported the prominent role of the Army and the single party, the Traditionalist Spanish Falange, in the development of archaeological research (Mederos 2003). The policy started from an indisputable maxim: those who control research control the construction of the history derived from it, and, as result, public opinion. Enlisting the military in this mission was a natural step, in the light of the prestige the Army had gained after its victory in the war and the power of the regime as its maximum guarantor. The idea of the Army was also important to the narrative of the renaissance of Imperial Spain. This narrative linked the present with the dynasty of the House of Austria between the sixteenth and early eighteenth centuries and the expansion in America, the period of the great Spanish Empire. This connection was especially true for the campaigns in the Spanish Protectorate in North Africa, the cornerstone of the Army's social standing since the middle of the nineteenth century, where many of the outstanding figures of the regime had forged their reputations (Gracia Alonso 2010).

The importance of *africanista* positions (a set of ideas on the regeneration of Spain, developed by the generals who fought in the colonial wars in Africa) in the ideological construction of the Franco regime, and the desire of the dictatorship after 1939 to maintain a colonial presence in Africa and thus establish Spain as a power of the first order on the international stage spurred on research in the Spanish Protectorate of Morocco, the Spanish Sahara, the enclaves of Ifni and Tarfaya, and Equatorial Guinea (Gozalbes Cravioto, Gozalbes García and Gozalbes García 2013). This was intended to demonstrate to the Spanish people that the country was on an equal footing with the colonial empires of Italy, France and the United Kingdom as regards the control of the southern banks of the Mediterranean. It was part of a political programme that would endure (admittedly on an increasingly reduced scale, due to the process of decolonisation) throughout the Franco regime, until the abandonment of the Western Sahara in 1975. Given its special political structure the Protectorate of Morocco did not constitute a Spanish province, and so it was not included in the General Commissariat of Archaeological Excavations (Comisaría General de Excavaciones Arqueológicas). The Commissariat had been created at the end of the Civil War on 9 March 1939, to take over the functions that the Heritage Act of 1933 had assigned to the Council for

Artistic Treasures (Junta Superior del Tesoro Artístico), a circumstance that would help define the links between the military, administrators and archaeologists and also the development of the research. Though he had no administrative control over the territory of the Protectorate, general commissioner Martínez Santa-Olalla, appointed on 7 March 1939, son of José Martínez Herrera who was an *africanista* soldier and Air Force General, wanted to expand Spanish archaeology in North Africa with the support of the Protectorate's political and military structure. He had already expressed this idea in his plan for the organisation of a National and Imperial Archaeological Institute (Instituto Arqueológico Nacional e Imperial) in 1938, in imitation of the German Archaeological Institute (Gracia Alonso and Munilla 2010). In this he also saw an opportunity to capitalise on the political weakness of France (Gracia Alonso 2010).

Without having authority in the Protectorate, Martínez Santa-Olalla made four trips to the region in 1939 and 1940, before the regime's cultural delegate, Tomás García Figueras (1892–1981), decided to appoint archaeologist Pelayo Quintero Atauri (1867–1946), former director of research work in the area of the city of Cádiz (Díaz-Andreu 2015; Gozalbes Cravioto 2015a; 2015b) to direct the archaeological activities in the territory, to be followed by Miquel Tarradell. Martínez Santa-Olalla also led the Spanish expedition to the territories of Ifni and Río de Oro between January and February 1941, the First Palaeoethnological Expedition to the Spanish Sahara between June and September 1943 (which would be repeated in September and October 1946) and the ethnographic and archaeological expedition to Guinea in July and August of the same year. All these visits to the Spanish Protectorate were carried out with the support of the military authorities, but they were short-lived projects that are not mentioned in Martínez Santa-Olalla's writings, probably because he was not able to consolidate his influence in the territory (Martínez Santa-Olalla 1947).

The interest in demonstrating the historical connections between the North of Africa and the Iberian Peninsula underpinned the archaeological and ethnographic expeditions to the Spanish Sahara. Almagro Basch participated in the trip organised in 1941 by the Institute of Political Studies (Instituto de Estudios Políticos, IEP) (Gracia Alonso 2012, 262–267). Furthermore, in 1943 he took on the 'patriotic' commission to expand the knowledge of the territory with the support of the director of the IEP, foreign affairs officer Fernando María Castiella (1907–1976), and of the General Directorate of Morocco and the Colonies led by government officer Juan Fontán Lobé (1904–1971). With the help of the Army units in the region, Almagro Basch carried out an extensive campaign of explorations during the winter of 1944. He defined the Army's relationship with the early Franco regime and the importance of *africanismo* in its ideological construction in the dedication of his monograph, *The Prehistory of North Africa and of the Spanish Sahara*, in 1946: 'to the Spanish Army of Africa, maintainer of the heroic, civilizing and missionary spirit of Spain'. Therefore, Almagro Basch made his contribution to the political project of recovery of the Spanish Empire, especially after the appointment of attorney Alberto Martín Artajo (1905–1979) as Minister of Foreign Affairs in July 1945, and in view of the need to reassess Spanish foreign policy after the end of the Second World War (Calvo 1997).

Julio Martínez Santa-Olalla and Almagro Basch competed over the work in Africa. With the scientific collaboration of archaeologist Lluís Pericot García (1899–1974) (Gracia Alonso 2017, 283–228) and his disciple Tarradell in the study of the prehistoric sites of the region, Almagro Basch was able to exert a decisive influence over the territory, and Pericot established himself as the Spanish reference point in the *africanista* meetings. Their collaboration considerably weakened the position of Martínez Santa-Olalla, due to the political influences of Almagro Basch and Pericot (Gracia Alonso 2019). In 1949 Almagro and Pericot won the Francisco Franco Prize, awarded by the High Commissariat in Morocco, for their *Moroccan Prehistory. A study of its different periods and relations with Spain and the rest of Africa*. Two new expeditions were carried out, one to the Sahara with the support of the Army in 1946, led by Almagro Basch and Panyella, and the other to Guinea in 1949 thanks to the support of the Institute of African Studies and the General Directorate of Morocco and the Colonies. The expeditions were possible because the military and political authorities of the Protectorate used archaeological research as one of the focal points of their cultural policy, in an attempt to outdo the research being carried out by the French in their Protectorate and in Algeria. Almagro obtained the necessary support for the expedition from the naturalist Joaquín Mateu Sanpere (1921–2015), who identified the rock carvings in the Smara area during his military service between 1944 and 1945. Later on, in 1951, they were also helped by archaeologists Antonio Arribas Palau (1926–2002) and Eduard Ripoll Perelló (1923–2006) (Gracia Alonso 2012, 201–202).

Martínez Santa-Olalla and Almagro Basch also competed for the support of the Air Force in the application of aerial photography to archaeological prospection after the Second World War. In *Ampurias*, written in 1943, Almagro Basch reported the first images taken by the Photographic Service of the Army of archaeological sites such as the Roman camp of Castra Caecilia (Cáceres), the Roman city of Segobriga (Saelices, Cuenca) and the hill fort of Monte Bernorio (Villarén de Valdivia, Palencia). In the same book, he also acknowledged the help given by the Minister of Air, General Juan Vigón Suero-Díaz (1880–1955) (Fig. 9.4), whom Almagro had met through his brother Jorge, who had links with monarchists inside the Francoist circles of power. In fact, in 1941 Almagro had already asked Vigón for the support of the Air Force for various projects, in an attempt to adopt the practices deployed before the war in the United Kingdom, Germany and North Africa and to apply them in Levante and, especially, in Ampurias. For his part, Martínez Santa-Olalla tried to win over Vigón by naming him a member of the Spanish Society of Anthropology, Ethnography and Prehistory (Sociedad Española de Antropología, Etnografía y Prehistoria) in 1942, of which Martínez Santa-Olalla was secretary. In addition, due to his links with Nazi archaeology and especially with the SS society Das Ahnenerbe (Gracia Alonso 2008a; 2008b; 2009), Martínez Santa-Olalla proposed in the early summer of 1942 the organisation of an exhibition in Madrid under the title *Aerial photography and prehistory* as a continuation of the one held in Berlin. For this event, he requested German support (specifically from the German Ministry of Air), as well as from archaeologist and Nazi Party official Herbert Jankuhn (1905–1990), who had been using aerial photography

Figure 9.4. General Juan Vigón Suero-Díaz (1880–1955). Source: Wikimedia Commons.

to investigate the Danish site of Haithabu since 1932. Invited by the Deputy Secretary of the Francoist education division (the Popular Education of the Movement; Vicesecretaría de Educación Popular del Movimiento), Martínez Santa-Olalla gave a lecture on 'Aviation and Archaeology' at the Naval Museum of Madrid (Museo Naval de Madrid) on 19 February 1942, in which he praised the work carried out by the Germans despite the limitations imposed on the development of their aviation by the Treaty of Versailles, and noted General Vigón's involvement with the General Commissariat of Archaeological Excavations. He even indicated that Franco himself had mentioned in their conversations his opinion on the organisation of archaeological research in Spain. He also lamented the lack of development of aerial archaeology in Spain, attributing it to the militant antimilitarism of the leading Spanish archaeologists before 1936. He would repeat this idea in 1945, in a discussion of the results obtained in aerial archaeology by the United Kingdom, France and Germany, and called for the organisation of an archaeological aerial photography service as a unit or service inside the Army itself (Martínez Santa-Olalla 1945). In the lecture he acknowledged the Ministry of Air and the Seminary of the Early History of Man at the University of Madrid as the pioneers of aerial photography in Spain. However, the cooperation of the military aviation in the flights in which Martinez-Olalla himself participated had come to an end in 1945, by express decision of the Minister Vigón. This was probably the consequence of the internal struggles between the different sectors of Spanish archaeology and their influences in the spheres of power (Gracia Alonso 2012, 138–139; 2017, 275–298).

The efforts of Martínez Santa-Olalla were opposed by the Diego Velázquez Institute (Instituto Diego Velázquez, IDV) of the Spanish Council for Scientific Research (Consejo Superior de Investigaciones Científicas, CSIC). On 2 February 1944, due to a collaboration agreement between the Ministry of Air under Vigón and the Ministry of National Education headed by José Ibáñez Martín (1896–1969), the IDV included in its organigram an Aerial Photography Section led by Lieutenant Colonel Juan Rodríguez Rodríguez, who would be replaced in 1946 by Colonel Pascual Girona Ortuño (?–1974) (Cabañas 2007). The IDV now received all the materials recorded in Army flights, including those corresponding to the Roman remains in Mérida (Badajoz), published by archaeologist Antonio Cristino Floriano Cumbreño (1892–1979) in 1944, and Roman city of Clunia (Burgos), used by archaeologist Blas Taracena in 1946. The newly created institution also encouraged photographic reconnaissance flights such as the ones made by the aircraft based in Reus over the city of Tarragona, published by archaeologist Samuel Ventura Solsona (1896–1972) in 1953 (González Reyero 2007, 227–232). This did not deter Martinez Santa-Olalla who, by taking advantage of the influence of his father, continued his attempts to gain control over the Armed Forces' involvement in aerial archaeology. For instance, he managed to persuade the Air Force to provide aerial photography equipment for the International Field Archaeology Course organised by the Ministry of Air in Granada between 15 and 30 September 1953, and later for the exhibition that he himself would stage at the headquarters of the Ministry of the Air on the occasion of the Fourth International Congress of Prehistoric and Protohistoric Sciences in Madrid in 1954 (Gracia Alonso 2009, 457–467).

A key factor in the development of the Spanish archaeology during the postwar period was the relationship between archaeologist Antonio Beltrán Martínez (1916–2006) and Admiral Francisco Bastarreche y Díez de Bulnes (1882–1962) (Fig. 9.5). The Archaeological Museum of Cartagena, which Beltrán founded in 1943 and directed between 1945 and 1950, became a major centre of activity thanks to Bastarreche's interest in archaeology. The admiral lent his support to the organisation of the Archaeological Congress of the Spanish Southeast (Congreso Arqueológico del Sudeste Español, CASE) between 1945 and 1950 (the starting point for the later National Congresses of Archaeology held from 1949 onwards) and of the publication of the Archaeological Bulletin of the Spanish Southeast (*Boletín Arqueológico del Sudeste Español*, BASE) which reported the results of the papers delivered at the congress. Given Spain's international isolation, the scientific meetings held in the country were an essential element of the regime's internal and external propaganda. The Course of Archaeology in the Southeast and Balearic Islands organised by the IDV between 28 May 28 and 16 June 1949 in Cartagena, Ibiza, Mahón, Palma de Mallorca and Valencia, had the support of the Navy thanks to Bastarreche, who allowed the organisers, archaeologists Blas Taracena Aguirre, Antonio Garcia y Bellido (1903–1972) and Beltrán to use the brand new gunboat *Magallanes* to transport the congress participants between the various venues. The captain, Juan Cervera, took the opportunity to stress to those present the need to 'continue to show the truth of Spain to the world', from a ship that was 'a messenger of peace [...] demonstrating that we care little about the slanders being spread regarding our country' (Gracia Alonso 2017, 343). In addition, the participants were able to visit the Navy's Diving Centre in Cartagena, where they were told of its involvement in the first works of underwater archaeology. In 1950, Bastarreche also lent a warship to transfer the participants in the Fourth International Course of Archaeology of Ampurias (organised by Almagro Basch and Pericot) between the Balearic Islands. In fact, the Navy was so heavily involved that archaeologist Nino Lamboglia (1912–1977), who had just carried out excavations at the Roman site of Albenga, suggested to Bastarreche the possibility that the Istituto di Studi Liguri might carry out research in Spain with the Navy's logistical support, even though the collaboration (Gracia Alonso 2012, 282) never materialised.

Figure 9.5. Admiral Francisco Bastarreche y Díez de Bulnes (1882-1962). Source: Wikimedia Commons.

The Navy, and especially its base at Cartagena, played an important role in the beginning of research in underwater archaeology (Nieto 2009; 2019). In 1947 the Navy carried out the first survey campaigns in the area of Escombreras Bay and the Corcos and Salinas anchorages of San Pedro del Pinatar (Murcia), in parallel with the development of the first works of this kind in the south of France and the north of Italy. The advances were not, however, the result of an official project, but the consequence of the personal interest of the Head of the Navy Chief of Staff, Juan José de Jáuregui y Gil Delgado (1898–1970), who had studied the Roman anchors preserved in the

Museum of Cartagena during his assignment at the naval base of Cartagena. One of the results of these underwater surveys was the Order of 9 July 1947, issued by Ministry of the Navy (Mederos and Escribano 2006, 365), which obliged Navy commanders to report any underwater findings; the actions of the Navy had little influence on the archaeological research, since 80% of the wrecks identified on the Spanish coasts were looted by divers. After the demonstration of the work methodology of the underwater research by the ship *Daino* of the Centro Sperimentale di Archaeologia Sottomarina and Spanish divers off the coasts of Rosas and Tarragona in Catalonia, the speakers at the Third International Congress of Underwater Archaeology in Barcelona in 1961 called on the government to enlist a Navy ship for the practice of archaeological research, to be carried out by an Experimental Centre of Underwater Archaeology. However, the request was ignored, and for more than three decades the Armed Forces played no part in any archaeological interventions. During this period, the Spanish Autonomous Communities developed their own research centres. Moreover, in 2008 the National Museum of Underwater Archaeology in Cartagena (Murcia) was also renovated, providing a more solid structure for the activities that this centre had been carrying out since 1970 (Nieto 2009).

A change in the paradigm (1977–2019)

The development of the Archaeology of Conflict in Spain over the last twenty years has created new links between researchers and the Armed Forces. Projects have been undertaken at the battlefields of Baecula (208 BC) (Bellón *et al.* 2015, 537–601) and the Ebro/Kesse (218 BC) (Noguera Guillén, Blé Gimeno and Valdés Matías 2013, 32–58) from the Second Punic War; as well as in sites where medieval battles took place in the 12th century: Alcalá la Vieja (Ramírez Galán 2017; Ramírez Galán, Montalvo Laguna and Benítez Galán 2018; Ramírez Galán and Montalvo Laguna 2019), Montiel (Gallego Valle 2017), Cutanda and Alarcos (Ramírez Galán 2016). There have also been studies on post-Medieval battles at Talamanca, the siege of the city of Barcelona from the War of the Spanish Succession, both in 1714; and Cardedéu (1808) from the Peninsular War. The Moroccan campaigns have also been the object of research, through the study of the remnants of the positions of the Spanish Army in the Rif cultural region between 1912 and 1956 (Blanco Vázquez and Sierra Piedra 2014). However, the vast majority of the research has focused on the Spanish Civil War (González Ruibal 2016), above all in two areas. The first is the archaeology of repression, in which the corpses buried in mass graves (the victims of executions carried out in the Francoist rearguard during the Spanish Civil War) are identified and exhumed, or the concentration camps and the war crimes committed during the conflict are investigated (for example, the events of Valdediós, Asturias, of 22 October 1937). The second area of study is the identification and analysis of structures such as trenches, bunkers, artillery positions, buildings used in any way in the war effort of both sides, anti-aircraft shelters, and so on (Pujadó 1998; 2006; Castellano Ruiz de la Torre and Schnell Querdant 2011; Miró Alaix and

Ramos Ruiz 2013; Ramos Ruiz 2016, 13–41), carried out using archaeological methods. This research area already has a long history and is by no means uncontroversial. Its political implications are significant in the context of the construction of the historical interpretation vision of the Civil War that has emerged since the democratic transition, and also in view of the attempts of governments to control the flow of information and the fate of human remains (see the excavation of the trenches of La Fatarella in Catalonia dug during the battle of the Ebro in 1938 (Solé 2010)).

In the case of Catalonia, the heritage policies regarding the Spanish Civil War have allowed the opening of a certain number of sites as museum spaces, in application of the concept of the 'duty of memory' to explain past events. They also enabled the creation of memorials centred on exile and the war's aftermath (for example in Figueras in Girona, or in the Camp de la Bota in Barcelona). Sometimes these policies have drawn on concepts developed in other European countries in relation to the Archaeology of the Holocaust, and therefore centres such as the Battle of the Ebro Museum in Corbera d'Ebre (Catalonia) have been set up. However, due to an anti-militarist, exclusionary concept of interpretation vision, this memorialist policy has sometimes been combined with the dismantling of centres such as the Ministry of Defence's military museums housed in the castles of Montjuïc (Barcelona) and Figueras; in both instances, no attempt was made to offer a redefinition of the spaces and the materials kept there, and the collections were either dispersed or moved elsewhere.[1]

In the field of the Archaeology of the Civil War, the main problem lies in the access to military documentary sources. Public archives such as the Documentary Centre of Historical Memory in Salamanca and the National Historical Archive in Madrid provide full access to their materials, but some of the documentation kept in the military archives of Ávila, Segovia, Guadalajara and Madrid remain classified. Certain government directives fail to comply with the 1985 Spanish National Heritage Act, and in particular with article 57 1C, for rather vague reasons of national security, under the protection of specific interpretations of Royal Decree 1708/2011 of 18 November. The application of the 1985 Spanish Heritage Act should allow free access to any document prior to 1969, thus including all the documentation generated during the Civil War and the subsequent repression. In the same way, the application of the 1977 Amnesty Act makes it difficult to investigate individual and collective responsibilities regarding actions that took place during the Civil War and the postwar period. At the same time, the 2007 Historical Memory Act has not introduced the necessary mechanisms to make the opening of graves a priority for the State, thus failing to implement the successive court orders presented for this purpose by international organisations such as the Rapporteur of Human Rights of the UN in 2011, 2013 and 2017[2] – in spite of the important results obtained, for example, in Málaga (Fernández Martín and Espinosa Jiménez 2019) and Seville.[3] The result of these actions is, in many cases, the interruption of the work of opening or exhumation of mass graves, and even of the pressing of criminal charges against those who analyse and publish the details of the events in question and expose the names of those responsible. These were also encouraged by the political decision not to allocate funds to these activities even if they are undertaken by private initiatives, and to uphold a policy of 'forgetting the past and not reopening old wounds' (wounds that are assumed to have been healed by the spirit of reconciliation attributed to the transition from Franco's dictatorship to democracy). The country's decentralisation into Autonomous Communities has favoured the creation of specific legislation in these regions, which apply divergent ideas on the question of historical memory and heritage maintenance. In the case of Catalonia, the process of location and exhumation envisaged in the 2009 *Common Graves Act on the location and identification of persons missing during the Civil War and the Francoist dictatorship and the dignification of common graves* (DOGC, July 9)[4] has been at a standstill for years due to the application of a policy that allowed private and public bodies to try to locate graves but not to open them, the latter being the exclusive competence of the Catalan government (with the exception of the test intervention carried out in Gurb in 2008) (Solé 2016). By 2017, interventions had begun at 21 of the 380 graves located in Catalonia, all of them consisting in small-scale operations due to the low number of bodies found in them. However, this policy has now changed and larger mass graves such as those at Soleràs (Lleida) and Pernafites de Miravet (Tarragona) have been opened and exhumed. The intention is to apply this model in future interventions as well, through the deployment of the *Mass Graves Plan 2017–2018*.[5] This is a large research project which aims to exhume and identify the persons who were murdered or killed in action during the war, as well as to return their bodies to the families (Etxebarría and Solé 2019; Solé 2019, 439–475).

Although the Armed Forces do not participate in the investigation of the common graves of the Civil War or in other classified aspects related to this conflict and Francoism, clearly for ideological reasons, they are strongly involved in a number of joint archaeological research projects promoted by the government and the Autonomous Communities. For instance, the Navy takes part in the National Plan for the Protection of the Underwater Heritage, approved on 30 November 2007,[6] as a result of a cooperation agreement signed by the Ministries of Education and Defense on 9 July 2009. Organised jointly with the Underwater Archaeology Centre of the Ministry and the Regional Government of Andalusia, with the aim of creating the archaeological map of the Gulf of Cadiz between Tarifa and the mouth of the Guadalquivir, this research project was a response to accusations of neglect levelled at government bodies as a result of Operation Black Swan (the illegal removal of the cargo of the frigate Nuestra Señora de las Mercedes and its subsequent recovery after the decision by the United States courts). The project also derived from the UNESCO Convention on the Protection of the Underwater Cultural Heritage of 2001. Another example of the cooperation of the Armed Forces is the participation of the members of the Ferrol Diving Unit (Unidad de Buceo de Ferrol, UBUFER) at the naval station of A Graña (Coruña) in the recovery of various items from the wreck of a late eighteenth-century vessel in Viveiro, a task undertaken in interdisciplinary cooperation with the Archaeological Service of the Regional Government of Galicia. In Viveiro, the Navy is in charge of periodically carrying out patrols to protect the underwater heritage in areas where the existence of wrecks has been detected. The cooperation between the Ministry of Defence and the Ministry of Education, Culture and Sport is an attempt to engage the resources and experience of the Navy in heritage protection. However, to a large extent this is also a public relations exercise, drawing attention to an activity that society in general does not normally associate with the Armed Forces. This change of focus is also reflected in the presence of the Navy in exhibitions and cultural events related to the research and dissemination of naval archaeology, especially at the Naval Museum of Madrid, or the participation of the Army in scientific meetings and cultural outreach activities, such as the conference 'The underwater archaeological heritage of Spain and the Navy' (El patrimonio arqueológico subacuático de España y la Armada) at National Archaeological Museum in Madrid, in 2016.[7] In recent years, the Institute of Military History and Culture and the Ministry of Defense have carried out extensive work on the history of the Spanish army in collaboration with researchers from different universities, but only on an individual level. For example, General Francisco Ramos Oliver participated in the interdisciplinary studies of history and archaeology concerning the development of the Cantabrian wars in the 1st century BC (Camino Mayor *et al.* 2007; Ramos Oliver 2016).

Conclusions

The three chronological phases examined in this chapter clearly show how, in contrast to other European or American spheres, the participation of the Spanish Armed Forces in archaeological research has been practically non-existent until very recent times, missing an excellent opportunity to deepen interdisciplinary connections in research. In France, for example, the participation of the army in archaeological research was very important due to the colonial expansion (Effros 2018), in the United States it served to develop a new historical analysis starting from theoretical discussions on the archaeology of conflict (Lambert 2002; Scott and McFeaters 2011), while in the United Kingdom it is currently part of the British Army's cultural projects, especially in relation to heritage protection (SGMI 2019). In the few instances in which this collaboration materialised in Spain, the Army has played a highly specific role. For both political and ideological reasons, the participation has sought to reaffirm the Army's position as a vital component of the structure of the State or has responded to personal motivations inside the various ideological currents of Franco's regime. As a result, the actions carried out were specific rather than structural. Some of them lasted over time, due to the public influence of their proponents and their contacts inside the government. In the last two decades we have seen a certain paradigm shift, deriving from the application of the Archaeology of Conflict to recent periods in the history of Spain, in which special attention has been given to the Spanish Civil War. With this change in paradigm and within the limits allowed by the application of the current legislation, the Army has become a research subject but has not been a part of it. In other words, the Armed Forces have not played a role in the attempts to resolve the problems arising from the civil conflict in Spain, and have not accepted the responsibilities that their counterparts in other countries have been willing to assume, even inside NATO through the Civil Military Cooperative Centre of Excellence and its cultural heritage protection programmes.[8] A second block, which involves the establishment of closer links with the society in order to foster a new culture of the Armed Forces, includes providing human and material support in various projects. One of these projects is the development of underwater archaeology, in the Navy's capacity as the protector of Spanish waters. However, there is still a long way to go before the Armed Forces finally shed their association with the past, and this is unlikely to be a straightforward process.

Acknowledgements

This chapter was written within the framework of the InterArq research project (HAR2016-80271-P) (interarqweb.wordpress.com) subsidised by the State Research Agency (AEI) and the European Regional Development Fund (ERDF, EU).

Notes

1. https://www.elmundo.es/elmundo/2009/05/15/barcelona/1242415895.html.
2. Texts available at: http://memoriahistorica.org.es/resoluciones-e-informes/; https://tbinternet.ohchr.org/_layouts/treatybodyexternal/Download.aspx?symbolno=CED/C/ESP/CO/1&Lang=En.
3. https://www.eldiario.es/andalucia/Gobierno-PP-Memoria-Historica-Presupuesto_0_880162343.html.
4. Text available at: https://www.parlament.cat/document/nom/TL092.pdf.
5. Text available at: http://exteriors.gencat.cat/web/.content/Noticia/RInstitucionals/Dossier-Premsa-Pla-Fosses-CASTELLA.pdf.
6. Text available at: http://www.culturaydeporte.gob.es/cultura-mecd/areas-cultura/patrimonio/patrimonio-subacuatico/plan-nacional-de-proteccion.html.
7. Lecture available at: https://www.youtube.com/watch?v=bycETdlXlKA.
8. Text available at: https://cimic-coe.org/wp-content/uploads/2015/11/CPP-Makes-Sense-final-version-29-10-15.pdf.

References

Almagro Basch, M. (1943) La colaboración de la aviación militar en el campo de la Arqueología. *Ampurias* 5, 247–251.

Bellón, J.P., Ruiz Rodríguez, A., Molinos, M., Rueda, M. and Gómez, F., eds (2015) *La Segunda Guerra Púnica en la Península Ibérica. Baecula: arqueología de una batalla*. Jaén, Publicaciones de la Universidad de Jaén.

Blanco Vázquez, L. and Sierra Piedra, G. (2014) La huella militar en el sector oriental del Protectorado Español de Marruecos (1912–1956). Fortificaciones, acuartelamientos y posiciones en el Rif. *Anejos de Nailos* 1, 19–41.

Cabañas, M. (2007) La Historia del Arte en el Centro de Estudios Históricos. In M.A. Puig-Samper (ed.) *Tiempos de investigación: JAE-CSIC, cien años de ciencia en España*, 143–154. Madrid, Consejo Superior de Investigaciones Científicas.

Calvo, L. (1997) *Historia de la Antropología en Cataluña*. Madrid, Consejo Superior de Investigaciones Científicas.

Camino Mayor, J., Viniegra, Y., Estrada, R., Ramos Oliver, F. and Jiménez, F.J. (2007) El campamento y la vía de la Carisa, reflexiones arqueológicas y militares. In J.A. Fernández Tresguerres Velasco (ed.) *Astures y romanos en el Principado de Asturias*, 61–94. Oviedo, Real Instituto de Estudios Asturianos.

Castellano Ruiz de la Torre, R. and Schnell Querdant, P. (2011) *Arquitectura militar de la Guerra Civil en la Comunidad de Madrid. Sector de la batalla de Brunete. Arqueología, Paletnología y Etnografía, 12*. Madrid, Comunidad de Madrid.

Colorado Castellary, A., ed. (2010) *Patrimonio, Guerra Civil y Posguerra*. Madrid, Universidad Complutense de Madrid.

Colorado Castellary, A. (2018) *Arte, revancha y propaganda. La instrumentalización franquista del patrimonio durante la Segunda Guerra Mundial*. Madrid, Cátedra.

Díaz-Andreu, M. (2015) The archaeology of the Spanish Protectorate of Morocco: a short history. *African Archaeological Review* 32 (1), 49–69.

Díaz-Andreu, M. and Ramírez Sánchez, M. (2004) Archaeological resource management under Franco's Spain: the Comisaría General de Excavaciones Arqueológicas. In M. Galaty and C. Watkinson (eds) *Archaeology under Dictatorship*, 109–130. Hingham, MA, Kluwer/Plenum.

Effros, B. (2018) *Incidental Archaeologists: French Officers and the Rediscovery of Roman North Africa*. Ithaca, Cornell University Press.

Etxebarría, F. and Solé, Q. (2019) Fosas comunes de la Guerra Civil en el Siglo XXI: antecedentes, interdisciplinariedad y legislación. *Historia contemporánea* 60, 401–438.

Fernández García, F. (2015) Fotografía aérea histórica e historia de la fotografía aérea en España. *Ería* 98, 217–240.

Fernández Martín, A. and Espinosa Jiménez, F. (2019) *San Rafael (Málaga). Las fosas. Febrero 1937-Noviembre 1955*. Málaga, Aratispi.

Gallego Valle, D. (2017) Fortificaciones y técnicas de asedio. *Desperta Ferro Antigua y Medieval* 44, 40–44.

Gómez-Barrera, J.A. (2014) *Tras los orígenes de la Arqueología soriana*. Soria, Diputación Provincial de Soria.

González Reyero, S. (2007) *La fotografía en la Arqueología Española (1860-1960). Cien años de discurso arqueológico a través de la imagen. Historia. Antiquaria Hispánica 15*. Madrid, Real Academia de la Historia.

González Ruibal, A. (2016) *Volver a las trincheras. Una arqueología de la Guerra Civil española*. Madrid, Alianza Editorial.

Gozalbes Cravioto, E. (2015a) Arqueología española para un nuevo régimen: Martínez Santa-Olalla y el norte de Marruecos. *Onoba* 3, 3–14.

Gozalbes Cravioto, E. (2015b) El africanismo del primer franquismo: la revista África (1942–1956). *Miscelánea de Estudios Árabes y Hebraicos* 64, 149–168.

Gozalbes Cravioto, E., Gozalbes García, H. and Gozalbes García, E. (2013) Arqueología y etnología en la colonia: la expedición de 1946 (Epaoe) a Guinea Ecuatorial. In *Proceedings International Conference Science in the Tropics. Glimpsing the Past Projecting the Future*. Lisboa.

Gracia Alonso, F. (2003) Arqueología de la memoria. Batallones disciplinarios de soldados-trabajadores y tropas del ejército en las excavaciones de Ampurias (1940-1943). In *Los campos de concentración y el mundo penitenciario en España durante la guerra civil y el franquismo. Congreso 21,22 y 23 de octubre de2002*, 209–245. Barcelona, Generalitat de Catalunya-Museu d'Història de Catalunya.

Gracia Alonso, F. (2008a) Las relaciones entre los arqueólogos españoles y la Alemania nazi (1939–1945). La influencia de Das Ahnenerbe en España. Un estudio preliminar. In G. Mora, C. Papí and M. Ayarzagüena (eds) *Documentos inéditos para la Historia de la Arqueología*, 129–154. Memorias de la Sociedad Española de Historia de la Arqueología 1. Madrid, Sociedad Española de Historia de la Arqueología.

Gracia Alonso, F. (2008b) Relations between Spanish archaeologists and Nazi Germany (1939–1945). A preliminary examination of the influence of Das Ahnenerbe in Spain. *Bulletin of the History of Archaeology* 18 (1), 4–24.

Gracia Alonso, F. (2009) *La arqueología durante el primer franquismo (1939-1956)*. Barcelona, Bellaterra.

Gracia Alonso, F. (2010) Contactos hispano-italianos en la arqueología durante la Guerra Civil y el primer franquismo. In R. Olmos, T. Tortosa and J.P. Bellón (eds) *Repensar la Escuela del CSIC en Roma. Cien años de memoria*, 425–440. Madrid, Consejo Superior de Investigaciones Científicas.

Gracia Alonso, F. (2012) *Arqueologia i politica. La gestió de Martín Almagro Basch al front del Museo Arqueològic Provincial de Barcelona (1939-1960)*. Barcelona, Universitat de Barcelona, Museo d'Arqueologia de Catalunya, Fundació Carles Pi i Sunyer.

Gracia Alonso, F. (2017) *Lluís Pericot García. Un prehistoriador entre dos épocas*. Pamplona, Urgoiti Editores.

Gracia Alonso, F. (2019) En el país de los Mau-Mau. Diario de viaje de Lluís Pericot al Primer Congreso Panafricano de Prehistoria. *Boletín del Museo Arqueológico Nacional* 39, 223–240.

Gracia Alonso, F. and Munilla, G. (2010) El Instituto Arqueológico Nacional e Imperial: Un intento fallido de reorganización de la protección y estudio del patrimonio arqueológico en 1938. In A. Colorado Castellary (ed.) *Patrimonio, Guerra Civil y posguerra: congreso internacional [Madrid, 2010]*, 175–186. Madrid.

Gracia Alonso, F. and Munilla, G. (2018) El Servicio de Recepción y Clasificación de Metales. La Generalitat de Catalunya y la destrucción del patrimonio artístico durante la Guerra Civil. In A. Colorado Castellary (ed.) *Patrimonio cultural, guerra civil y posguerra*, 457–486. Madrid, Fragua.

Gracia Alonso, F. and Munilla, G. (2011) *Salvem l'art. La protecció del patrimoni cultural calatà durant la Guerra Civil (1936-1939)*. Barcelona, Ed. La Magrana– RBA.

Gracia Alonso, F. and Munilla, G. (2013) *El tesoro del «Vita». La protección y expolio del patrimonio histórico-arqueológico durante la Guerra Civil*. Barcelona, Universidad de Barcelona.

Jimeno, A. and Torre, J.I.d.l. (2005) *Numancia, símbolo e historia*. Madrid, Akal.

Lambert, P.M. (2002) The archaeology of war. A North American perspective. *Journal of Archaeological Research* 10 (3), 207–241.

Martínez Santa-Olalla, J. (1945) Aviación y Arqueología. *Boletín Arqueológico del Sureste Español* 3, 229–249.

Martínez Santa-Olalla, J. (1947) *África en las actividades del Seminario de Historia Primitiva del Hombre*. Madrid, Publicaciones del Seminario de Historia Primitiva del Hombre

Mederos, A. (2003) Julio Martínez Santa-Olalla y la interpretación aria de la Prehistoria de España (1939–1945). *Boletín del Seminario de Arte y Arqueología* 69, 13–56.

Mederos, A. (2017) Martín Almagro Basch, un balance de su trayectoria científica (1934–1984). *Cuadernos de Prehistoria y Arqueología de la Universidad Autónoma de Madrid* 43, 251–289.

Mederos, A. and Escribano, G. (2006) Los inicios de la arqueología subacuática en España (1947–1948). *Mayurqa* 31 359–395.

Miró Alaix, C. and Ramos Ruiz, J. (2013) Cronotipologia dels refugis antiaeris de Barcelona. Els refugis antiaeris de Barcelona. Criteris d'intervenció patrimonial. *MUHBA documents* 6.

Nieto, X. (2009) La arqueología subacuática en España. In X. Nieto and M.Á. Cau Ontiveros (eds) *Arqueología Nàutica Mediterrània*, 17–32. Monografies del CASC 8. Barcelona, Museu d'Arqueologia de Catalunya.

Nieto, X. (2019) La evolución conceptual de la arqueología subacuática. *Pyrenae* 50 (1), 7–29.

Noguera Guillén, J., Blé Gimeno, E. and Valdés Matías, P., eds (2013) *La Segona Guerra Púnica al nordest d'Ibèria: una revisió necessària*. Barcelona, Societat Catalana d'Arqueologia.

Pujadó, J. (1998) *Oblits de rereguarda: els refugis antiaeris a Barcelona (1936-1939)*. Barcelona, Publicacions de l'Abadia de Montserrat.

Pujadó, J. (2006) *Contra l'oblit. Els refugis antiaèris poble a poble*. Barcelona, Publicacions de l'Abadia de Montserrat.

Quirós Linares, F. and Fernández García, F. (1996) Los orígenes de la fotografía aérea en España. El Servicio de Aerostación Militar (1896-1913). *Ería* 41, 173-188.

Ramírez Galán, M. (2016) Archaeology and battlefields in Ciudad Real. *Archaeological Research and Ethnographic Studies* 4, 63-74.

Ramírez Galán, M. (2017) *Los yacimientos olvidados: registro y musealización de campos de batalla*. Access Archaeology. Oxford, Archaeopress.

Ramírez Galán, M. and Montalvo Laguna, R. (2019) Las posiciones cristianas de los cerros de Malvecino y La Veracruz en el asedio de Alcalá la Vieja: un estudio de visibilidad. *Cuadernos de Prehistoria y Arqueología de la UAM* 45, 249-266.

Ramírez Galán, M., Montalvo Laguna, R. and Benítez Galán, M. (2018) The battle of Alcalá la Vieja. Location and undestanding of a medieval battle. In N. Moreira, M. Derderian and A. Bissonnette (eds) *Fields of Conflict*, 23-43. Mashantucket, Mashantucket Pequot Museum and Research Center.

Ramos Oliver, F. (2016) La logística romana en las guerras astur-cántabras (siglo I a.C.). In E. Martínez Ruiz, J. Cantera Montenegro, M. De Pazzis and L. Sánchez (eds) *La organización de los ejércitos* 225-273. Madrid, Ministerio de Defensa.

Ramos Ruiz, J. (2016) *Turó de la Rovira. Arqueologia d'un conflicte*. Barcelona Societat Catalana d'Arqueologia.

Scott, D.D. and McFeaters, A. (2011) The archaeology of historic battlefields: a history and theoretical development in conflict archaeology. *Journal of Archaeological Research* 19 (1), 103-132.

SGMI (2019) BAR Special Report: culture in conflict. *British Army Report* 2019, 1-129.

Solé, Q. (2010) Usos polítics dels morts de la Guerra Civil. *Via. Revista del Centre d'Estudis Jordi Pujol* 14, 119-130.

Solé, Q. (2016) Gobiernos democráticos del Estado español frente a la persistencia de la memoria y la historia de las fosas comunes de la guerra civil española. La actuación de la Generalitat en Cataluña (2004-2015). *Munibe Antropología-Arkeologia* 67, 199-214.

Solé, Q. (2019) Pervivencia de las fosas comunes de la guerra civil española en el siglo XXI. Evidencia cultural, particularidad académica. *Historia contemporánea* 60, 439-475.

Chapter 10

The decline of epistemology in archaeology: comments on an ongoing discussion

Oscar Moro Abadía and Emma Lewis-Sing

Abstract

During most of the twentieth century, epistemology and philosophy of science were central in archaeological theory. 'New' or 'processual' archaeologists used models of explanation developed by philosophers of science as reference to make archaeology a Science with a capital 'S'. Starting in the 1980s, many archaeologists became sceptical of interpreting past human behaviour using law-like statements. While these post-processual archaeologists called into question logical positivism, epistemological questions remained at the centre of the theoretical debate. However, two interrelated developments have recently challenged the privileged position of epistemology as a focus for research. First, today there is no singular, dominant archaeological theory but rather a plurality of theories and viewpoints, some of which are openly anti-epistemological. Second, archaeology has increasingly become a public-oriented discipline with a growing commitment to extra-academic audiences, participants and partners. We consider the sustainability of epistemological discussion and whether it can overcome criticism and contribute to recent debates in archaeological theory.

Keywords: epistemology; philosophy of science; archaeology; theory; logical positivism; twentieth century.

Introduction

Archaeology is probably the most interdisciplinary of all human and social sciences. This is related to the fact that this science was born under the influence of several well-established disciplines, including geology, paleontology, anthropology and history (Vašiček 1994, 33–40; Coye 1997, 6–10). For this reason, archaeologists and historians of science have reflected on and examined the relationships between archaeology and the natural sciences (Blanckaert 2000; Hurel and Coye 2011), the exchanges between archaeology and other social sciences (Delley and Plutniak 2018) and the methodological borrowings from other disciplines (Lyman and O'Brien 2006; Reubi 2012). Philosophy of science constitutes one of the disciplines with which archaeology has been reciprocally engaged in more intense and productive ways. On the one hand, as Bruce G. Trigger pointed out, philosophers of science have historically been interested in archaeological research (Trigger 2001, 630). Philosophers such as Wesley Salmon, Alison Wylie, William Krieger and Marsha Hanen have argued that archaeology constitutes a privileged area of research to understand some important philosophical and epistemological problems. On the other hand, as we examine in the following pages, archaeologists have extensively read and commented on the work of philosophers of science. In this chapter we examine the complex relationships between archaeology and the philosophy of science in the context of recent developments and theoretical discussions in the wider 'archaeological theory'.

The field of archaeological theory has gone through important changes over the past two decades. As many commentators have suggested, since the beginning of the twenty-first century, 'archaeological theory and theorizing is changing course' (Pétursdóttir and Olsen 2018, 99), 'theoretical debates have shifted and mutated to the point where the issues under discussion are now strikingly distinct from the preoccupations of 30 years ago' (Thomas 2015a, 1287), and 'there is a real sense of a sea change happening in [archaeological theory]' (Lucas 2015a, 13). The complexity of this change is better illustrated by the contradictory diagnoses about the current state of the field. While some archaeologists postulate the 'death' of archaeological theory as a unified field of research (Bintliff and Pearce 2011), others provide a 'more optimistic perspective on the future' (Kristiansen 2014, 12) and see 'recent debates in theory as exciting, vibrant and absolutely essential to the discipline of archaeology' (Harris and Cipolla 2017, 1). While some of these statements are rather different, most commentators tend to agree that we are *in* a turning point in archaeological theory. This moment of change is marked by a number of interrelated developments.

To begin, as Julian Thomas has pointed out, archaeological theory is continuing to develop, although incrementally rather than as a sweeping paradigmatic change (Thomas 2015b). In other words, if the history of archaeology during the twentieth century was marked by a number of well-defined paradigms (culture-historical archaeology, processual archaeology, post-processual archaeology), the past twenty years have witnessed a theoretical diversification that cannot be easily explained in terms of major paradigm revolutions. Instead, archaeologists are gradually divided into a number of 'disparate communities defined by diverse epistemologies, methods and interests' (Moro Abadía 2017, 1; see also Kristiansen 2004; Bintliff and Pearce 2011). This plurality of 'non-communicating discourses' (Hodder 2001, 11) has led to 'a sort of peaceful coexistence based on both mutual recognition and reciprocal indifference' (Moro Abadía 2017, 1). Moreover, and related to the previous point, since the turn of the twenty-first century we have witnessed a substitution of old questions and problems for new ones. In particular, if twentieth-century theoretical debates were largely dominated by epistemological questions (*e.g.* how objective knowledge is possible, what scientific models are the most adequate fit for archaeological research, how non-epistemological questions impact the making of archaeological knowledge), it seems that, in the twenty-first century, 'archaeologists [...] have grown weary of the jousts between the champions of reflexivity and the defenders of positivism, and of the constant skirmishing over what we can know and how we can know it' (Atalay *et al.* 2014, 1).

Our perspective in these matters is localised and largely reflects the current situation of epistemology and archaeological theory in North America (where discussions on epistemology and theory of knowledge have been largely replaced by other theoretical questions), but similar ideas are being expressed elsewhere, as evidenced by Gavin Lucas' statement that 'epistemic issues in archaeological theory have greatly diminished in importance' (Lucas 2019, 49). As we interpret it, the decline of epistemology in archaeology is related to a number of interrelated factors. First, as Sonya Atalay and others (2014) have pointed out, archaeologists seem somewhat tired to repeat the same questions over and over. Second, in a context marked by a plurality of theories and viewpoints, there is an increasing awareness that everything cannot be reduced to epistemology. Finally, some of the most popular theoretical positions in contemporary archaeology are anti-epistemological, including a number of ontological approaches.

This chapter examines the causes for the decline of traditional epistemology in archaeological theory as well as some of the new paths that archaeological theory is currently taking. In the second section, we examine the privileged position of epistemology in archaeology during the second half of the twentieth century. Starting in the 1950s, a number of 'new' or 'processual' archaeologists, especially in North America, took as reference the models of explanation developed by philosophers of science in their search to transform archaeology into a 'hard' science. It was in this context that, during the 1960s and the 1970s, they discussed Hempel's covering-law model (Hempel and Oppenheim 1948), Salmon's statistical-relevance model (Salmon 1967; 1971) and Braithwaite's probability propositions (Braithwaite 1955). Philosophical discussions took a turn in the 1980s when post-processual archaeologists questioned new archaeologists' positivism. Under the influence of authors such as Thomas Kuhn (1962 (1996)) and David Bloor (1976 (1991)), this new generation of archaeologists insisted that archaeological knowledge could not be disentangled from archaeologists' own prejudices and biases. While they called into question positivism (replicating what had happened in the field of the philosophy of science in the 1960s), discussions on the theory of knowledge remained at the core of the theoretical debate.

With these ideas in mind, we examine in the third section the loss of strength of epistemological questions in archaeology. We argue that this decrease can be explained with reference to two main processes. In the first place, the emergence of a great variety of theorical positions over the past two decades (such as ontology, realism, new materialism, symmetrical archaeology as well as a variety of Indigenous knowledges) has transformed and continues to transform the landscape of archaeological theory. In a context marked by the 'mobility of theory', epistemological questions have become just some among many others. Moreover, some of the abovementioned positions are bluntly anti-epistemological. For instance, some theorists have claimed that 'ontology [...] is both an anti-epistemological and counter-cultural (in both senses of 'counter-culture') philosophical war machine' (Viveiros de Castro 2015, 9). In the second place, as with many other human and social sciences, archaeology has recently evolved from a purely academic science into a more public-oriented discipline. In this setting, archaeologists are increasingly committed towards a 'greater involvement with contemporary communities, political controversies, and social demands' (González-Ruibal 2018, 345). Moreover, today it is generally accepted that scientists have the ethical obligation to share their knowledge with the public. This has led to 'an increasing media attention for scientific issues' and 'an increasing orientation of science towards the mass media' (Rödder 2011, 835). In other words, during the past two decades 'the opening up of science to the public has become the accepted expectation' in most Western societies (Weingart 2012, 17). This has generated a number of effects, including the development of community archaeology (perceived by most as an important advance in archaeological research) and the increasing impact of research funding bodies in scientists' agendas (Palmer and Schibeci 2014).

In this context, the traditional epistemological concern of the philosophy of science (at least in its positivist side), generally perceived as uninteresting and too technical, has been replaced by new theoretical and practical interrogations about the role and the responsibilities of archaeologists in the public sphere. In the final section, we conclude with some thoughts about the role of epistemology in the field of archaeological theory. While, in a context of increasing diversification, epistemological questions cannot aspire to maintain their traditional privileged position, we argue that they still have a role to play in our theoretical (and practical) discussions.

The golden age of epistemology and philosophy of science in archaeology: 1960–2000

As some commentators have pointed out, 'there is an old and deeply rooted inferiority complex among some archaeologists, encapsulated in a self-image of archaeology as a second-rate, social science' (Olsen et al. 2012, 2). The origins of this lack of self-esteem (that is less widespread today) lies in the process of the institutionalisation of archaeology at the end of the nineteenth century. At that time, modern archaeology emerged in a context of competition with other well-consolidated sciences. For instance, as late as 1870, John Evans pointed out that, 'two other provinces that at the present seem almost excluded from the federation of the sciences- [are] those of History and Archaeology' (Evans 1870, 4). As a result, archaeologists put together a number of interrelated strategies to reinforce the scientific status of their discipline, including the critique of religious and mythical approaches to the past, the construction of a disciplinary history and the constant affirmation of the scientific nature of their research (for a more detailed account of these questions, see Murray 2002; Schlanger 2002; Moro Abadía 2013).

In the spirit of strengthening the scientific foundations of their discipline, early archaeologists looked at the models and theories devoted to the study of scientific inquiry. While explicit references to the work of philosophers were sparse during the first half of the twentieth century, archaeologists discussed epistemological questions related to the interpretation of the archaeological record. These questions played a central role, for instance, in the work of Clyde Kluckhohn (who was influenced by Alfred North Whitehead), Raymond Thompson (influenced by John Dewey), Walter Taylor (who was a reader of Cohen and Nagel), William Duncan Strong and Christopher Hawkes. However, it was not until the 1960s that archaeologists began to discuss philosophical issues in an explicit (and intensive) way. At that time, new/processual archaeologists insisted on the importance of adopting a scientific approach in archaeological research (*e.g.* Binford 1968; Fritz and Plog 1970; Martin 1971; Watson, Leblanc and Redman 1971; Plog 1974). They advocated for 'the conscious use of the hypothetic-deductive methods in seeking confirmation for ideas used in explanations, [and] the development of the theoretical laws [to offer] explanations in covering-law form' (Binford 1978, 631).

In their attempt to transform archaeology into a Science with a capital 'S' (Flannery 1973), processual archaeologists looked for inspiration in the work of philosophers of science. In particular, Hempel and Oppenheim's Deductive-Nomological model (Hempel and Oppenheim 1948) became a reference for them. Hempel's starting point was the critique of 'the narrow inductivist conception of scientific inquiry' (Hempel 1966) according to which scientific inquiry was based on the observation and recording of all the facts. This view of science was untenable for 'all the facts up to now cannot be collected, since there are an infinite number and variety of them' (Hempel 1966, 11). Furthermore, Hempel suggested that scientific facts were neither prior to nor independent of theories, but rather that 'empirical "facts" or findings […] can be qualified as logically relevant or irrelevant only in reference to a given hypothesis' (Hempel 1966, 12).

Following Hempel, processual archaeologists called into question the 'strict empiricist position' (Binford 1985, 583) that 'believes that *to be a good scientist one must clear his mind of bias and observe nature objectively*; if this is done properly and the observer is astute and honest, then the truths of natural history will be clearly apprehended' (Binford 1983, 372). Processual archaeologists rejected empiricism for two main reasons. In the first place, they argued that empiricism was fatally flawed because facts are infinite and, therefore, archaeologists cannot collect them all. In the second place, they suggested that archaeological facts were determined by archaeological theories and, therefore, they were not 'objective'. They advocated for a shift from an inductive procedure, or from one in which undirected data collection forms the first, and the 'abstraction' of laws from data forms the last research step, to a deductive procedure in which the explicit formulation of potential laws and their empirical consequences precedes and directs the collection of data (Fritz and Plog 1970, 405).

Processual archaeologists' support of the Deductive-Nomological model opened an intense debate about scientific explanation in archaeology. For instance, in *Analytical Archaeology*, David Clarke argued that, while the deductive model was the most reliable, 'archaeological propositions were made by inference and induction rather than by classic deduction' (Clarke 1968 (2015), 16). He suggested that archaeological observations were 'very rarely "general propositions" of the kind "all *As* are *Bs*" or "all *As* have *Bs*"'. Instead, they typically took 'the form "some *As* are *Bs*" or "some *As* have *Bs*"' (Clarke 1968 (2015), 16). According to Clarke, these kinds of statements 'are equally respectable and are really "low-level" laws or principles' (Clarke 1968 (2015), 15). Following Clarke, a number of scholars called into question the idea that the Deductive-Nomological model was the most adequate for archaeology. Merrilee Salmon and Wesley Salmon considered that 'it was somewhat unfortunate that discussion among archaeologists of Hempel's models of explanation has focused so exclusively on this D-N model, given the prevalence of statistical laws in the behavioral sciences' (Salmon and Salmon 1979, 63). Instead, they proposed to apply Wesley Salmon's statistical-relevance model of scientific explanation to archaeological research. This model sought to 'accommodate events of high, middling, or low probability as amenable to explanation' (Salmon and Salmon 1979, 63). In other words, Salmon's model considered archaeological explanations in terms of their statistical relevance.

As these examples illustrate, epistemological issues largely dominated the theoretical debate in archaeology during the 1960s and the 1970s. Archaeologists were preoccupied with the competing models elaborated by philosophers of science to characterise the structure of scientific explanations. While these models offered different definitions of scientific research, they all considered science through the lens of positivism. This situation changed in the 1980s, when the so-called post-processual approaches became popular in archaeology. As Robert Preucel mentioned, 'if anything can be said to unite these archaeologies, it is that most share a common dissatisfaction with the standard positivist paradigm' (Preucel 1995, 147). In other words, during the 1980s, scholars reacted against positivism and began to explore a number of alternative philosophical perspectives. The assimilation of a plethora of new philosophers and their ideas into archaeological theory that followed illustrates this shift.

If processual archaeologists exclusively referred to the work of philosophers of science associated with different versions of positivism (such as Hempel, Oppenheim and Salmon), post-processual archaeologists drew on philosophers associated with postmodernism (including Thomas Kuhn, Michel Foucault, Pierre Bourdieu, Claude Lévi-Strauss, Hans-Georg Gadamer and Martin Heidegger). Archaeologists such as Ian Hodder, Michael Shanks and Christopher Tilley suggested that, by the time new/

processual archaeologists embraced positivism, philosophers, historians and sociologists of science will have already called into question virtually every axiom on which positivism was based (see also Kelley and Hanen 1988, 2). As Shapere explained, 'already by the 1950s [...] the notion of "observational facts" as brute undeniable givens was all but surrendered' (Shapere 1986, 1). The works of Lakatos (1978), Feyerabend (1975) and other philosophers (including Hempel himself) have made clear that facts are theory dependent. Moreover, the belief in the possibility of performing 'objective' observations was also thrown in jeopardy in the 1960s. The publication of Gadamer's *Truth and Method* in 1960 attested that what one observer sees depends on their previous knowledge and expectations (Gadamer 1969 (2006)). Finally, post-processual archaeologists insisted on the fact that, by the 1960s, philosophers of science had abandoned the attempts to give an exact definition of the scientific method. In particular, Thomas Kuhn's *The Structure of Scientific Revolution* (1962) demonstrated that scientific theories are dependent on the different paradigms that orient research. Therefore, scientists' theories are the result of 'a consensus position which has little to do with a non-subjectively defined reality' (Shanks and Tilley 1992, 37). In short, during the 1980s and 1990s, post-processual archaeologists transferred the postmodernist critique of science to archaeology in order to dismantle the positivist framework that had oriented the discipline since the early twentieth century.

To summarise, questions about how archaeologists should evaluate knowledge claims dominated theoretical discussions during the second half of the twentieth century. Archaeologists passionately debated what kind of science archaeology was, what models of scientific explanation might be applied to archaeological research and whether (or not) an objective knowledge of the past was possible. In this setting, a new trend of discussion emerged in the 1980s. At that time, a number of archaeologists began to discuss the impact of non-epistemological factors in the making of archaeological knowledge. Historians of archaeology took the lead in these discussions. Historical studies provided numerous examples of how social conditions had historically shaped the interpretation of archaeological data. In particular, Bruce G. Trigger's *A History of Archaeological Thought*, first published in 1989, marked the agenda of this new historiography. Trigger examined the 'relations between archaeology and its social milieu from a historical perspective' (Trigger 1989, 1). He argued that 'the development of archaeology has corresponded temporally with the rise to power of the middle classes in Western societies' (Trigger 1989, 15). While he stated that there were a number of potential factors to have influenced archaeological interpretations, he suggested that the history of archaeology has been mainly shaped by imperialism, colonialism and nationalism (Trigger 1984; Díaz-Andreu 2007). Following this lead, during the 1980s and 1990s, historians of archaeology examined the role of nationalism in the development of archaeology (Atkinson, Banks and O'Sullivan 1996; Díaz-Andreu and Champion 1996), the impact of imperialism in the early development of archaeological research (Trigger 1984), and the connections between colonialism and archaeology (Trigger 1980; 1984; Fagan 1981; Murray and White 1981; Bray and Glover

1987; Díaz-Andreu 2007). Simultaneously, other scholars analysed how a number of non-epistemological factors have marked archaeologists' agendas, including gender prejudices (Gero 1985; Nelson, Nelson and Wylie 1994; Díaz-Andreu and Sørensen 1998), and social classes' interests (Patterson 1986; 1995; Kehoe 1998; 1999). While these sociological approaches became more common in the late 1990s, they were still considered as secondary to archaeology by late twentieth-century archaeologists. As we will see in the next section, it has only been in the past twenty years that discussions on the socio-politics of the past have significantly modified the way in which we perceive and practice archaeological research.

The decline of epistemology in archaeology

In this section, we argue that the decline of epistemology in archaeological theory is related to two main trends. The first trend has to do with an increasing commitment towards theoretical plurality that, in some cases, has resulted in anti-epistemological positions. The second trend has to do with the reevaluation of the role of science in general, and archaeology in particular, in a globalised and multicultural world. We distinguish these trends for the sake of explanation but, in reality, they are interrelated and fuel each other.

Plurality and mobility of archaeological theory

As we have seen in the previous section, discussions on different epistemological questions were at the core of the theoretical divide (the 'processual/post-processual debate') that separated late twentieth-century archaeologists into two irreconcilable groups. The earlier generation of processual archaeologists became the champions of positivism and the new generation of post-processual archaeologists were anxious to demonstrate that archaeology was a form of power seeking to legitimate the interests of Euro-Western scholars. This characterisation of the history of archaeology is really a caricature but, as any stereotype, it contains some pieces of truth. Broadly speaking, most late twentieth-century archaeologists (especially in America and the United Kingdom) tended to identify with one of the two abovementioned theoretical positions (processualism and post-processualism). This is related to the fact that the positivist paradigm was so entrenched in archaeology that, when post-processual archaeology emerged in the 1980s, archaeologists were somewhat forced to take positions in a very polarised debate. Moreover, at the end of the twentieth century, theory in human sciences was conceived in terms of Kuhn's paradigm model, *i.e.* as a succession of programs of research that engendered specific modes of inquiry incommensurable with each other.

This situation has changed in the past twenty years, when archaeological theory 'has grown increasingly diverse and complicated' (Harris and Cipolla 2017, 1). It is not only that we are moving towards a plurality of theoretical positions but, more importantly perhaps, we have changed the way in which we think about theory in archaeology. First, the time of 'big' theoretical frameworks has passed and archaeological theory has become plural and varied (see, however, Lucas' interesting discussion about the concept of 'paradigm' in archaeology, Lucas 2017). Second, the relationships between archaeological theory and practice have also changed. The traditional 'top-down approach' in which theory dictates practice has been, if not replaced, at least complemented by a 'bottom-up approach' in which archaeological practices orient and shape theorical questions (see Chapman and Wylie 2015; Lucas 2015a; Wylie 2015). This is exemplified, not only in the so-called 'return to things', but 'it is also a focus on our engagement with [things] in the context of archaeological practice' (Lucas 2015a, 18). Finally, the source of theory in archaeology has also diversified beyond the traditional epistemological framework. Today there is a wide-range of new theoretical proposals currently circulating in archaeology. For instance, the increasing impact of ontological approaches in this field (Olsen 2010; Alberti *et al.* 2011; Olsen and Whitmore 2015; Alberti 2016; Caraher 2016; Jones 2017) has generated a significant deal of interest, including research on the archaeological body (Harris and Robb 2012; Marshall and Alberti 2014), relational ontologies (Watts 2013; Porr 2018), humans and 'other-than-human' entities (Harrison-Buck and Hendon 2018) and alterity (Cipolla 2019). Ontological approaches have largely been fueled by the increasing impact of Aboriginal and Indigenous knowledges in archaeological research. In countries such as Australia, Canada, the United States and South Africa (just to quote a few), collaboration between archaeologists and Aboriginal and Indigenous communities is increasing (Colwell 2016), allowing for more voices and experiences to inform research objectives and design. However, there is still much work to be done by archaeologists to ensure that these collaborations are conducted respectfully and ethically. Successful collaborations have resulted in a number of practical and technical effects that, as we examine below, are essential for understanding on-going discussions about the role of epistemology in archaeology.

In a different vein, archaeologists have also drawn inspiration from recent developments in Science and Technology Studies. For instance, a group of scholars have engaged with the idea of 'symmetrical archaeology' (Shanks 2007; Witmore 2007; Olsen *et al.* 2012; Hodder 2014; Hodder and Lucas 2017), a 'new "ecology" packed with things, mixed with things, mixed with humans and companion species, and which prioritizes the multi-temporal and multi-sensorial qualities, the multiplicity, of the material world' (Witmore 2007, 547). Correspondingly, recent works have called into question the dichotomies that oriented archaeological research in the past (humans/things, culture/nature, animate/inanimate, etc.) and have proposed new approaches based on concepts such as entanglement (Hodder 2012), assemblage (Hamilakis and Jones 2017) and network (Hodder and Mol 2016). Discussions on new materialism(s) (Witmore 2014; Bauer and Kosiba 2016; Bauer and Bhan 2018; Alt and Pauketat 2020), agential realism (Immonen 2012; Marshall and Alberti 2014), critical realism (Wallace 2011) and other movements complete the picture of this heterogenous theoretical landscape (for a general overview, please see Lucas 2015b).

This theoretical plurality might be interpreted as the consequence of the overweening focus on epistemology that was the epicenter of the processual/post-processual debate. After the passionate controversies of the 1980s and the 1990s, 'archaeologists have become tired of the polemical war that ended the twentieth century' (Atalay et al. 2014, 7). It seems that, after two decades of processual/post-processual discussions, scholars have moved on from what is today generally perceived as a highly polarised (and polarising), unproductive and exhausted controversy. In this setting marked by the exploration of new questions and issues, the centrality of epistemology can no longer be assumed.

Moreover, some of the theoretical standpoints that archaeologists are currently exploring are bluntly anti-epistemological. This is the case of a number of ontological approaches. For instance, some authors have explicitly argued for 'the analytic advantages of shifting focus from questions of knowledge and epistemology toward those of ontology' (Henare, Holbaard and Wastell 2007, 8). As Benjamin Alberti has pointed out, we can identify two main stimuli for ontological research in archaeology. First, the so-called 'metaphysical archaeologists' (Alberti 2016, 164) who seek to elaborate alternatives to the modern Cartesian ontology within the Western intellectual tradition. Second, the 'ontological anthropology-inspired approach' that seek to 'theorize and practice archaeology on the basis of Indigenous theories' (Alberti 2016, 171). The problem that these authors have with epistemology is mainly related to their theory of reality. The concept behind traditional epistemological accounts is what some scholars refer to as 'mono-realism'; that is, the assumption that there is one, and only one, reality that we can discover thanks to the scientific method (Hage 2011, 8). This was, for instance, the position of processual archaeologists. At the end of the twentieth century, constructivist theories called into question the objectivist view and suggested that there is no single reality but 'multiple subjectivities that are themselves the only realities that matter' (Hage 2011, 9). This was the position of post-processual archaeologists. More recently, scholars interested in ontology have gone one step further and have argued that 'there are multiple realities or worlds, period' (Blaser 2014, 52). In this view, people do not interpret or understand reality differently but they live in different realities. Needless to say, this idea is incompatible with the mono-realist view of traditional epistemology.

Archaeology as a public discipline

A second factor explaining why epistemological questions are losing their appeal in archaeological theory has to do with the fact that a number of approaches concerned with the political, ethical and public dimensions of archaeological research are assuming a central position in current disciplinary debates. Paraphrasing Robert Preucel's quotation in this chapter, if something can be said to unite these approaches, it is that they seek to promote a non-epistemological approach to archaeology. In other words, they focus on a number of factors that, in the past, would have been considered 'external' to archaeological science. The increasing interest in the public impact of archaeology is related to a fundamental change in the conceptualisation of this science. To put it simply, archaeology has shifted from being considered the science of the *past* to being defined as a discipline mainly concerned with the *present* (with a concern for the future). A brief summary of some recent developments in archaeology may be useful to understand this process.

Broadly speaking, until the end of the twentieth century, archaeology was considered the science 'which [dealt] with the material remains of man's past' (Daniel 1981, 13). While there were intense discussions about whether archaeology was a branch of history or a subfield of anthropology, most people agreed that, following its Greek etymology, archaeology was the science of ancient things. Consequently, archaeologists' main goal was to decipher the past beyond the inferences of the present. This consensus began to fragment in the late 1980s, when some archaeologists suggested that 'the past is both completed and still living. But in concentrating on the time of the past, the time of archaeology tends to be forgotten, *i.e.* archaeology as social practice and personal experience which take up people's time in the present' (Shanks and Tilley 1992, 7). They argued that either the past is physically present with us or, strictly speaking, it is nothing. Moreover, archaeologists are always influenced by the ideas, categories and language of their time and, therefore, they cannot escape the present in their interpretations of the past. In Shanks' words, 'since there is no direct route to the past we must remember that archaeology is something done in the present' (Shanks and Tilley 1992, 15). Following Shanks and Tilley, a number of authors in the 1990s and the early 2000s suggested that archaeologists did not discover the past; they 'created', 'produced' or 'made' it *in* and *for* the present.

The focus on the present, under different forms, now seems to dominate archaeological theory. For instance, in Europe, the concern for the present has resulted in a number of theoretical approaches, including the archaeology of the present (Harrison 2011), the archaeology of the contemporary past (Harrison and Schofield 2009), archaeologies of the contemporary world (Harrison and Breithoff 2017) and the archaeology of super-modernity (González-Ruibal 2008). Simplifying for the purposes of the argument, these 'archaeologies' examine the different ways in which memory is managed within living communities. This interest in living collective memory has forced archaeologists 'to take living people seriously and expand the scope of archaeological ethics, from mere objects to human beings' (González-Ruibal 2018, 346). Concurrently, in countries such as Canada, the United States and Australia, the political mobilisation of Aboriginal and Indigenous peoples has marked recent developments in archaeology, as well as in many other social and human sciences. While, in these places, Indigenous peoples have been increasingly politically active since the 1970s, it has only been during the past two decades that archaeologists have paid unprecedented attention to their claims. In the United States, for instance, the turning point was Magistrate John Jelderks's ruling in August 2002 stating that Kennewick Man could not be considered as a Native American under the Native American Graves Protection and Repatriation Act (NAGPRA). This decision had a huge impact on the relationships between archaeologists and Indigenous communities (see Watkins 2004; Bruning 2006). Stemming from this, community archaeology emerged as 'the only way that Indigenous people, descendant communities and other local interest groups will be able to own the pasts archaeologists are employed to create' (Marshall 2002, 218).

In the past fifteen years, community archaeology has abandoned its originally small theoretical niche to be incorporated into, and inseparable from, much archaeological research. As González-Ruibal has pointed out, collaboration 'is an ethical mandate that has become widely accepted, at least in theory' (González-Ruibal 2018, 348). This last statement, 'at least in theory', is extremely important for it correctly suggests that collaboration as an ethical mandate is accepted in the *minds* of archaeologists but not always put into practice. This has become immensely stark and impossible to ignore following the spring and summer of 2020. Protests against racism and discrimination, fueled by the Black Lives Matter movements in the United States have spread internationally. Demands for action to confront and eliminate racial and social discrimination have shook the Humanities and Social Sciences to the core, necessitating non-marginalised practitioners (the majority of academic practitioners in general) in these fields to not only acknowledge the privilege of their voices and actions in the research body but also take immediate meaningful and effective action to change this situation and support, prioritise, defend and champion marginalised voices. Archaeologists need to intensively rise to these demands if they wish to live up to their own theoretical mandate of community collaboration. Archaeologists must seriously evaluate and negotiate their and the discipline's presents and futures, so that they might ethically interpret the many pasts, presents and futures of many peoples. The protests of 2020 have underlined the great amount of work that still needs to be done to align the praxis of archaeology with the stated and mandated commitments to ethical and community-based research. This journey will necessarily shift the theoretical landscape of archaeology.

It is, therefore, precisely in the context of community archaeology that discontent against epistemology has flourished. Indigenous scholars (as well as archaeologists working with Indigenous communities) have called into question the traditional epistemological paradigm grounded on the idea that Western knowledge is superior to all others (because of its superior access to reality). According to them, this paradigm has served to justify the political hegemony of the Western upper-middle classes over other peoples and has promoted 'epistemic violence' (Marker 2003; Hunt 2014) and 'epistemic injustice' (Kidd, Medina and Pohlhaus 2017). For this reason, some of these scholars have called 'for a complementary epistemology that equally integrates and recognizes the potentials and limitations of different approaches of analysis and understanding' (Porr and Bell 2012, 184). Others, however, have suggested that the current epistemological framework of scientific research is intrinsically linked to the colonialism of Euro-Western thinking and, therefore, needs to be discarded (Atalay *et al.* 2014). This has provoked a reaction from some archaeologists associated with critical realism (Sayer 2011) who have argued that 'the history of science illustrates that later theories or technical solutions are more effective than earlier ones' (Stump 2013, 284; see also McGhee 2008; Holtorf 2009).

The increasing impact of diverse knowledges in archaeological research, of course, is a positive aspect of archaeologists' contemporary commitment to diversity and inclusion. There are, however, other facets of the relationship between archaeology and the public that are more problematic. As several authors have pointed out, during the last twenty years, the relationships between science and society have been reformulated. In most Western countries, there is a widespread 'commitment to improve the involvement of diverse elements of democratic civil society in [...] science and government' (Felt *et al.* 2007, 9). This involvement has translated into the widespread impact of governmental funding bodies' priorities, policies and rules upon research agendas.

Epistemological questions are certainly not among the priorities of research funding bodies. In the context of this new paradigm of public engagement with science, communication has become one of the main demands for scientists and scientific organisations (Franzen, Weingart and Rödder 2012, 5). Since communication in Western societies largely depends on mass media, this demand has resulted in the 'medialization' of scientific research; that is, in the intensification of the relationships between science and the mass media. The current impact of mass media in scientific research is particularly relevant in archaeology, a discipline in which many projects often make global news. While the medialisation of science is neither a good or a bad thing *per se*, the fact is that this process is having a number of effects on the orientation, organisation and presentation of scientific research. For instance, the medialisation of science often results in an over-simplification of scientific results, reduced to sensational headlines. Understandably, epistemological and theoretical questions, commonly perceived as difficult to communicate to, and irrelevant for, the public, are being excluded from scientific (and archaeological) research.

Conclusions

As Liv Nilsson Stuzt has recently pointed out, 'archaeology has a long history with interdisciplinarity. It is in our bones. Where other academic disciplines are eloquently debating how to do inter- and transdisciplinary work and how to define it [...] archaeology is doing business as usual, often without much fanfare' (Stutz 2018, 49). However, research concerning archaeology and interdisciplinarity has mainly focused on (A) the methods and techniques that archaeologists borrowed from other sciences and (B) the ideas that have influenced archaeological research. Without calling into question the importance of this research, we believe that there is a pressing need to examine, from an interdisciplinary viewpoint, the models of scientific research used in archaeological inquiry. For this reason, in this chapter we have focused on the relationships between archaeologists and philosophers of science, with a reference to an ongoing discussion about the role of epistemology in archaeological theory.

The fragile position of epistemology in archaeology is the logical outcome of the history of archaeological research. During a long period of time (the second half of the twentieth century), epistemological questions were at the centre of the theoretical debate. Moreover, epistemology was understood in a narrow way (using one of Binford's favorite expressions); that is, largely linked to the positivist program. In particular Epistemology (with a capital 'E') was a key part of processual archaeologists' project of making archaeology a Science (with a capital 'S'). They established a clear-cut distinction between scientific and non-scientific (or objective and subjective) that excluded other forms of knowledge from the exclusive realm of archaeological explanation. Moreover, they treated past and present people 'as objects rather than as subjects of research' (Trigger 1980, 662). The 'New' archaeology's strong commitment to logical-positivism engendered the reaction of post-processual archaeologists in the 1980s and 1990s. At that time, archaeologists such as Shanks and Tilley argued that archaeological research could not be reduced to epistemic terms. In so doing, they initiated a discussion that dominated theoretical debates for almost twenty years. Epistemology reached its paroxysm in archeology.

However, twenty years after the processual/post-processual debate, the popularity of epistemological issues has seriously declined. In the first place, questions about how we know what we know about the past seems to have reached a point of exhaustion. Today, archaeologists prefer to explore other possibilities as a way of reviving disciplinary debates. New theoretical positions have emerged and the primacy of epistemology has been contested. In the second place, in a context in which our understanding of the social and ethical role of archaeology has changed and continues to change, the superiority and exclusiveness of epistemological questions is no longer acceptable. If we agree that archaeological research is not just about the past but instead mainly about the present, then we have to incorporate new and different kinds of questions into the debate. Moreover, if we concur that we need to take past and living people seriously, we also need to take their knowledges and realities seriously.

In short, the traditional epistemological project has been seriously undermined by a number of critiques, including the connections between epistemology and colonialism, the epistemological contempt for other forms of knowledge and the impossibility of facing important political and ethical issues within an epistemological frame of reference. The question is whether we should move from an epistemological paradigm to other theoretical frameworks. This is, for instance, what a number of scholars interested in ontology have proposed. This position, however, is not without problems. To begin, it promotes a monolithic view of epistemology that does not reflect the current plurality of positions concerning the theory of knowledge, from Paul Boghossian's 'classical picture of knowledge' (2006, 19) to Hasok Chang's 'active normative epistemic pluralism' (2012, 253). Moreover, by arguing that Indigenous knowledge can only be discussed in terms of the theory of reality (not in terms of the theory of knowledge), one could wonder whether ontological theorists are fueling the idea that Indigenous knowledges cannot contribute to a more adequate understanding of archaeological materials and places. Our point, however, is that Indigenous knowledges are, in fact, *knowledges* and, therefore, they should not be overlooked. For this reason, instead of opposing epistemology and ontology, it is probably more productive to examine the complex relationships between them. After all, this is what authors such as Karen Barad (2007) and Donna Haraway (2016) have proposed in their discussions about onto-epistemologies. However, in order to do so, epistemological questions need to be reformulated with reference to some of the challenges that we have examined in this chapter. In short, we argue that we need to move from a single and monolithic Epistemology to critical, plural and practical epistemologies.

First, epistemology needs to become *critical*, i.e. it needs to reevaluate its postulates in the light of some of the serious charges that have been raised against it. For instance, it is hard not to see a significant part of the history of archaeology and anthropology as an example of colonial imposition and cultural appropriation. Similarly, it is equally difficult not to see the connections between the positivist program and the traditional overlooking of Indigenous ways of knowing. Epistemological discussions need to be critical with their own tradition. This is, for instance, what Lucas (2019), Chapman and Wylie (2015), and Murray and Spriggs (2017) are doing in archaeological theory from different standpoints.

Second, epistemology needs to embrace *plurality*. As Hasok Chang has pointed out, there are at least two main benefits in the cultivation of plurality: 1) the 'benefits of toleration' that arise from 'simply allowing multiple systems simultaneously, which provides insurance against unpredictability, compensation for the limitations of each system, and multiple satisfaction of any given aim' (Chang 2012, 253) and; 2) the 'benefits of interaction' that result from 'the integration of different systems for specific purposes, the co-optation of beneficial elements across systems, and the productive competition between systems' (Chang 2012, 253). In a science with such a colonial past (and such an aspiration for a collaborative present) as archaeology, both the benefits of toleration and interaction seem particularly desirable. Archaeologists need to embrace 'a plurality of pluralisms', using Alison Wylie's words (2015).

Third, epistemology needs to become *practical*. As Robert Chapman and Alison Wiley have recently argued, 'the epistemic status of archaeological evidence has been conducted at a level of abstraction that provides little useful guidance for practice' (Chapman and Wiley 2015, 7). The need for practice is also related to the fact that the point of access for archaeologists into epistemic pluralism has been the practical context of collaborative archaeology, not the theoretical discussions about the status of our science (see, for instance, Wiley 2014). In other words, it is not only that collaborative practice is expanding our way of doing archaeology but it is also enriching our ways of thinking about archaeology. In this context, we agree with Robert Chapman and Alison Wylie when they wrote that

> what is needed [...] is resolutely case-based analysis of actual practice – key instances of exemplary practice, critical turning points, innovations, and instructive failures in the use of

archaeological data as evidence – aimed at making explicit the norms of evidential reasoning that have taken shape in the context of evolving traditions of practical experience working with archaeological material (Chapman and Wiley 2015, 7).

In short, we believe that there is justification for claiming that archaeologists should not completely renounce discussions of epistemological issues. Epistemologies of different kinds may provide scientists with a number of valuable tools to examine a variety of questions. Additionally, there is no contradiction between the legitimate goal of making a socially-responsible science and the claim that epistemological arguments should be relevant for archaeological research. It is exactly the opposite. It is when we embrace epistemic plurality that we are likely to make an impact in the wider community. Third, in a setting defined by increasing demands concerning social involvement, public communication and community participation, we need some critical tools to approach these recent developments. In this setting, it is important to remember that epistemology has a long tradition of critical thought with its exigence of rigor and relevance. This, in a moment in which we are witnessing a number of worrying developments in scientific research (from the expansion of neoliberalism to the impact of mass media), may be a precious tool to navigate our changing world.

Acknowledgements

This chapter was written within the framework of the InterArq research project (HAR2016-80271-P) (interarqweb.wordpress.com) subsidised by the State Research Agency (AEI) and the European Regional Development Fund (ERDF, EU). The final version of this chapter has greatly benefitted from the comments of those who participated in the Inter-Arq seminar held in Barcelona in June 2019, including Margarita Díaz-Andreu, Ana Cristina Martins, Eduardo Palacio Pérez, Nathan Schlanger, Oliver Hochadel, Alessandro Guidi and Tim Murray. The authors would like to thank the two anonymous reviewers for their comments on this contribution.

References

Alberti, B. (2016) Archaeologies of ontologies. *Annual Review of Anthropology* 45, 163–179.
Alberti, B., Fowles, S., Holbraad, M., Marshall, Y. and Witmore, C. (2011) 'Worlds Otherwise': archaeology, anthropology, and ontological difference. *Current Anthropology* 52 (6), 896–912.
Alt, S.M. and Pauketat T.R., eds (2020) *New Materialisms Ancient Urbanisms*. London and New York, Routledge.
Atalay, S.L., Clauss, L.R., McGuire, R. and Welch, J.R., eds (2014) *Transforming Archaeology. Activist Practices and Prospects*. Walnut Creek, CA, Left Coast Press.
Atkinson, J.A., Banks, I. and O'Sullivan, J., eds (1996) *Nationalism and Archaeology*. Glasgow, Cruithne Press.
Barad, K. (2007) *Meeting the Universe Halfway. Quantum Physics and the Entanglement of Matter and Meaning*. Durham, Duke University Press.
Bauer, A.M. and Bhan, M. (2018) *Climate Without Nature: A Critical Anthropology of the Anthropocene*. Cambridge, Cambridge University Press.

Bauer, A.M. and Kosiba, S. (2016) How things act: an archaeology of materials in political life. *Journal of Social Archaeology* 16 (2), 115–141.

Binford, L.R. (1968) Archaeological perspectives. In S.R. Binford and L.R. Binford (eds) *New Perspectives in Archaeology*, 5–32. Chicago, New York, Aldine, Atherton.

Binford, L.R. (1978) On covering law and theories in archaeology. *Current Anthropology* 19 (3), 631–632.

Binford, L.R. (1983) Reply to 'More on the Mousterian: Flaked Bone From Cueva Morin' by L.G. Freeman. *Current Anthropology* 24 (3), 372–376.

Binford, L.R. (1985) 'Brand X' versus the recommended product. *American Antiquity* 50 (3), 580–590.

Bintliff, J. and Pearce, M., eds (2011) *Death of Archaeological Theory*. Oxford, Oxbow Books.

Blanckaert, C. (2000) 1800 – Le moment 'naturaliste' des sciences de l'homme. *Revue d'Histoire des Sciences Humaines* 3 (2), 117–160.

Blaser, M. (2014) Ontology and indigeneity: on the political ontology of heterogeneous assemblages. *Cultural Geographies* 21 (1), 49–58.

Bloor, D. (1976 (1991)) *Knowledge and Social Imagery*. Chicago and London, The University of Chicago Press.

Boghossian, P.A. (2006). *Fear of Knowledge: Against Relativism and Constructivism*. Oxford, Oxford University Press.

Braithwaite, R.V. (1955) *Scientific Explanation: A Study of the Function of Theory, Probability and Law in Science*. Cambridge, Cambridge Universty Press.

Bray, W. and Glover, I.C. (1987) Scientific investigation or cultural imperialism: British archaeology in the Third World. *Bulletin of the Institute of Archaeology* 24, 109–125.

Bruning, S.B. (2006) Complex legal legacies: the Native American Graves Protection and Repatriation Act, Scientific Study and Kennewick Man. *American Antiquity* 71 (3), 501–521.

Caraher, W. (2016) Review: Ontology, World Archaeology, and the Recent Past. *American Journal of Archaeology* 120 (2), 325–331.

Chang, H. (2012) *Is Water H2O? Evidence, Realism and Pluralism*. New York, Springer.

Chapman, R. and Wylie, A. (2015) *Material Evidence. Learning from Archaeological Practice*. New York, Routledge.

Cipolla, C.N. (2019) Taming the ontological wolves: learning from Iroquoian Effigy Objects. *American Anthropologists* 121 (3), 613–627.

Clarke, D.L. (1968 (2015)) *Analytical Archaeology*. London, Routledge.

Colwell, C. (2016) Collaborative archaeologies and descendant communities. *Annual Review of Anthropology* 45, 113–127.

Coye, N. (1997) *La Préhistoire en parole et en acte. Méthodes et enjeux de la practique archéologique (1830-1950). Histoire des Sciences Humaines*. Paris, L'Harmattan.

Daniel, G.E., ed. (1981) *A Short History of Archaeology*. London, Thames and Hudson.

Delley, G. and Plutniak, S. (2018) History and sociology of science. In S.L. López Varela (ed.) *The Encyclopedia of Archaeological Sciences*. Oxford, John Wiley & Son.

Díaz-Andreu, M. (2007) *A World History of Nineteenth-Century Archaeology. Nationalism, Colonialism and the Past. Oxford Studies in the History of Archaeology*. Oxford, Oxford University Press.

Díaz-Andreu, M. and Champion, T., eds (1996) *Nationalism and Archaeology in Europe*. London, Boulder, Co., UCL Press, Westview Press.

Díaz-Andreu, M. and Sørensen, M.L.S., eds (1998) *Excavating Women. A History of Women in European Archaeology*. London, Routledge.

Evans, J. (1870) *An Address Delivered in the Department of Ethnology and Anthropology. Liverpool (September 15, 1870, British Association for the Advancement of Science)*. London, Virtue & Co.

Fagan, B. (1981) Two hundred and four years of African archaeology. In J.D. Evans, B. Cunliffe and C. Renfrew (eds) *Antiquity and Man. Essays in Honour of Glyn Daniel*, 42–51. London, Thames and Hudson.

Felt, U., Wynne, B., Callon, M., Gonçalves, M.E., Jasanoff, S., Jepsen, M., Joly, P.-B., Konopasek, Z., May, S., Neubauer, C., Rip, A., Siune, K., Stirling, A. and Tallacchini, M. (2007) *Taking European Knowledge Society Seriously: Report of the Expert Group on Science and Governance to the Science, Economy and Society Directorate, Directorate-General for Research, European Commission*. Brussels, European Communities, European Commission.

Feyerabend, P. (1975) *Against Method: Outline of an Anarchistic Theory of Knowledge*. London, New Left Book.

Flannery, K.V. (1973) Archaeology with a capital S. In C.L. Redman (ed.) *Research and Theory in Current Archaeology*, 47–58. New York, Wiley.

Franzen, M., Weingart, P. and Rödder, S. (2012) Exploring the impact of science communication on scientific knowledge production: an introduction. In S. Rödder, M. Franzen and P. Weingart (eds) *The Sciences' Media Connection: Public Communication and its Repercussions*, 3–14. London, Springer.

Fritz, J.M. and Plog, F.T. (1970) The nature of archaeological explanation. *American Antiquity* 35, 405–412.

Gadamer, H.-G. (1969 (2006)) *Truth and Method*. New York, Continuum.

Gero, J. (1985) Socio-politics and the woman-at-home ideology. *American Antiquity* 50 (2), 342–350.

González-Ruibal, A. (2008) Time to destroy. An archaeology of super-modernity. *Current Anthropology* 49 (2), 247–263.

González-Ruibal, A. (2018) Ethics of archaeology. *Annual Review of Anthropology* 47, 345–360.

Hage, G. (2011) Dwelling in the reality of utopian thought. *Traditional Dwelllings and Settlement Review* 23 (1), 7–13.

Hamilakis, Y. and Jones, A.Y. (2017) Archaeology and assemblage. *Cambridge Archaeological Journal* 27 (1), 77–84.

Haraway, D.J. (2016) *Staying with the Trouble: Making Kin in the Chthulucene*. London, Duke University Press.

Harris, O.J.T. and Robb, J. (2012) Multiple ontologies and the problem of the body in history. *American Anthropologist* 114 (4), 668–679.

Harris, O.J.T. and Cipolla, C., eds (2017) *Archaeological Theory in the New Millennium: Introducing Current Perspectives*. London, Routledge.

Harrison, R. (2011) Surface assemblages. Towards an archaeology in and of the present. *Archaeological Dialogues* 18 (2), 141–161.

Harrison, R. and Breithoff, E. (2017) Archaeologies of the contemporary world. *Annual Review of Anthropology* 46, 203–221.

Harrison, R. and Schofield, J. (2009) Archaeo-Ethnography, auto-archaeology: introducing archaeologies of the contemporary past. *Archaeologies: Journal of the World Archaeological Congress* 5 (2), 185–209.

Harrison-Buck, E. and Hendon, J.A. eds (2018) *Relational Identities and Other-than-Human Agency in Archaeology*. Boulder, University of Colorado Press.

Henare, A, Holbaard, M. and Wastell. S. (2007) Introduction: thinking through things. In A. Henare, M. Holbraad and S. Wastell (eds) *Thinking through Things: Theorizing Artefacts Ethnographically*, 1–31. London, Routledge.

Hempel, C. (1966) *Philosophy of Natural Science*. Princeton, Princeton University Press.

Hempel, C. and Oppenheim, P. (1948) Studies in the logic of explanation. *Philosophy of Science* 15, 135–175.

Hodder, I., ed. (2001) *Archaeological Theory Today*. London, Routledge.

Hodder, I. (2012) *Entangled: An Archaeology of the Relationships between Humans and Things*. Oxford, Wiley-Blackwell.

Hodder, I. (2014) The asymmetries of symmetrical archaeology. *Journal of Contemporary Archaeology* 1 (2), 228–230.

Hodder, I. and Lucas, G. (2017) The symmetries and asymetries of human-thing relations. A dialogue. *Archaeological Dialogues* 24 (2), 119–137.

Hodder, I. and Mol, A. (2016) Network analysis and entanglement. *Journal of Archaeological Method and Theory* 23, 1066–1094.

Holtorf, C. 2009. A European perspective on indigenous and immigrant archaeologies. *World Archaeology* 41 (4), 672–681.

Hunt, S. (2014). Ontologies of indigeneity: the politics of embodying a concept. *Cultural Geographies* 21 (1), 27–32.

Hurel, A. and Coye, N. (2011) *Dans l'épaisseur du temps. Archéologues et géologues inventent la préhistoire. Publications scientifiques du muséum*. Paris, Muséum national d'Histoire naturelle.

Immonen, V. (2012) The mess before the modern – Karen Barad's agential realism, and periodization in medieval archaeology in Finland. In T. Äikäs, S. Lipkin and A.-K. Salmi (eds) *Archaeology of Social Relations: Ten Case Studies by Finnish Archaeologists*, 7–32. Oulu, University of Oulu.

Jones, A.M. (2017) Rock art and ontology. *Annual Review of Anthropology* 46 (1), 167–181.

Kehoe, A.B. (1998) *The Land of Prehistory: A Critical History of American Archaeology*. London, Routledge.

Kehoe, A.B. (1999) *Assembling the Past: Studies in the Professionalization of Archaeology*. New Mexico, University of New Mexico Press.

Kelley, J.H. and Hanen, M.P. (1988) *Archaeology and the Methodology of Science*. Alburquerque, University of New Mexico Press.

Kidd, J., Medina, J. and Pohlhaus, G., eds (2017) *The Routledge Handbook of Epistemic Injustice*. London, Routledge.

Kristiansen, K. (2004) Genes versus agents. A discussion of the widening theoretical gap in archaeology. *Archaeological Dialogues* 11 (2), 77–98.

Kristiansen, K. (2014) Towards a new paradigm? The Third Science Revolution and its possible consequences in Archaeology. *Current Swedish Archaeology* 22, 11–71.

Kuhn, T.S. (1962 (1996)) *The Structure of Scientific Revolutions*, 3rd edition (1st edition 1962). Chicago, University of Chicago Press.

Lakatos, I. (1978) *The Methodology of Scientific Research Programmes*. Cambridge, Cambridge University Press.

Lucas, G. (2015a) The mobility of theory. *Current Swedish Archaeology* 23, 13–32.

Lucas, G. (2015b) The future of archaeological theory. *Antiquity* 89 (348), 1287–1296.

Lucas, G. (2017) The paradigm concept in archaeology, *World Archaeology*, 49 (2), 260–270.

Lucas, G. (2019) *Writing the Past. Knowledge and Literary Production in Archaeology*. New York, Routledge.

Lyman, R.L. and O'Brien, M.J. (2006) *Measuring Time with Artifacts. A History of Methods in American Archaeology*. Lincoln, University of Nebraska Press.

Marker, M. (2003) Indigenous voice, community, and epistemic violence: the ethnographer's 'interests' and what 'interests' the ethnographer. *International Journal of Qualitative Studies in Education* 16 (3), 361–375.

Marshall, Y. (2002) What is community archaeology? *World Archaeology [special issue: Community Archaeology]* 34 (2), 211–219.

Marshall, Y. and Alberti, B. (2014) A matter of difference: Karen Barad, ontology and archaeological bodies. *Cambridge Archaeological Journal* 24 (1), 19–36.

Martin, P.S. (1971) The revolution in archaeology. *American Antiquity* 3 (1), 1–8.

McGhee, R. (2008) Aboriginalism and the problems of Indigenous archaeology. *American Antiquity* 73 (4), 579–597.

Moro Abadía, O. (2013) The history of archaeology as a field: from marginality to recognition. In S. Chrisomalis and A. Costopoulos (eds) *Human Expeditions: Inspired by Bruce Trigger*, 90–101. Toronto, University of Toronto Press.

Moro Abadía, O. (2017) Bridging the gap in archaeological theory: an alternative account of scientific 'progress' in archaeology. *World Archaeology* 49, 1–10.

Murray, T. (2002) Epilogue: why the history of archaeology matters. *Antiquity (special section: 'Ancestral Archives. Explorations in the History of Archaeology')* 76, 234–238.

Murray, T. and White, J.P. (1981) Cambridge in the Bush? Archaeology in Australia and New Guinea. *World Archaeology* 13 (2), 255–263.

Murray, T. and Spriggs, M. (2017) The historiography of archaeology: exploring theory, contingency and rationality. *World Archaeology* 49 (2), 151–157.

Nelson, M.C., Nelson, S.M. and Wylie, A., eds (1994) *Equity Issues for Women in Archaeology*. Washington, American Anthropological Association (Archaeological Papers of the American Anthropological Association 5).

Olsen, B. (2010) *In Defense of Things: Archaeology and the Ontology of Objects*. Lanham, AltaMira Press.

Olsen, B. and Whitmore, C. (2015) Archaeology, symmetry and the ontology of things: a response to critics. *Archaeological Dialogues* 22 (2), 187–197.

Olsen, B., Shanks, M., Webmoor, T. and Witmore, C. (2012) *The Discipline of Things*. Berkeley, CA, University of California Press.

Palmer, S.E. and Schibeci, R.A. (2014) What conceptions of science communication are espoused by science research funding bodies? *Public Understanding of Science* 23 (5), 511–527.

Patterson, T.C. (1986) The last sixty years: towards a social history of Americanist archaeology in the United States. *American Anthropologist* 88, 7–26.

Patterson, T.C. (1995) *Toward a Social History of Archaeology in the United States*. Fort Worth, Texas, Hartcourt Brace College Publishers.

Pétursdóttir, T. and Olsen, B. (2018) Theory adrift: the matter of archaeological theorizing. *Journal of Social Archaeology* 18 (1), 97–117.

Plog, F.T. (1974) *The Study of Prehistoric Change*. New York, Academic Press.

Porr, M. (2018) Country and relational ontology in the Kimberley, Northwest Australia: implications for understanding and representing archaeological evidence. *Cambridge Archaeological Journal* 28 (3), 395–409.

Porr, M. and Bell, H.R. (2012) 'Rock-art', 'animism' and two-way thinking: towards a complementary epistemology in the understanding of material culture and 'rock-art' of hunting and gathering people. *Journal of Archaeological Method and Theory* 19, 161–205.

Preucel, R.W. (1995) The post-processual condition. *Journal of Archaeological Research* 32 (2), 147–175.

Reubi, S. (2012) Exploring the disciplinary significance of fieldwork methods: a case from the history of Swiss anthropology. In M. Harbsmeier, C. Ries and K. Nielsen (eds) *Scientists and Scholars in the Field: Studies in the History of Fieldwork and Expeditions*, 309–328. Aarhus, Aarhus University Press.

Rödder, S. (2011) Science and the mass media. 'Medialization' as a new perspective on an intricate relationship. *Sociology Compass* 5 (9), 834–845.

Salmon, M.H. and Salmon, W. (1979) Alternative models of Scientific Explanation. *American Anthropologist* 81 (1), 61–74.

Salmon, W.C. (1967) *The Foundations of Scientific Inference*. Pittsburgh, University of Pittsburgh Press.

Salmon, W.C. (1971) *Statistical Explanation and Statistical Relevance*. Pittsburgh, University of Pittsburgh Press.

Sayer, A. (2011) *Why Things Matter to People: Social Science, Values and Ethical Life*. Cambridge, Cambridge University Press.

Schlanger, N. (2002) Special section: 'Ancestral Archives. Explorations in the History of Archaeology'. *Antiquity (special section: 'Ancestral Archives. Explorations in the History of Archaeology')* 76, 127–131.

Shanks, M. (2007) Symmetrical archaeology. *World Archaeology* 39 (4), 589–596.

Shanks, M. and Tilley, C. (1992) *Re-constructing Archaeology. Theory and Practice*, 2nd edition (1st edition 1987). Cambridge, Cambridge University Press.

Shapere, D. (1986) External and internal factors in the development of science. *Science & Technology Studies* 4 (1), 1–9.

Stump, D. (2013) On applied archaeology, Indigenous knowledge, and the usable past. *Current Anthropology* 54 (3), 268–298.

Stutz, L.G.N. (2018) A future for archaeology: in defense of an intellectually engaged, collaborative and confident archaeology. *Norwegian Archaeological Review* 51 (1–2), 48–56.

Thomas, J. (2015a). The future of archaeological theory. *Antiquity* 89 (348), 1287–1296.

Thomas, J. (2015b). Why 'the death of archaeological theory'? In C. Hillerdal and J. Siapkas (eds) *Debating Archaeological Empiricism: The Ambiguity of Material Evidence*, 11–31. New York, Routledge.

Trigger, B.G. (1980) Archaeology and the image of the American Indian. *American Antiquity* 45, 662–676.

Trigger, B.G. (1984) Alternative archaeologies: nationalist, colonialist, imperialist. *Man* 19 (3), 355–370.

Trigger, B.G. (1989) *A History of Archaeological Thought*. Cambridge, Cambridge University Press.

Trigger, B. (2001) Historiography. In T. Murray (ed.) *Encyclopedia of Archaeology. History and Discoveries.* Volume II, 630–639. Santa Barbara, ABC-CLIO.

Vašiček, Z. (1994) *L'archéologie, l'histoire, le passé. Chapitres sur la présentation, l'épistémologie et l'ontologie du temps perdu*. Sceaux, Kronos Éditions.

Viveiros de Castro, E. (2015). Who's afraid of the ontological wolf: Some comments on an ongoing anthropological debate. *Cambridge Anthropology* 33 (1), 2–17.

Wallace, S. (2011) *Contradictions of Archaeological Theory: Engaging Critical Realism and Archaeological Theory*. New York, Routledge.

Watkins, J. (2004) Becoming American or becoming Indian?: NAGPRA, Kennewick and Cultural Affiliation. *Journal of Social Archaeology* 4, 60–80.

Watts, C, ed. (2013) *Relational Archaeologies. Humans, Animals, Things.* London, Routledge.

Watson, P.J., Leblanc, S.A. and Redman, C.L. (1971) *Explanation in Archeology: An Explicitly Scientific Approach*. New York, Columbia University Press.

Weingart, P. (2012) The lure of the mass media and its repercussions on science. In S. Rödder, M. Franzen and P. Weingart (eds) *The Sciences' Media Connection: Public Communication and its Repercussions*, 17–32. London, Springer.

Witmore, C. (2007) Symmetrical archaeology: excerpts of a manifesto. *World Archaeology* 39 (4), 546–562.

Witmore, C. (2014) Archaeology and the new materialisms. *Journal of Contemporary Archaeology* 1 (2), 203–246.

Wylie, A. (2014) Community-based collaborative archeology. In N. Cartwright and E. Montuschi (eds) *Philosophy of Social Science. A New Introduction*, 68–82. Oxford, Oxford University Press.

Wylie, A. (2015) A plurality of pluralism: collaborative practice in archaeology. In F. Padovani, A. Richardson, and J.Y. Tsou (eds) *Objectivity in Science: New Perspectives from Science and Technology Studies*, 189–210. New York, Springer.